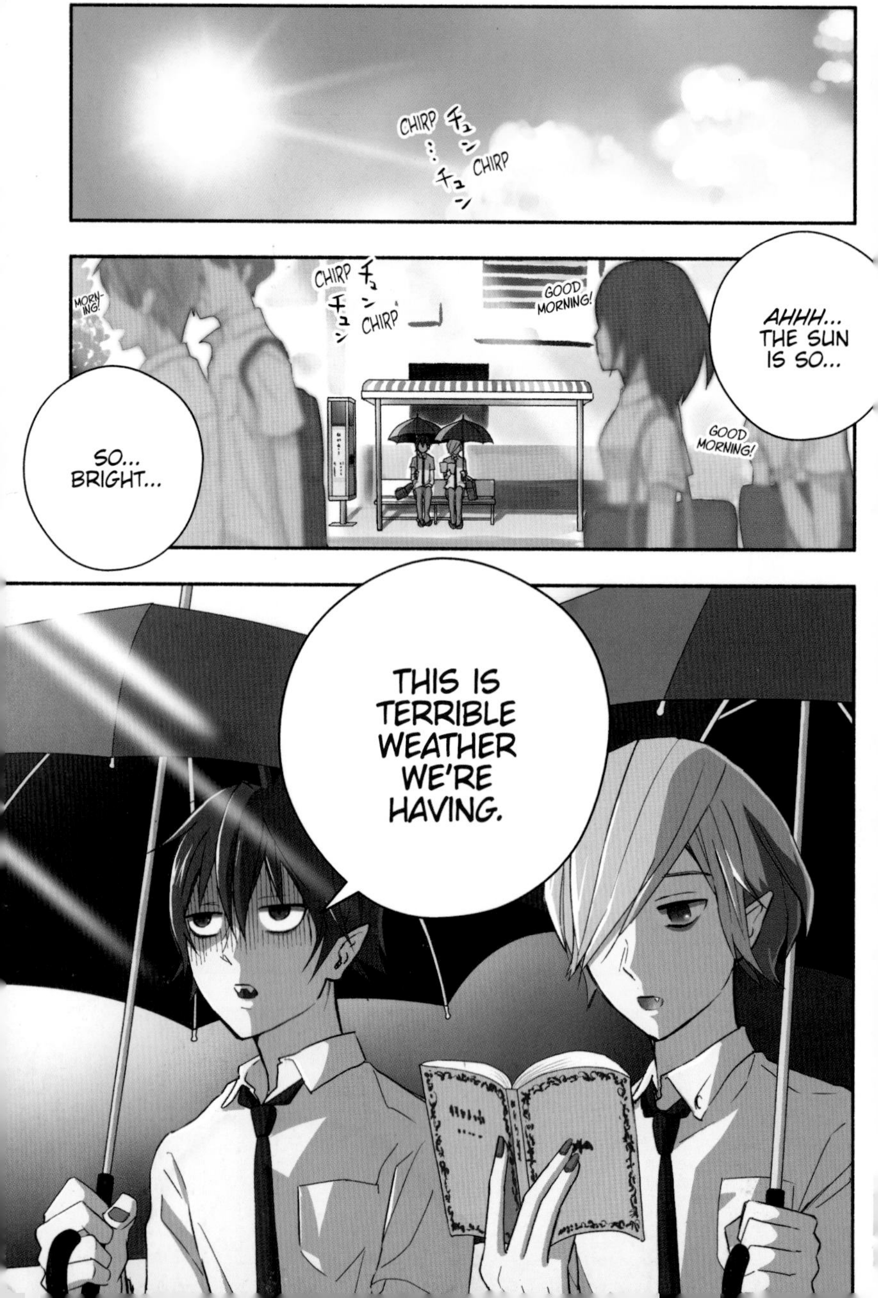
CHIRP チュン…チュン CHIRP
AHHH... THE SUN IS SO...
GOOD MORNING!
GOOD MORNING!
CHIRP チュンチュン CHIRP
MORNING!
SO... BRIGHT...
THIS IS TERRIBLE WEATHER WE'RE HAVING.

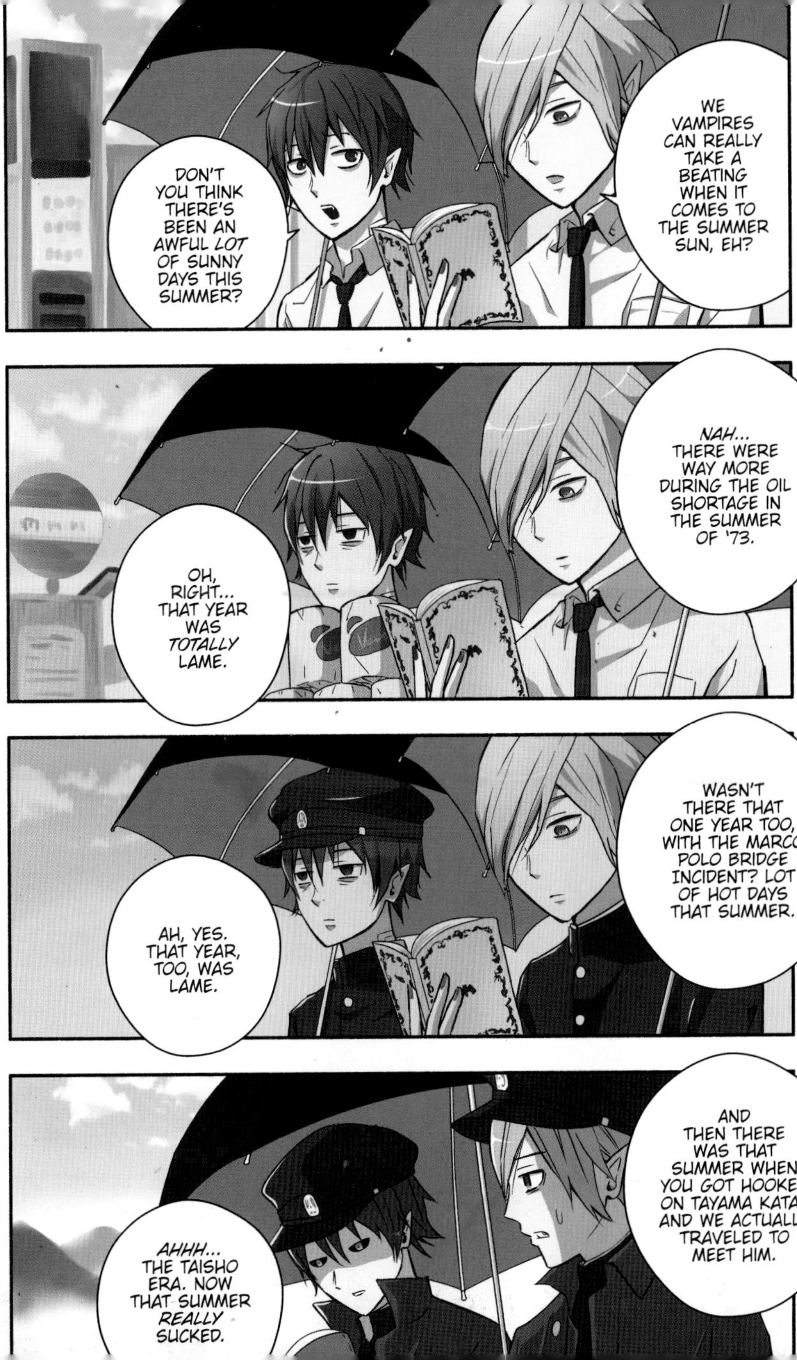
WE VAMPIRES CAN REALLY TAKE A BEATING WHEN IT COMES TO THE SUMMER SUN, EH?
DON'T YOU THINK THERE'S BEEN AN AWFUL LOT OF SUNNY DAYS THIS SUMMER?
NAH... THERE WERE WAY MORE DURING THE OIL SHORTAGE IN THE SUMMER OF '73.
OH, RIGHT... THAT YEAR WAS TOTALLY LAME.
WASN'T THERE THAT ONE YEAR TOO, WITH THE MARCO POLO BRIDGE INCIDENT? LOT OF HOT DAYS THAT SUMMER.
AH, YES. THAT YEAR, TOO, WAS LAME.
AND THEN THERE WAS THAT SUMMER WHEN YOU GOT HOOKED ON TAYAMA KATAI, AND WE ACTUALLY TRAVELED TO MEET HIM.
AHHH... THE TAISHO ERA. NOW THAT SUMMER REALLY SUCKED.

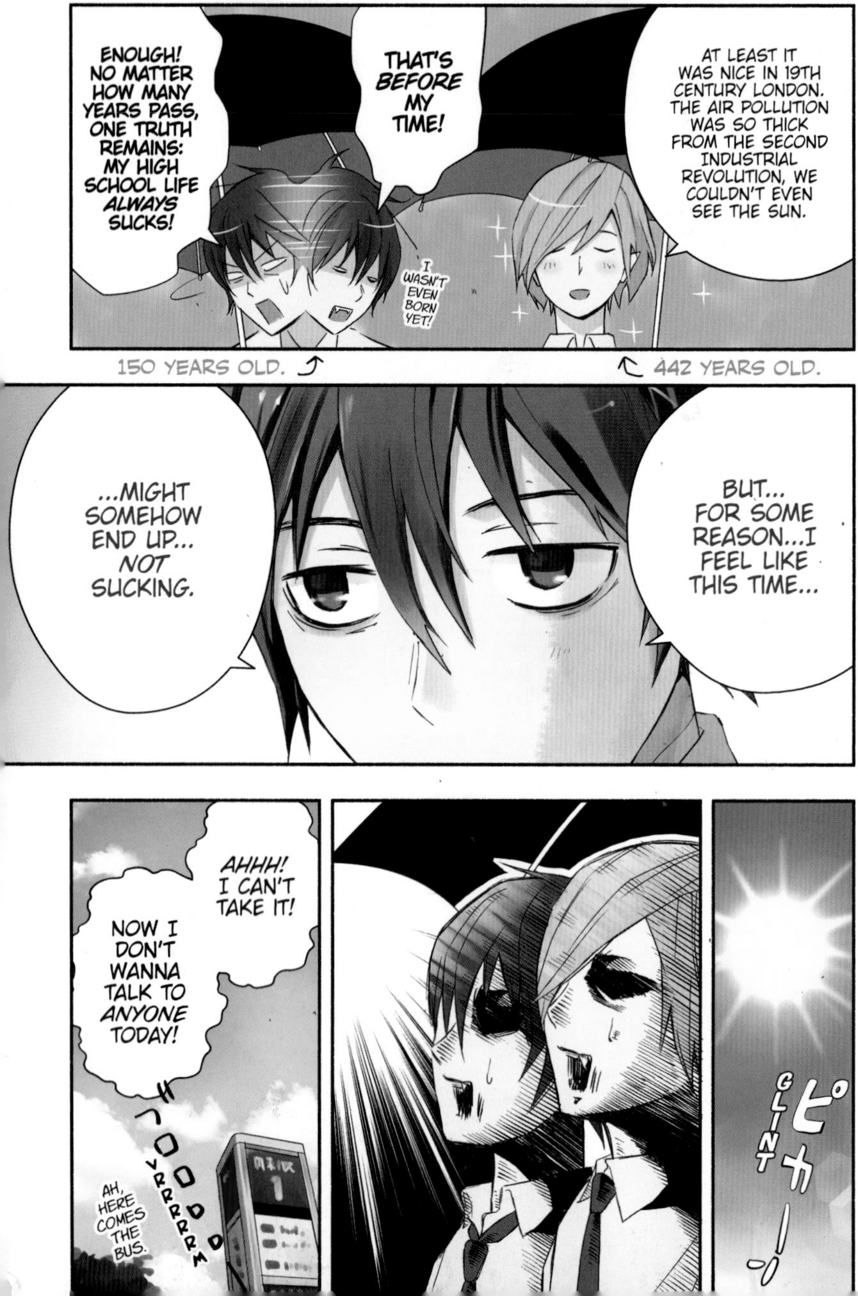
AT LEAST IT WAS NICE IN 19TH CENTURY LONDON. THE AIR POLLUTION WAS SO THICK FROM THE SECOND INDUSTRIAL REVOLUTION, WE COULDN'T EVEN SEE THE SUN.
THAT'S *BEFORE* MY TIME!
ENOUGH! NO MATTER HOW MANY YEARS PASS, ONE TRUTH REMAINS: MY HIGH SCHOOL LIFE *ALWAYS* SUCKS!
I WASN'T EVEN BORN YET!
442 YEARS OLD.
150 YEARS OLD.
BUT... FOR SOME REASON...I FEEL LIKE THIS TIME...
...MIGHT SOMEHOW END UP... *NOT* SUCKING.
GLINT
AHHH! I CAN'T TAKE IT!
NOW I DON'T WANNA TALK TO *ANYONE* TODAY!
VRRRRRM
AH, HERE COMES THE BUS.

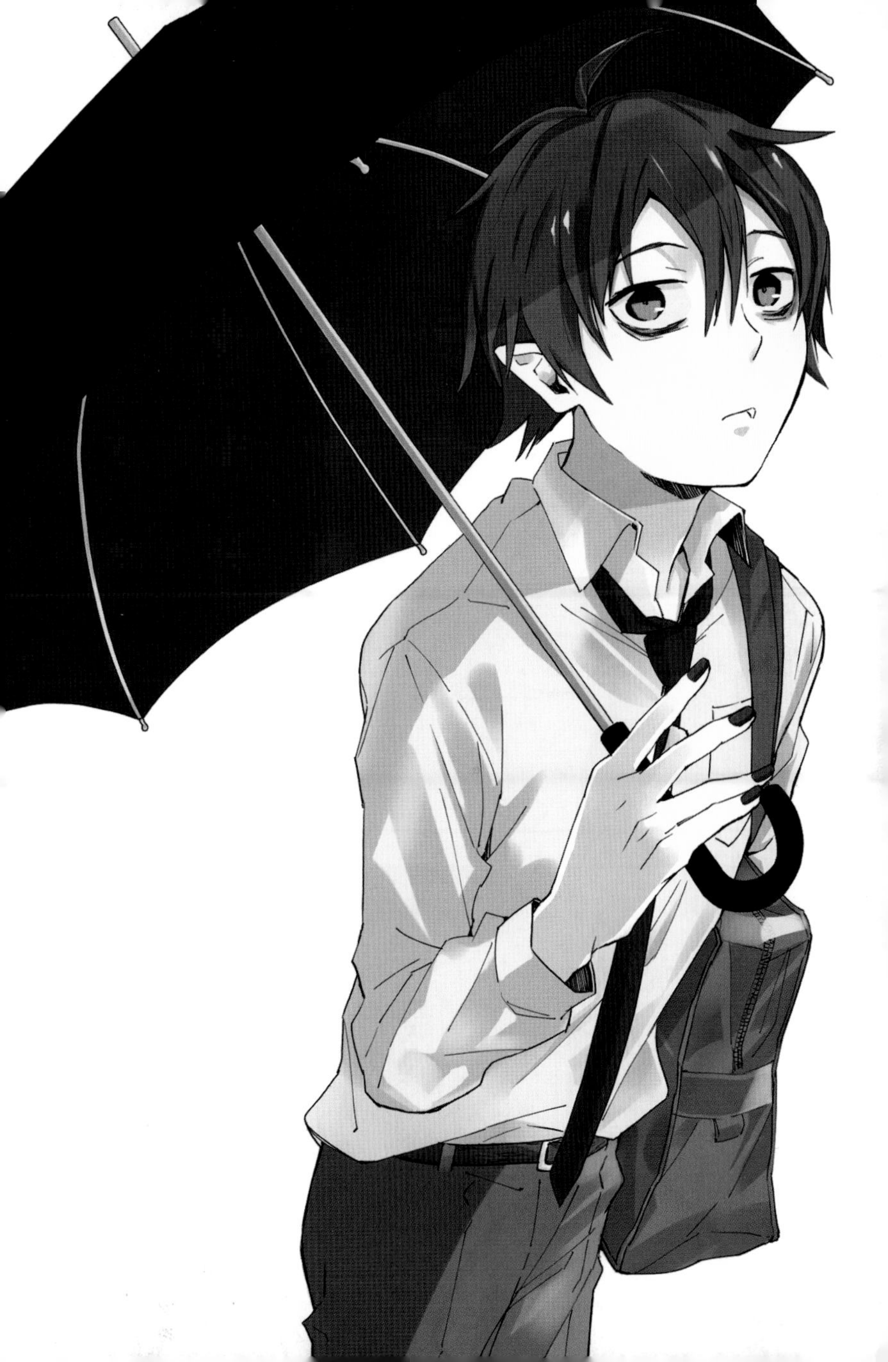

CHAPTER 1 / 3RD WEEK OF JUNE (134TH TIME)

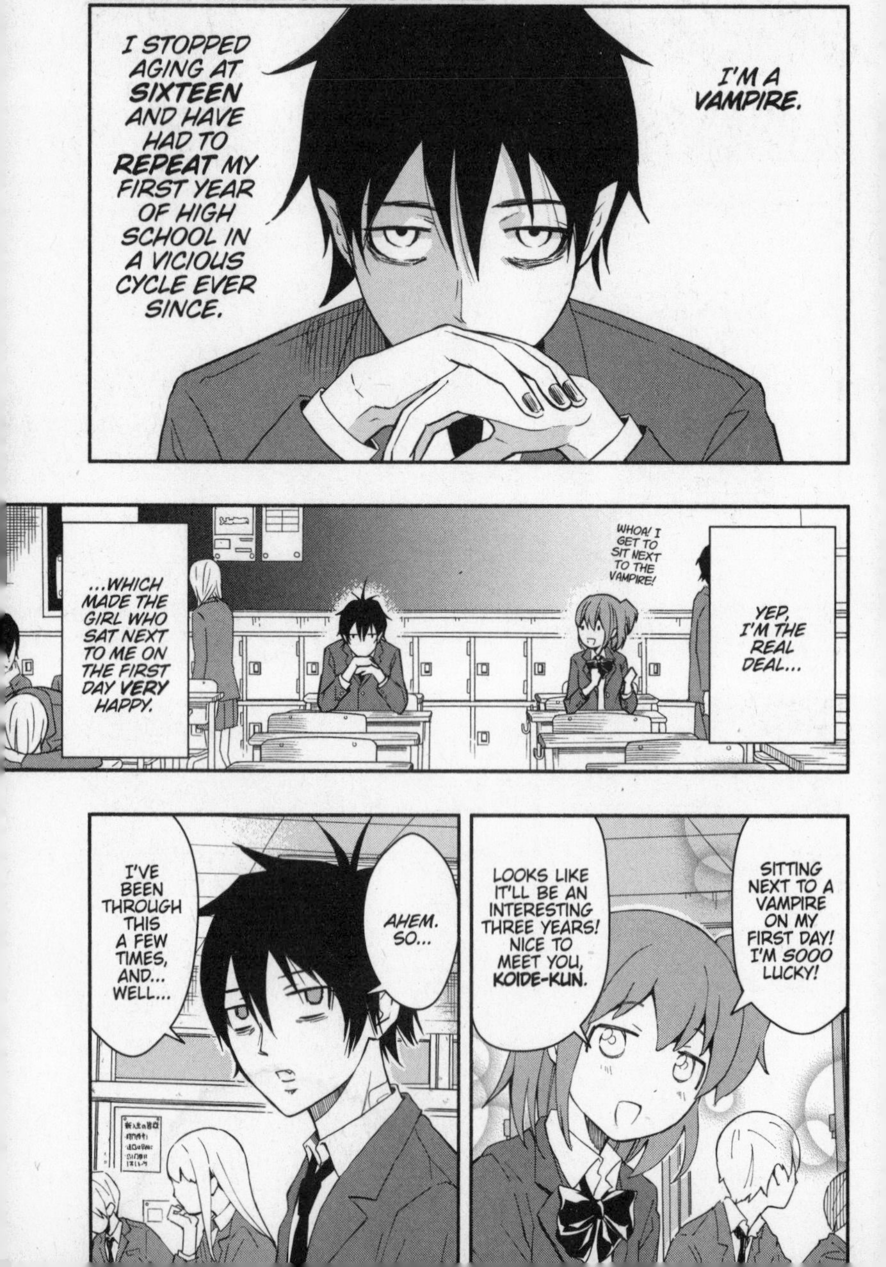
I'M A VAMPIRE.
I STOPPED AGING AT SIXTEEN AND HAVE HAD TO REPEAT MY FIRST YEAR OF HIGH SCHOOL IN A VICIOUS CYCLE EVER SINCE.
YEP, I'M THE REAL DEAL...
WHOA! I GET TO SIT NEXT TO THE VAMPIRE!
...WHICH MADE THE GIRL WHO SAT NEXT TO ME ON THE FIRST DAY VERY HAPPY.
SITTING NEXT TO A VAMPIRE ON MY FIRST DAY! I'M SOOO LUCKY!
LOOKS LIKE IT'LL BE AN INTERESTING THREE YEARS! NICE TO MEET YOU, KOIDE-KUN.
AHEM. SO...
I'VE BEEN THROUGH THIS A FEW TIMES, AND... WELL...

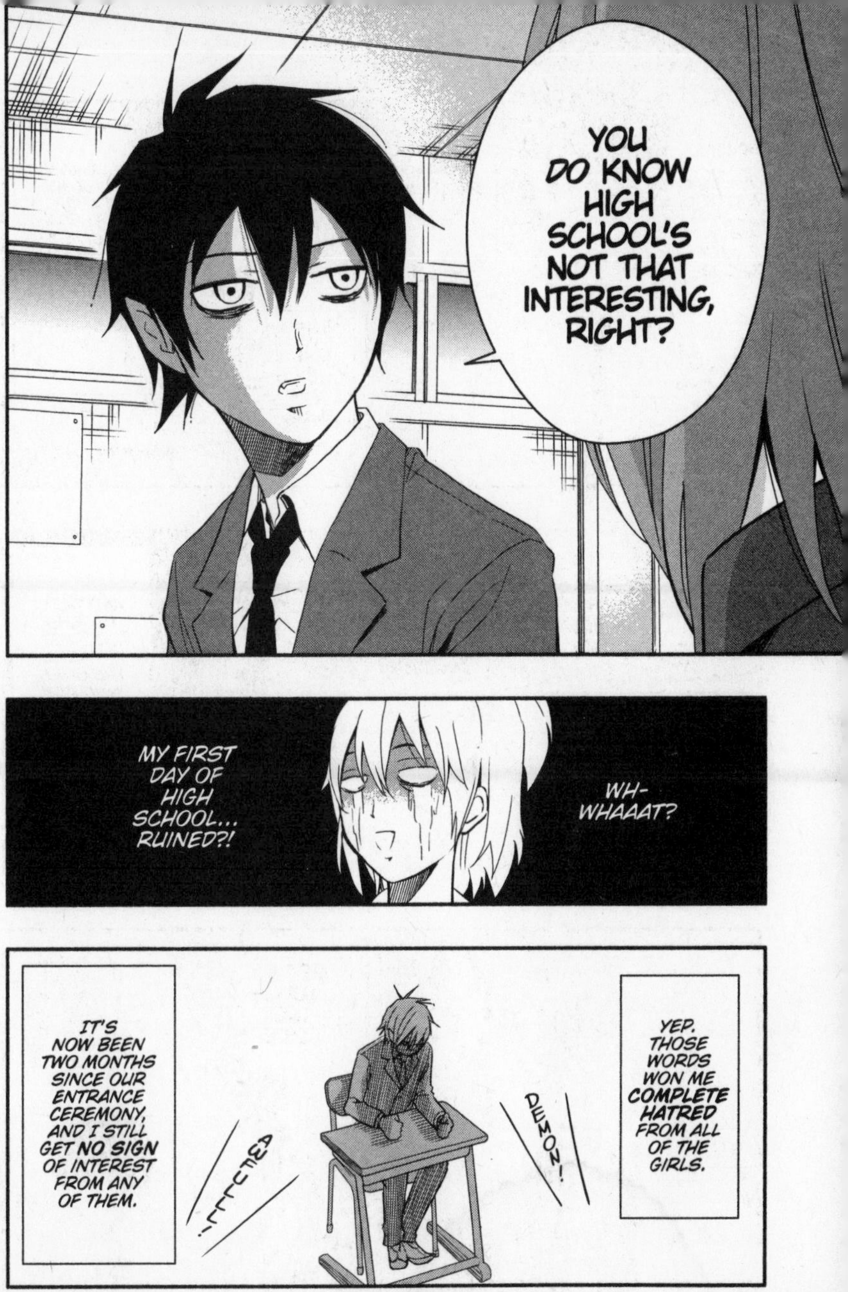
YOU DO KNOW HIGH SCHOOL'S NOT THAT INTERESTING, RIGHT?
WH- WHAAAT?
MY FIRST DAY OF HIGH SCHOOL... RUINED?!
YEP. THOSE WORDS WON ME COMPLETE HATRED FROM ALL OF THE GIRLS.
DEMON!
AWFULLL!
IT'S NOW BEEN TWO MONTHS SINCE OUR ENTRANCE CEREMONY, AND I STILL GET NO SIGN OF INTEREST FROM ANY OF THEM.

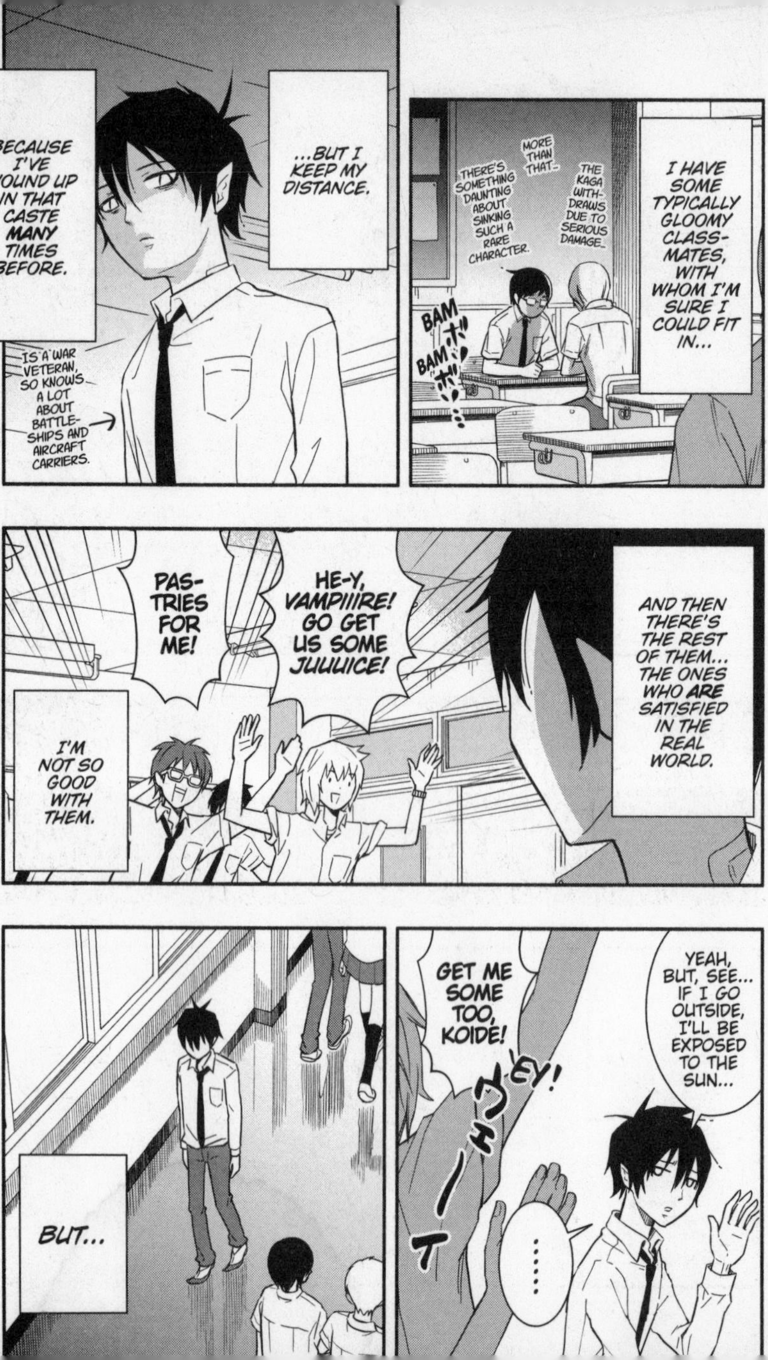
I HAVE SOME TYPICALLY GLOOMY CLASSMATES, WITH WHOM I'M SURE I COULD FIT IN...
THE KAGA WITHDRAWS DUE TO SERIOUS DAMAGE...
MORE THAN THAT...
THERE'S SOMETHING DAUNTING ABOUT SINKING SUCH A RARE CHARACTER.
BAM
BAM
...BUT I KEEP MY DISTANCE.
BECAUSE I'VE WOUND UP IN THAT CASTE MANY TIMES BEFORE.
IS A WAR VETERAN, SO KNOWS A LOT ABOUT BATTLESHIPS AND AIRCRAFT CARRIERS.
AND THEN THERE'S THE REST OF THEM... THE ONES WHO ARE SATISFIED IN THE REAL WORLD.
HE-Y, VAMPIIIRE! GO GET US SOME JUUUICE!
PASTRIES FOR ME!
I'M NOT SO GOOD WITH THEM.
YEAH, BUT, SEE... IF I GO OUTSIDE, I'LL BE EXPOSED TO THE SUN...
GET ME SOME TOO, KOIDE!
'EY!
......
BUT...

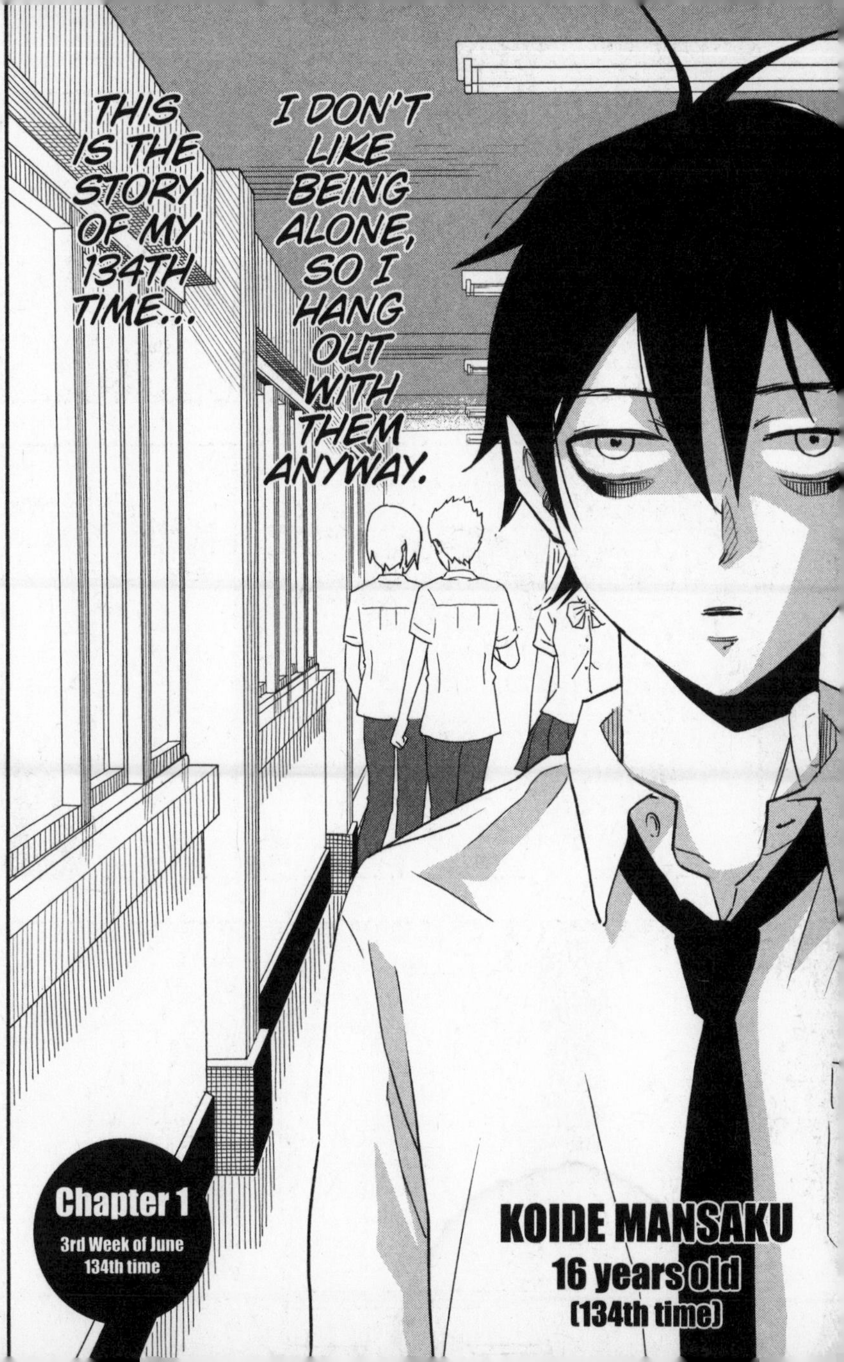
I DON'T LIKE BEING ALONE, SO I HANG OUT WITH THEM ANYWAY.
THIS IS THE STORY OF MY 134TH TIME...
KOIDE MANSAKU
16 years old
(134th time)
Chapter 1
3rd Week of June
134th time

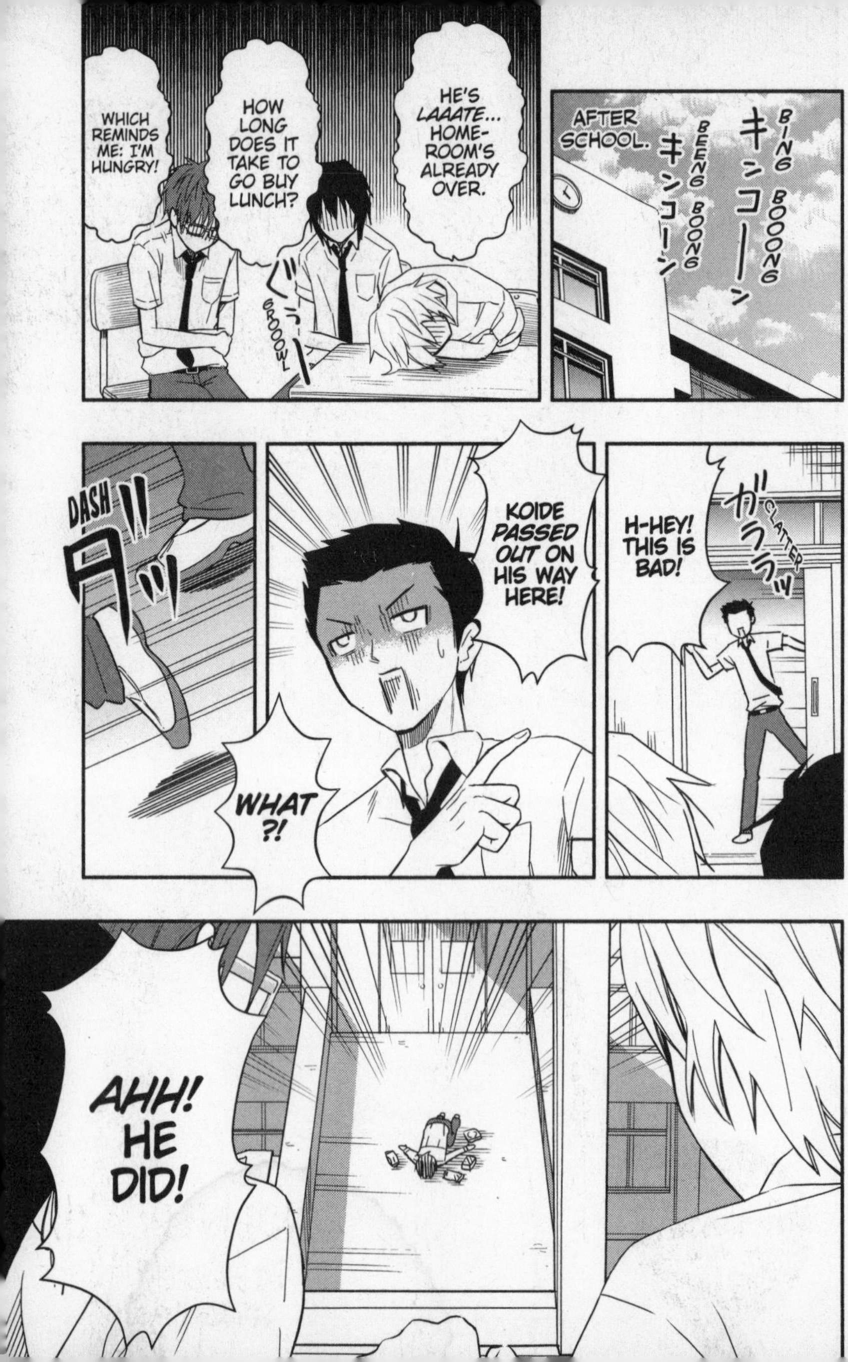
AFTER SCHOOL.
BING BOOONG
キンコーン
BEENG BOONG
キンコーン
HE'S LAAATE... HOME-ROOM'S ALREADY OVER.
HOW LONG DOES IT TAKE TO GO BUY LUNCH?
WHICH REMINDS ME: I'M HUNGRY!
GROOOWL
H-HEY! THIS IS BAD!
CLATTER
KOIDE PASSED OUT ON HIS WAY HERE!
WHAT?!
DASH
AHH! HE DID!

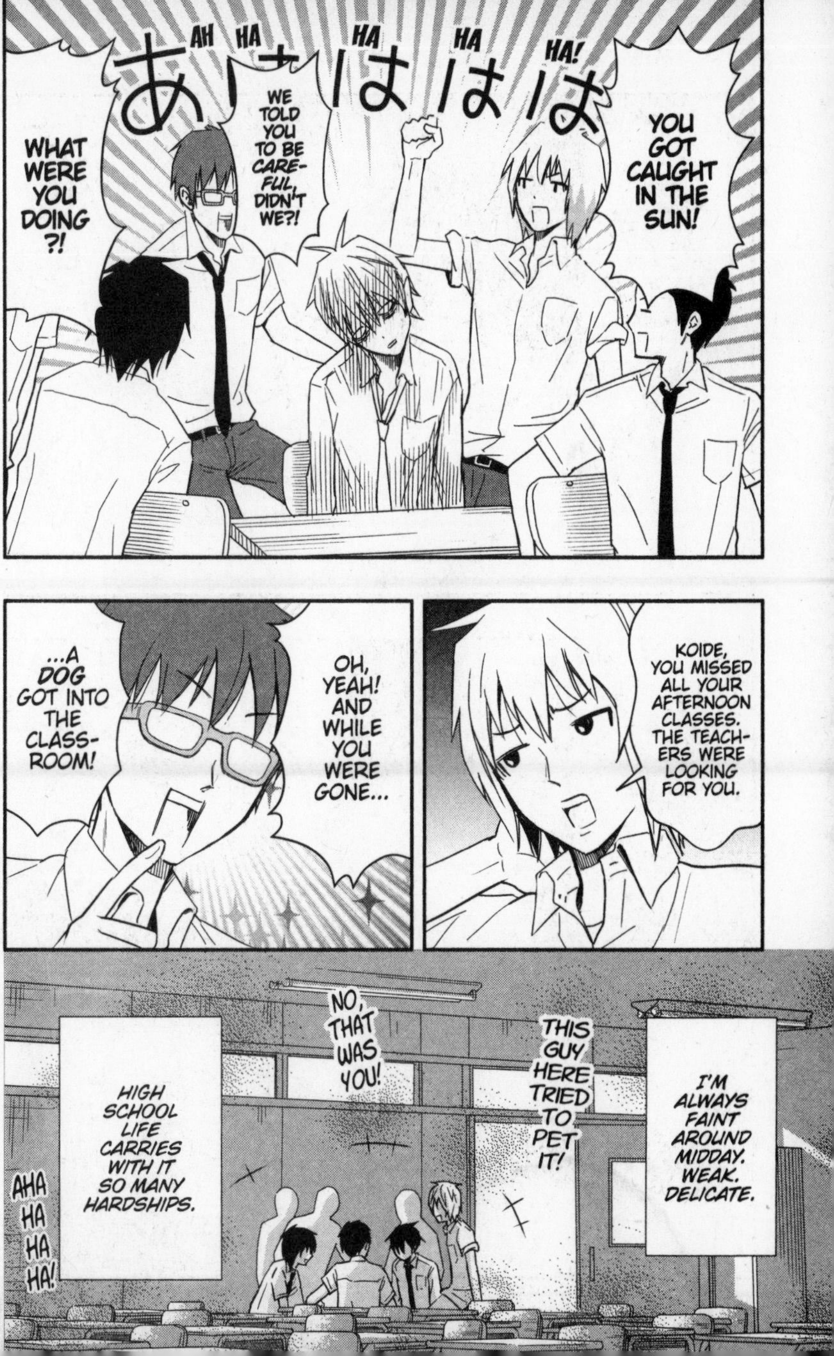
AH HA HA HA HA!
あーははは
YOU GOT CAUGHT IN THE SUN!
WE TOLD YOU TO BE CAREFUL, DIDN'T WE?!
WHAT WERE YOU DOING?!
KOIDE, YOU MISSED ALL YOUR AFTERNOON CLASSES. THE TEACHERS WERE LOOKING FOR YOU.
OH, YEAH! AND WHILE YOU WERE GONE...
...A DOG GOT INTO THE CLASSROOM!
I'M ALWAYS FAINT AROUND MIDDAY. WEAK. DELICATE.
THIS GUY HERE TRIED TO PET IT!
NO, THAT WAS YOU!
HIGH SCHOOL LIFE CARRIES WITH IT SO MANY HARDSHIPS.
AHA HA HA HA HA!

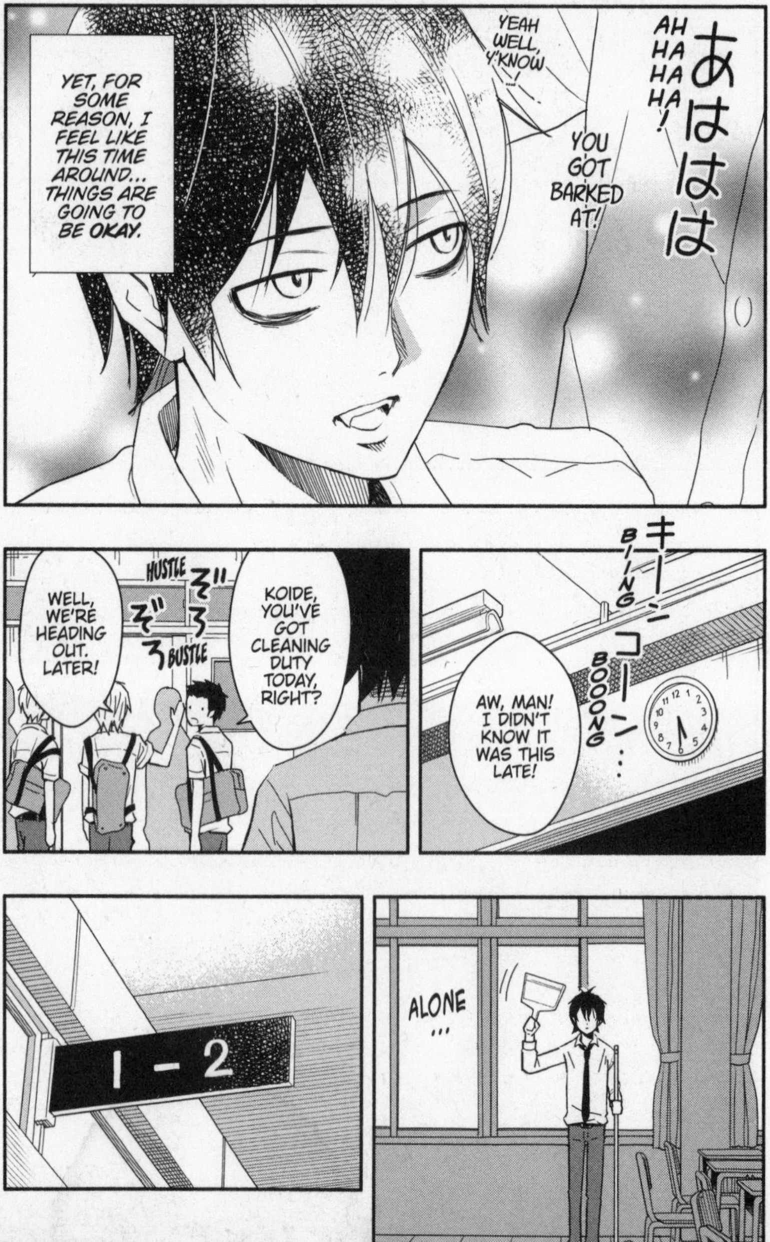
あははは
AH HA HA HA!
YEAH WELL, Y'KNOW ...!
YOU GOT BARKED AT!
YET, FOR SOME REASON, I FEEL LIKE THIS TIME AROUND... THINGS ARE GOING TO BE OKAY.
キーンコーン…
BIING BOOONG
AW, MAN! I DIDN'T KNOW IT WAS THIS LATE!
KOIDE, YOU'VE GOT CLEANING DUTY TODAY, RIGHT?
ぞろぞろ
HUSTLE BUSTLE
WELL, WE'RE HEADING OUT. LATER!
ALONE ...
1-2

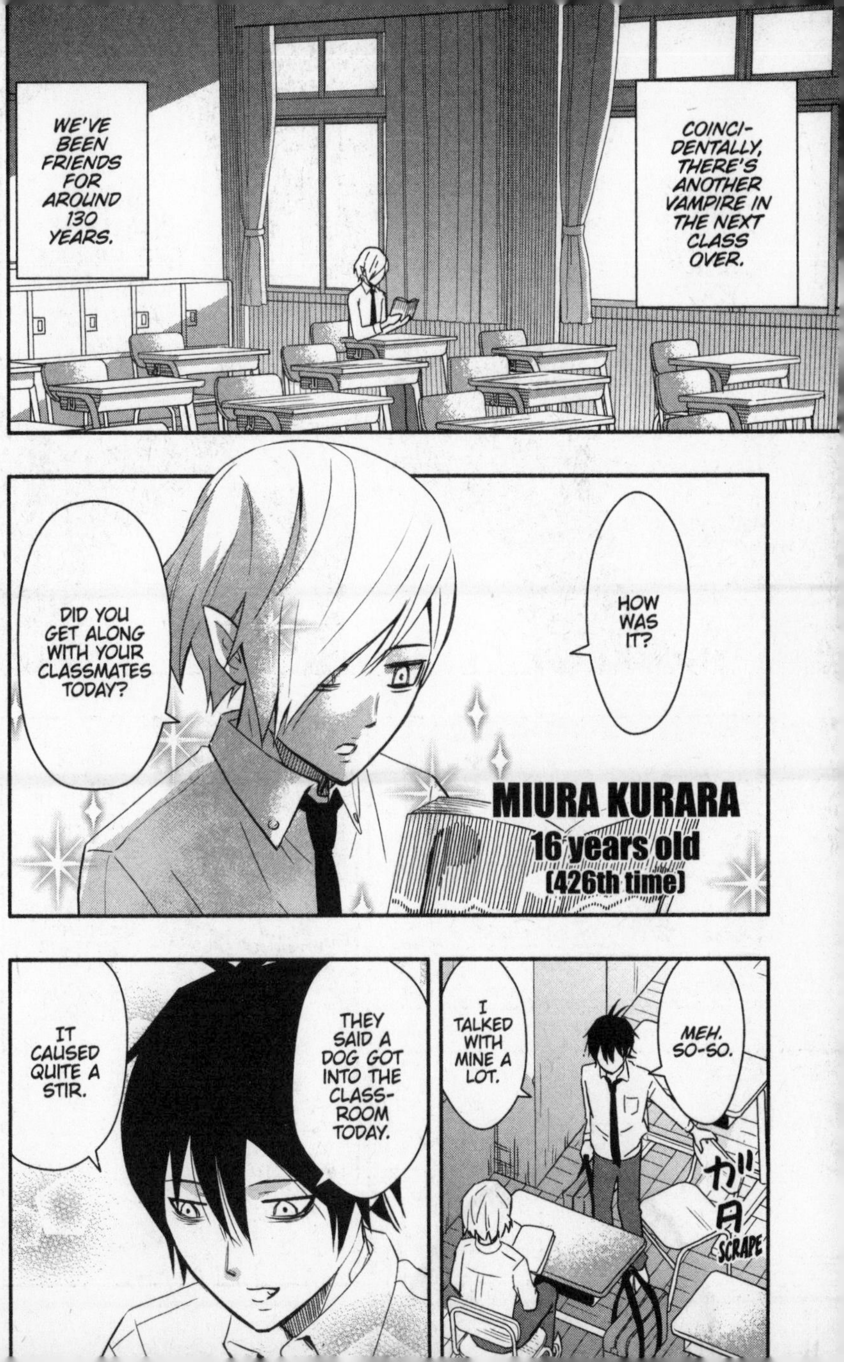
COINCI-DENTALLY, THERE'S ANOTHER VAMPIRE IN THE NEXT CLASS OVER.
WE'VE BEEN FRIENDS FOR AROUND 130 YEARS.
HOW WAS IT?
DID YOU GET ALONG WITH YOUR CLASSMATES TODAY?
MIURA KURARA
16 years old
(426th time)
MEH. SO-SO.
I TALKED WITH MINE A LOT.
ガリ
SCRAPE
THEY SAID A DOG GOT INTO THE CLASS-ROOM TODAY.
IT CAUSED QUITE A STIR.

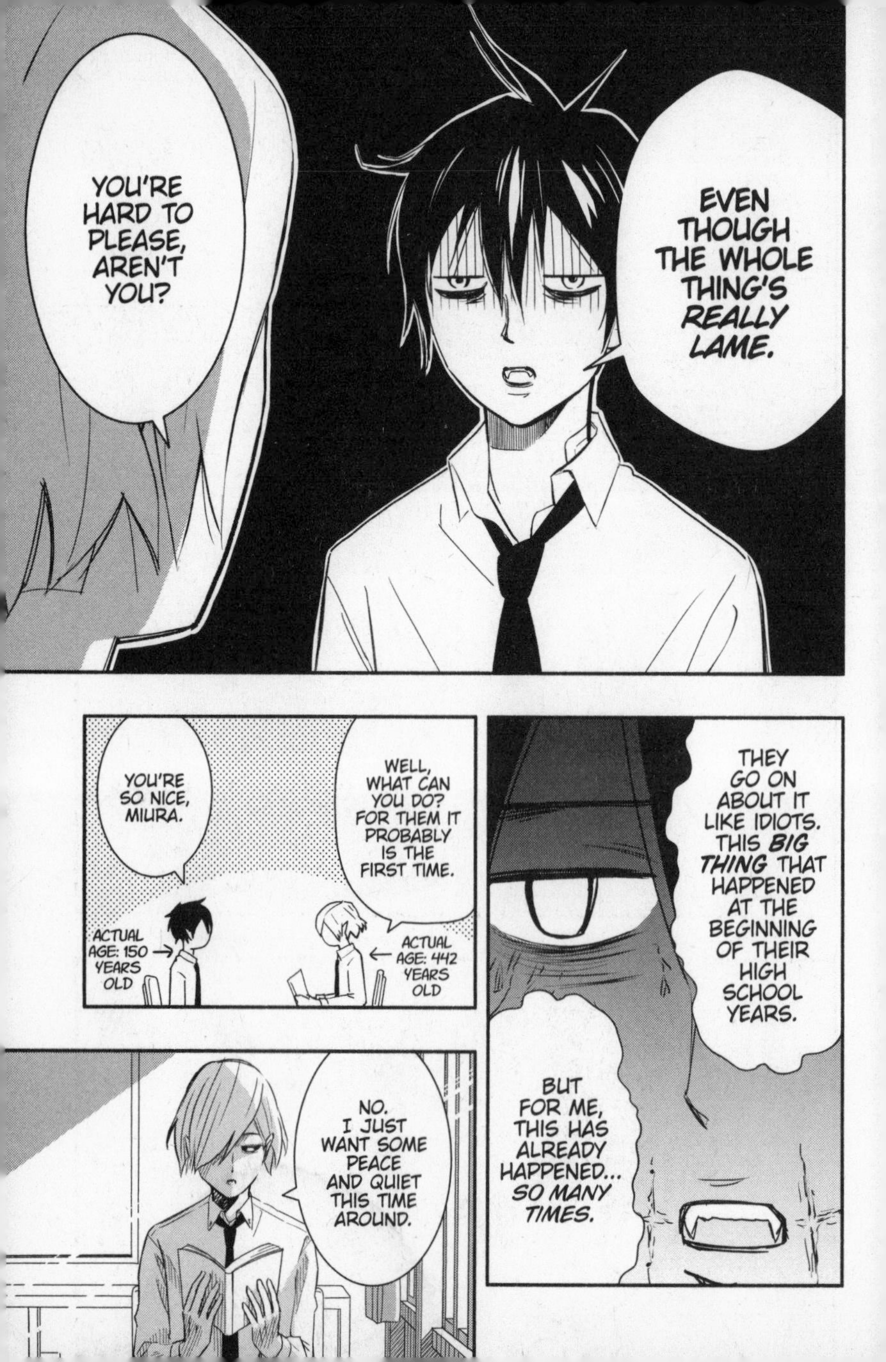
EVEN THOUGH THE WHOLE THING'S REALLY LAME.
YOU'RE HARD TO PLEASE, AREN'T YOU?
THEY GO ON ABOUT IT LIKE IDIOTS. THIS BIG THING THAT HAPPENED AT THE BEGINNING OF THEIR HIGH SCHOOL YEARS.
BUT FOR ME, THIS HAS ALREADY HAPPENED... SO MANY TIMES.
WELL, WHAT CAN YOU DO? FOR THEM IT PROBABLY IS THE FIRST TIME.
YOU'RE SO NICE, MIURA.
ACTUAL AGE: 442 YEARS OLD
ACTUAL AGE: 150 YEARS OLD
NO. I JUST WANT SOME PEACE AND QUIET THIS TIME AROUND.

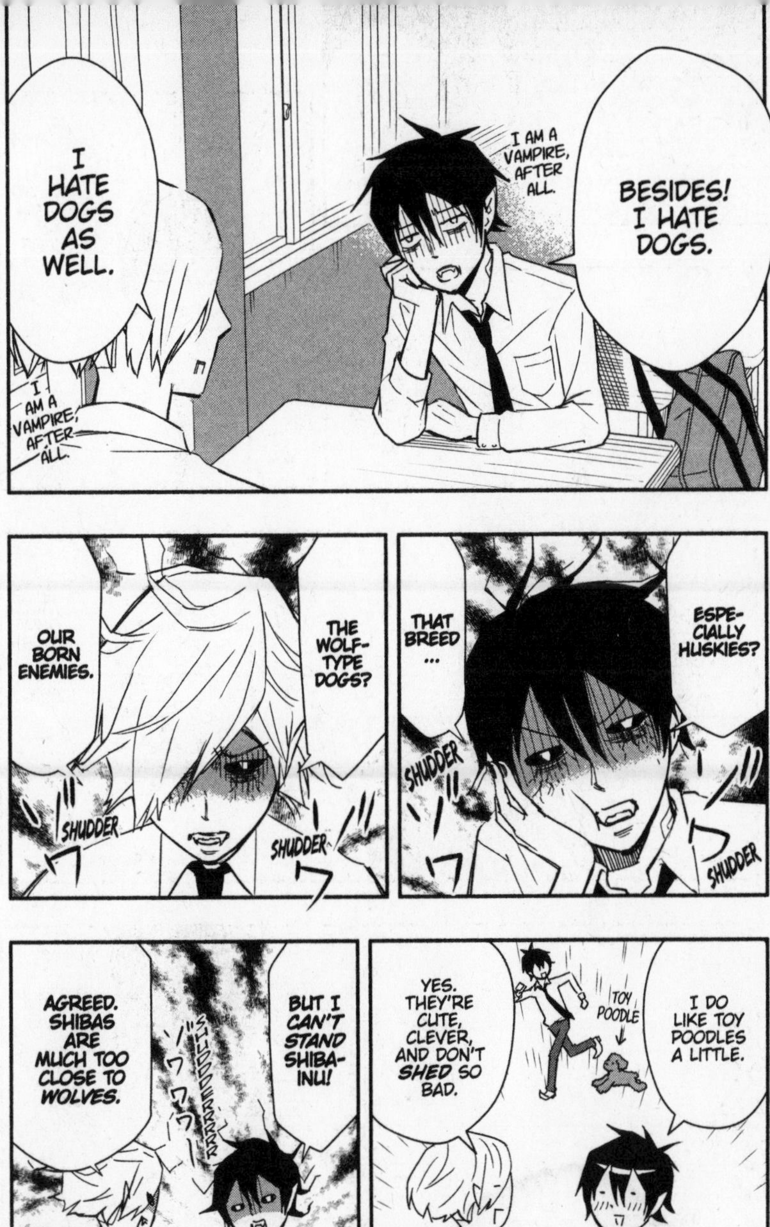
BESIDES! I HATE DOGS.
I AM A VAMPIRE, AFTER ALL.
I HATE DOGS AS WELL.
I AM A VAMPIRE, AFTER ALL.
ESPECIALLY HUSKIES?
THAT BREED ...
SHUDDER
SHUDDER
THE WOLF-TYPE DOGS?
OUR BORN ENEMIES.
SHUDDER
SHUDDER
I DO LIKE TOY POODLES A LITTLE.
TOY POODLE
YES. THEY'RE CUTE, CLEVER, AND DON'T *SHED* SO BAD.
BUT I *CAN'T STAND* SHIBA-INU!
SHUDDERRRR
AGREED. SHIBAS ARE MUCH TOO CLOSE TO *WOLVES*.

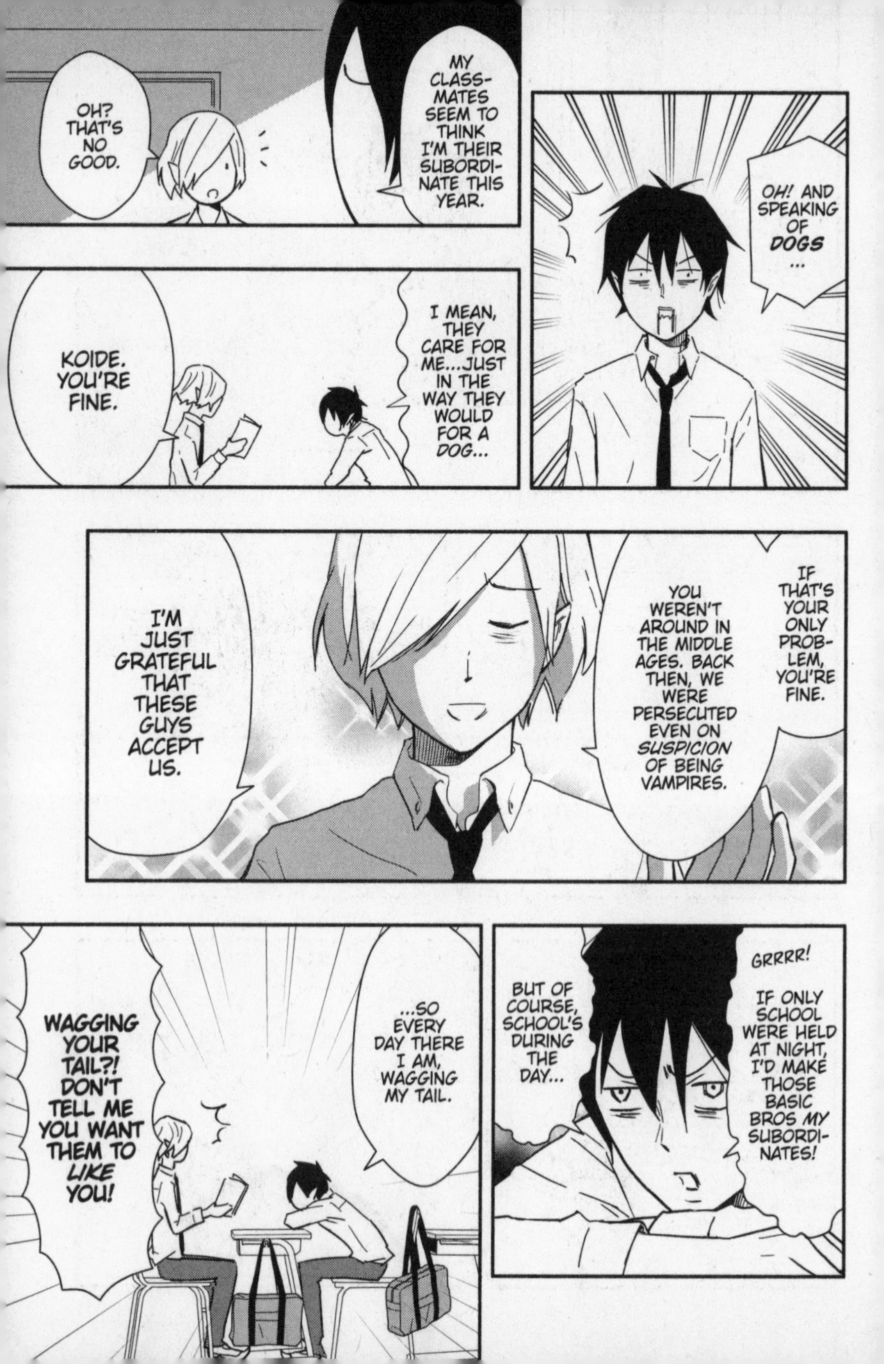
OH! AND SPEAKING OF DOGS...
MY CLASSMATES SEEM TO THINK I'M THEIR SUBORDINATE THIS YEAR.
OH? THAT'S NO GOOD.
I MEAN, THEY CARE FOR ME...JUST IN THE WAY THEY WOULD FOR A DOG...
KOIDE. YOU'RE FINE.
IF THAT'S YOUR ONLY PROBLEM, YOU'RE FINE.
YOU WEREN'T AROUND IN THE MIDDLE AGES. BACK THEN, WE WERE PERSECUTED EVEN ON SUSPICION OF BEING VAMPIRES.
I'M JUST GRATEFUL THAT THESE GUYS ACCEPT US.
GRRRR!
IF ONLY SCHOOL WERE HELD AT NIGHT, I'D MAKE THOSE BASIC BROS MY SUBORDINATES!
BUT OF COURSE, SCHOOL'S DURING THE DAY...
...SO EVERY DAY THERE I AM, WAGGING MY TAIL.
WAGGING YOUR TAIL?! DON'T TELL ME YOU WANT THEM TO LIKE YOU!

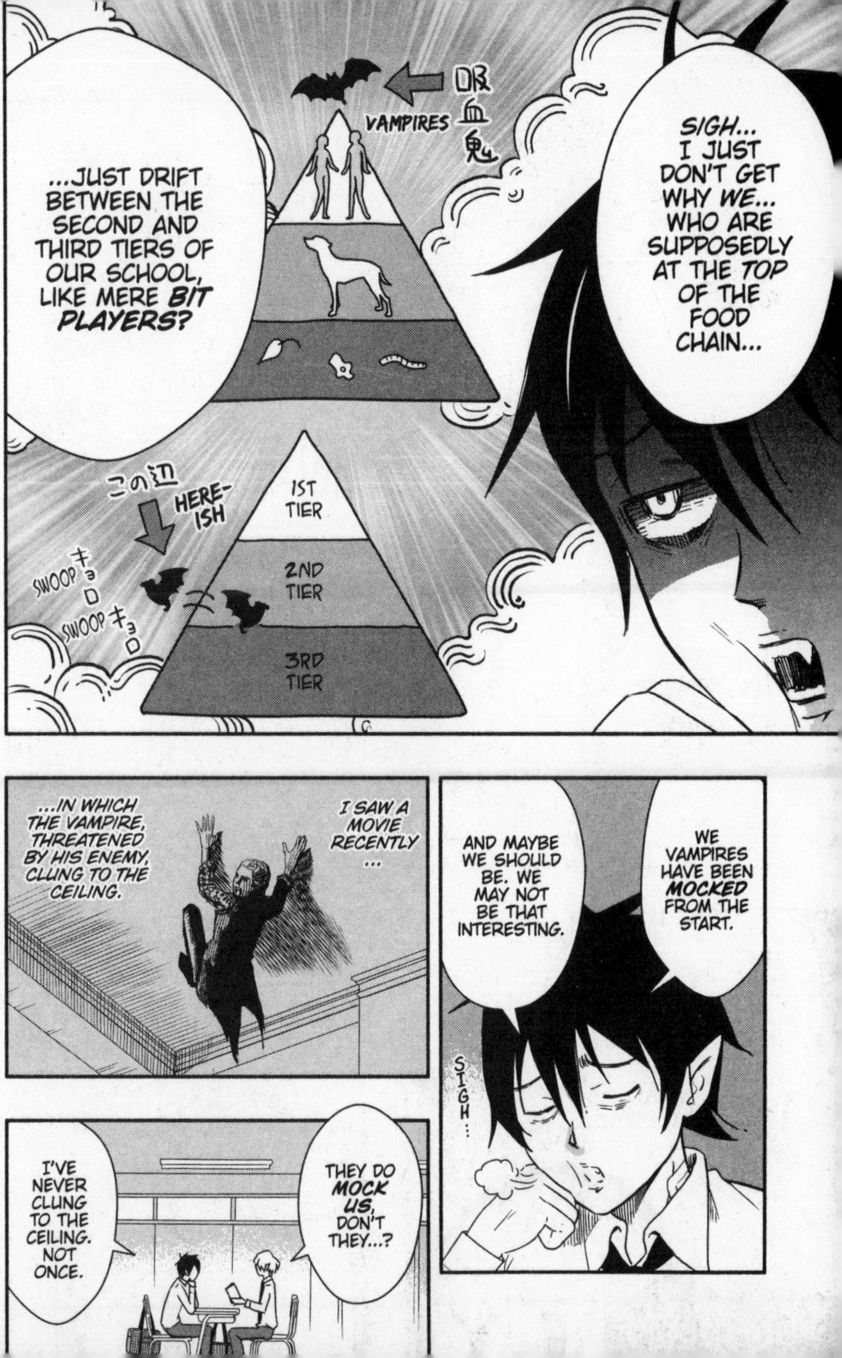
SIGH... I JUST DON'T GET WHY *WE*... WHO ARE SUPPOSEDLY AT THE *TOP* OF THE FOOD CHAIN...
吸血鬼
VAMPIRES
...JUST DRIFT BETWEEN THE SECOND AND THIRD TIERS OF OUR SCHOOL, LIKE MERE *BIT PLAYERS?*
1ST TIER
2ND TIER
3RD TIER
この辺
HERE-ISH
キョロ
SWOOP
キョロ
SWOOP
WE VAMPIRES HAVE BEEN ***MOCKED*** FROM THE START.
AND MAYBE WE SHOULD BE. WE MAY NOT BE THAT INTERESTING.
SIGH...
I SAW A MOVIE RECENTLY...
...IN WHICH THE VAMPIRE, THREATENED BY HIS ENEMY, CLUNG TO THE CEILING.
THEY DO ***MOCK US,*** DON'T THEY...?
I'VE NEVER CLUNG TO THE CEILING. NOT ONCE.

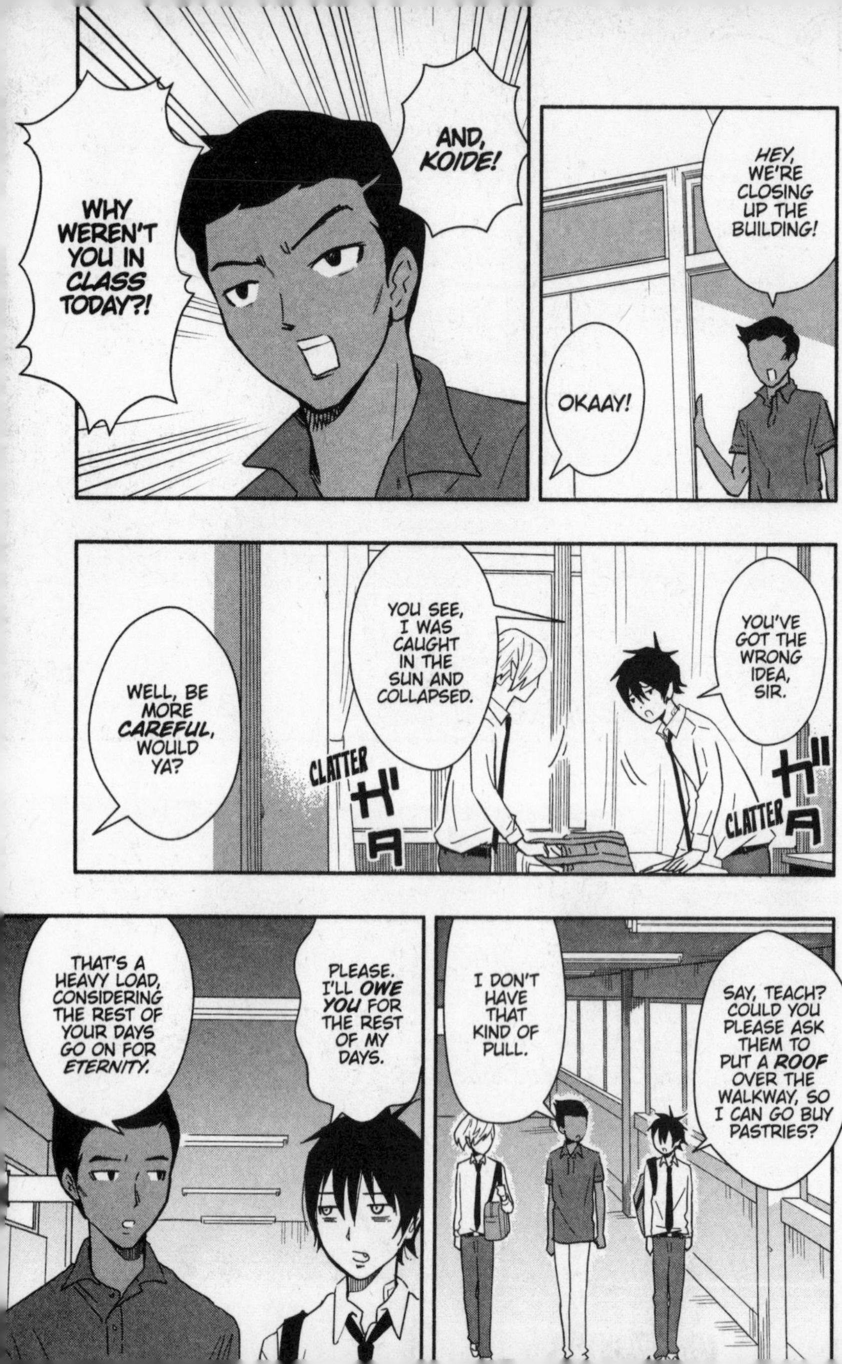
HEY, WE'RE CLOSING UP THE BUILDING!
OKAAY!
AND, KOIDE!
WHY WEREN'T YOU IN CLASS TODAY?!
YOU'VE GOT THE WRONG IDEA, SIR.
CLATTER ガタ
YOU SEE, I WAS CAUGHT IN THE SUN AND COLLAPSED.
CLATTER ガタ
WELL, BE MORE CAREFUL, WOULD YA?
SAY, TEACH? COULD YOU PLEASE ASK THEM TO PUT A ROOF OVER THE WALKWAY, SO I CAN GO BUY PASTRIES?
I DON'T HAVE THAT KIND OF PULL.
PLEASE. I'LL OWE YOU FOR THE REST OF MY DAYS.
THAT'S A HEAVY LOAD, CONSIDERING THE REST OF YOUR DAYS GO ON FOR ETERNITY.

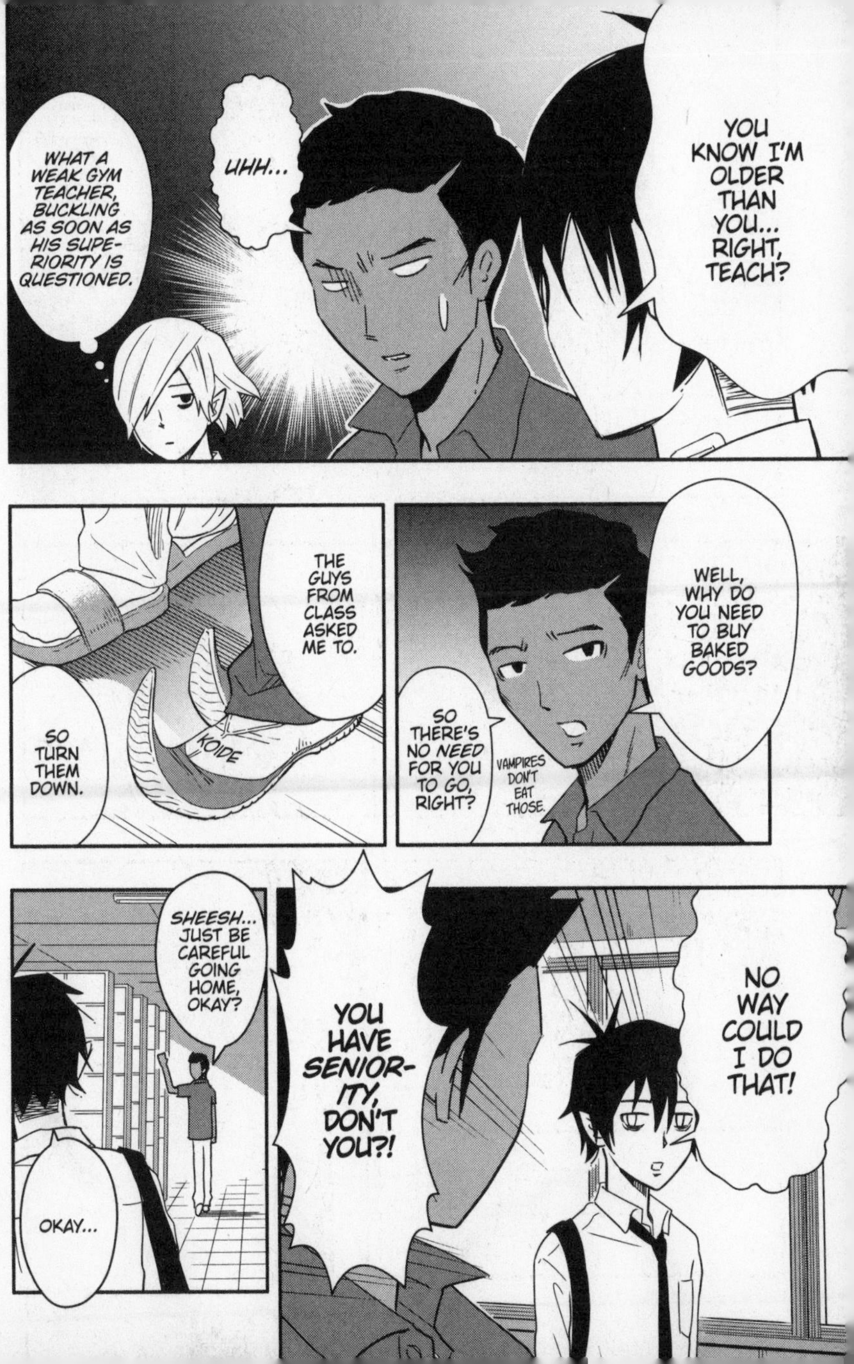
YOU KNOW I'M OLDER THAN YOU... RIGHT, TEACH?
UHH...
WHAT A WEAK GYM TEACHER, BUCKLING AS SOON AS HIS SUPER-IORITY IS QUESTIONED.
WELL, WHY DO YOU NEED TO BUY BAKED GOODS?
VAMPIRES DON'T EAT THOSE.
SO THERE'S NO NEED FOR YOU TO GO, RIGHT?
THE GUYS FROM CLASS ASKED ME TO.
KOIDE
SO TURN THEM DOWN.
NO WAY COULD I DO THAT!
YOU HAVE SENIOR-ITY, DON'T YOU?!
SHEESH... JUST BE CAREFUL GOING HOME, OKAY?
OKAY...

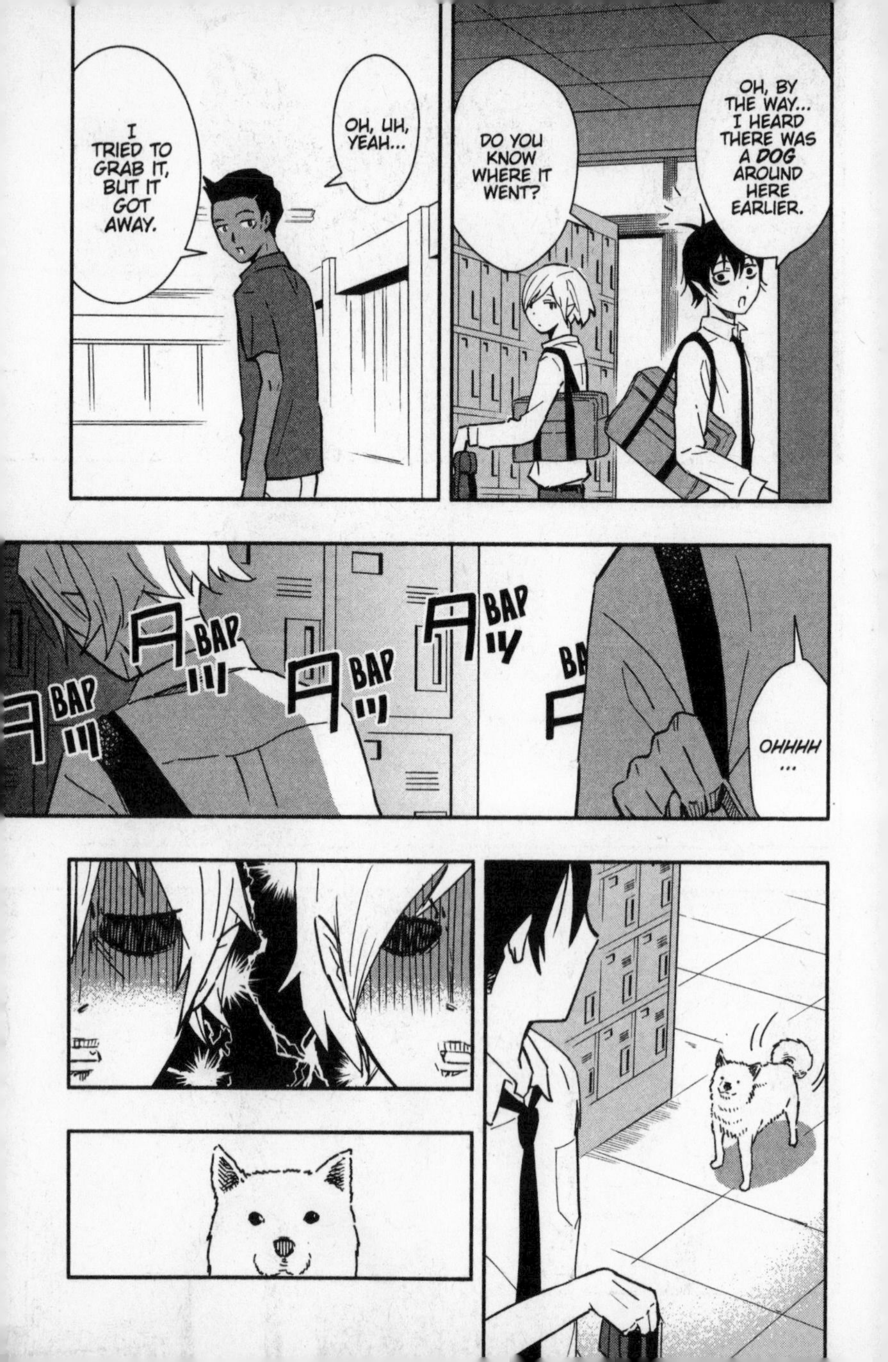
OH, BY THE WAY... I HEARD THERE WAS A DOG AROUND HERE EARLIER.
DO YOU KNOW WHERE IT WENT?
OH, UH, YEAH...
I TRIED TO GRAB IT, BUT IT GOT AWAY.
OHHHH...
BA
BAP
BAP
BAP
BAP

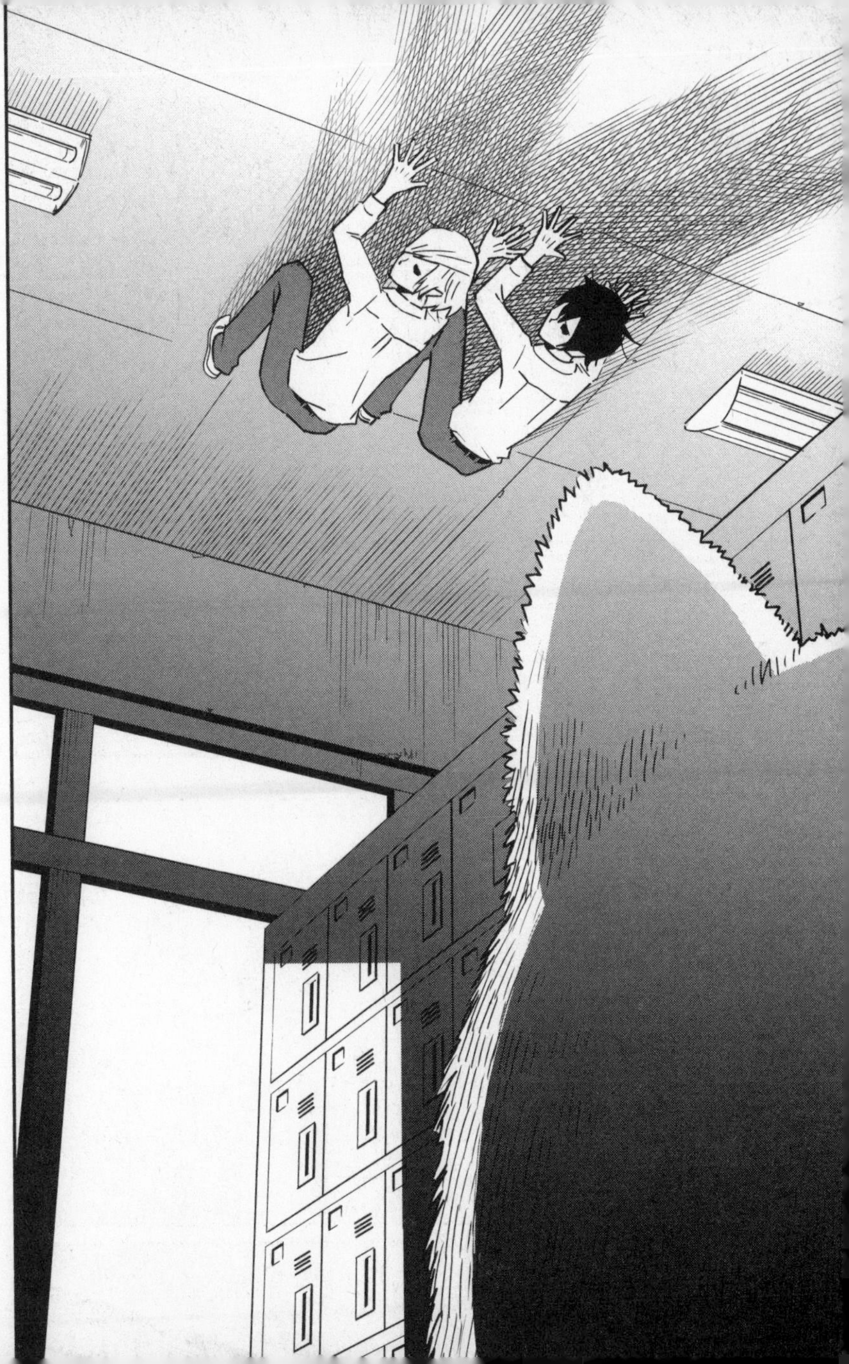

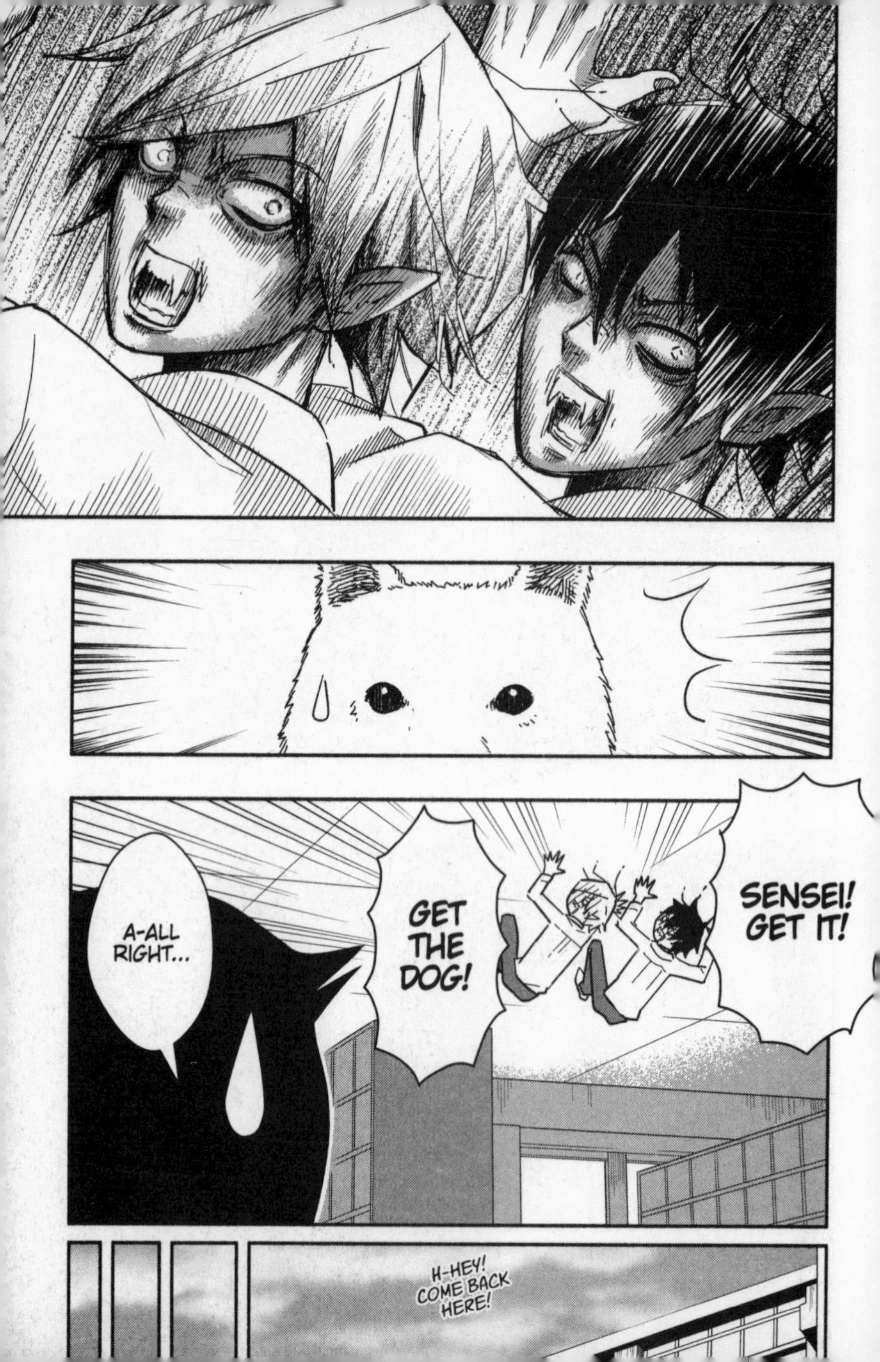
SENSEI! GET IT!
GET THE DOG!
A-ALL RIGHT...
H-HEY! COME BACK HERE!

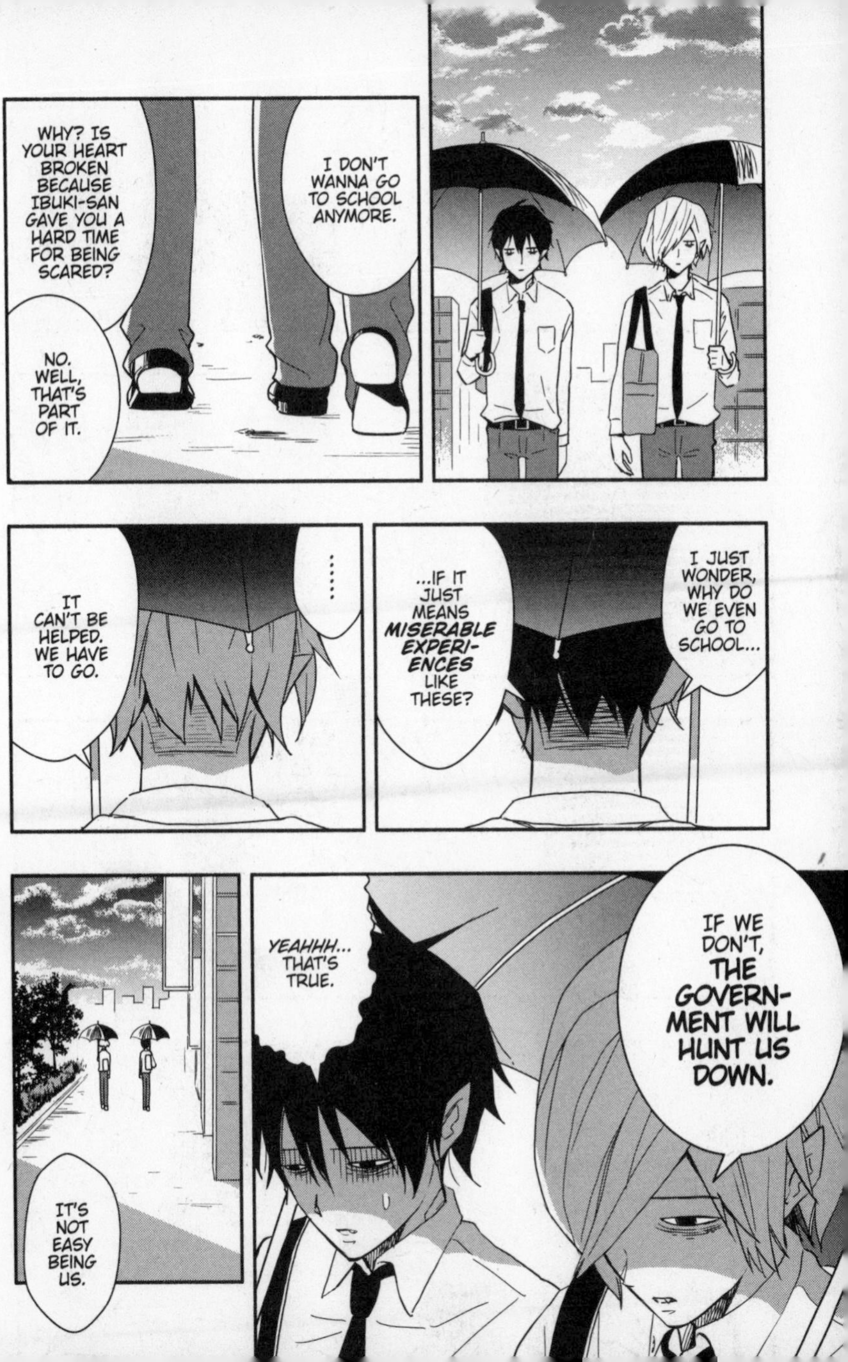
I DON'T WANNA GO TO SCHOOL ANYMORE.
WHY? IS YOUR HEART BROKEN BECAUSE IBUKI-SAN GAVE YOU A HARD TIME FOR BEING SCARED?
NO. WELL, THAT'S PART OF IT.
I JUST WONDER, WHY DO WE EVEN GO TO SCHOOL...
...IF IT JUST MEANS *MISERABLE EXPERIENCES* LIKE THESE?
......
IT CAN'T BE HELPED. WE HAVE TO GO.
IF WE DON'T, **THE GOVERNMENT WILL HUNT US DOWN.**
YEAHHH... THAT'S TRUE.
IT'S NOT EASY BEING US.

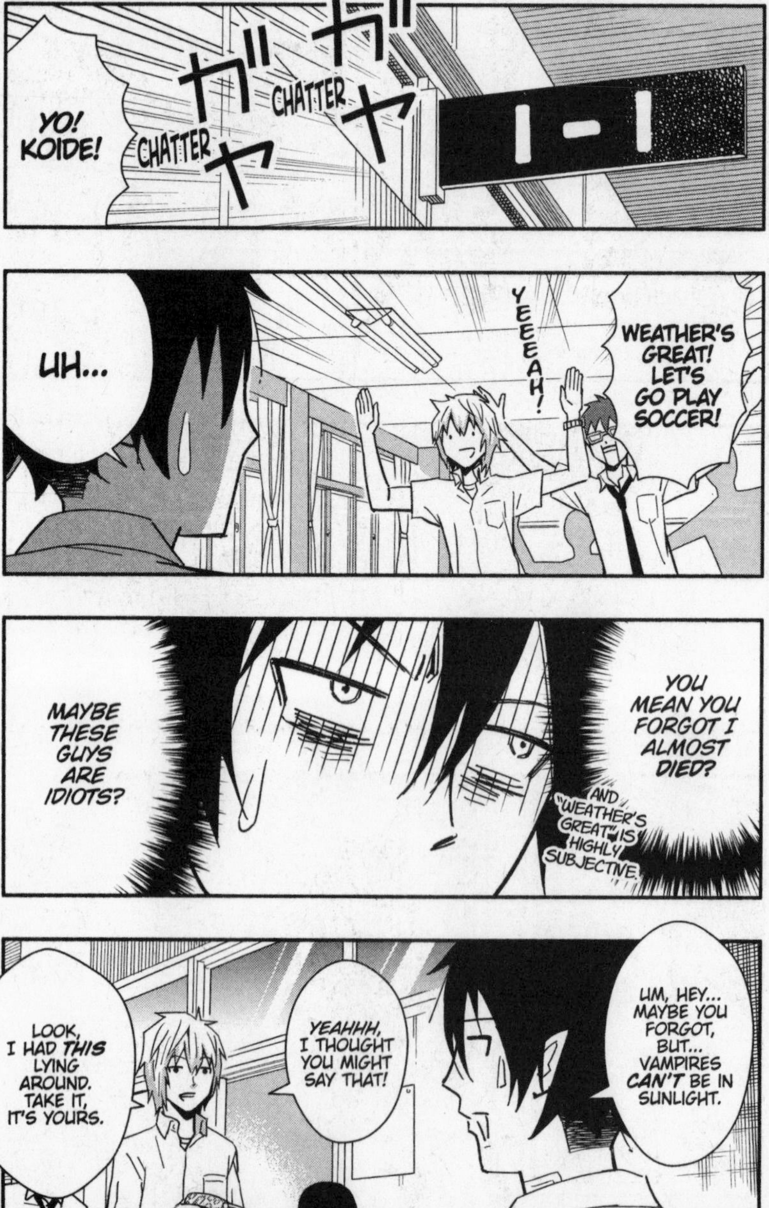

1-1
ガヤ
CHATTER
ガヤ
CHATTER
YO! KOIDE!
WEATHER'S GREAT! LET'S GO PLAY SOCCER!
YEEEAH!
UH...
YOU MEAN YOU FORGOT I ALMOST DIED?
AND "WEATHER'S GREAT" IS HIGHLY SUBJECTIVE.
MAYBE THESE GUYS ARE IDIOTS?
UM, HEY... MAYBE YOU FORGOT, BUT... VAMPIRES CAN'T BE IN SUNLIGHT.
YEAHHH, I THOUGHT YOU MIGHT SAY THAT!
LOOK, I HAD THIS LYING AROUND. TAKE IT, IT'S YOURS.

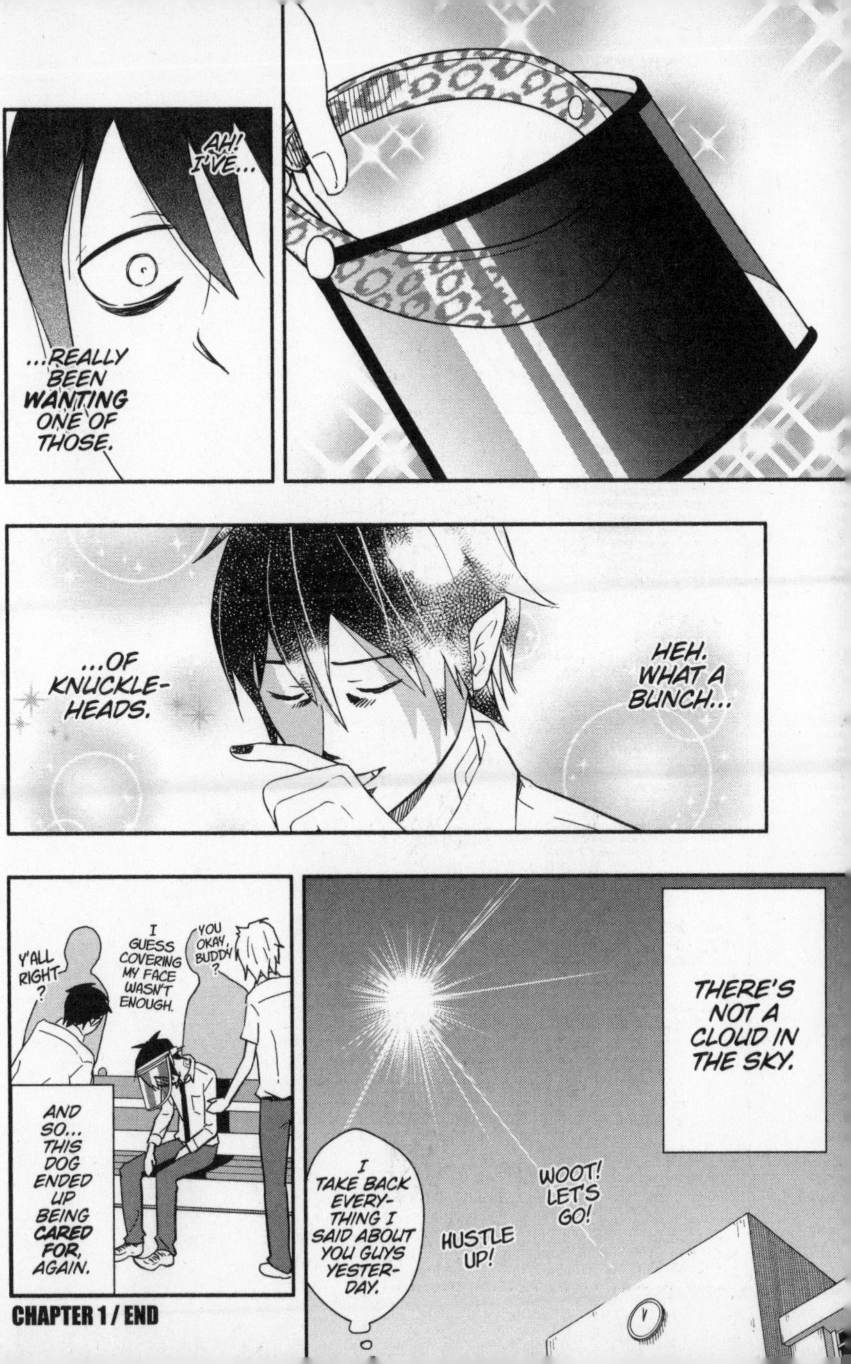
AH! I'VE...
...REALLY BEEN WANTING ONE OF THOSE.
HEH. WHAT A BUNCH...
...OF KNUCKLE-HEADS.
THERE'S NOT A CLOUD IN THE SKY.
WOOT! LET'S GO!
HUSTLE UP!
I TAKE BACK EVERY-THING I SAID ABOUT YOU GUYS YESTER-DAY.
YOU OKAY, BUDDY?
I GUESS COVERING MY FACE WASN'T ENOUGH.
Y'ALL RIGHT?
AND SO... THIS DOG ENDED UP BEING CARED FOR, AGAIN.

CHAPTER 1 / END

THE TRANSFER OF ENERGY

MORNING.
MORNIN'!
MORN!
KOIDE
AVERAGE HIGH SCHOOL STUDENT
LUNCH.
WOOOOO!
KOIDE
AVERAGE HIGH SCHOOL STUDENT
AFTER SCHOOL.
YEAH! LET'S GOOOO!
KOIDE
AVERAGE HIGH SCHOOL STUDENT
NIGHT.
KOIDE
AVERAGE HIGH SCHOOL STUDENT
BUT NO ONE'S AROUND TO SEE, BECAUSE IT'S NIGHT.

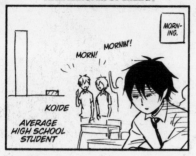

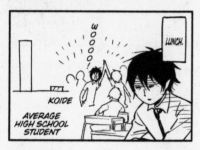

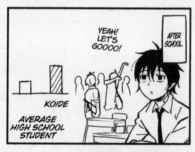

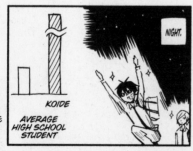

MY
PATHETIC
VAMPIRE
LIFE

THE GOVERNMENT'S POSITION ON VAMPIRES

TEENAGE VAMPIRES ARE SENT TO SCHOOL
TO KEEP THEM FOCUSED ON STUDIES AND
OFF THE STREETS. IN OTHER WORDS, TO
KEEP THEM FROM TERRORIZING THE PUBLIC
AT LARGE.

 IF VAMPIRES DON'T ATTEND SCHOOL,
THE GOVERNMENT—WORKING
CLOSELY WITH ITS CONTRACTOR,
HELSING CORP.—HUNTS THEM DOWN.

CHAPTER 2 / 2ND WEEK OF APRIL (134TH TIME)

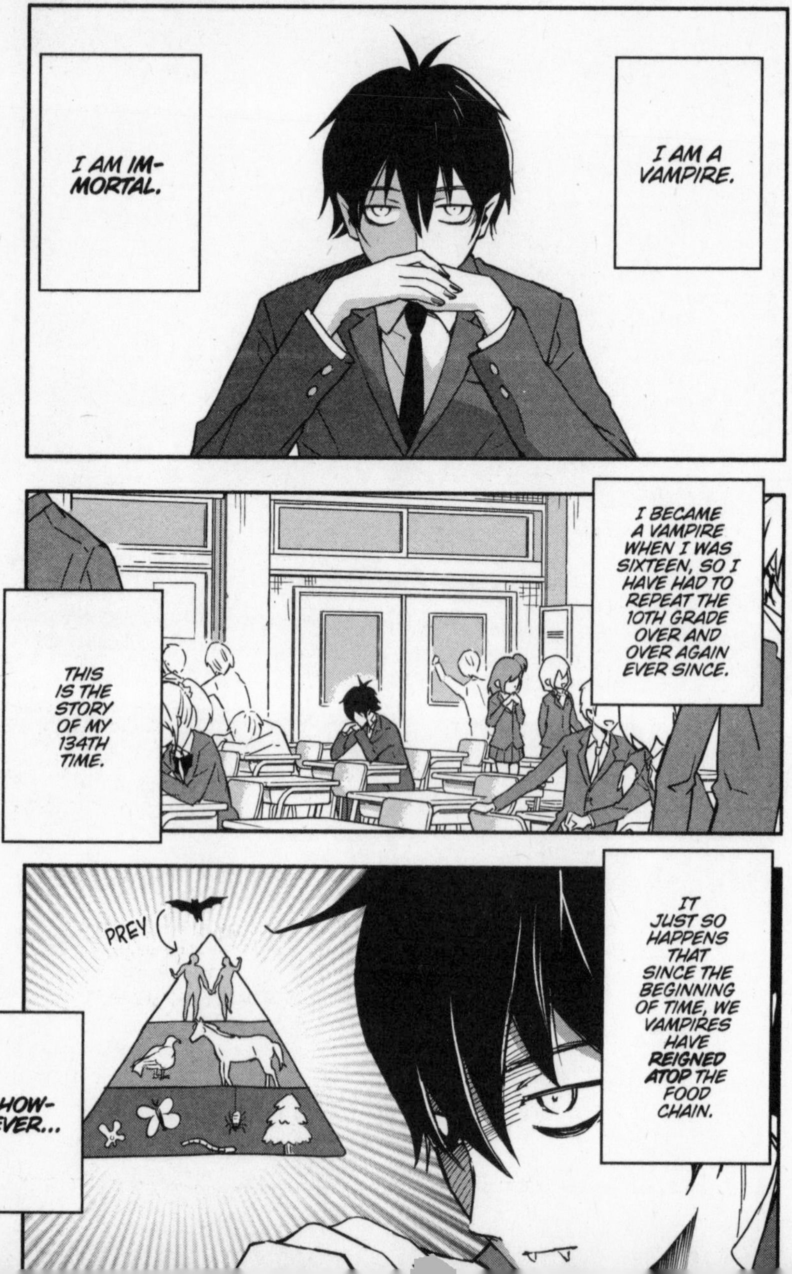
I AM A VAMPIRE.
I AM IM-MORTAL.
I BECAME A VAMPIRE WHEN I WAS SIXTEEN, SO I HAVE HAD TO REPEAT THE 10TH GRADE OVER AND OVER AGAIN EVER SINCE.
THIS IS THE STORY OF MY 134TH TIME.
IT JUST SO HAPPENS THAT SINCE THE BEGINNING OF TIME, WE VAMPIRES HAVE **REIGNED ATOP** THE FOOD CHAIN.
PREY
HOW-EVER...

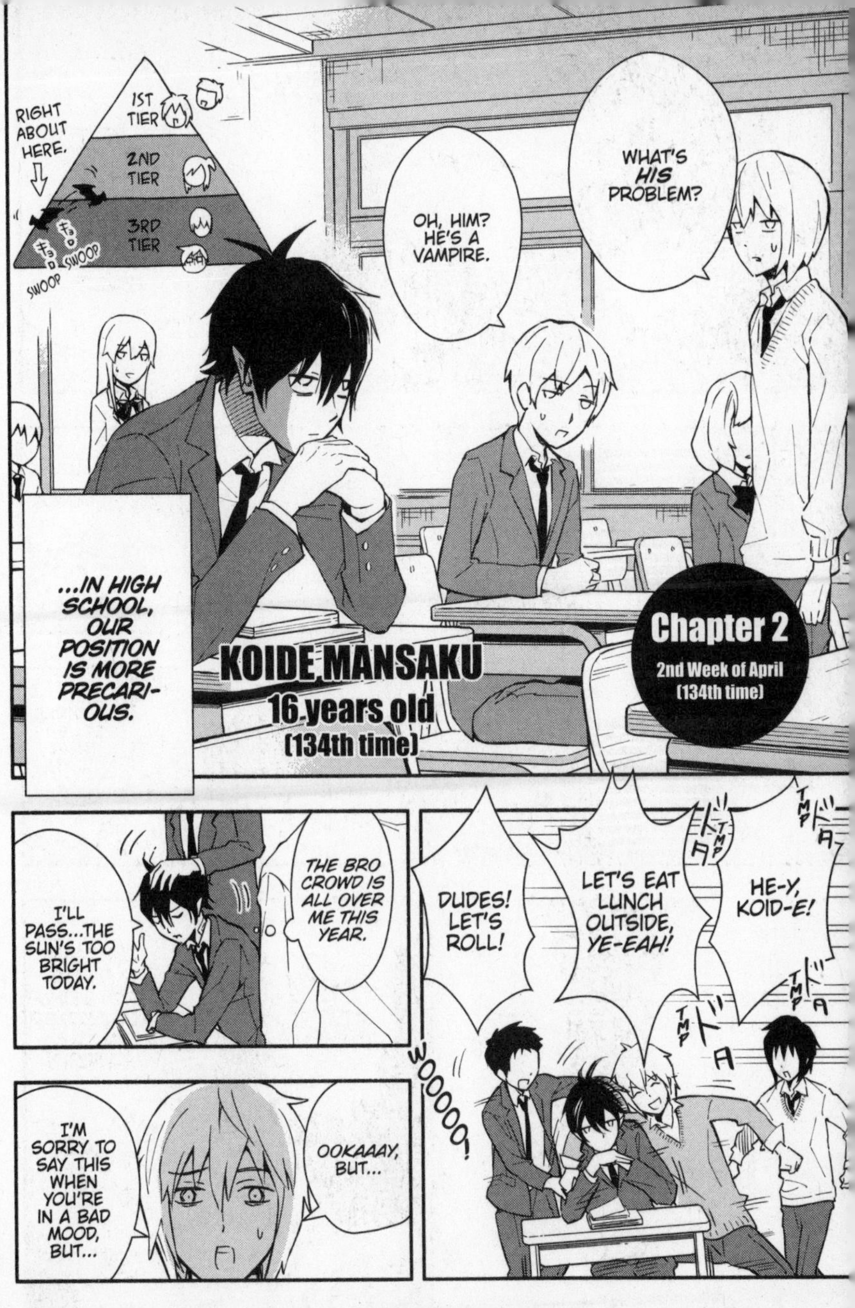

WHAT'S HIS PROBLEM?
OH, HIM? HE'S A VAMPIRE.
1ST TIER
2ND TIER
3RD TIER
RIGHT ABOUT HERE.
SWOOP
SWOOP
Chapter 2
2nd Week of April (134th time)
KOIDE MANSAKU
16 years old (134th time)
...IN HIGH SCHOOL, OUR POSITION IS MORE PRECARIOUS.
TMP TMP
HE-Y, KOID-E!
TMP TMP
LET'S EAT LUNCH OUTSIDE, YE-EAH!
DUDES! LET'S ROLL!
WOOOOOO!
THE BRO CROWD IS ALL OVER ME THIS YEAR.
I'LL PASS...THE SUN'S TOO BRIGHT TODAY.
OOKAAAY, BUT...
I'M SORRY TO SAY THIS WHEN YOU'RE IN A BAD MOOD, BUT...

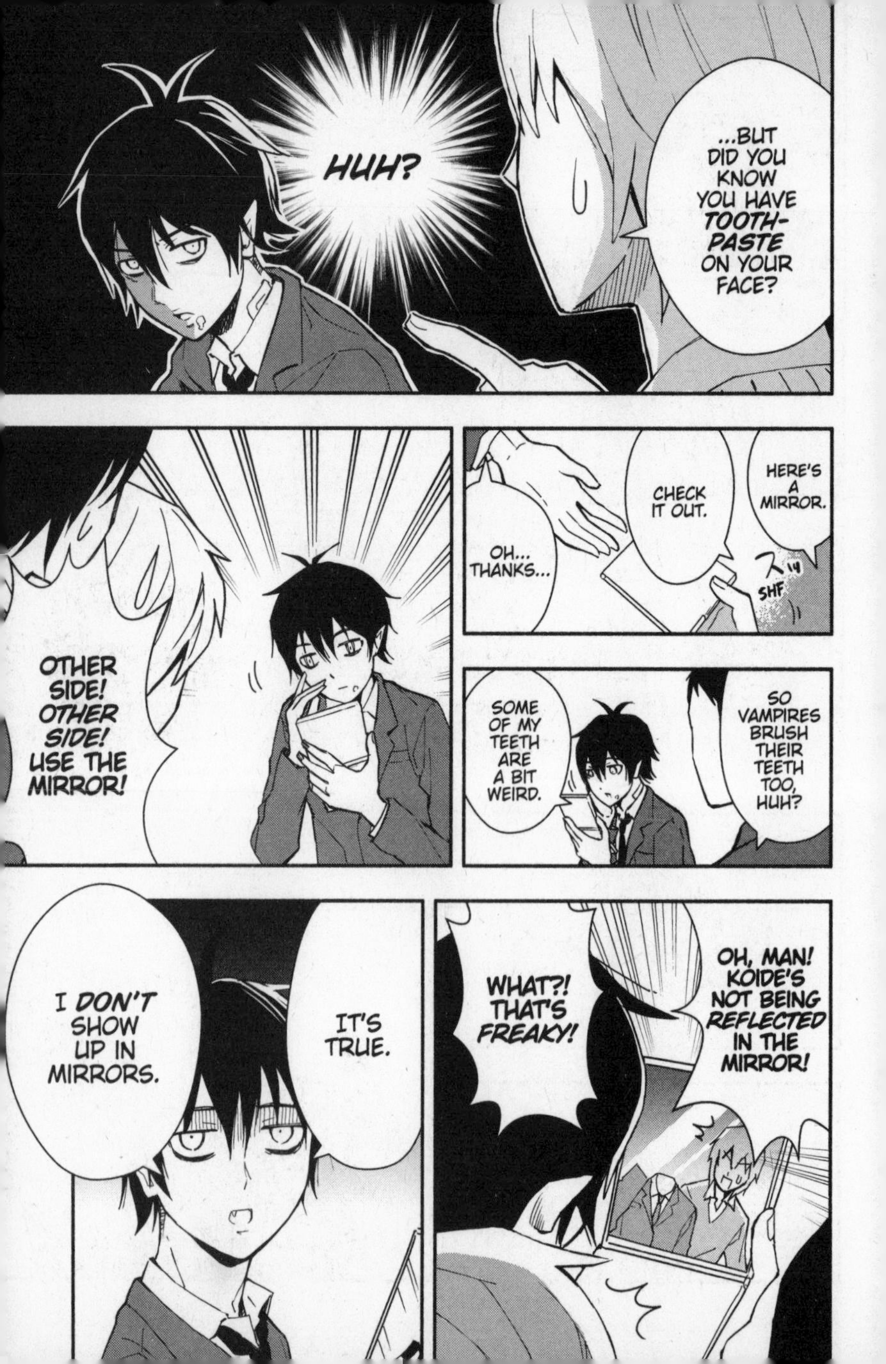
...BUT DID YOU KNOW YOU HAVE *TOOTH-PASTE* ON YOUR FACE?
HUH?
HERE'S A MIRROR.
CHECK IT OUT.
SHF
OH... THANKS...
SO VAMPIRES BRUSH THEIR TEETH TOO, HUH?
SOME OF MY TEETH ARE A BIT WEIRD.
OTHER SIDE! *OTHER SIDE!* USE THE MIRROR!
OH, MAN! KOIDE'S NOT BEING *REFLECTED* IN THE MIRROR!
WHAT?! THAT'S *FREAKY!*
IT'S TRUE.
I *DON'T* SHOW UP IN MIRRORS.

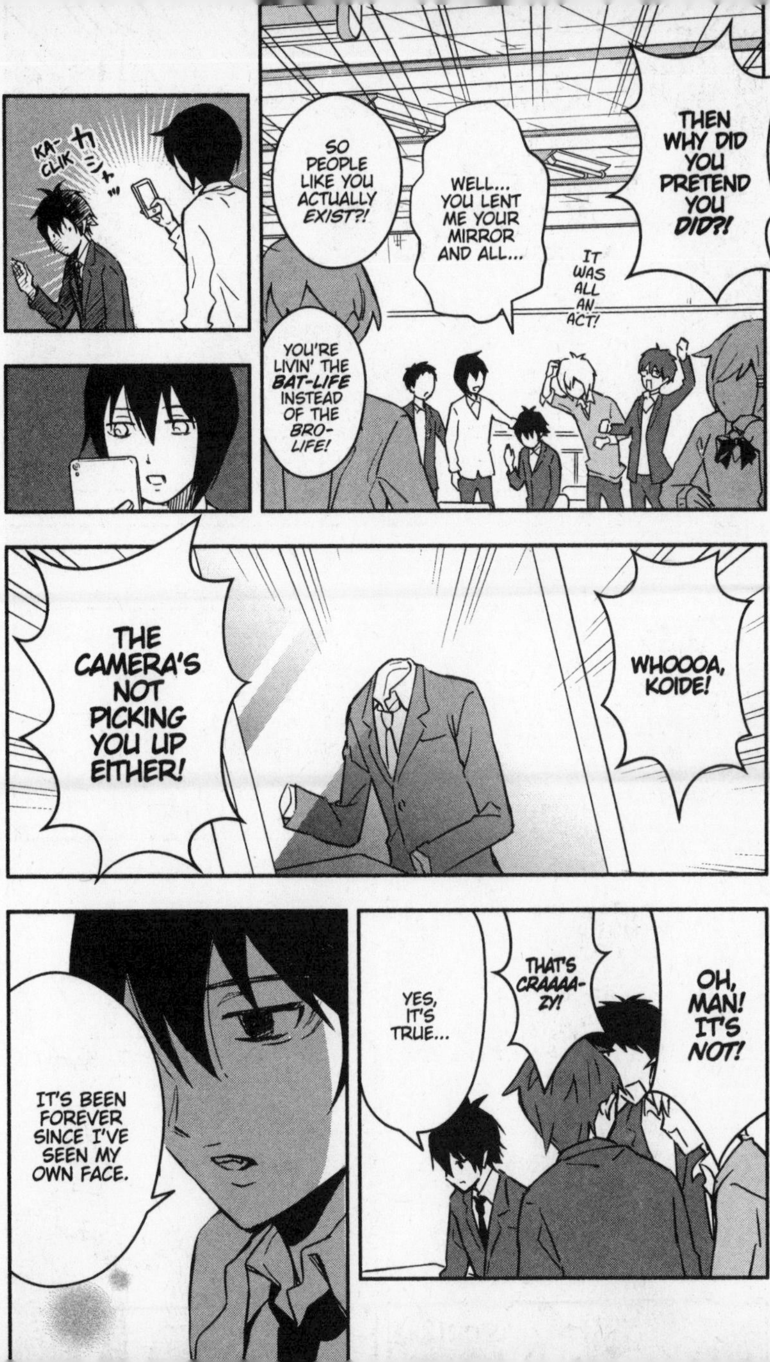
THEN WHY DID YOU PRETEND YOU DID?!
WELL... YOU LENT ME YOUR MIRROR AND ALL...
SO PEOPLE LIKE YOU ACTUALLY EXIST?!
IT WAS ALL AN ACT!
YOU'RE LIVIN' THE BAT-LIFE INSTEAD OF THE BRO-LIFE!
KA-CLIK
カシャッ
WHOOOA, KOIDE!
THE CAMERA'S NOT PICKING YOU UP EITHER!
OH, MAN! IT'S NOT!
THAT'S CRAAAAZY!
YES, IT'S TRUE...
IT'S BEEN FOREVER SINCE I'VE SEEN MY OWN FACE.

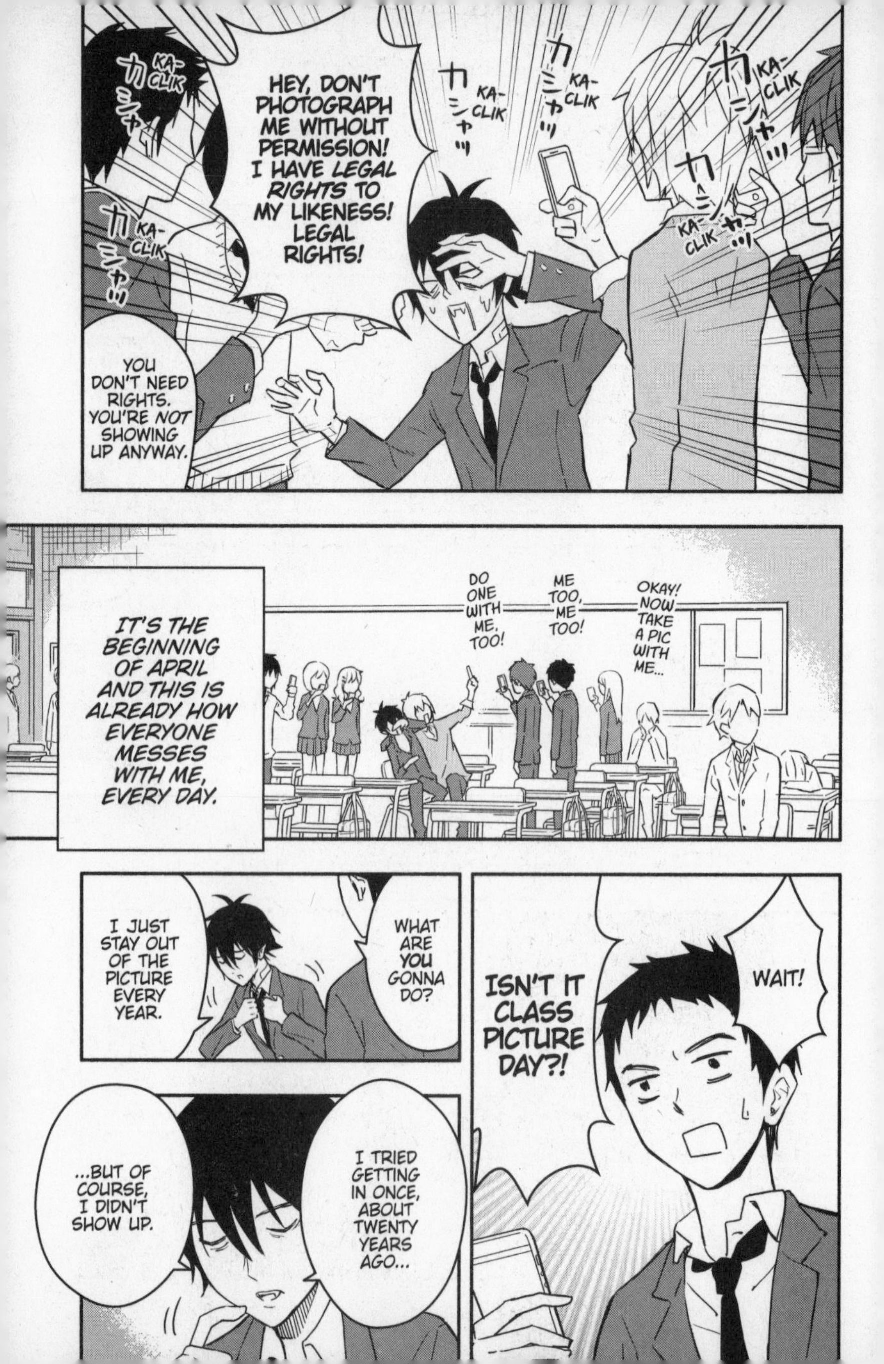

KA-CLIK
カシャッ
KA-CLIK
カシャッ
KA-CLIK
カシャッ
KA-CLIK
カシャッ
HEY, DON'T PHOTOGRAPH ME WITHOUT PERMISSION! I HAVE *LEGAL RIGHTS* TO MY LIKENESS! LEGAL RIGHTS!
KA-CLIK
カシャッ
KA-CLIK
カシャッ
YOU DON'T NEED RIGHTS. YOU'RE *NOT* SHOWING UP ANYWAY.
OKAY! NOW TAKE A PIC WITH ME...
ME TOO, ME TOO!
DO ONE WITH ME, TOO!
IT'S THE BEGINNING OF APRIL AND THIS IS ALREADY HOW EVERYONE MESSES WITH ME, EVERY DAY.
WAIT!
ISN'T IT CLASS PICTURE DAY?!
WHAT ARE *YOU* GONNA DO?
I JUST STAY OUT OF THE PICTURE EVERY YEAR.
I TRIED GETTING IN ONCE, ABOUT TWENTY YEARS AGO...
...BUT OF COURSE, I DIDN'T SHOW UP.

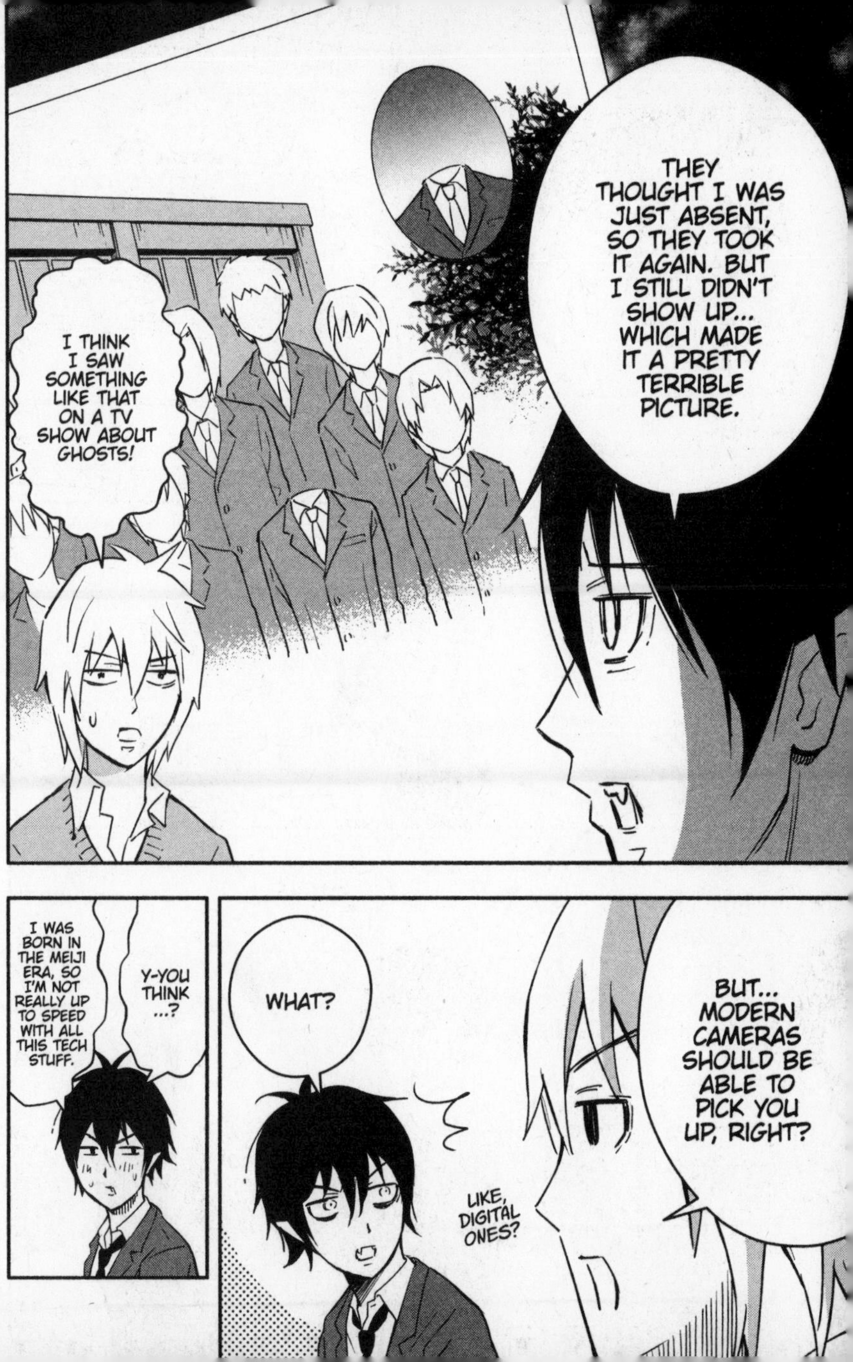
THEY THOUGHT I WAS JUST ABSENT, SO THEY TOOK IT AGAIN. BUT I STILL DIDN'T SHOW UP... WHICH MADE IT A PRETTY TERRIBLE PICTURE.
I THINK I SAW SOMETHING LIKE THAT ON A TV SHOW ABOUT GHOSTS!
BUT... MODERN CAMERAS SHOULD BE ABLE TO PICK YOU UP, RIGHT?
LIKE, DIGITAL ONES?
WHAT?
Y-YOU THINK ...?
I WAS BORN IN THE MEIJI ERA, SO I'M NOT REALLY UP TO SPEED WITH ALL THIS TECH STUFF.

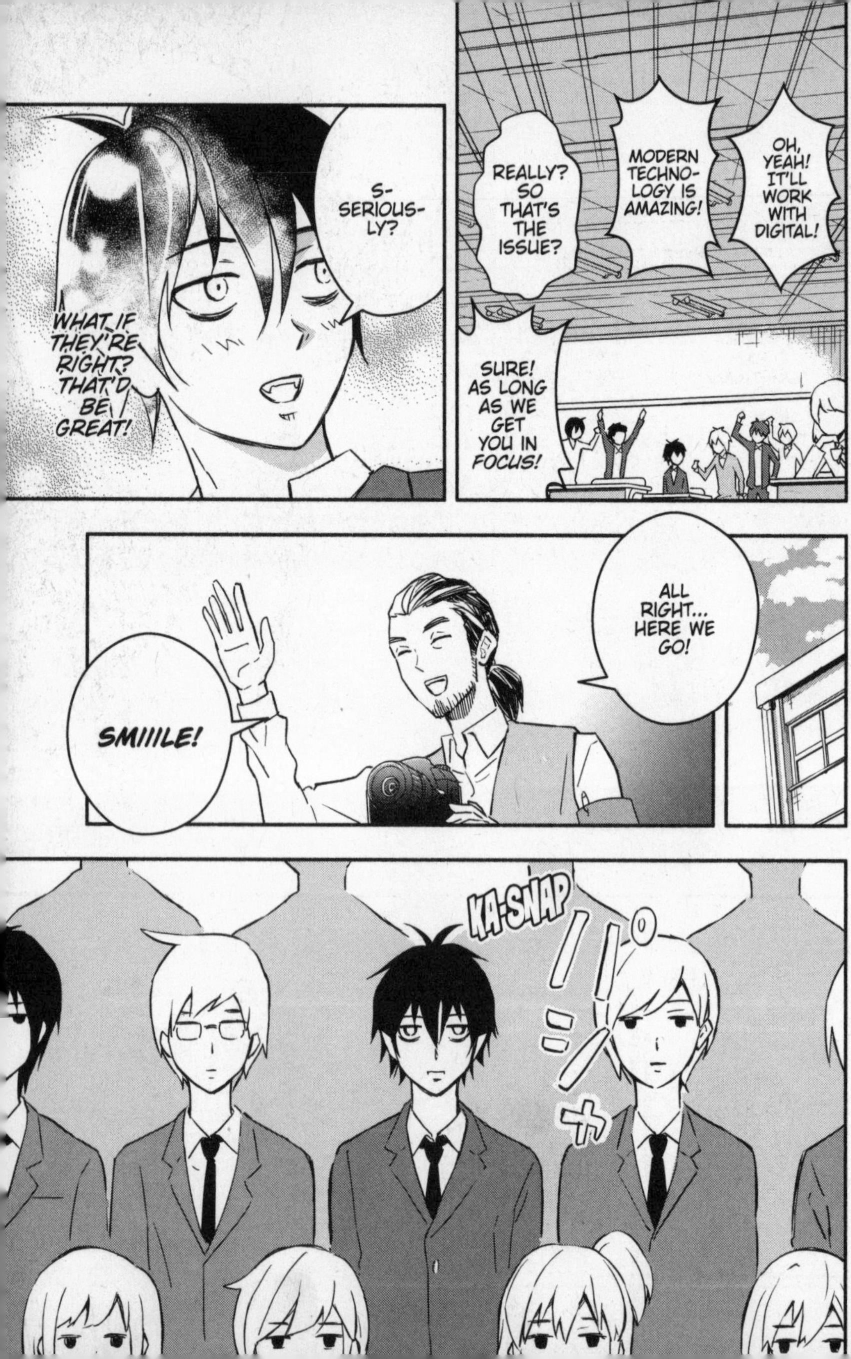
OH, YEAH! IT'LL WORK WITH DIGITAL!
MODERN TECHNOLOGY IS AMAZING!
REALLY? SO THAT'S THE ISSUE?
SURE! AS LONG AS WE GET YOU IN FOCUS!
S-SERIOUSLY?
WHAT IF THEY'RE RIGHT? THAT'D BE GREAT!
ALL RIGHT... HERE WE GO!
SMIIILE!
KA-SNAP

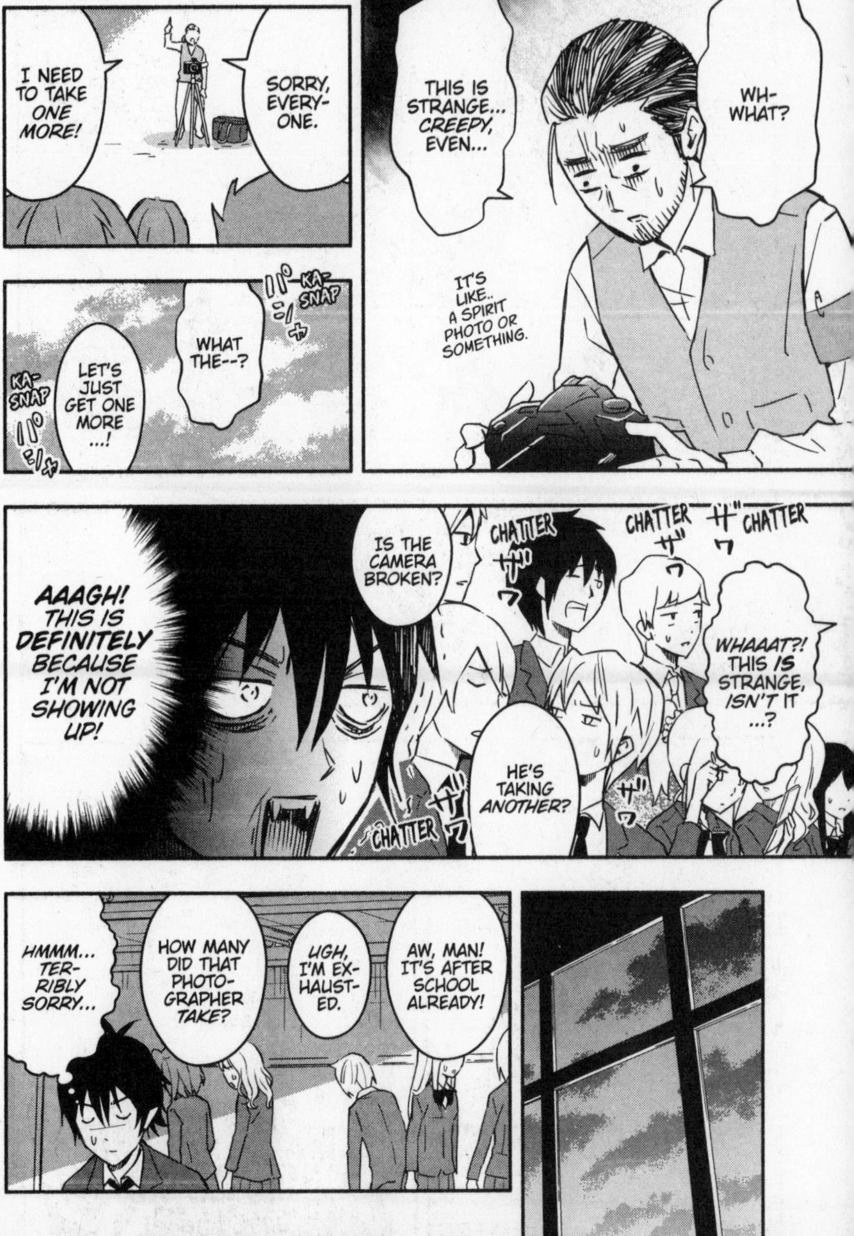
WH-WHAT?
THIS IS STRANGE... CREEPY, EVEN...
IT'S LIKE.. A SPIRIT PHOTO OR SOMETHING.
SORRY, EVERY-ONE.
I NEED TO TAKE ONE MORE!
KA-SNAP
WHAT THE--?
LET'S JUST GET ONE MORE ...!
KA-SNAP
CHATTER
CHATTER
WHAAAT?! THIS IS STRANGE, ISN'T IT ...?
CHATTER
IS THE CAMERA BROKEN?
HE'S TAKING ANOTHER?
CHATTER
AAAGH! THIS IS DEFINITELY BECAUSE I'M NOT SHOWING UP!
AW, MAN! IT'S AFTER SCHOOL ALREADY!
UGH, I'M EX-HAUST-ED.
HOW MANY DID THAT PHOTO-GRAPHER TAKE?
HMMM... TER-RIBLY SORRY...

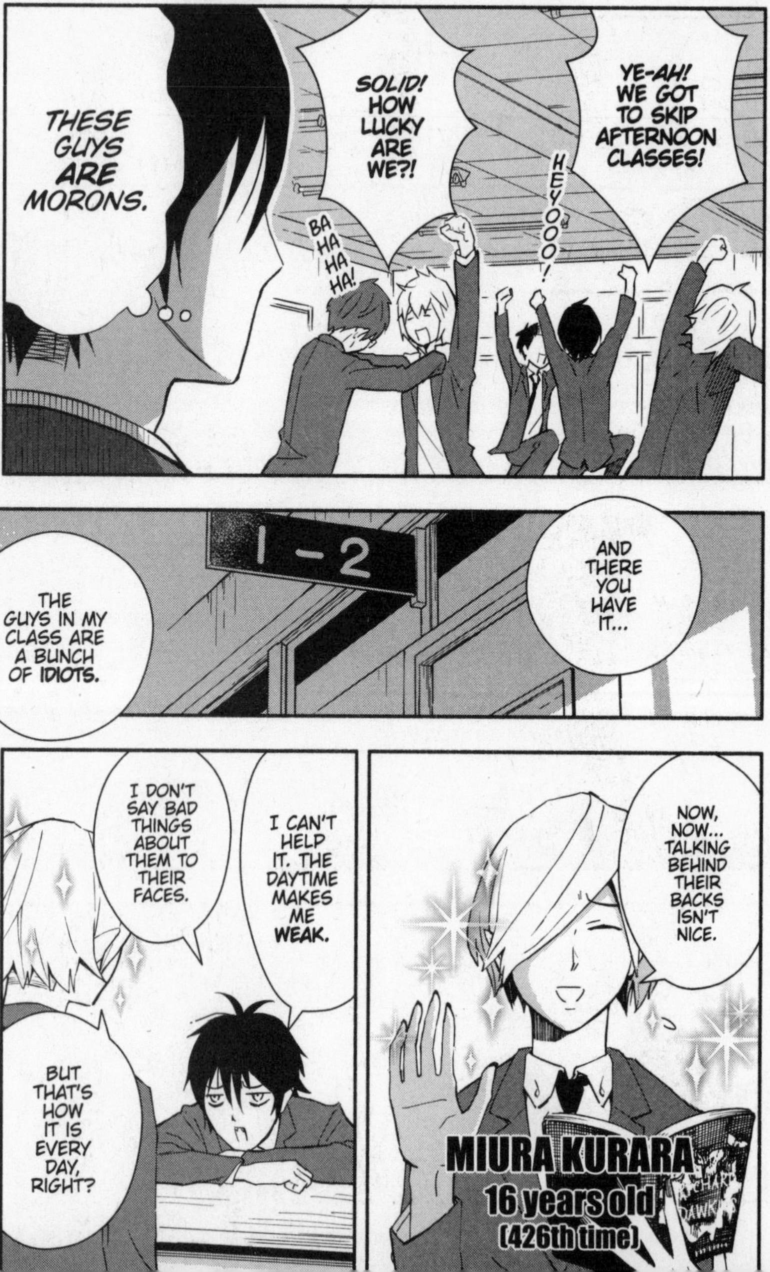

YE-AH! WE GOT TO SKIP AFTERNOON CLASSES!
HEYOOO!
SOLID! HOW LUCKY ARE WE?!
BA HA HA HA!
THESE GUYS ARE MORONS.
AND THERE YOU HAVE IT...
1-2
THE GUYS IN MY CLASS ARE A BUNCH OF IDIOTS.
NOW, NOW... TALKING BEHIND THEIR BACKS ISN'T NICE.
MIURA KURARA
16 years old
(426th time)
I CAN'T HELP IT. THE DAYTIME MAKES ME WEAK.
I DON'T SAY BAD THINGS ABOUT THEM TO THEIR FACES.
BUT THAT'S HOW IT IS EVERY DAY, RIGHT?

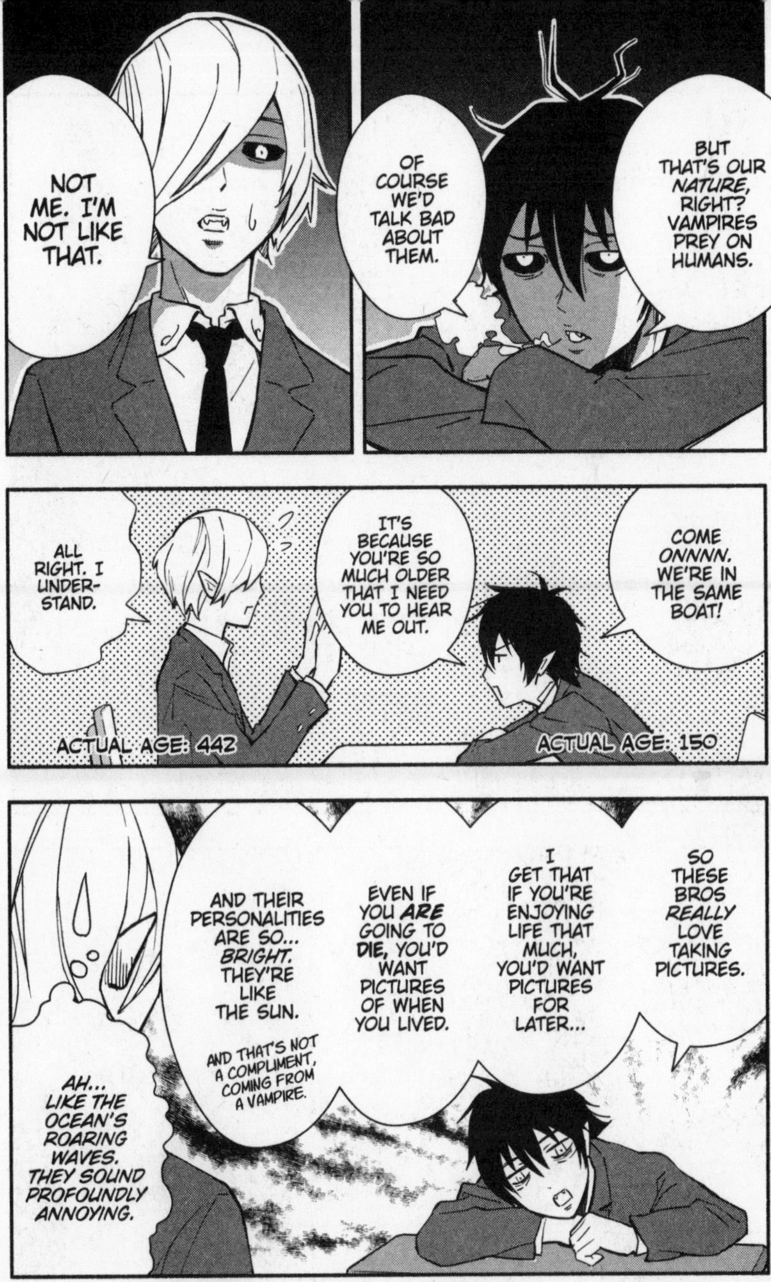

BUT THAT'S OUR NATURE, RIGHT? VAMPIRES PREY ON HUMANS.
OF COURSE WE'D TALK BAD ABOUT THEM.
NOT ME. I'M NOT LIKE THAT.
COME ONNNN. WE'RE IN THE SAME BOAT!
ACTUAL AGE: 150
IT'S BECAUSE YOU'RE SO MUCH OLDER THAT I NEED YOU TO HEAR ME OUT.
ALL RIGHT. I UNDER-STAND.
ACTUAL AGE: 442
SO THESE BROS REALLY LOVE TAKING PICTURES.
I GET THAT IF YOU'RE ENJOYING LIFE THAT MUCH, YOU'D WANT PICTURES FOR LATER...
EVEN IF YOU ARE GOING TO DIE, YOU'D WANT PICTURES OF WHEN YOU LIVED.
AND THEIR PERSONALITIES ARE SO... BRIGHT. THEY'RE LIKE THE SUN.
AND THAT'S NOT A COMPLIMENT, COMING FROM A VAMPIRE.
AH... LIKE THE OCEAN'S ROARING WAVES. THEY SOUND PROFOUNDLY ANNOYING.

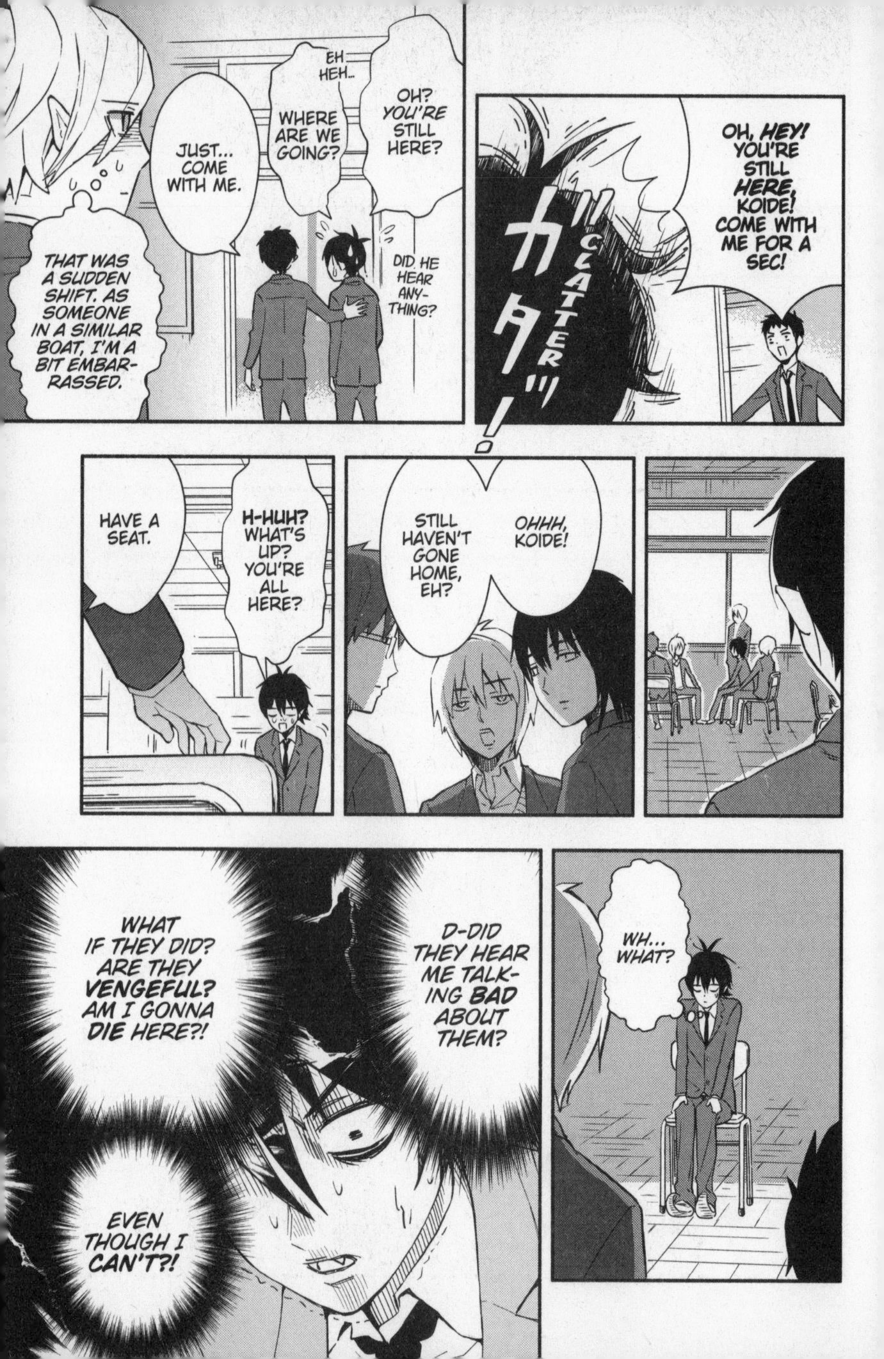

OH, HEY! YOU'RE STILL HERE, KOIDE! COME WITH ME FOR A SEC!
CLATTER
OH? YOU'RE STILL HERE?
EH HEH..
WHERE ARE WE GOING?
JUST... COME WITH ME.
DID HE HEAR ANYTHING?
THAT WAS A SUDDEN SHIFT. AS SOMEONE IN A SIMILAR BOAT, I'M A BIT EMBARRASSED.
OHHH, KOIDE!
STILL HAVEN'T GONE HOME, EH?
H-HUH? WHAT'S UP? YOU'RE ALL HERE?
HAVE A SEAT.
WH... WHAT?
D-DID THEY HEAR ME TALKING BAD ABOUT THEM?
WHAT IF THEY DID? ARE THEY VENGEFUL? AM I GONNA DIE HERE?!
EVEN THOUGH I CAN'T?!

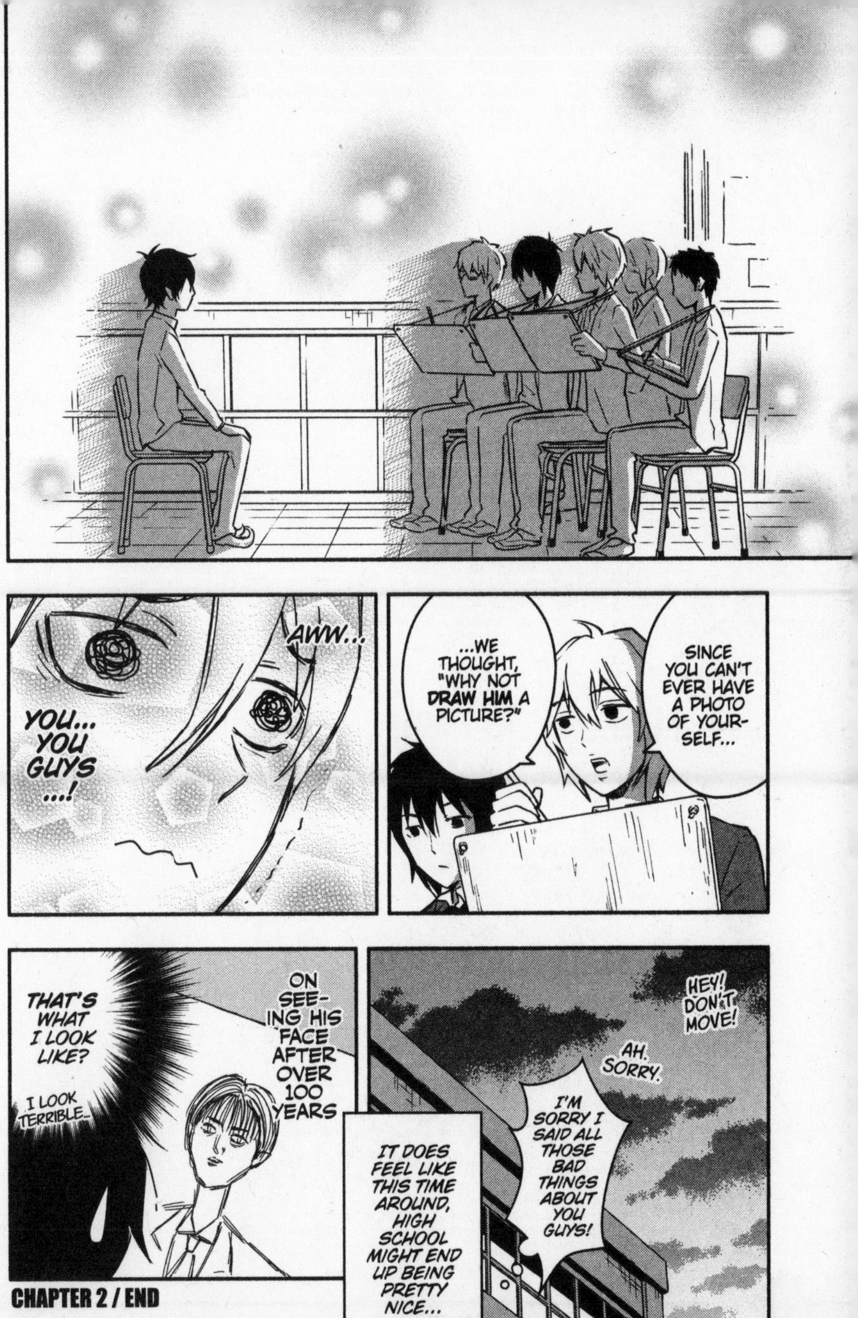
SINCE YOU CAN'T EVER HAVE A PHOTO OF YOUR-SELF...
...WE THOUGHT, "WHY NOT DRAW HIM A PICTURE?"
AWW...
YOU... YOU GUYS ...!
HEY! DON'T MOVE!
AH. SORRY.
I'M SORRY I SAID ALL THOSE BAD THINGS ABOUT YOU GUYS!
ON SEE-ING HIS FACE AFTER OVER 100 YEARS
THAT'S WHAT I LOOK LIKE?
I LOOK TERRIBLE...
IT DOES FEEL LIKE THIS TIME AROUND, HIGH SCHOOL MIGHT END UP BEING PRETTY NICE...

CHAPTER 2 / END

MIURA   KOIDE

My Pathetic
Vampire Life

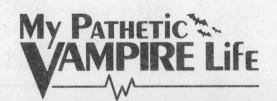

CHAPTER 3 / THE LAST WEEK OF JUNE (134TH TIME)

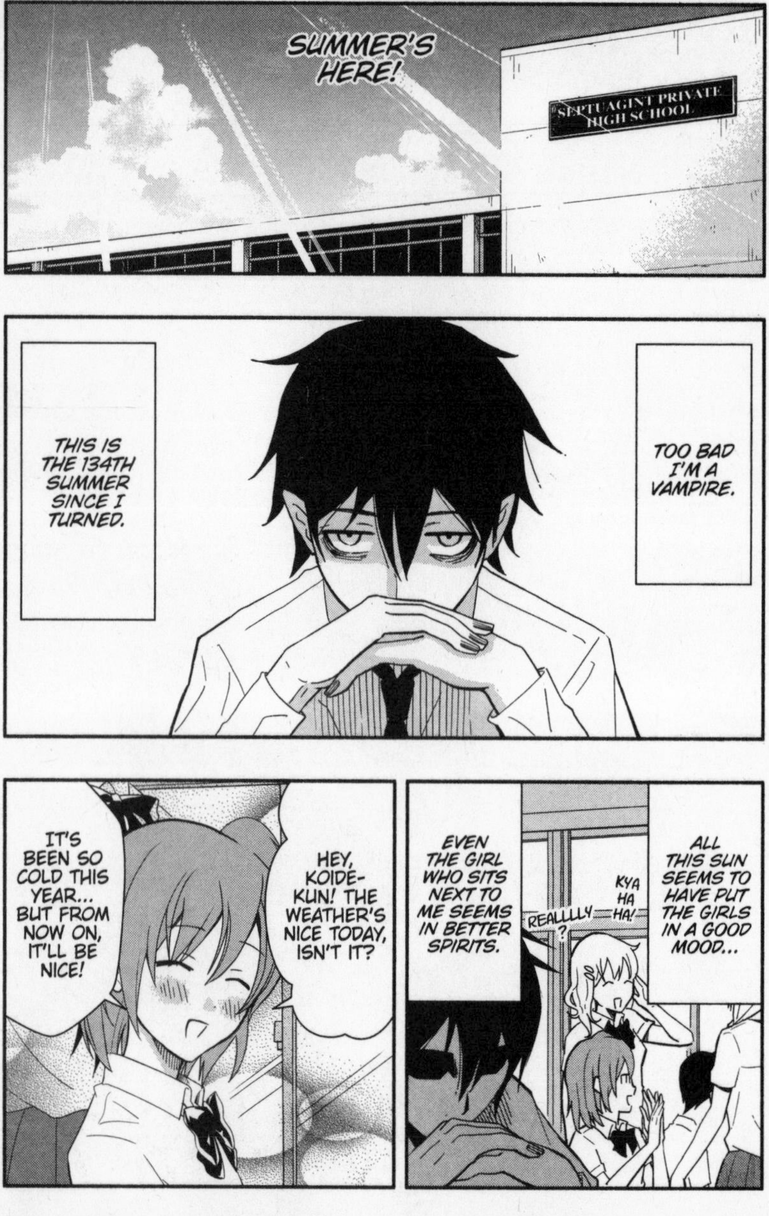
SUMMER'S HERE!
SEPTUAGINT PRIVATE HIGH SCHOOL
TOO BAD I'M A VAMPIRE.
THIS IS THE 134TH SUMMER SINCE I TURNED.
ALL THIS SUN SEEMS TO HAVE PUT THE GIRLS IN A GOOD MOOD...
KYA HA HA!
REALLLLY?
EVEN THE GIRL WHO SITS NEXT TO ME SEEMS IN BETTER SPIRITS.
HEY, KOIDE-KUN! THE WEATHER'S NICE TODAY, ISN'T IT?
IT'S BEEN SO COLD THIS YEAR... BUT FROM NOW ON, IT'LL BE NICE!

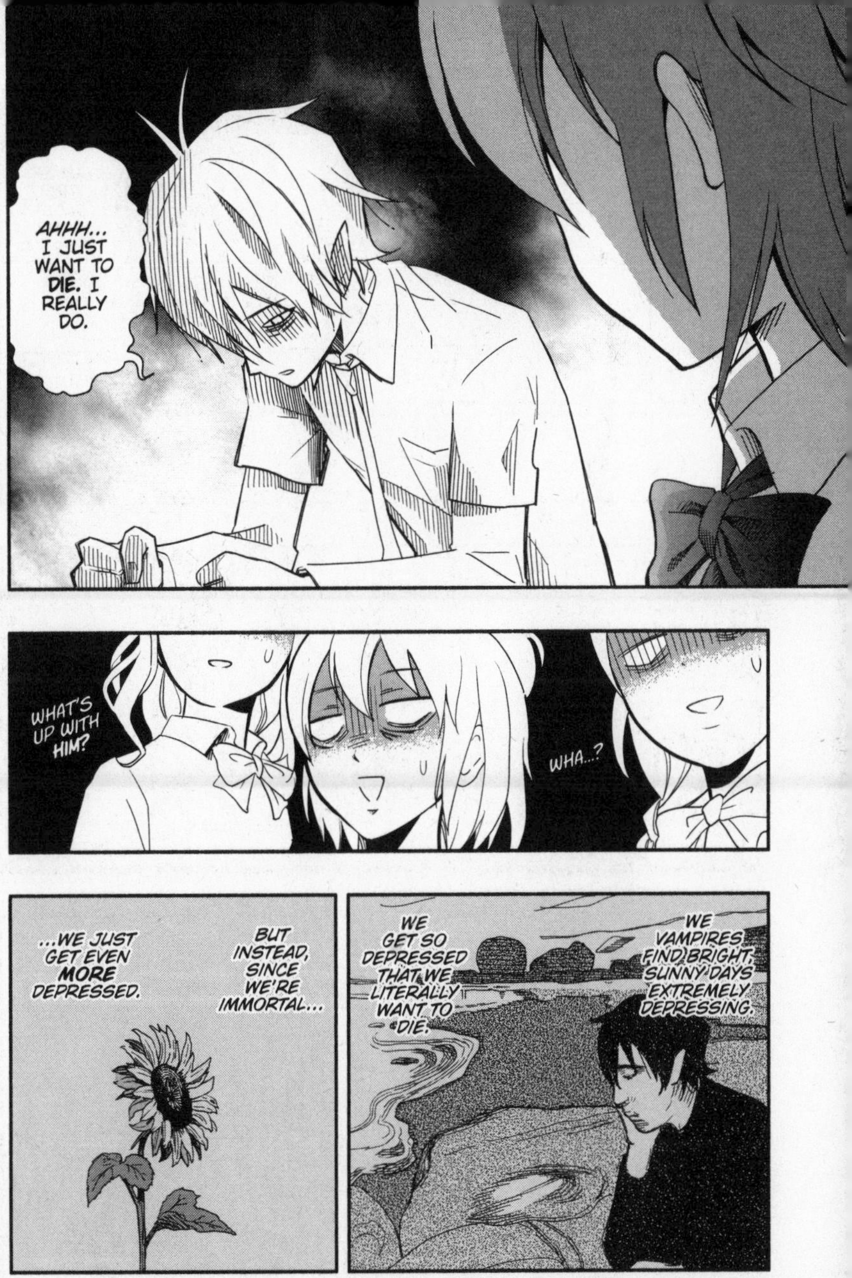
AHHH... I JUST WANT TO DIE. I REALLY DO.
WHA...?
WHAT'S UP WITH HIM?
WE VAMPIRES FIND BRIGHT, SUNNY DAYS EXTREMELY DEPRESSING.
WE GET SO DEPRESSED THAT WE LITERALLY WANT TO DIE.
BUT INSTEAD, SINCE WE'RE IMMORTAL...
...WE JUST GET EVEN MORE DEPRESSED.

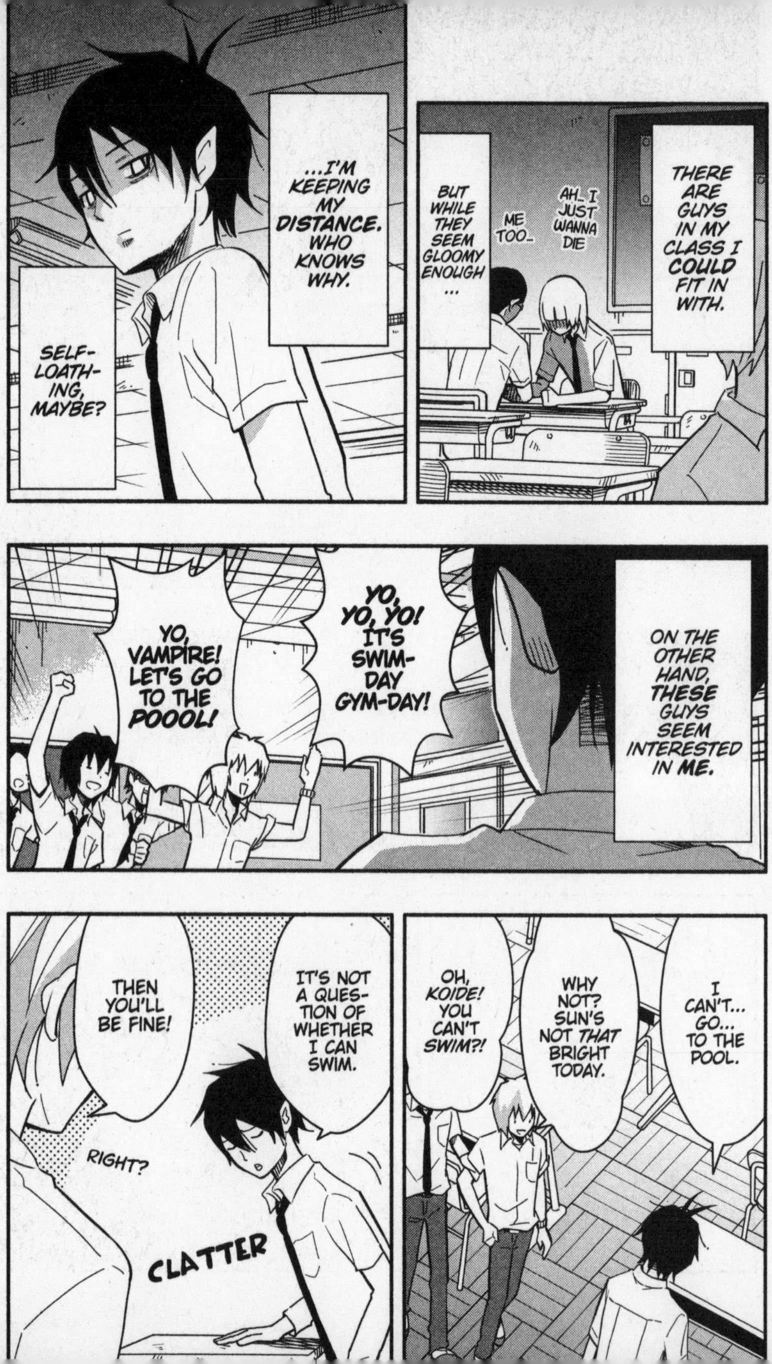
THERE ARE GUYS IN MY CLASS I COULD FIT IN WITH.
AH.. I JUST WANNA DIE
ME TOO..
BUT WHILE THEY SEEM GLOOMY ENOUGH ...
...I'M KEEPING MY DISTANCE. WHO KNOWS WHY.
SELF-LOATHING, MAYBE?
ON THE OTHER HAND, THESE GUYS SEEM INTERESTED IN ME.
YO, YO, YO! IT'S SWIM-DAY GYM-DAY!
YO, VAMPIRE! LET'S GO TO THE POOOL!
I CAN'T... GO... TO THE POOL.
WHY NOT? SUN'S NOT THAT BRIGHT TODAY.
OH, KOIDE! YOU CAN'T SWIM?!
IT'S NOT A QUESTION OF WHETHER I CAN SWIM.
THEN YOU'LL BE FINE!
RIGHT?
CLATTER

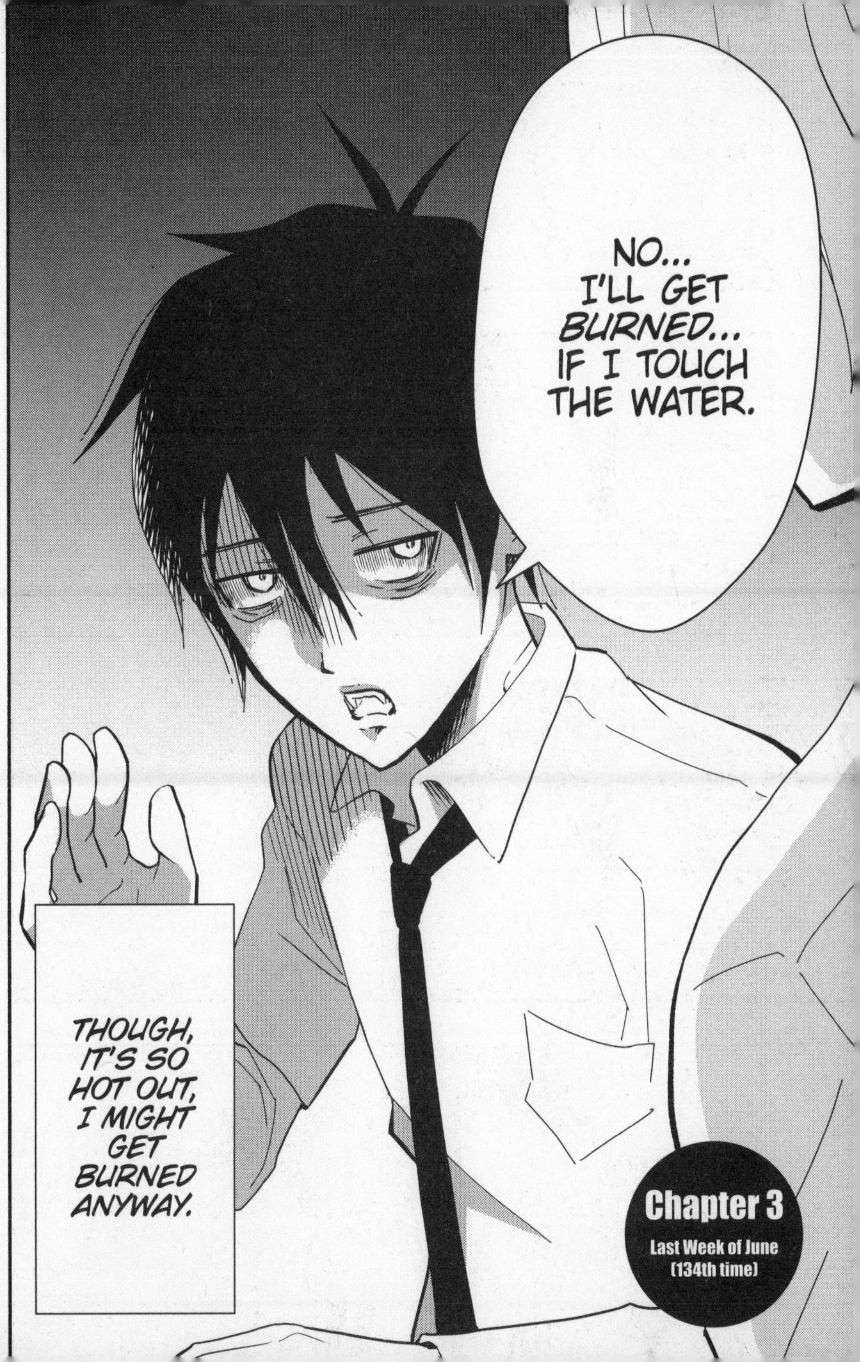
NO... I'LL GET BURNED... IF I TOUCH THE WATER.
THOUGH, IT'S SO HOT OUT, I MIGHT GET BURNED ANYWAY.
Chapter 3
Last Week of June (134th time)

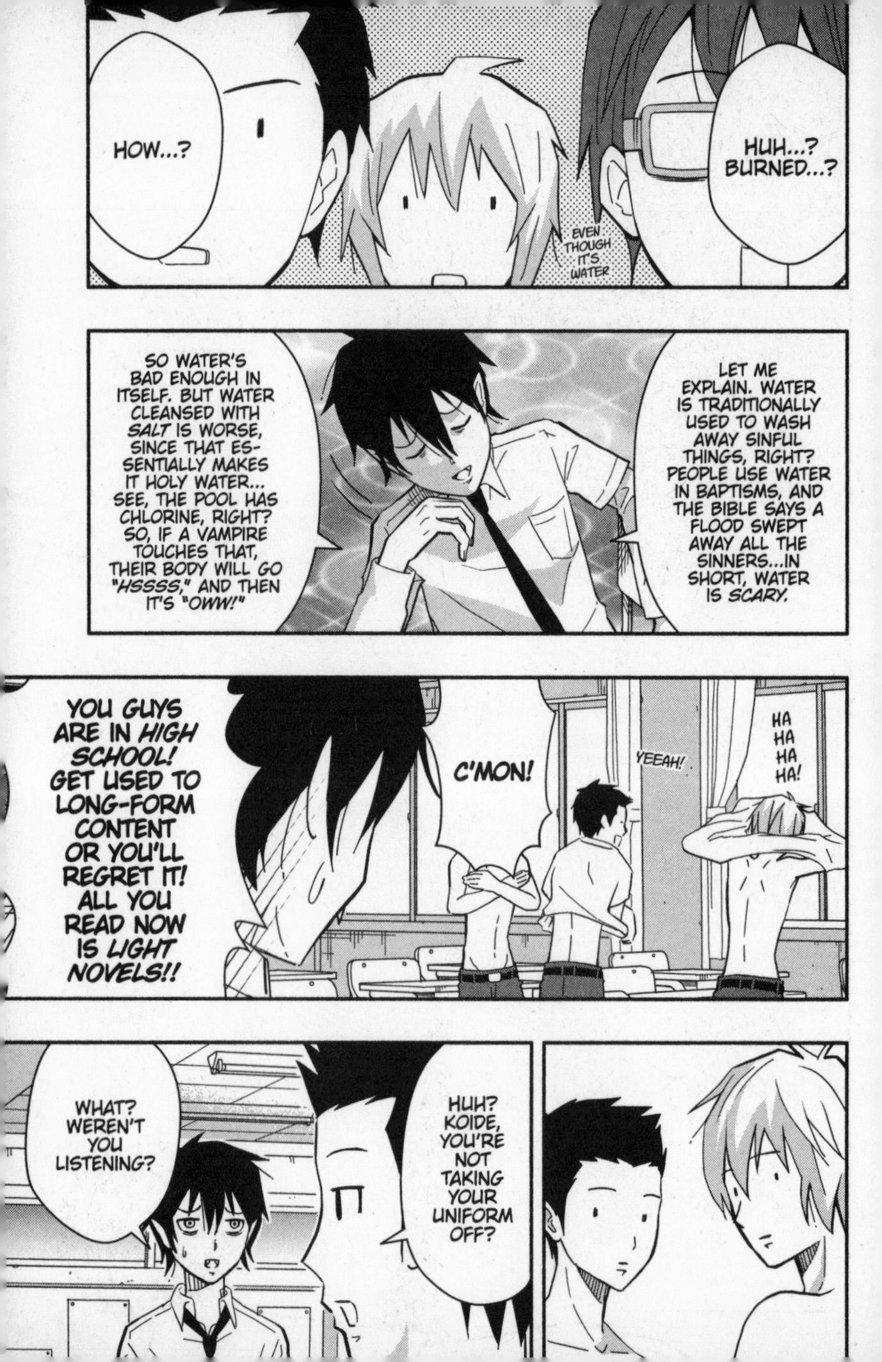
HUH...? BURNED...?
EVEN THOUGH IT'S WATER
HOW...?
LET ME EXPLAIN. WATER IS TRADITIONALLY USED TO WASH AWAY SINFUL THINGS, RIGHT? PEOPLE USE WATER IN BAPTISMS, AND THE BIBLE SAYS A FLOOD SWEPT AWAY ALL THE SINNERS...IN SHORT, WATER IS *SCARY.*
SO WATER'S BAD ENOUGH IN ITSELF. BUT WATER CLEANSED WITH *SALT* IS WORSE, SINCE THAT ESSENTIALLY MAKES IT HOLY WATER... SEE, THE POOL HAS CHLORINE, RIGHT? SO, IF A VAMPIRE TOUCHES THAT, THEIR BODY WILL GO *"HSSSS,"* AND THEN IT'S *"OWW!"*
HA HA HA HA!
YEEAH!
C'MON!
YOU GUYS ARE IN *HIGH SCHOOL!* GET USED TO LONG-FORM CONTENT OR YOU'LL REGRET IT! ALL YOU READ NOW IS *LIGHT NOVELS!!*
HUH? KOIDE, YOU'RE NOT TAKING YOUR UNIFORM OFF?
WHAT? WEREN'T YOU LISTENING?

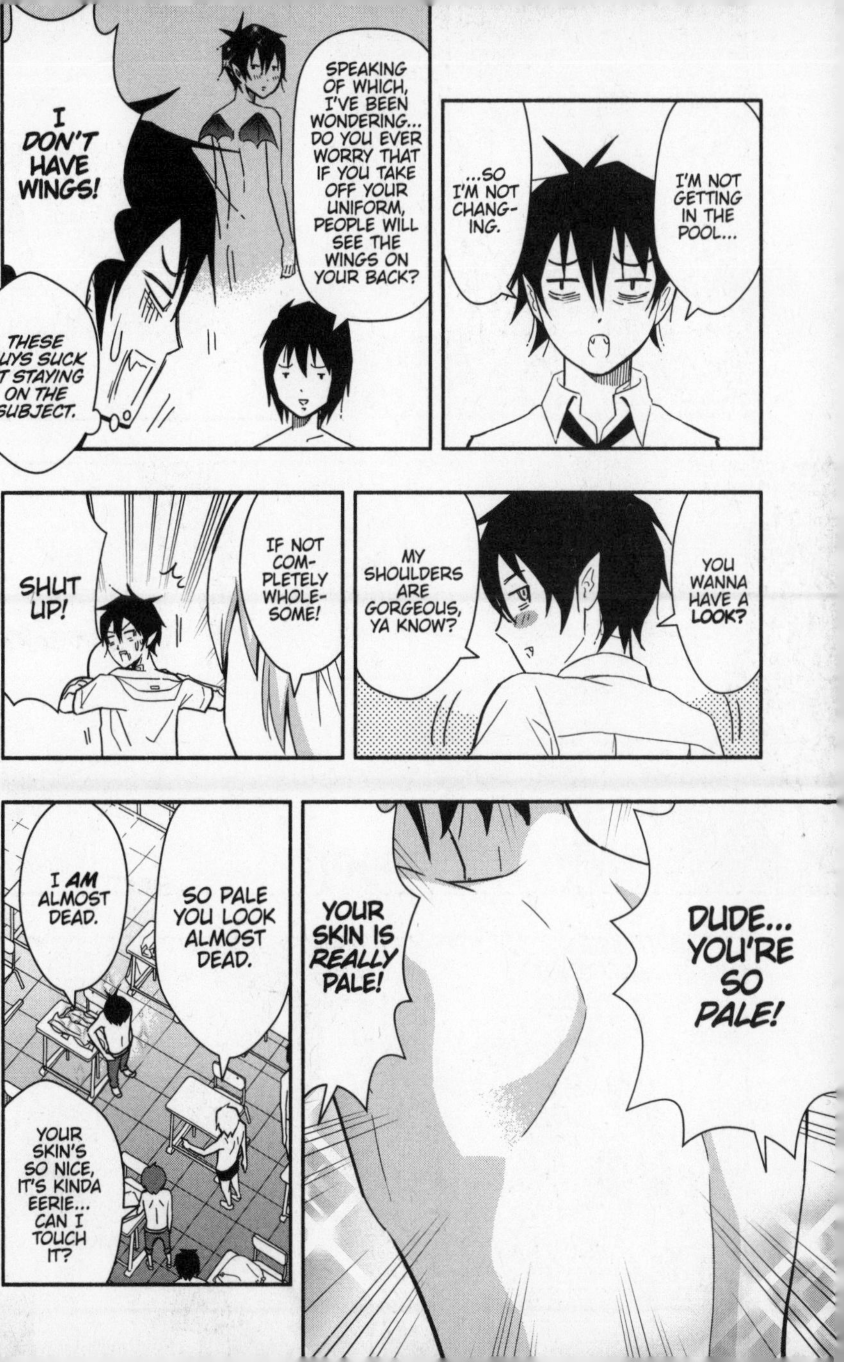
I'M NOT GETTING IN THE POOL...
...SO I'M NOT CHANGING.
SPEAKING OF WHICH, I'VE BEEN WONDERING... DO YOU EVER WORRY THAT IF YOU TAKE OFF YOUR UNIFORM, PEOPLE WILL SEE THE WINGS ON YOUR BACK?
I *DON'T* HAVE WINGS!
THESE GUYS SUCK AT STAYING ON THE SUBJECT.
YOU WANNA HAVE A LOOK?
MY SHOULDERS ARE GORGEOUS, YA KNOW?
IF NOT COMPLETELY WHOLESOME!
SHUT UP!
DUDE... YOU'RE SO *PALE!*
YOUR SKIN IS *REALLY* PALE!
SO PALE YOU LOOK ALMOST DEAD.
I *AM* ALMOST DEAD.
YOUR SKIN'S SO NICE, IT'S KINDA EERIE... CAN I TOUCH IT?

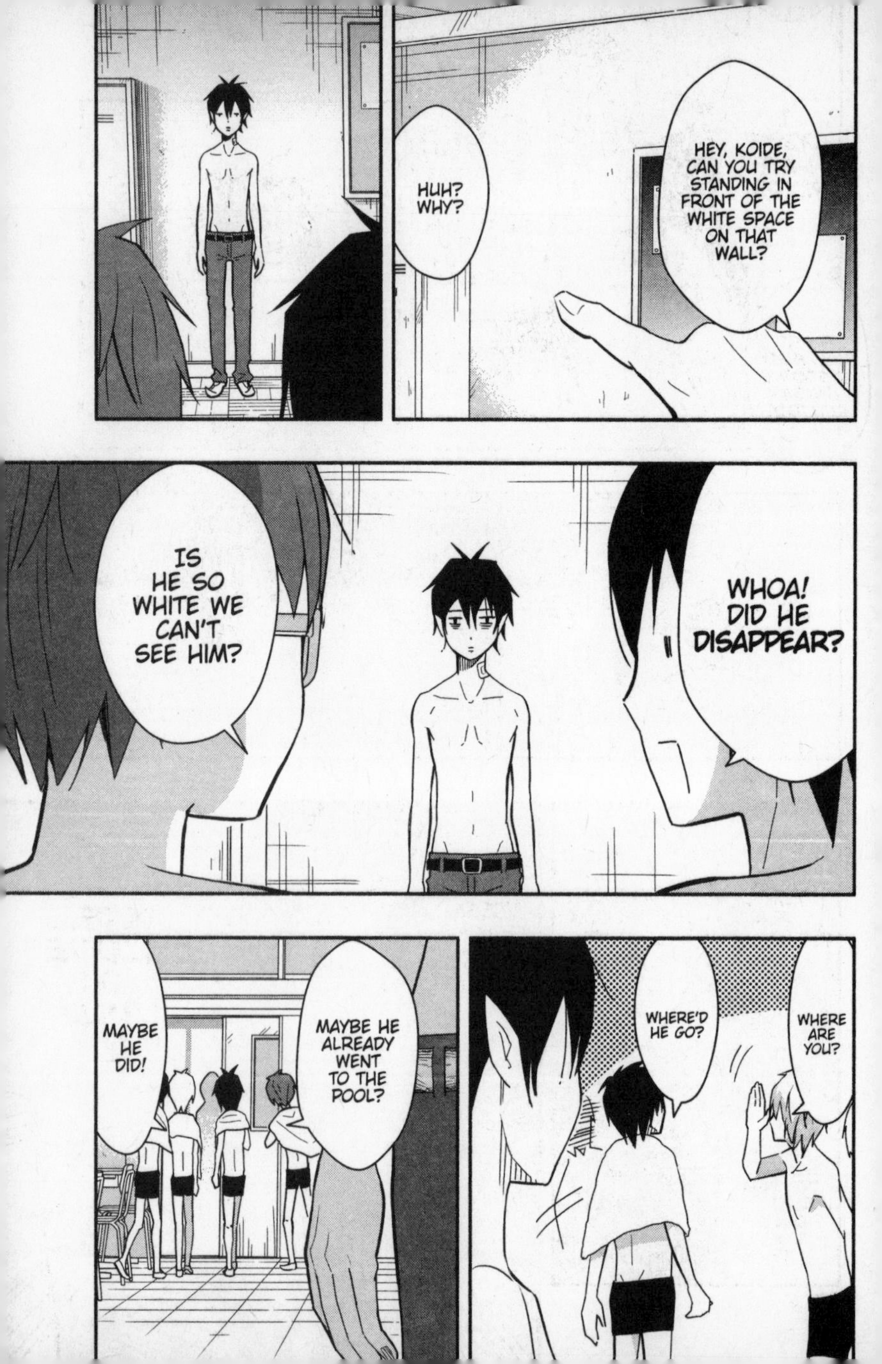
HEY, KOIDE, CAN YOU TRY STANDING IN FRONT OF THE WHITE SPACE ON THAT WALL?
HUH? WHY?
WHOA! DID HE DISAPPEAR?
IS HE SO WHITE WE CAN'T SEE HIM?
WHERE ARE YOU?
WHERE'D HE GO?
MAYBE HE ALREADY WENT TO THE POOL?
MAYBE HE DID!

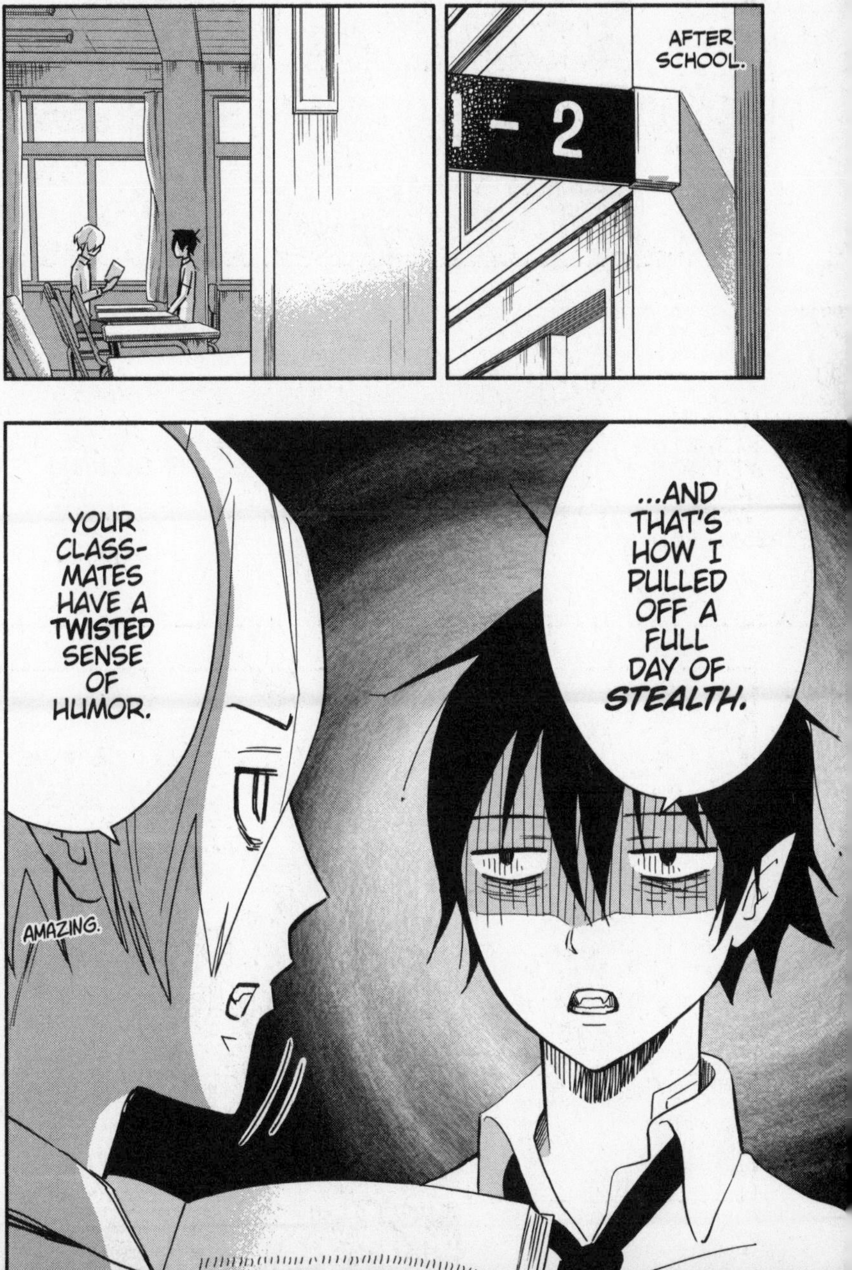
AFTER SCHOOL.
...AND THAT'S HOW I PULLED OFF A FULL DAY OF STEALTH.
YOUR CLASSMATES HAVE A TWISTED SENSE OF HUMOR.
AMAZING.

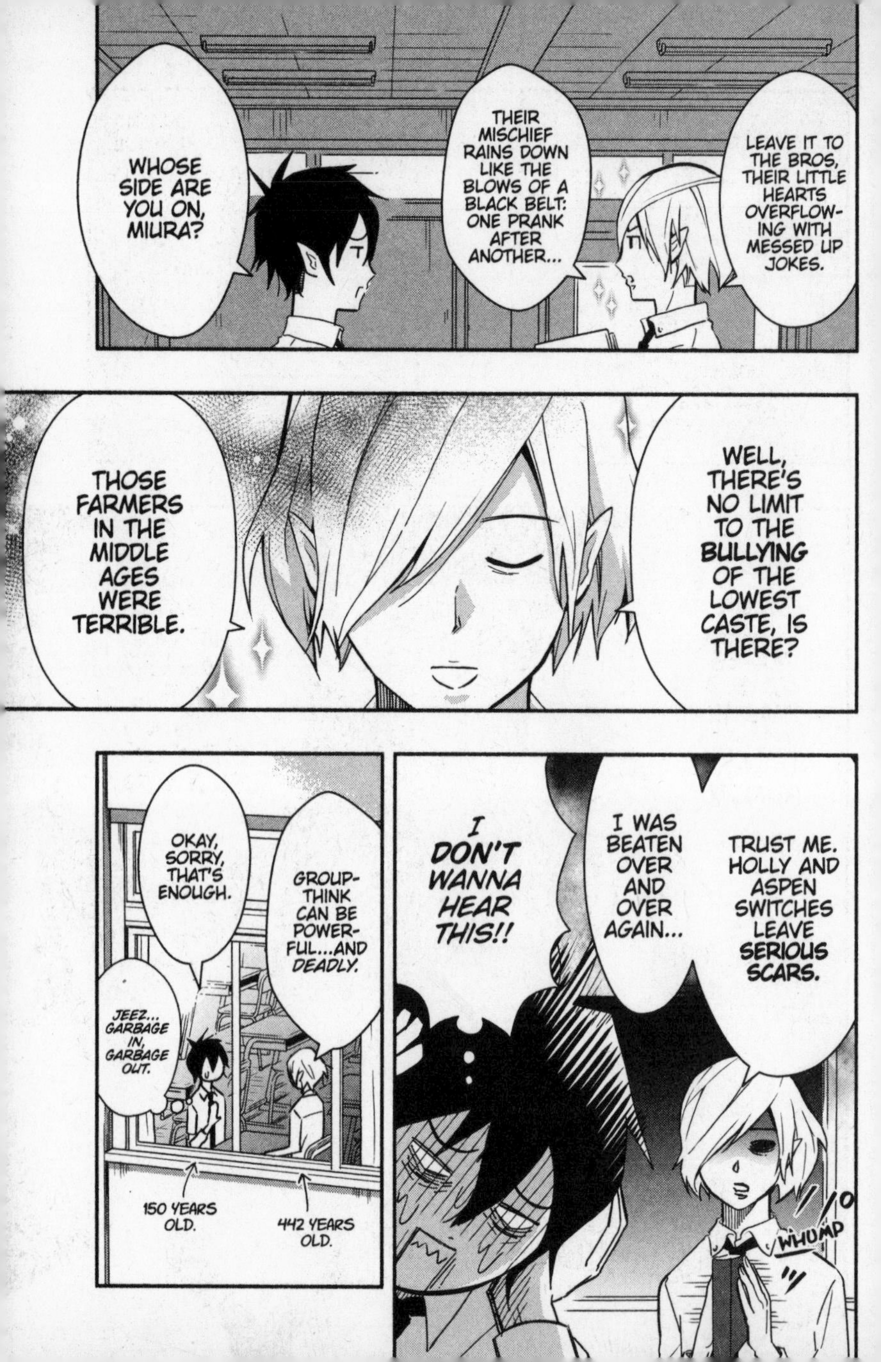
LEAVE IT TO THE BROS, THEIR LITTLE HEARTS OVERFLOWING WITH MESSED UP JOKES.
THEIR MISCHIEF RAINS DOWN LIKE THE BLOWS OF A BLACK BELT: ONE PRANK AFTER ANOTHER...
WHOSE SIDE ARE YOU ON, MIURA?
WELL, THERE'S NO LIMIT TO THE **BULLYING** OF THE LOWEST CASTE, IS THERE?
THOSE FARMERS IN THE MIDDLE AGES WERE TERRIBLE.
TRUST ME. HOLLY AND ASPEN SWITCHES LEAVE **SERIOUS** SCARS.
I WAS BEATEN OVER AND OVER AGAIN...
I DON'T WANNA HEAR THIS!!
WHUMP
GROUP-THINK CAN BE POWERFUL...AND *DEADLY.*
OKAY, SORRY, THAT'S ENOUGH.
JEEZ... GARBAGE IN, GARBAGE OUT.
442 YEARS OLD.
150 YEARS OLD.

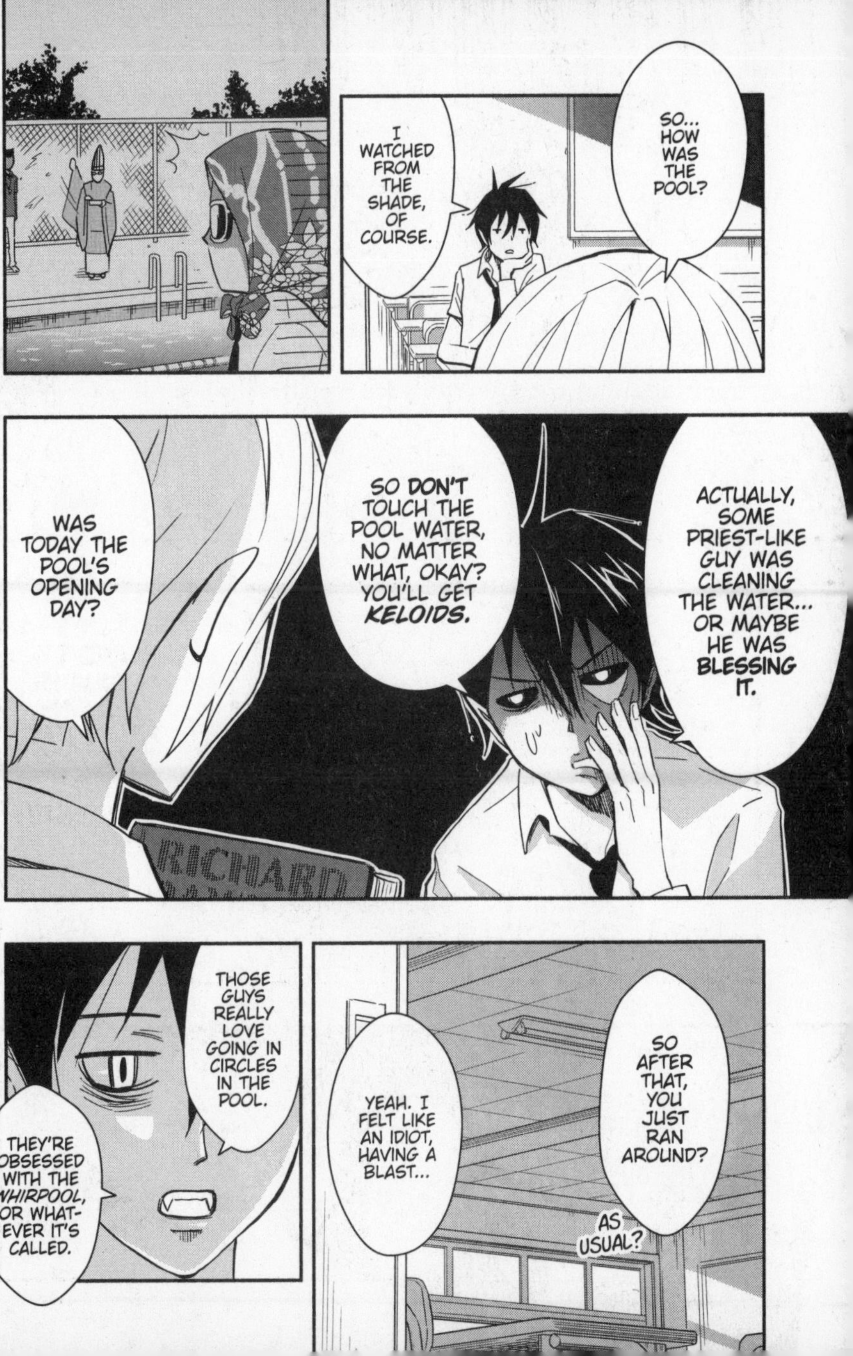
SO... HOW WAS THE POOL?
I WATCHED FROM THE SHADE, OF COURSE.
ACTUALLY, SOME PRIEST-LIKE GUY WAS CLEANING THE WATER... OR MAYBE HE WAS BLESSING IT.
SO DON'T TOUCH THE POOL WATER, NO MATTER WHAT, OKAY? YOU'LL GET KELOIDS.
WAS TODAY THE POOL'S OPENING DAY?
RICHARD
SO AFTER THAT, YOU JUST RAN AROUND?
AS USUAL?
YEAH. I FELT LIKE AN IDIOT, HAVING A BLAST...
THOSE GUYS REALLY LOVE GOING IN CIRCLES IN THE POOL.
THEY'RE OBSESSED WITH THE WHIRPOOL, OR WHATEVER IT'S CALLED.

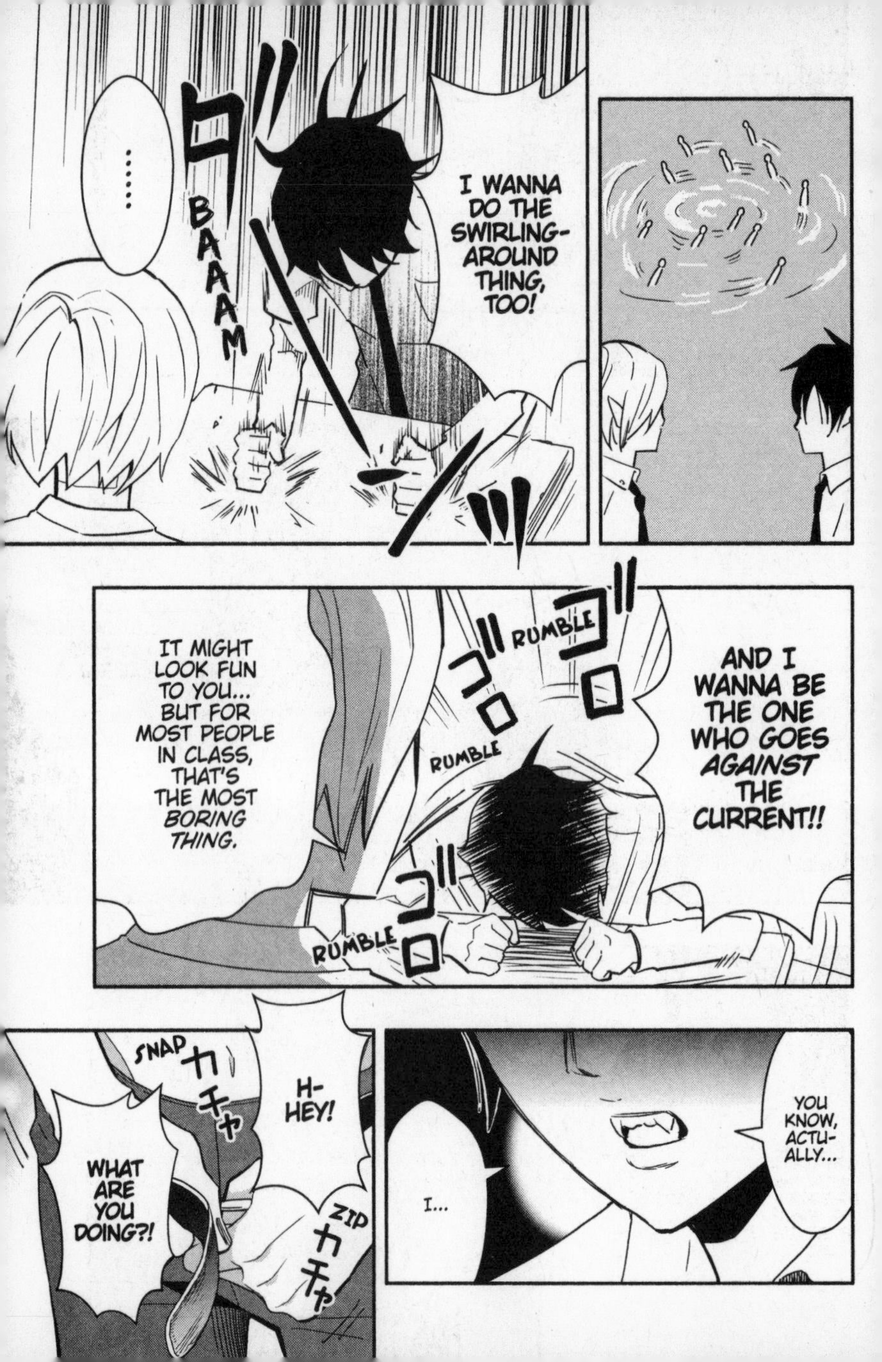

I WANNA DO THE SWIRLING-AROUND THING, TOO!
BAAAAM
......
AND I WANNA BE THE ONE WHO GOES AGAINST THE CURRENT!!
RUMBLE
RUMBLE
RUMBLE
IT MIGHT LOOK FUN TO YOU... BUT FOR MOST PEOPLE IN CLASS, THAT'S THE MOST BORING THING.
YOU KNOW, ACTUALLY...
I...
H-HEY!
SNAP
WHAT ARE YOU DOING?!
ZIP

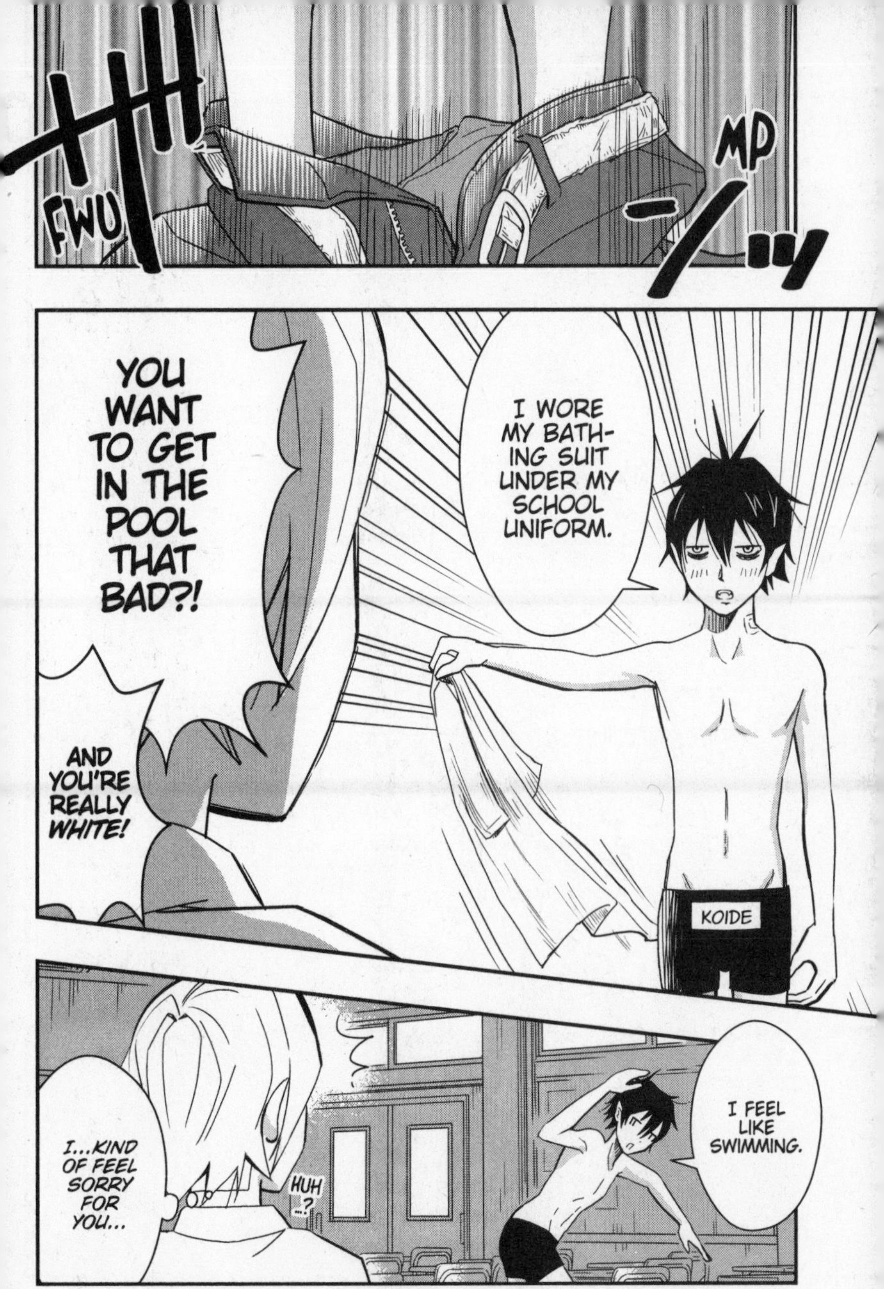
FWU
MP
I WORE MY BATHING SUIT UNDER MY SCHOOL UNIFORM.
YOU WANT TO GET IN THE POOL THAT BAD?!
AND YOU'RE REALLY WHITE!
KOIDE
I FEEL LIKE SWIMMING.
HUH...?
I...KIND OF FEEL SORRY FOR YOU...

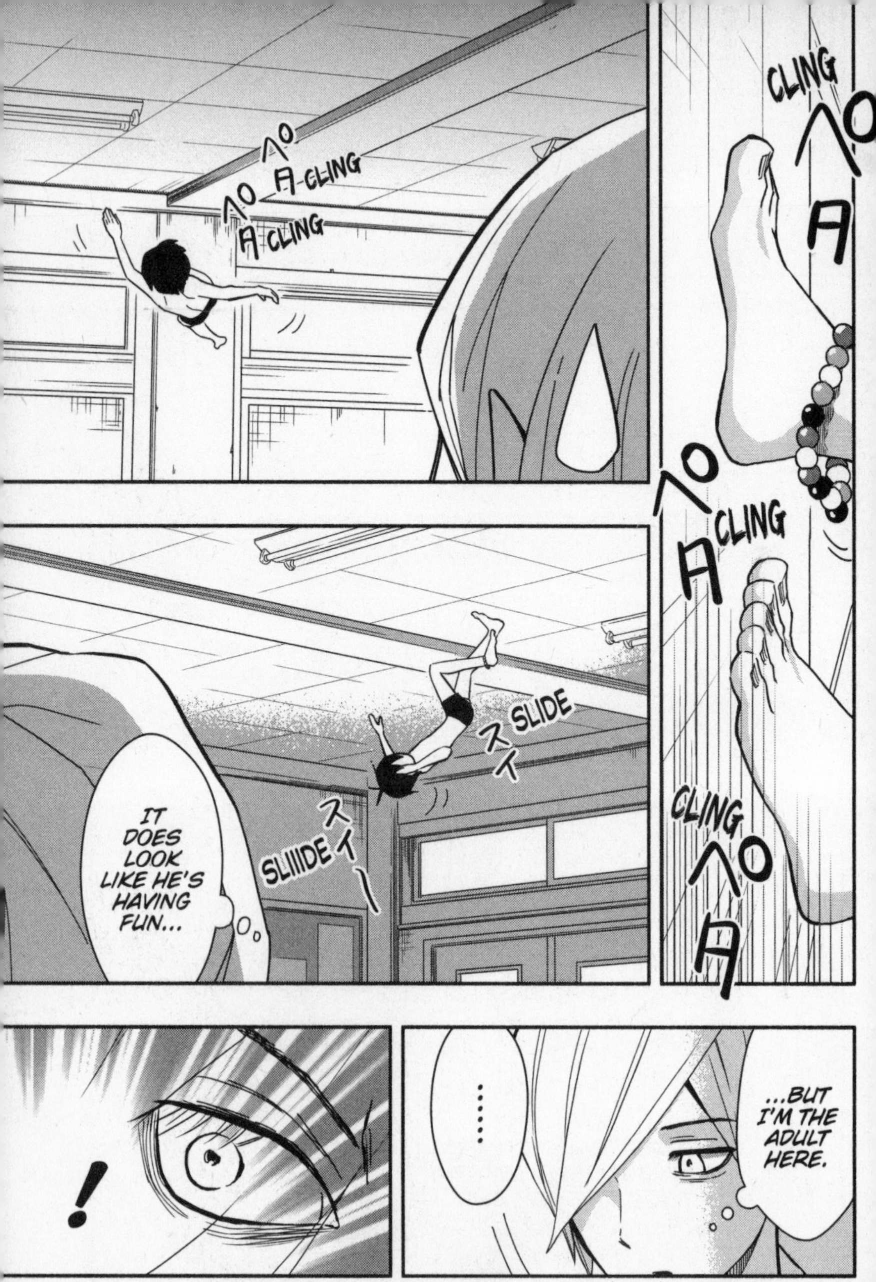
CLING
CLING
CLING
CLING
CLING
SLIDE
スイ
SLIIIDE
スイー
IT DOES LOOK LIKE HE'S HAVING FUN...
......
...BUT I'M THE ADULT HERE.
!

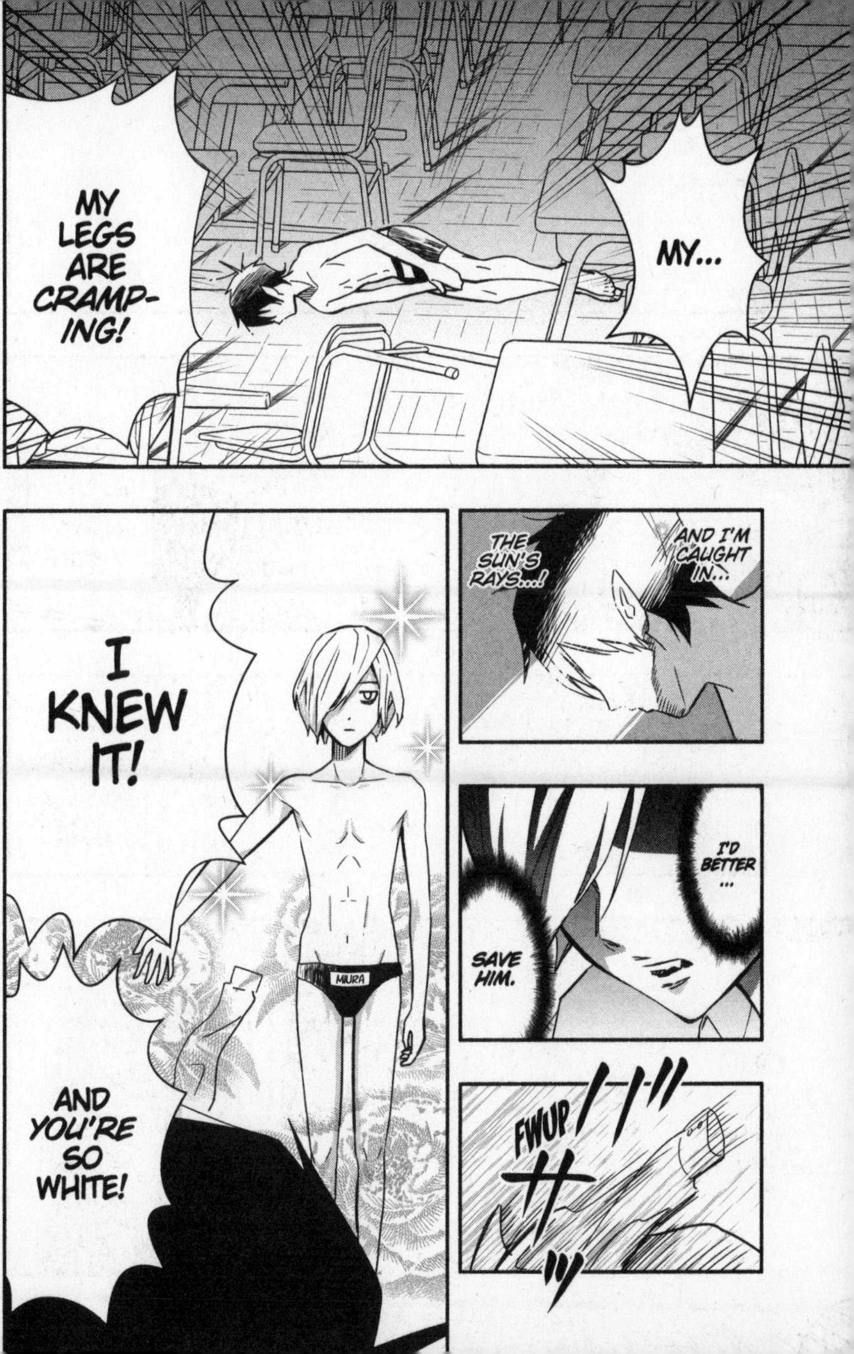
MY...
MY LEGS ARE CRAMPING!
AND I'M CAUGHT IN...
THE SUN'S RAYS...!
I'D BETTER...
SAVE HIM.
FWUP
I KNEW IT!
AND YOU'RE SO WHITE!

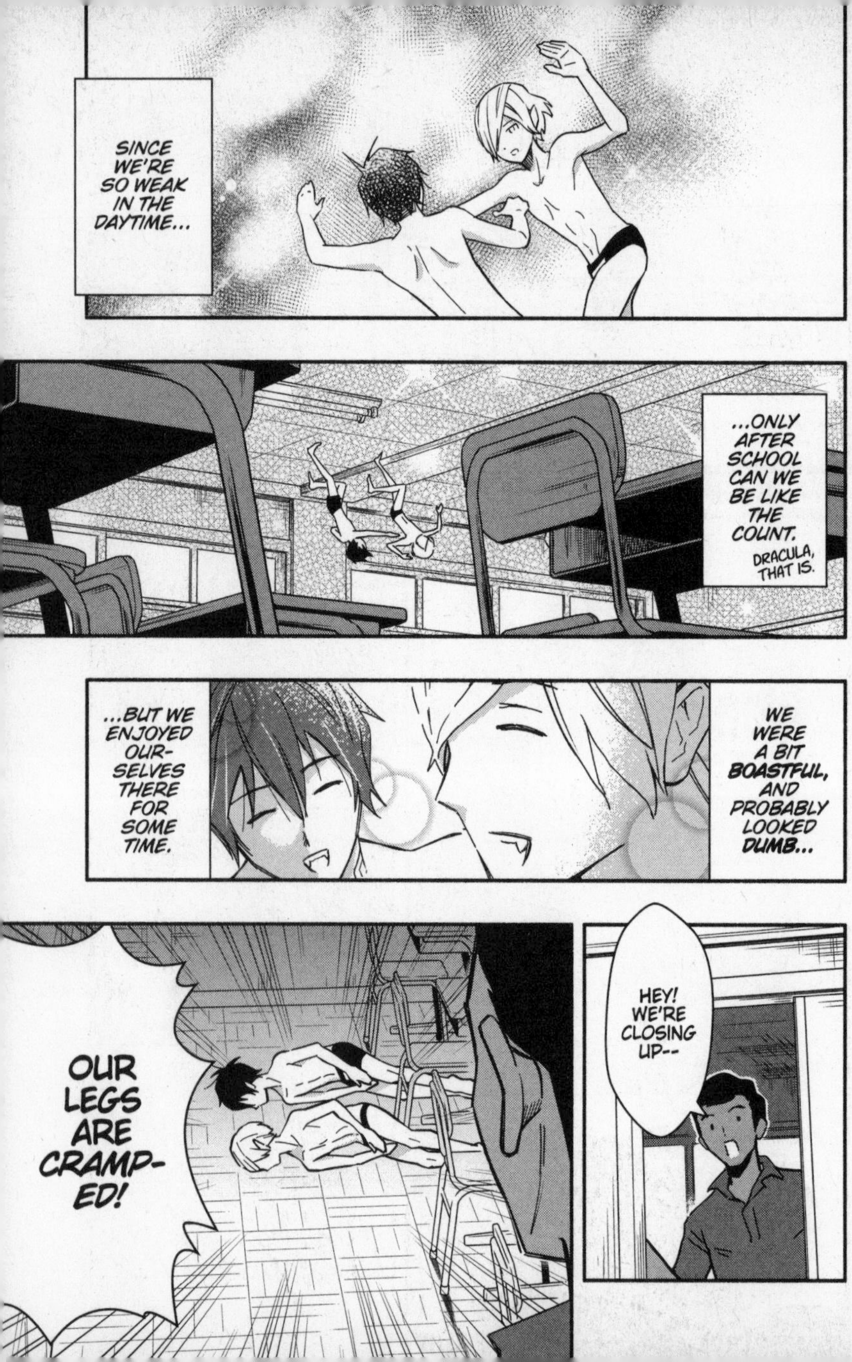
SINCE WE'RE SO WEAK IN THE DAYTIME...
...ONLY AFTER SCHOOL CAN WE BE LIKE THE COUNT.
DRACULA, THAT IS.
WE WERE A BIT BOASTFUL, AND PROBABLY LOOKED DUMB...
...BUT WE ENJOYED OUR-SELVES THERE FOR SOME TIME.
HEY! WE'RE CLOSING UP--
OUR LEGS ARE CRAMP-ED!

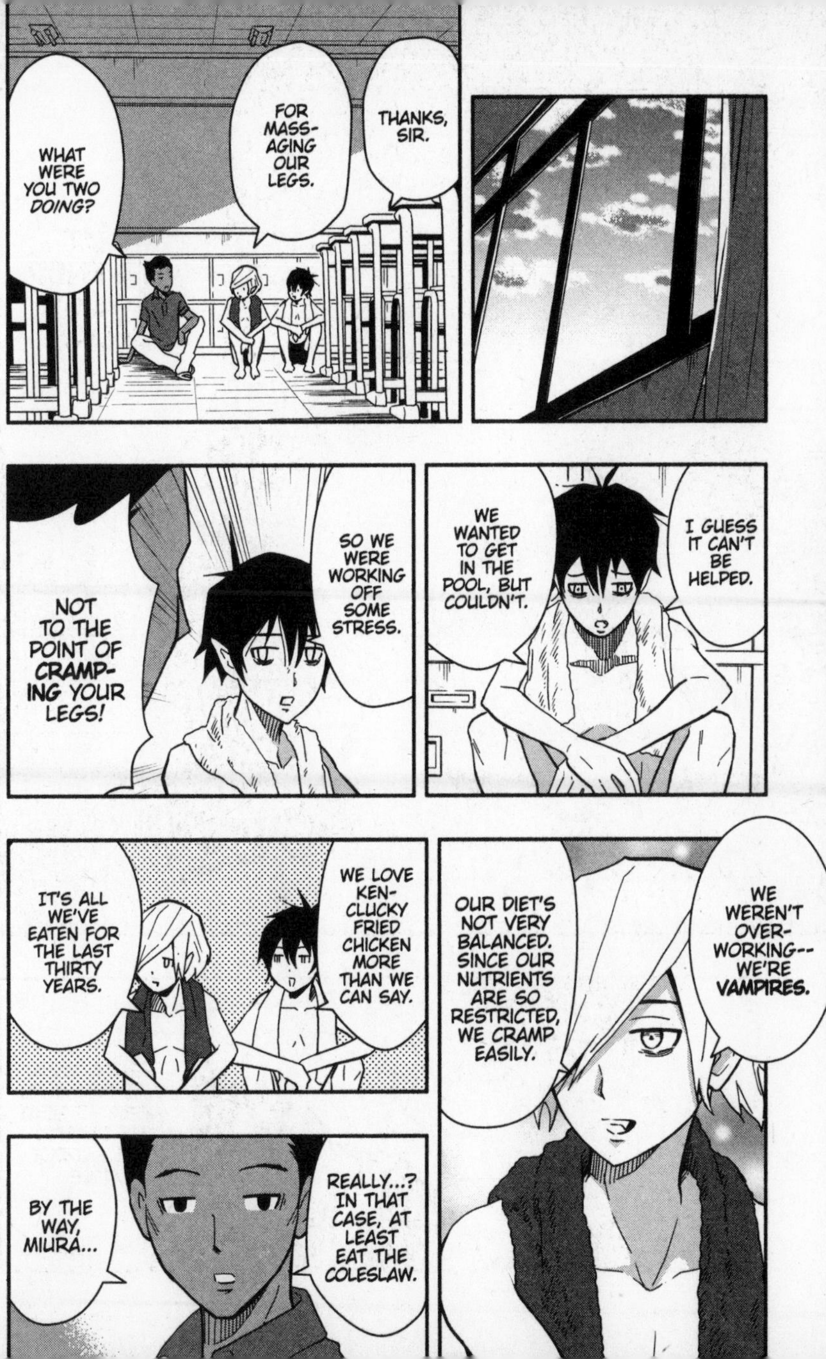
THANKS, SIR.
FOR MASSAGING OUR LEGS.
WHAT WERE YOU TWO *DOING?*
I GUESS IT CAN'T BE HELPED.
WE WANTED TO GET IN THE POOL, BUT COULDN'T.
SO WE WERE WORKING OFF SOME STRESS.
NOT TO THE POINT OF **CRAMPING** YOUR LEGS!
WE WEREN'T OVERWORKING-- WE'RE **VAMPIRES.**
OUR DIET'S NOT VERY BALANCED. SINCE OUR NUTRIENTS ARE SO RESTRICTED, WE CRAMP EASILY.
WE LOVE KEN-CLUCKY FRIED CHICKEN MORE THAN WE CAN SAY.
IT'S ALL WE'VE EATEN FOR THE LAST THIRTY YEARS.
REALLY...? IN THAT CASE, AT LEAST EAT THE COLESLAW.
BY THE WAY, MIURA...

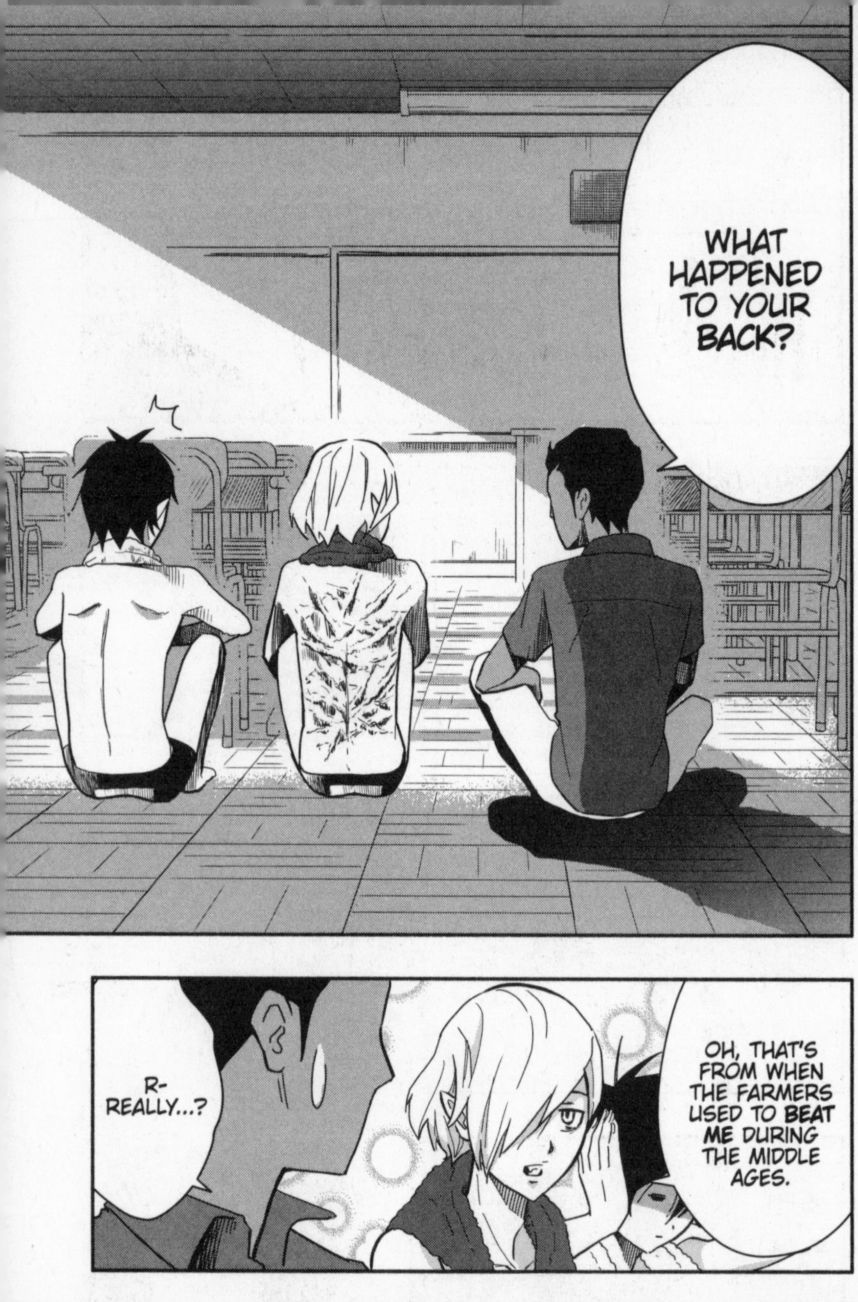
WHAT HAPPENED TO YOUR BACK?
OH, THAT'S FROM WHEN THE FARMERS USED TO BEAT ME DURING THE MIDDLE AGES.
R-REALLY...?

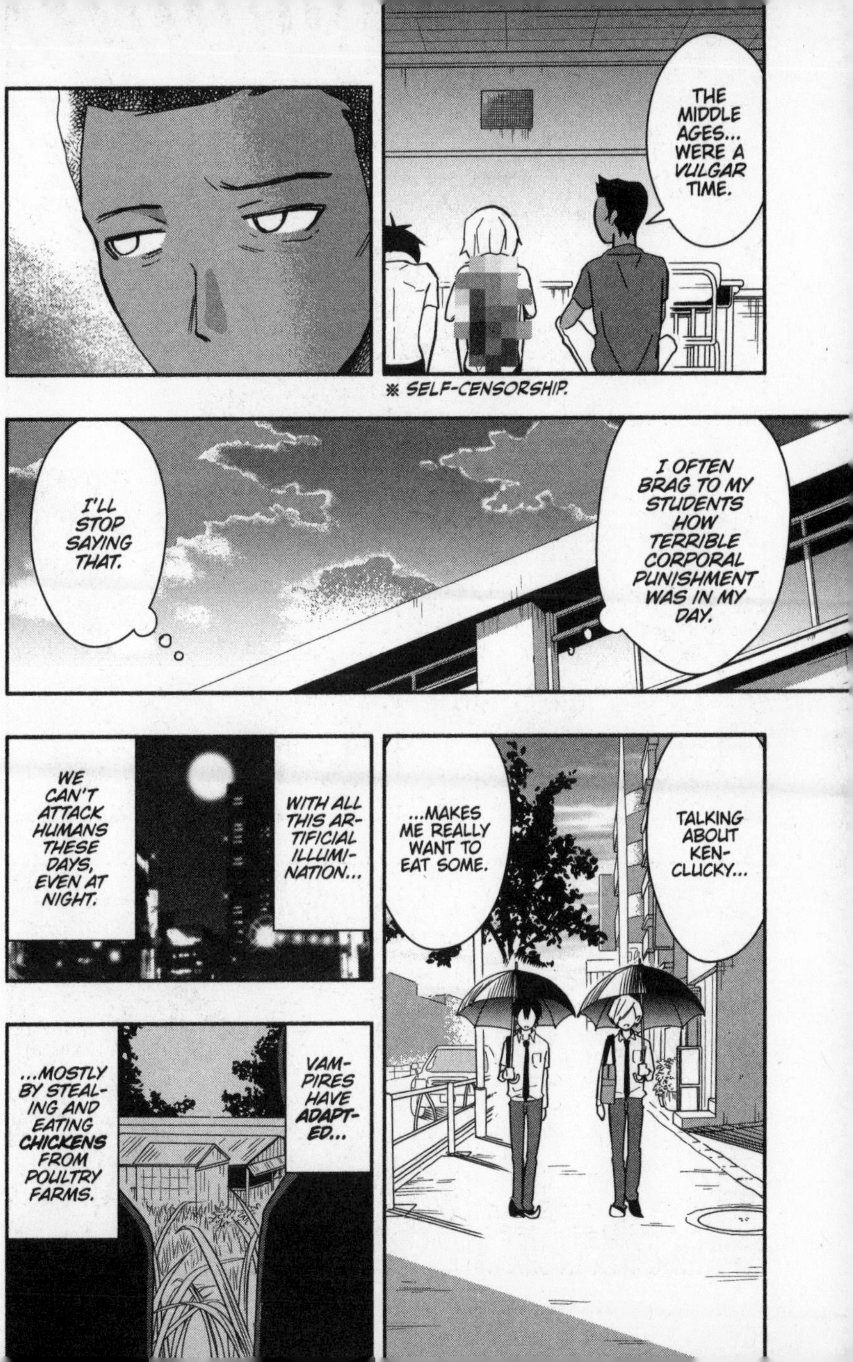
THE MIDDLE AGES... WERE A VULGAR TIME.
※ SELF-CENSORSHIP.
I OFTEN BRAG TO MY STUDENTS HOW TERRIBLE CORPORAL PUNISHMENT WAS IN MY DAY.
I'LL STOP SAYING THAT.
TALKING ABOUT KEN-CLUCKY...
...MAKES ME REALLY WANT TO EAT SOME.
WITH ALL THIS ARTIFICIAL ILLUMINATION...
WE CAN'T ATTACK HUMANS THESE DAYS, EVEN AT NIGHT.
VAMPIRES HAVE ADAPTED...
...MOSTLY BY STEALING AND EATING CHICKENS FROM POULTRY FARMS.

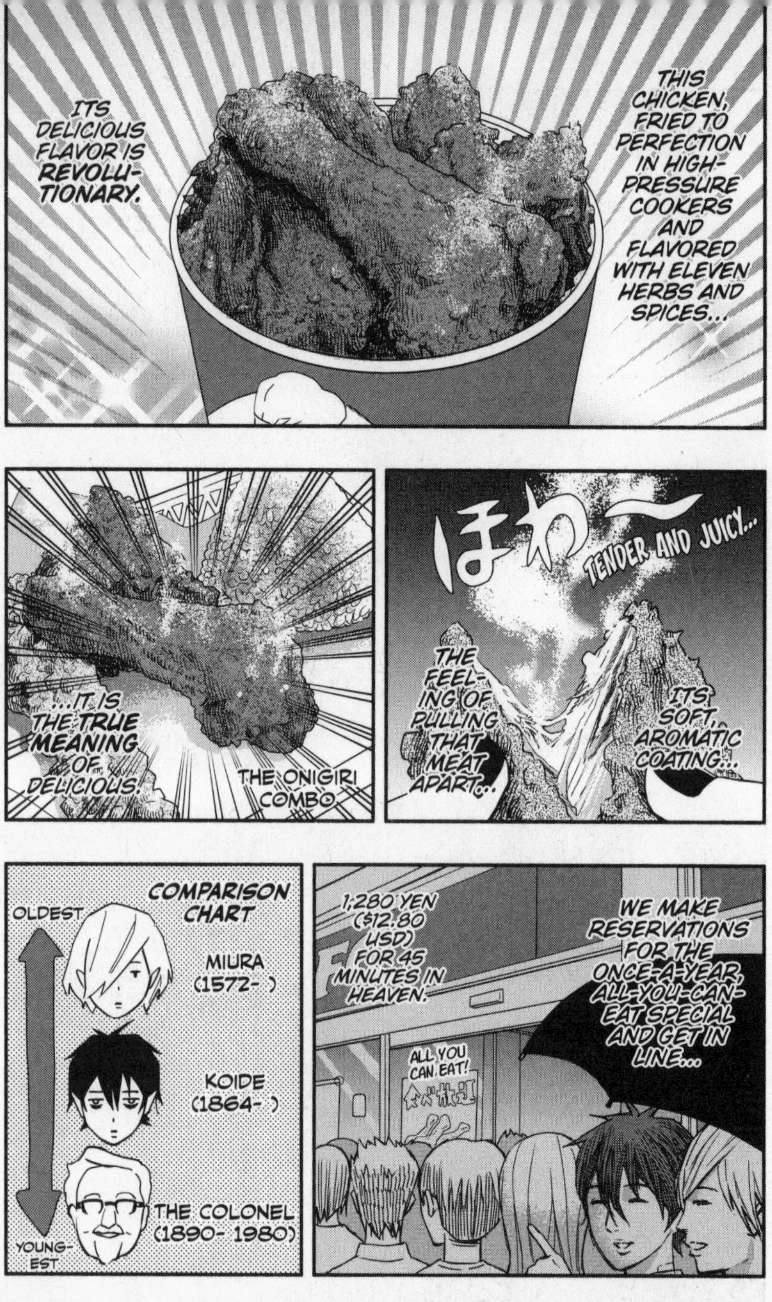
THIS CHICKEN, FRIED TO PERFECTION IN HIGH-PRESSURE COOKERS AND FLAVORED WITH ELEVEN HERBS AND SPICES...
ITS DELICIOUS FLAVOR IS REVOLUTIONARY.
ほわ~
TENDER AND JUICY...
ITS SOFT, AROMATIC COATING...
THE FEELING OF PULLING THAT MEAT APART...
...IT IS THE TRUE MEANING OF DELICIOUS!
THE ONIGIRI COMBO
WE MAKE RESERVATIONS FOR THE ONCE-A-YEAR, ALL-YOU-CAN-EAT SPECIAL AND GET IN LINE...
1,280 YEN ($12.80 USD) FOR 45 MINUTES IN HEAVEN.
ALL YOU CAN EAT!
COMPARISON CHART
OLDEST
MIURA (1572-)
KOIDE (1864-)
THE COLONEL (1890- 1980)
YOUNG-EST

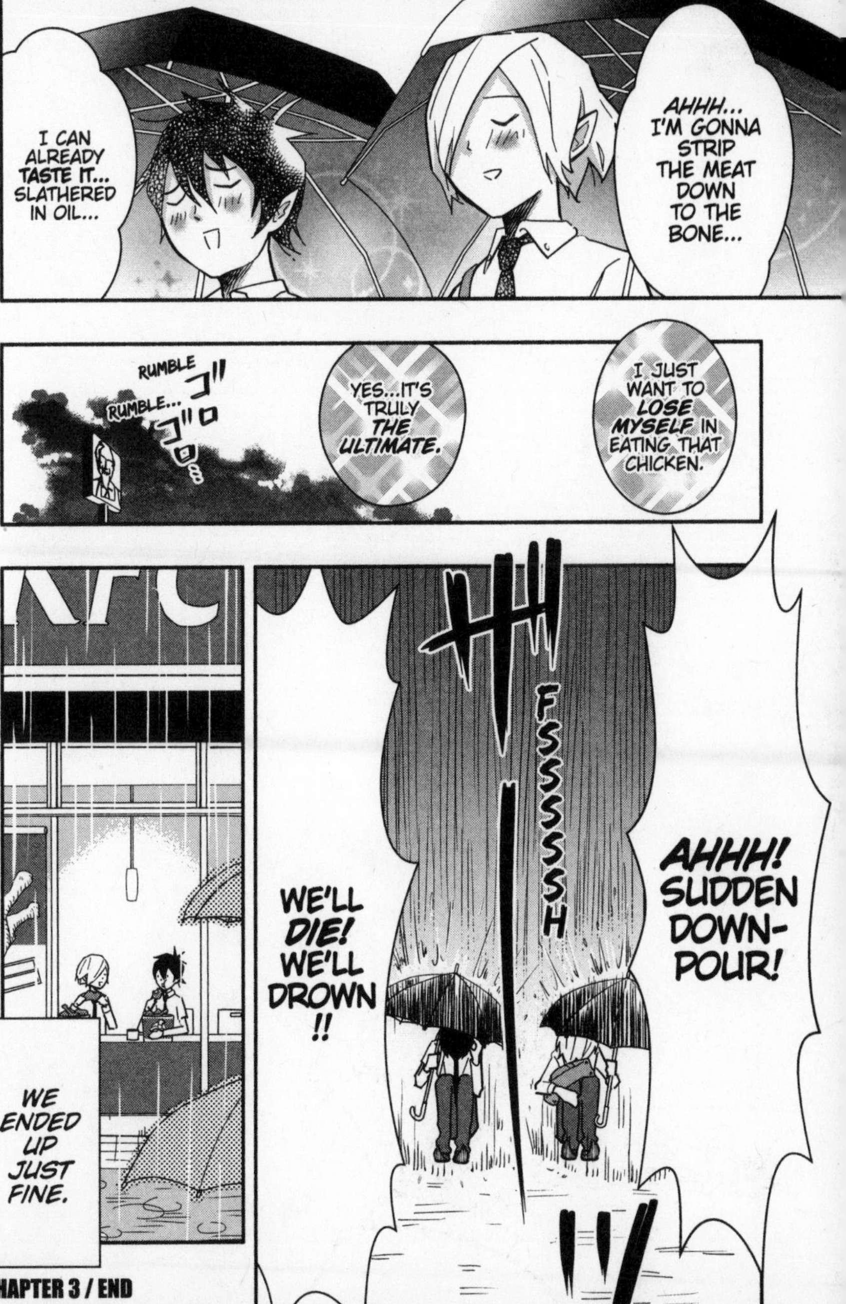
AHHH... I'M GONNA STRIP THE MEAT DOWN TO THE BONE...
I CAN ALREADY TASTE IT... SLATHERED IN OIL...
I JUST WANT TO LOSE MYSELF IN EATING THAT CHICKEN.
YES...IT'S TRULY THE ULTIMATE.
RUMBLE RUMBLE... ゴロゴロ...
AHHH! SUDDEN DOWN-POUR!
FSSSSSH
WE'LL DIE! WE'LL DROWN!!
WE ENDED UP JUST FINE.

CHAPTER 3 / END

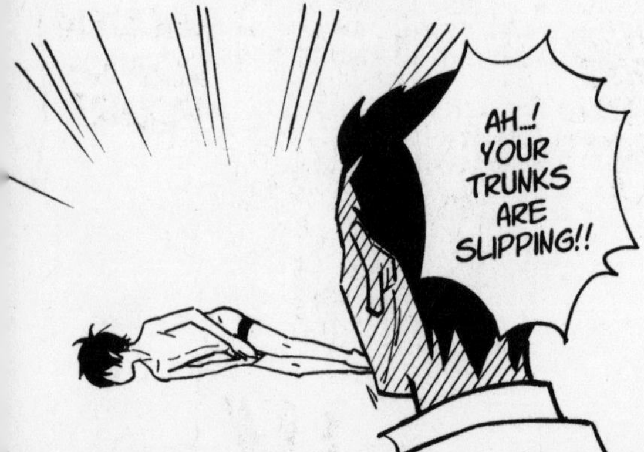
AH...! YOUR TRUNKS ARE SLIPPING!!

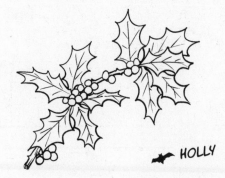

MY PATHETIC VAMPIRE LIFE

HOLLY

VAMPIRES ESPECIALLY HATE CERTAIN PLANTS, INCLUDING HOLLY, ASPEN, AND WILD ROSES.

HOLLY'S THORNY LEAVES REPRESENT CHRIST'S SUFFERING, AND ITS BERRIES REPRESENT THE BLOOD OF CHRIST.

BEING HIT WITH A WHIP MADE OF HOLLY IS EXTREMELY PAINFUL FOR VAMPIRES— AND FOR HUMANS.

BUT FOR VAMPIRES, THEIR WOUNDS REMAIN FOR ETERNITY.

CHAPTER 4 / 1ST WEEK OF JULY (134TH TIME)

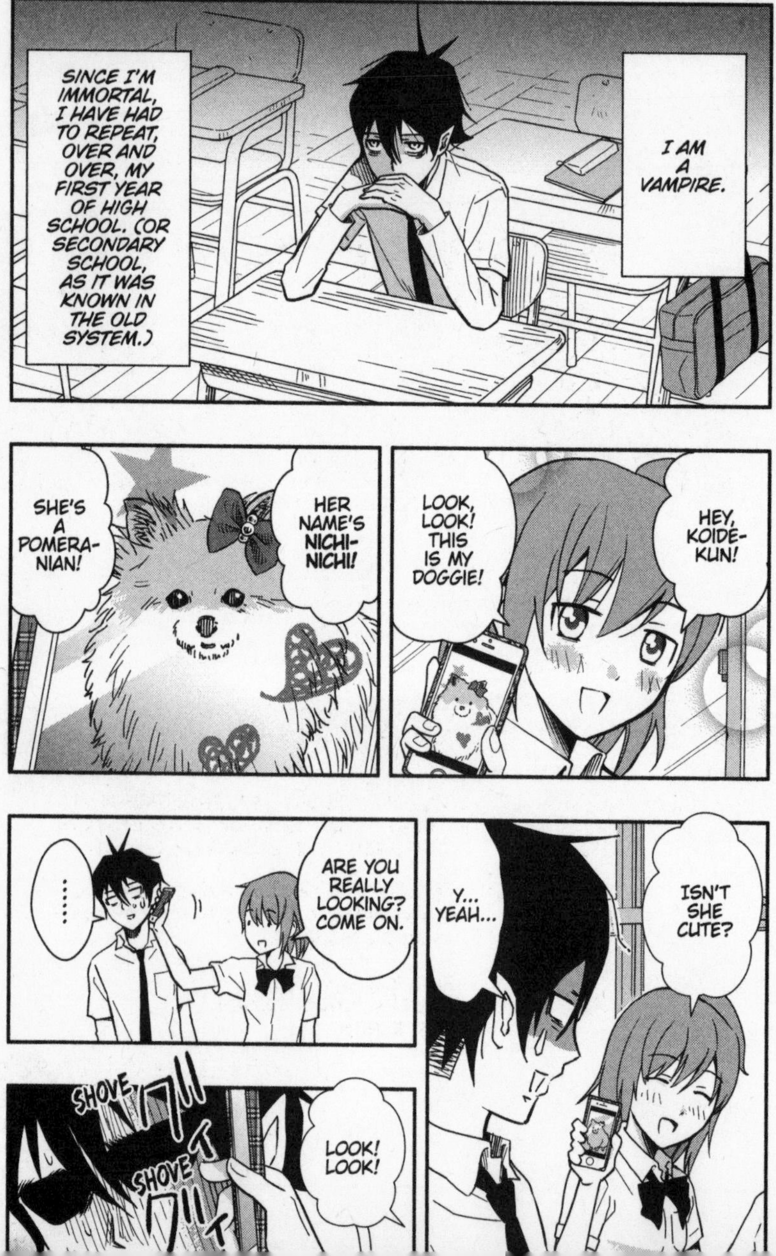
I AM A VAMPIRE.
SINCE I'M IMMORTAL, I HAVE HAD TO REPEAT, OVER AND OVER, MY FIRST YEAR OF HIGH SCHOOL. (OR SECONDARY SCHOOL, AS IT WAS KNOWN IN THE OLD SYSTEM.)
HEY, KOIDE-KUN!
LOOK, LOOK! THIS IS MY DOGGIE!
HER NAME'S NICHI-NICHI!
SHE'S A POMERANIAN!
ISN'T SHE CUTE?
Y... YEAH...
ARE YOU REALLY LOOKING? COME ON.
......
LOOK! LOOK!
SHOVE
SHOVE

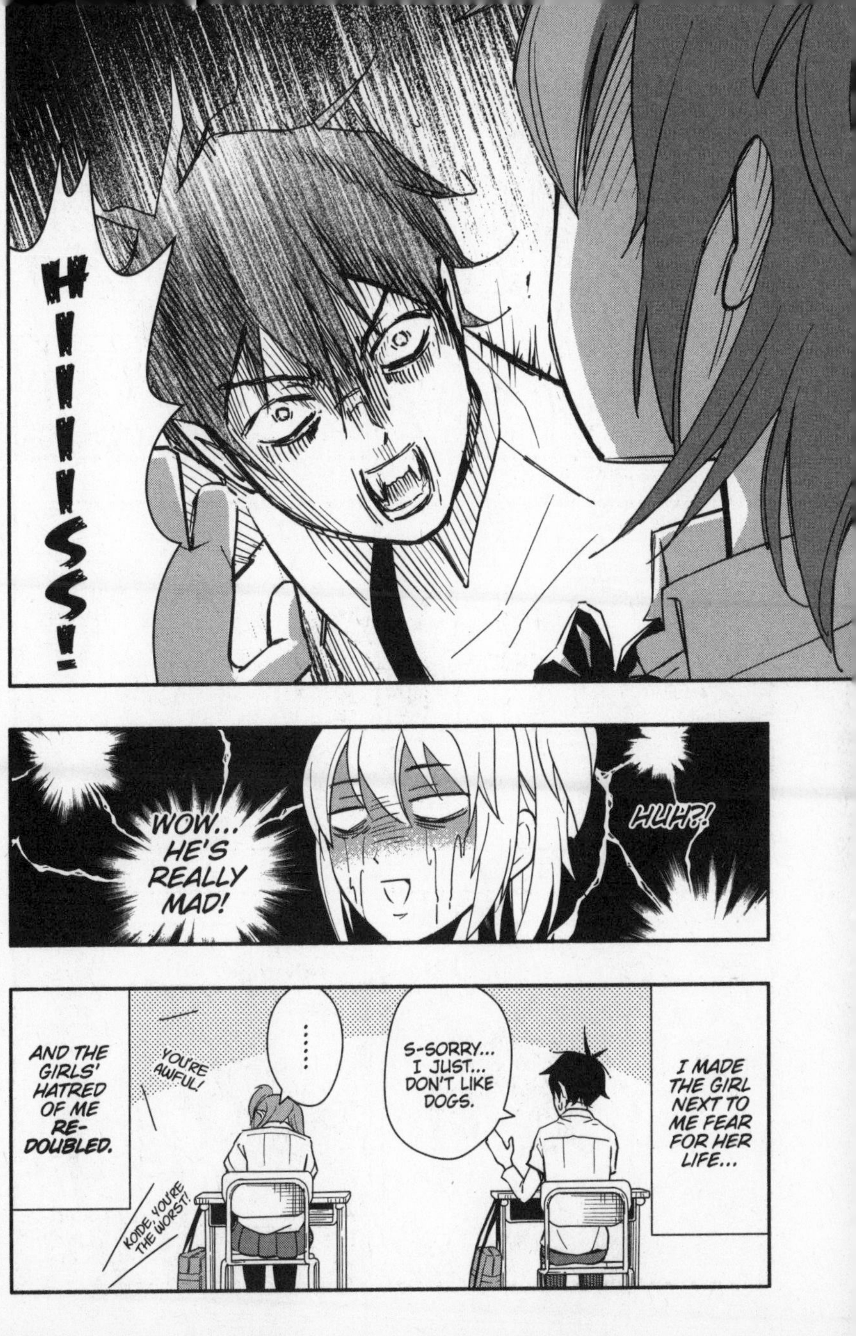
HIIIIISS!
HUH?!
WOW... HE'S REALLY MAD!
I MADE THE GIRL NEXT TO ME FEAR FOR HER LIFE...
S-SORRY... I JUST... DON'T LIKE DOGS.
......
YOU'RE AWFUL!
KOIDE, YOU'RE THE WORST!
AND THE GIRLS' HATRED OF ME RE-DOUBLED.

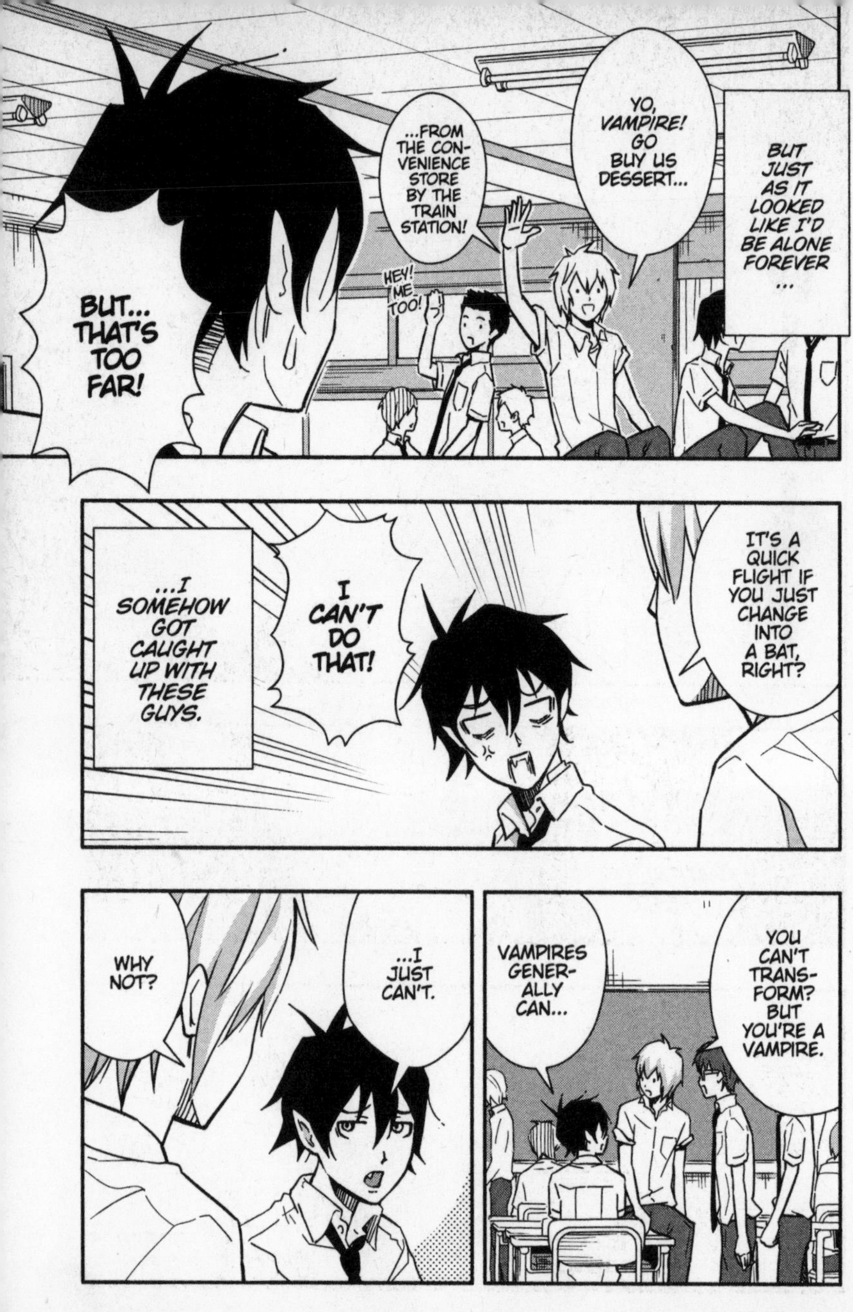
BUT JUST AS IT LOOKED LIKE I'D BE ALONE FOREVER ...
YO, VAMPIRE! GO BUY US DESSERT...
...FROM THE CONVENIENCE STORE BY THE TRAIN STATION!
HEY! ME TOO!
BUT... THAT'S TOO FAR!
IT'S A QUICK FLIGHT IF YOU JUST CHANGE INTO A BAT, RIGHT?
I CAN'T DO THAT!
...I SOMEHOW GOT CAUGHT UP WITH THESE GUYS.
YOU CAN'T TRANSFORM? BUT YOU'RE A VAMPIRE.
VAMPIRES GENERALLY CAN...
WHY NOT?
...I JUST CAN'T.

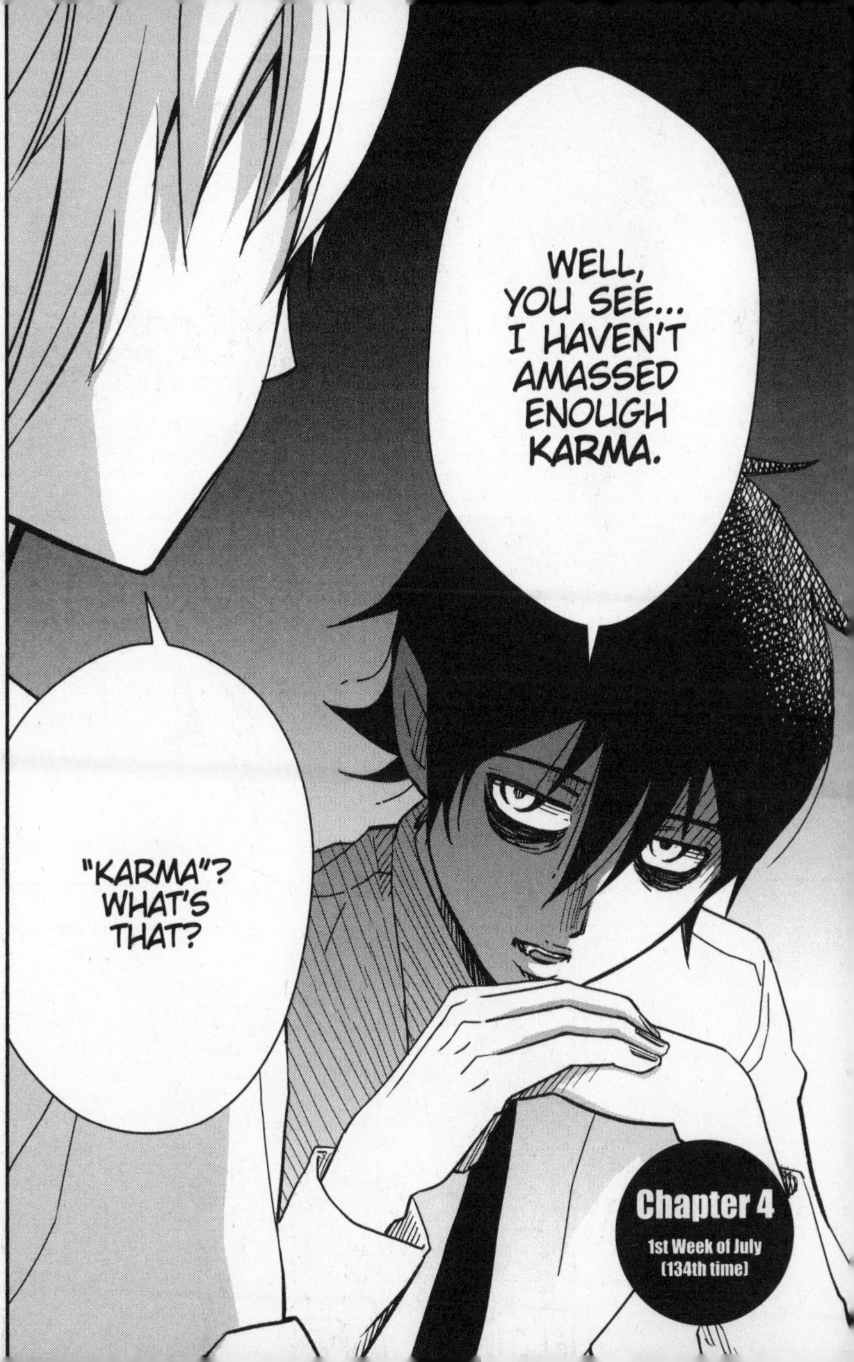
WELL, YOU SEE... I HAVEN'T AMASSED ENOUGH KARMA.
"KARMA"? WHAT'S THAT?
Chapter 4
1st Week of July (134th time)

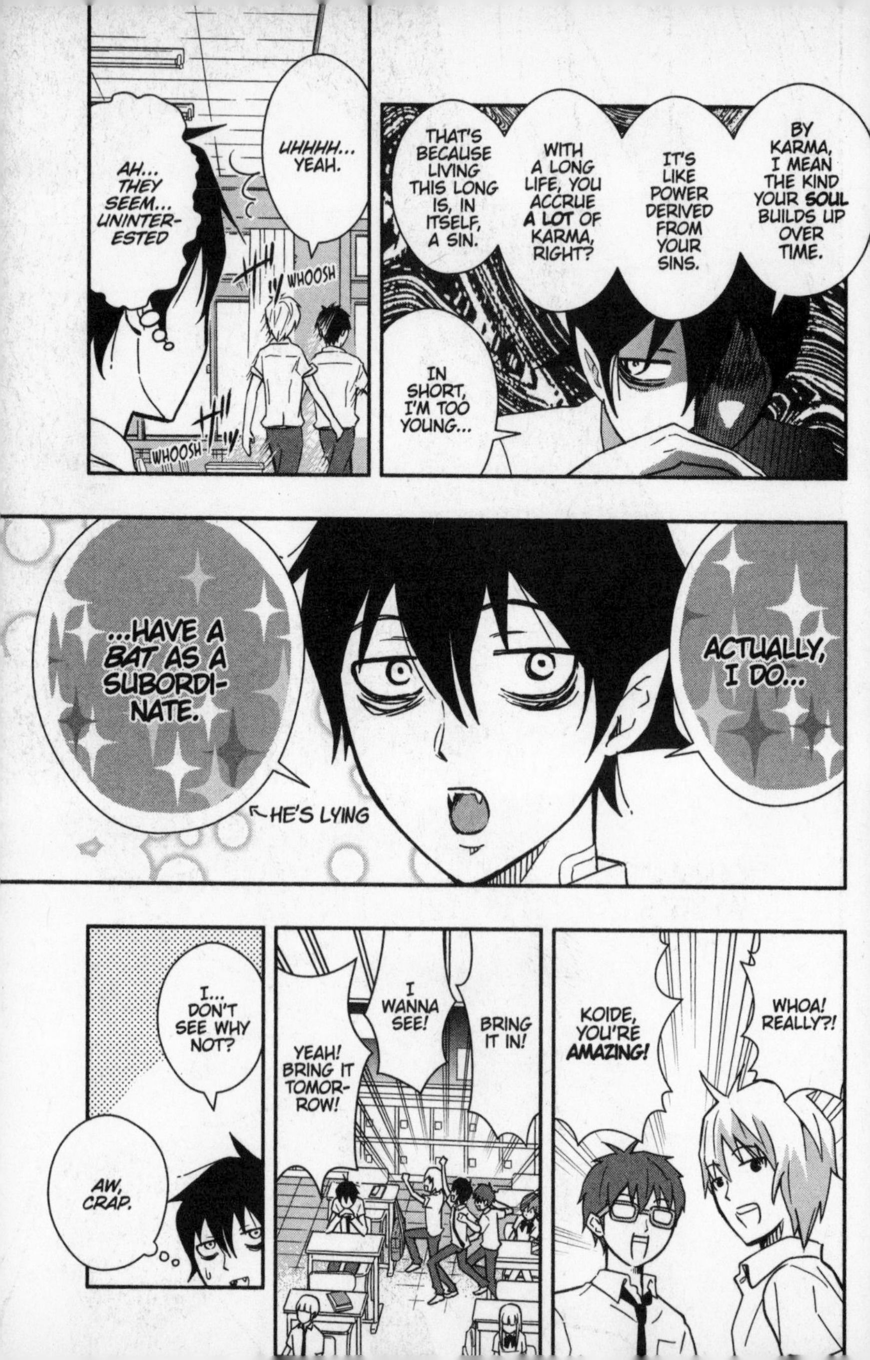
BY KARMA, I MEAN THE KIND YOUR SOUL BUILDS UP OVER TIME.
IT'S LIKE POWER DERIVED FROM YOUR SINS.
WITH A LONG LIFE, YOU ACCRUE A LOT OF KARMA, RIGHT?
THAT'S BECAUSE LIVING THIS LONG IS, IN ITSELF, A SIN.
IN SHORT, I'M TOO YOUNG...
UHHHH... YEAH.
AH... THEY SEEM... UNINTER-ESTED
WHOOSH
WHOOSH
ACTUALLY, I DO...
...HAVE A BAT AS A SUBORDI-NATE.
HE'S LYING
WHOA! REALLY?!
KOIDE, YOU'RE AMAZING!
BRING IT IN!
I WANNA SEE!
YEAH! BRING IT TOMOR-ROW!
I... DON'T SEE WHY NOT?
AW, CRAP.

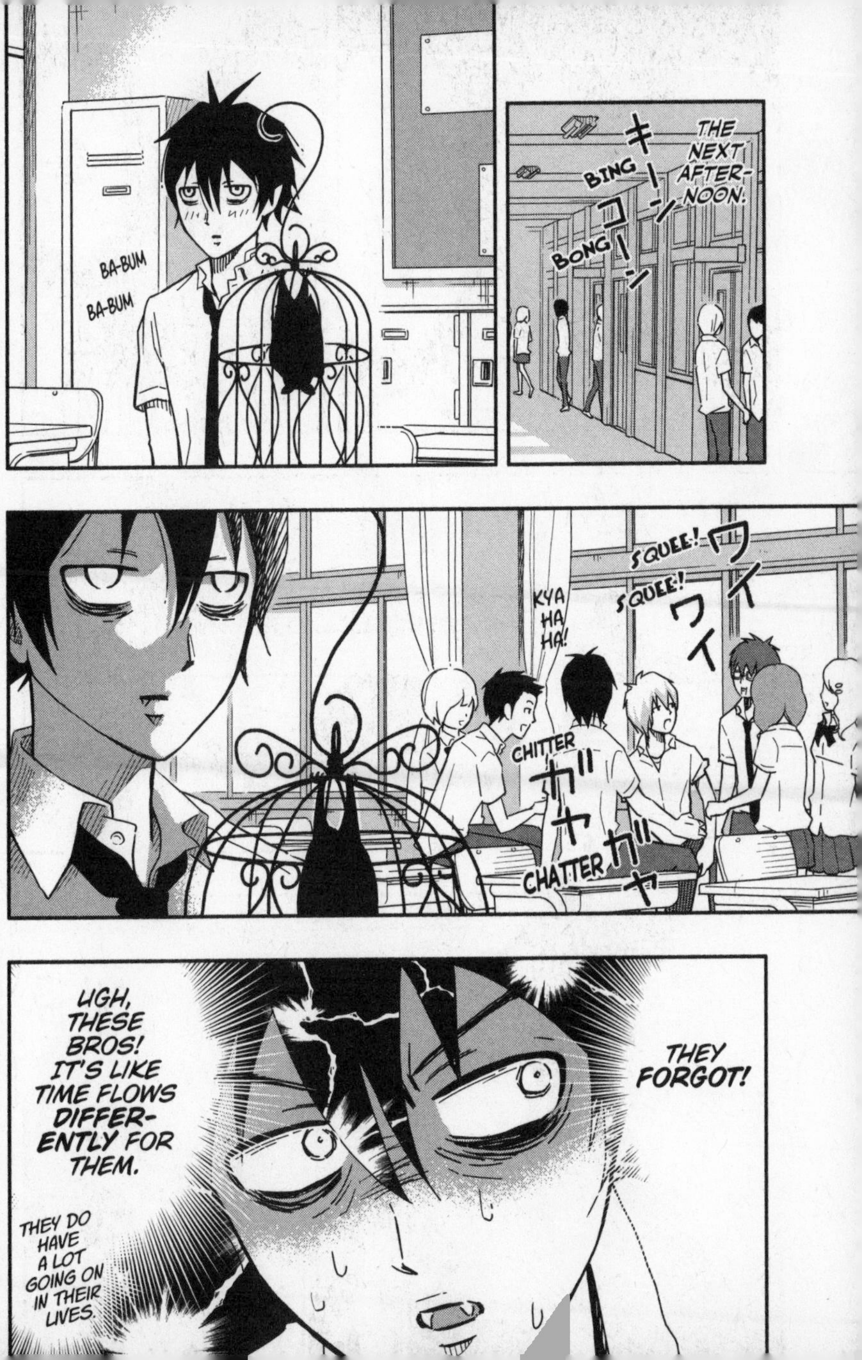
THE NEXT AFTERNOON.
BING BONG
キーンコーン
BA-BUM BA-BUM
SQUEE! SQUEE!
ワイワイ
KYA HA HA!
CHITTER CHATTER
ガヤガヤ
THEY FORGOT!
UGH, THESE BROS! IT'S LIKE TIME FLOWS DIFFERENTLY FOR THEM.
THEY DO HAVE A LOT GOING ON IN THEIR LIVES.

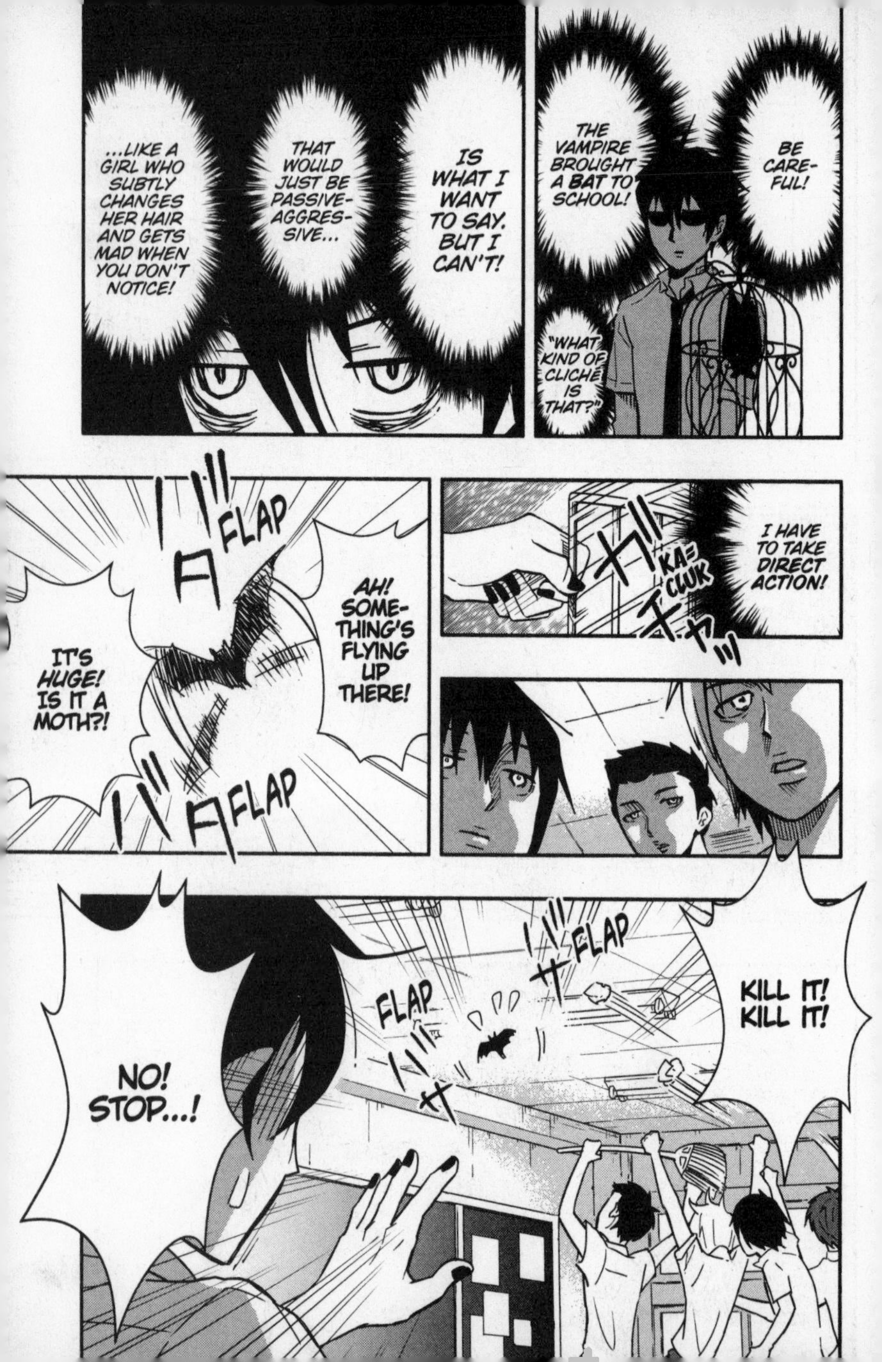
BE CARE-FUL!
THE VAMPIRE BROUGHT A BAT TO SCHOOL!
"WHAT KIND OF CLICHE IS THAT?"
IS WHAT I WANT TO SAY. BUT I CAN'T!
THAT WOULD JUST BE PASSIVE-AGGRESSIVE...
...LIKE A GIRL WHO SUBTLY CHANGES HER HAIR AND GETS MAD WHEN YOU DON'T NOTICE!
I HAVE TO TAKE DIRECT ACTION!
KA-CLUK
FLAP
AH! SOMETHING'S FLYING UP THERE!
IT'S HUGE! IS IT A MOTH?!
FLAP
KILL IT! KILL IT!
FLAP
FLAP
NO! STOP...!

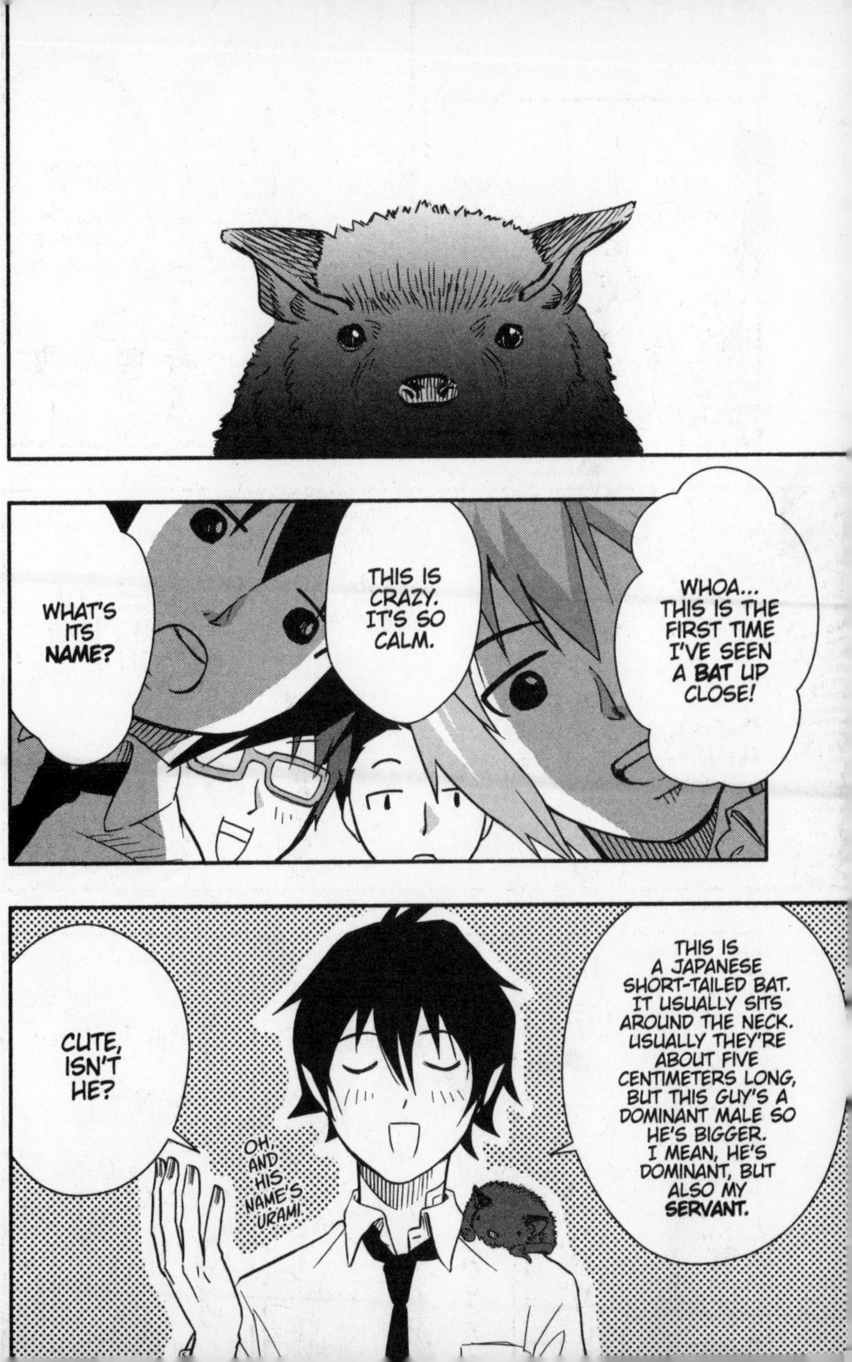
WHOA... THIS IS THE FIRST TIME I'VE SEEN A BAT UP CLOSE!
THIS IS CRAZY. IT'S SO CALM.
WHAT'S ITS NAME?
THIS IS A JAPANESE SHORT-TAILED BAT. IT USUALLY SITS AROUND THE NECK. USUALLY THEY'RE ABOUT FIVE CENTIMETERS LONG, BUT THIS GUY'S A DOMINANT MALE SO HE'S BIGGER. I MEAN, HE'S DOMINANT, BUT ALSO MY SERVANT.
CUTE, ISN'T HE?
OH, AND HIS NAME'S URAMI.

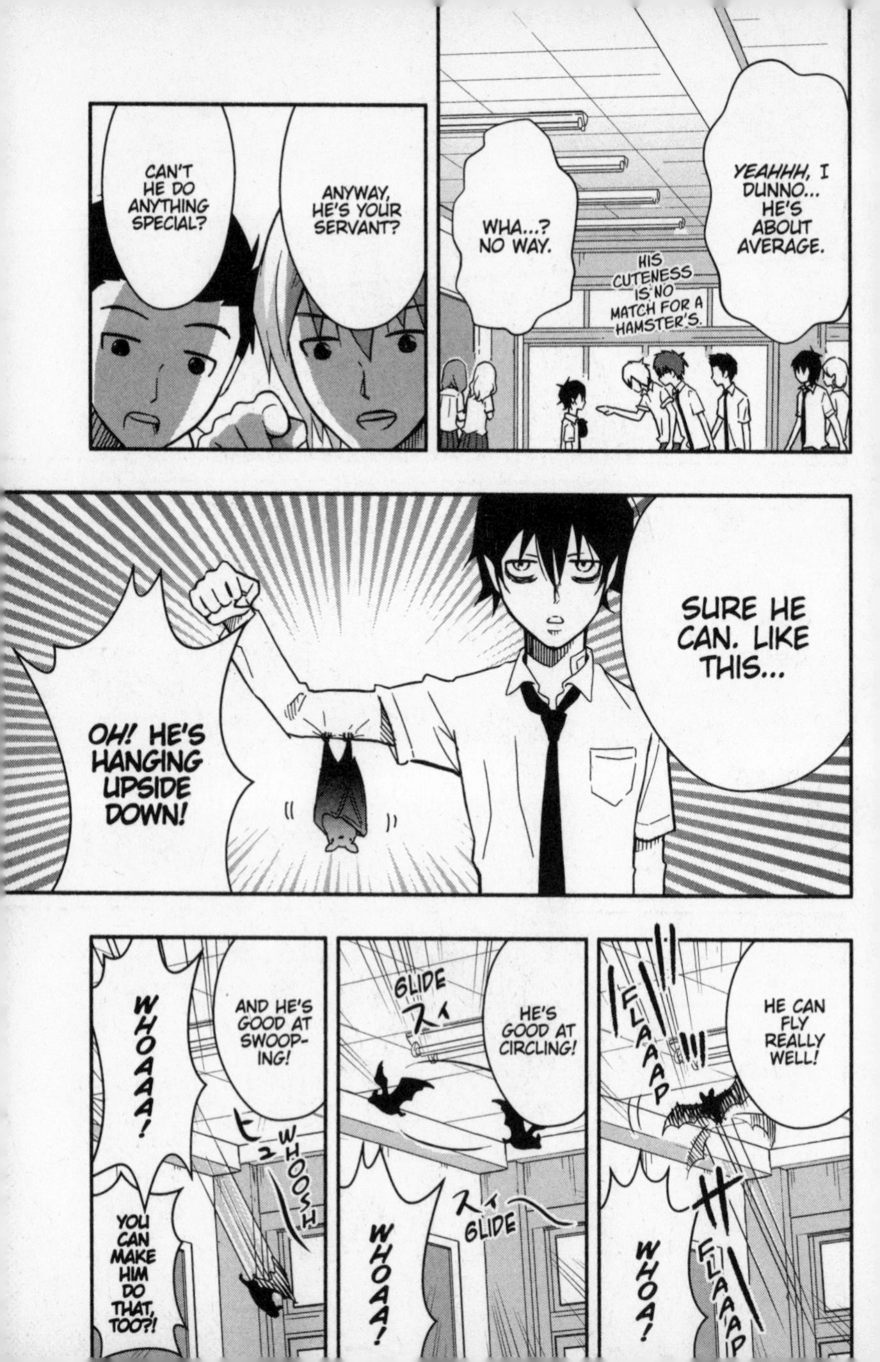
YEAHHH, I DUNNO... HE'S ABOUT AVERAGE.
HIS CUTENESS IS NO MATCH FOR A HAMSTER'S.
WHA...? NO WAY.
ANYWAY, HE'S YOUR SERVANT?
CAN'T HE DO ANYTHING SPECIAL?
SURE HE CAN. LIKE THIS...
OH! HE'S HANGING UPSIDE DOWN!
HE CAN FLY REALLY WELL!
FLAAAP
FLAAAAP
WHOA!
GLIDE
HE'S GOOD AT CIRCLING!
GLIDE
WHOAA!
AND HE'S GOOD AT SWOOP-ING!
WHOAAA!
WHOOSH
YOU CAN MAKE HIM DO THAT, TOO?!

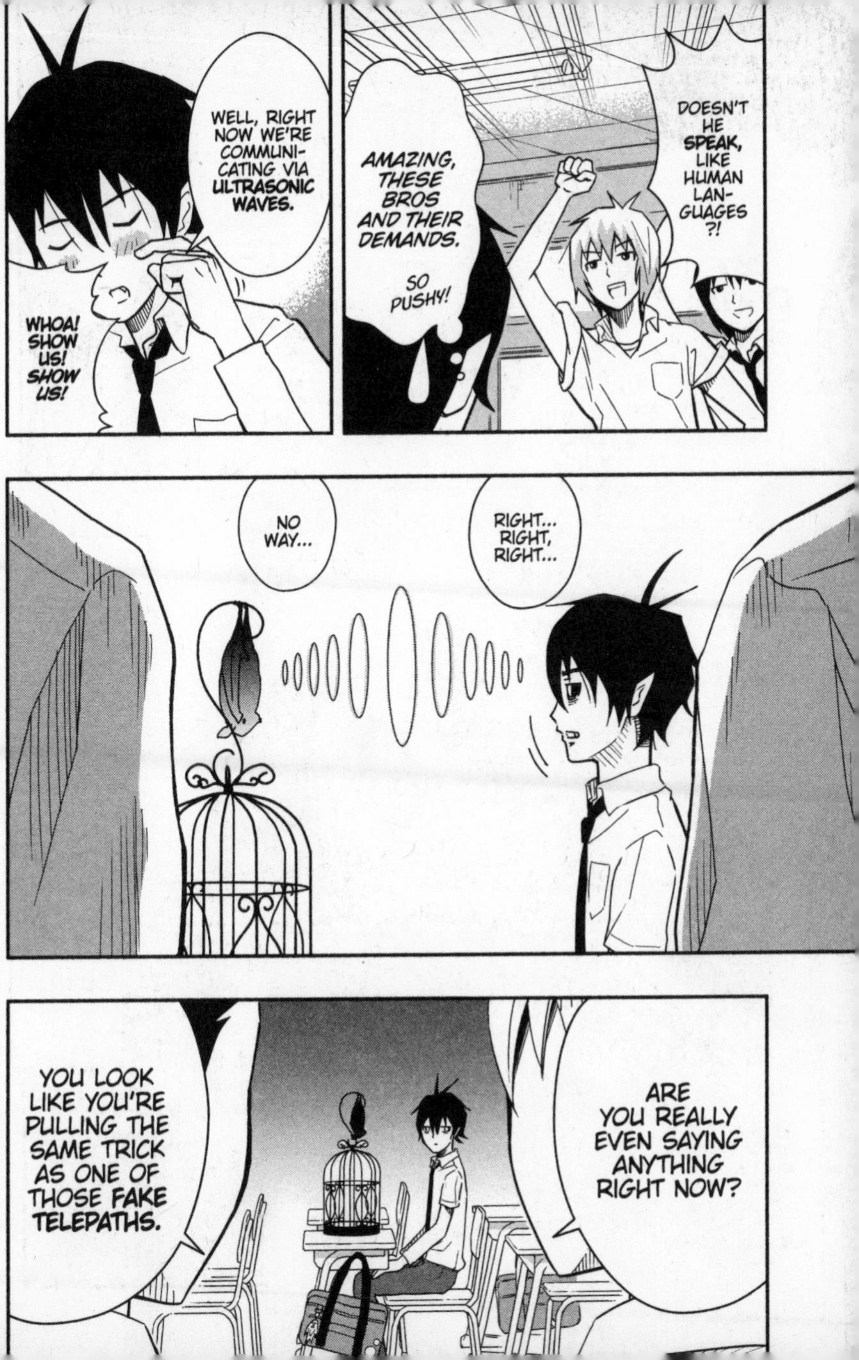
DOESN'T HE SPEAK, LIKE HUMAN LANGUAGES?!
AMAZING, THESE BROS AND THEIR DEMANDS.
SO PUSHY!
WELL, RIGHT NOW WE'RE COMMUNI-CATING VIA ULTRASONIC WAVES.
WHOA! SHOW US! SHOW US!
RIGHT... RIGHT, RIGHT...
NO WAY...
ARE YOU REALLY EVEN SAYING ANYTHING RIGHT NOW?
YOU LOOK LIKE YOU'RE PULLING THE SAME TRICK AS ONE OF THOSE FAKE TELEPATHS.

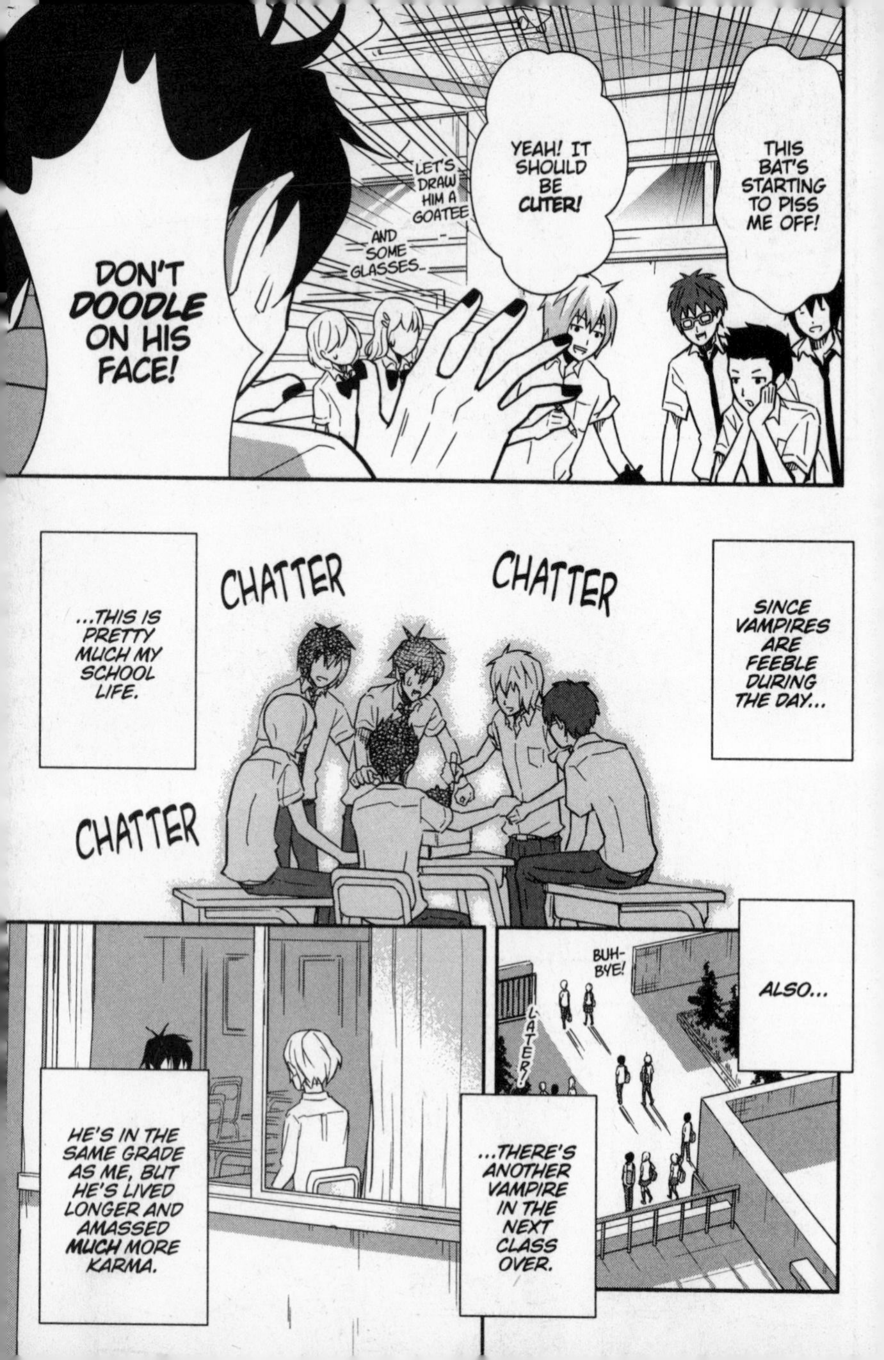
THIS BAT'S STARTING TO PISS ME OFF!
YEAH! IT SHOULD BE CUTER!
LET'S DRAW HIM A GOATEE
AND SOME GLASSES.
DON'T DOODLE ON HIS FACE!
SINCE VAMPIRES ARE FEEBLE DURING THE DAY...
CHATTER
CHATTER
CHATTER
...THIS IS PRETTY MUCH MY SCHOOL LIFE.
ALSO...
BUH-BYE!
LATER!
...THERE'S ANOTHER VAMPIRE IN THE NEXT CLASS OVER.
HE'S IN THE SAME GRADE AS ME, BUT HE'S LIVED LONGER AND AMASSED MUCH MORE KARMA.

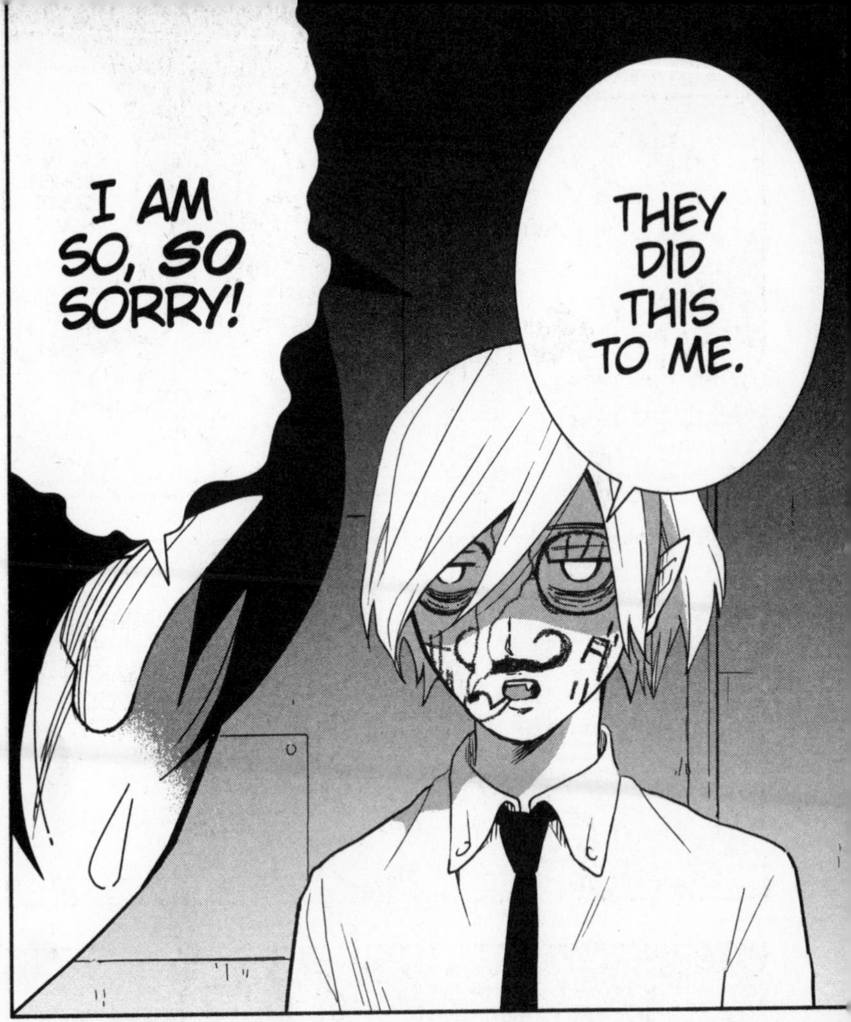
THEY DID THIS TO ME.
I AM SO, SO SORRY!
Face doodles: SALV DALI.

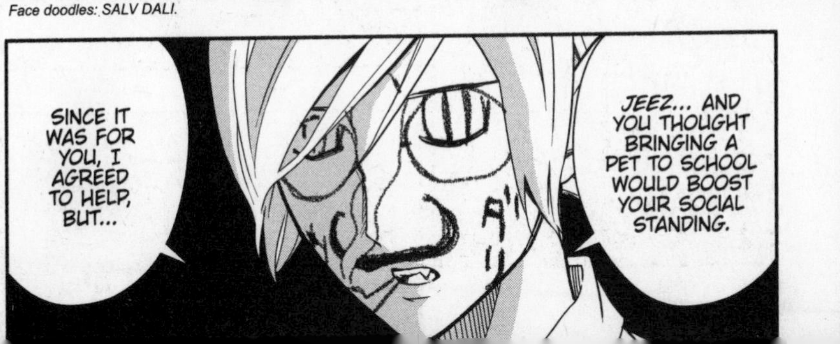
JEEZ... AND YOU THOUGHT BRINGING A PET TO SCHOOL WOULD BOOST YOUR SOCIAL STANDING.
SINCE IT WAS FOR YOU, I AGREED TO HELP, BUT...

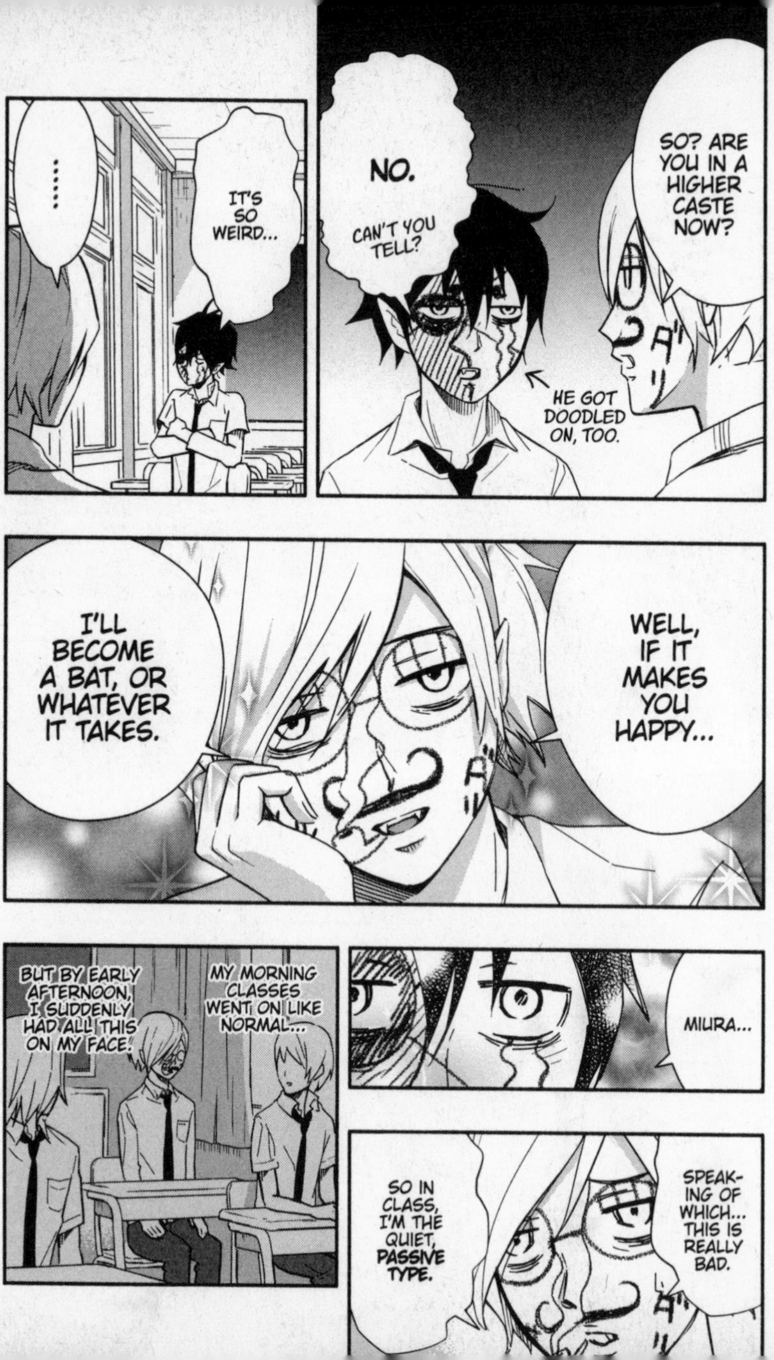
SO? ARE YOU IN A HIGHER CASTE NOW?
NO.
CAN'T YOU TELL?
HE GOT DOODLED ON, TOO.
IT'S SO WEIRD...
......
WELL, IF IT MAKES YOU HAPPY...
I'LL BECOME A BAT, OR WHATEVER IT TAKES.
MIURA...
SPEAK-ING OF WHICH... THIS IS REALLY BAD.
SO IN CLASS, I'M THE QUIET, PASSIVE TYPE.
MY MORNING CLASSES WENT ON LIKE NORMAL...
BUT BY EARLY AFTERNOON, I SUDDENLY HAD ALL THIS ON MY FACE.

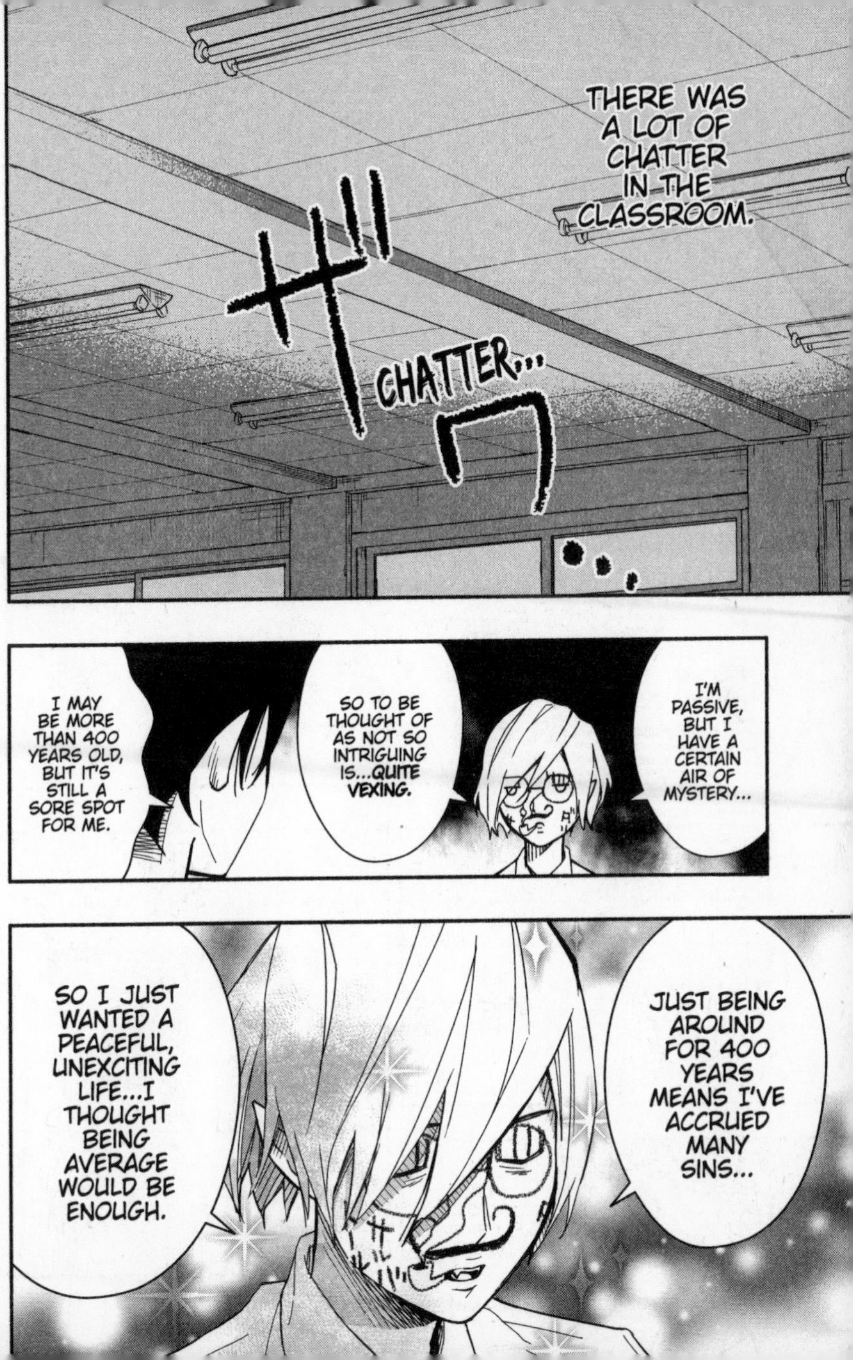
THERE WAS A LOT OF CHATTER IN THE CLASSROOM.
ザワ…
CHATTER...
I'M PASSIVE, BUT I HAVE A CERTAIN AIR OF MYSTERY...
SO TO BE THOUGHT OF AS NOT SO INTRIGUING IS...**QUITE VEXING.**
I MAY BE MORE THAN 400 YEARS OLD, BUT IT'S STILL A SORE SPOT FOR ME.
JUST BEING AROUND FOR 400 YEARS MEANS I'VE ACCRUED MANY SINS...
SO I JUST WANTED A PEACEFUL, UNEXCITING LIFE...I THOUGHT BEING AVERAGE WOULD BE ENOUGH.

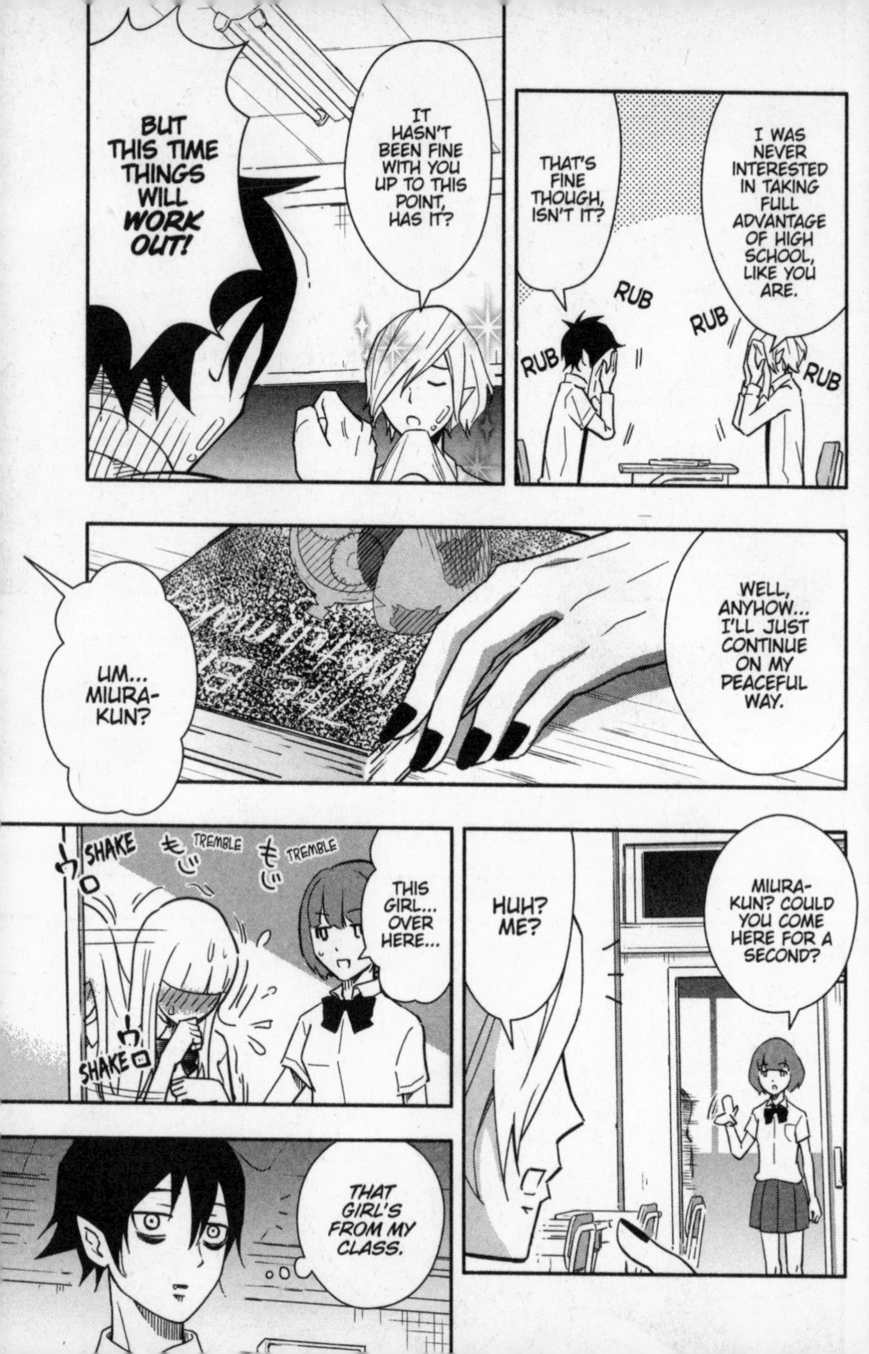
I WAS NEVER INTERESTED IN TAKING FULL ADVANTAGE OF HIGH SCHOOL, LIKE YOU ARE.
THAT'S FINE THOUGH, ISN'T IT?
RUB
RUB
RUB
RUB
IT HASN'T BEEN FINE WITH YOU UP TO THIS POINT, HAS IT?
BUT THIS TIME THINGS WILL **WORK OUT!**
WELL, ANYHOW... I'LL JUST CONTINUE ON MY PEACEFUL WAY.
UM... MIURA-KUN?
MIURA-KUN? COULD YOU COME HERE FOR A SECOND?
HUH? ME?
THIS GIRL... OVER HERE...
もじ TREMBLE
もじ TREMBLE
ウロ SHAKE
ウロ SHAKE
THAT GIRL'S FROM MY CLASS.

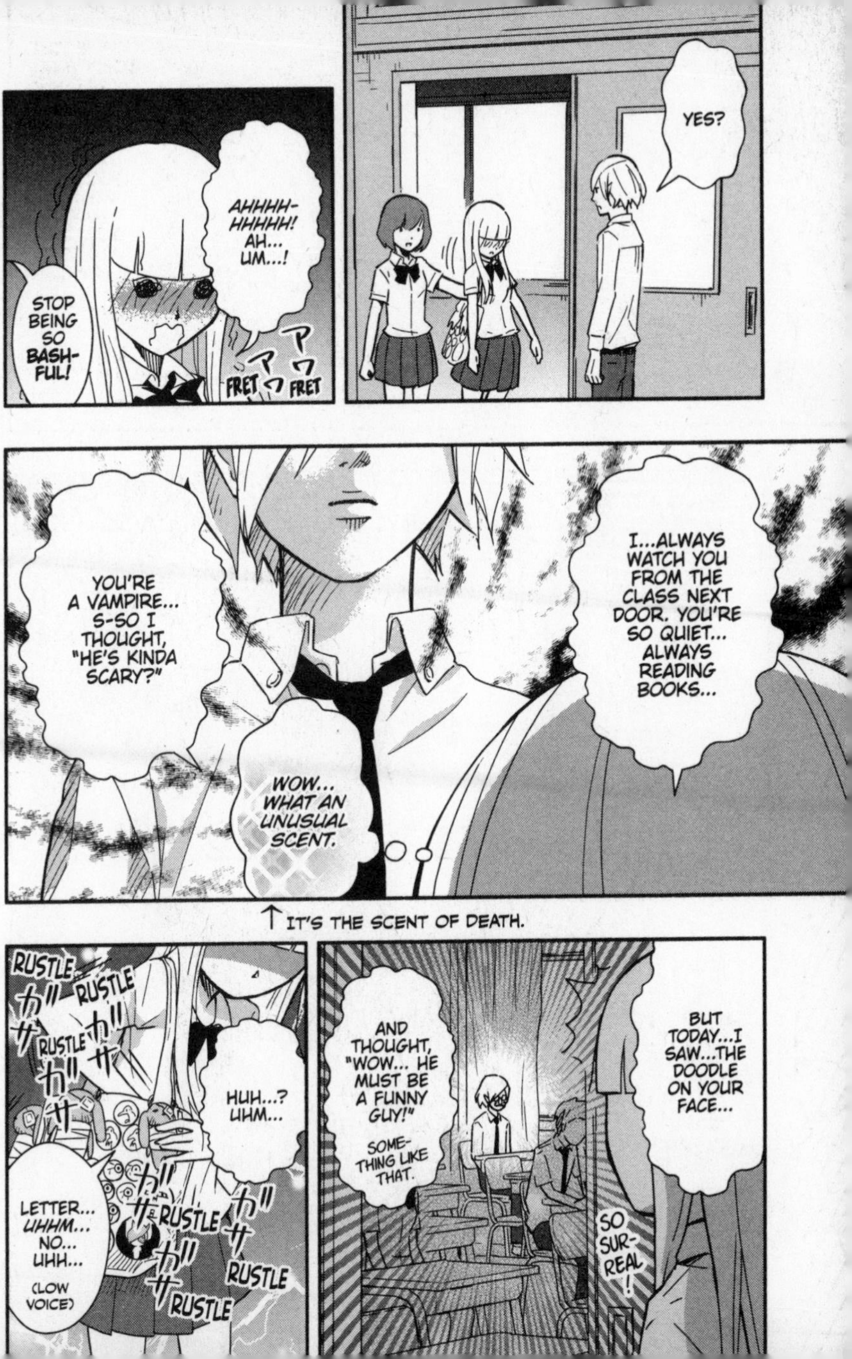
YES?
AHHHH-HHHHH! AH... UM...!
STOP BEING SO BASH-FUL!
FRET FRET
I...ALWAYS WATCH YOU FROM THE CLASS NEXT DOOR. YOU'RE SO QUIET... ALWAYS READING BOOKS...
YOU'RE A VAMPIRE... S-SO I THOUGHT, "HE'S KINDA SCARY?"
WOW... WHAT AN UNUSUAL SCENT.
↑ IT'S THE SCENT OF DEATH.
BUT TODAY...I SAW...THE DOODLE ON YOUR FACE...
SO SUR-REAL!
AND THOUGHT, "WOW... HE MUST BE A FUNNY GUY!"
SOME-THING LIKE THAT.
HUH...? UHM...
RUSTLE RUSTLE RUSTLE
LETTER... UHHM... NO... UHH... (LOW VOICE)
RUSTLE RUSTLE RUSTLE

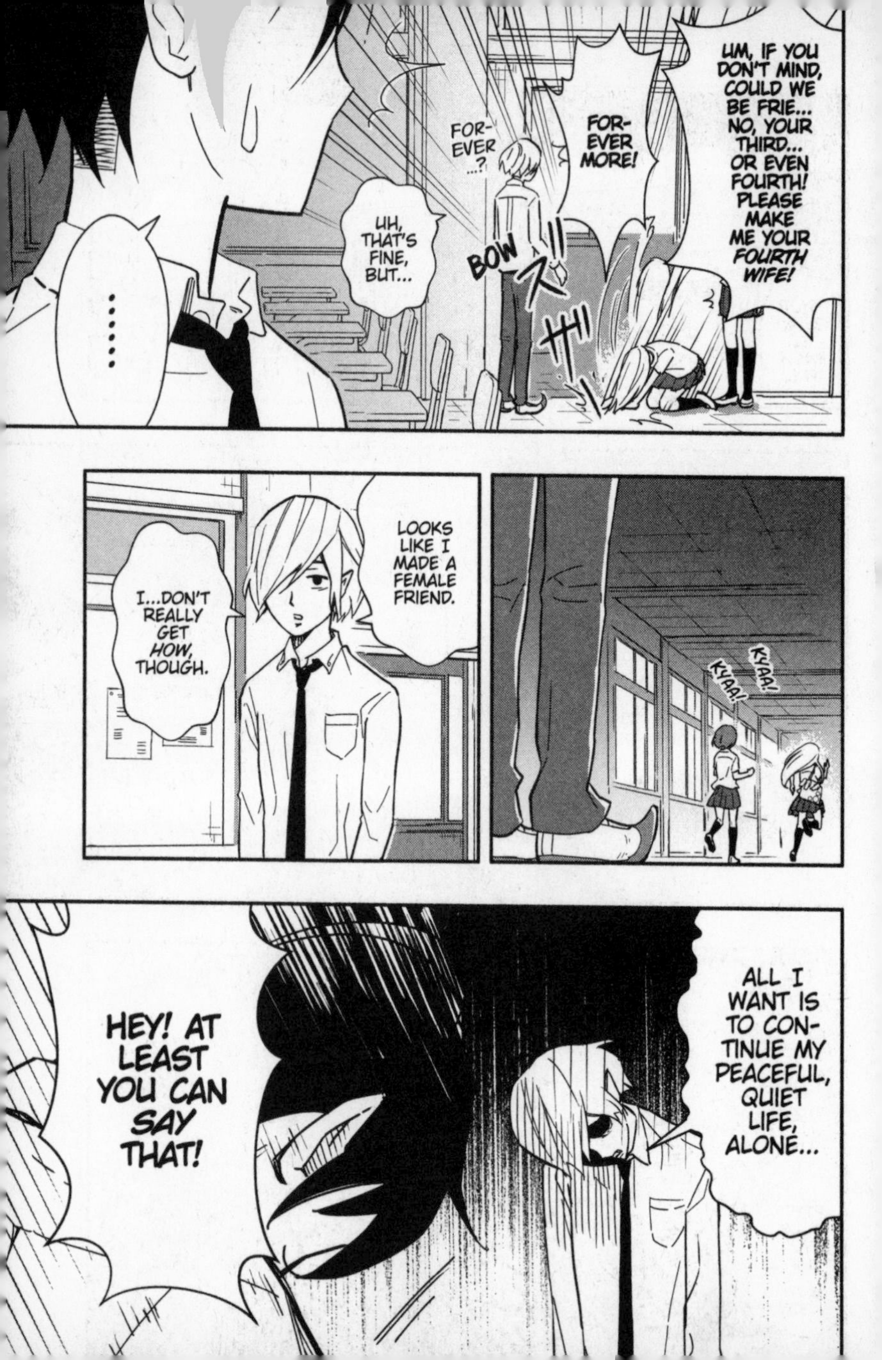
UM, IF YOU DON'T MIND, COULD WE BE FRIE... NO, YOUR THIRD... OR EVEN FOURTH! PLEASE MAKE ME YOUR FOURTH WIFE!
BOW
FOR-EVER MORE!
FOR-EVER ...?
UH, THAT'S FINE, BUT...
......
KYAA!
KYAA!
LOOKS LIKE I MADE A FEMALE FRIEND.
I...DON'T REALLY GET *HOW*, THOUGH.
ALL I WANT IS TO CON-TINUE MY PEACEFUL, QUIET LIFE, ALONE...
HEY! AT LEAST YOU CAN *SAY* THAT!

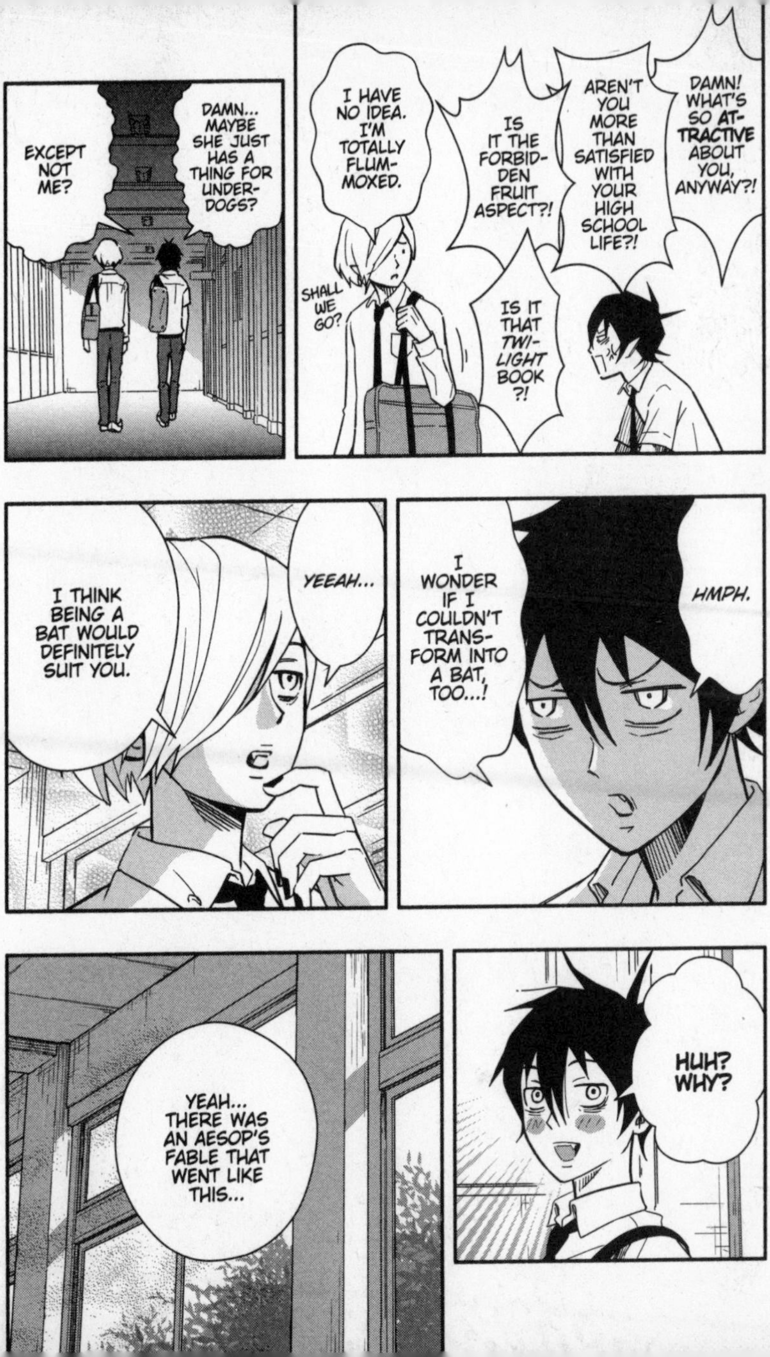
DAMN! WHAT'S SO ATTRACTIVE ABOUT YOU, ANYWAY?!
AREN'T YOU MORE THAN SATISFIED WITH YOUR HIGH SCHOOL LIFE?!
IS IT THE FORBIDDEN FRUIT ASPECT?!
IS IT THAT TWILIGHT BOOK?!
I HAVE NO IDEA. I'M TOTALLY FLUMMOXED.
SHALL WE GO?
DAMN... MAYBE SHE JUST HAS A THING FOR UNDERDOGS?
EXCEPT NOT ME?
HMPH.
I WONDER IF I COULDN'T TRANSFORM INTO A BAT, TOO...!
YEEAH...
I THINK BEING A BAT WOULD DEFINITELY SUIT YOU.
HUH? WHY?
YEAH... THERE WAS AN AESOP'S FABLE THAT WENT LIKE THIS...

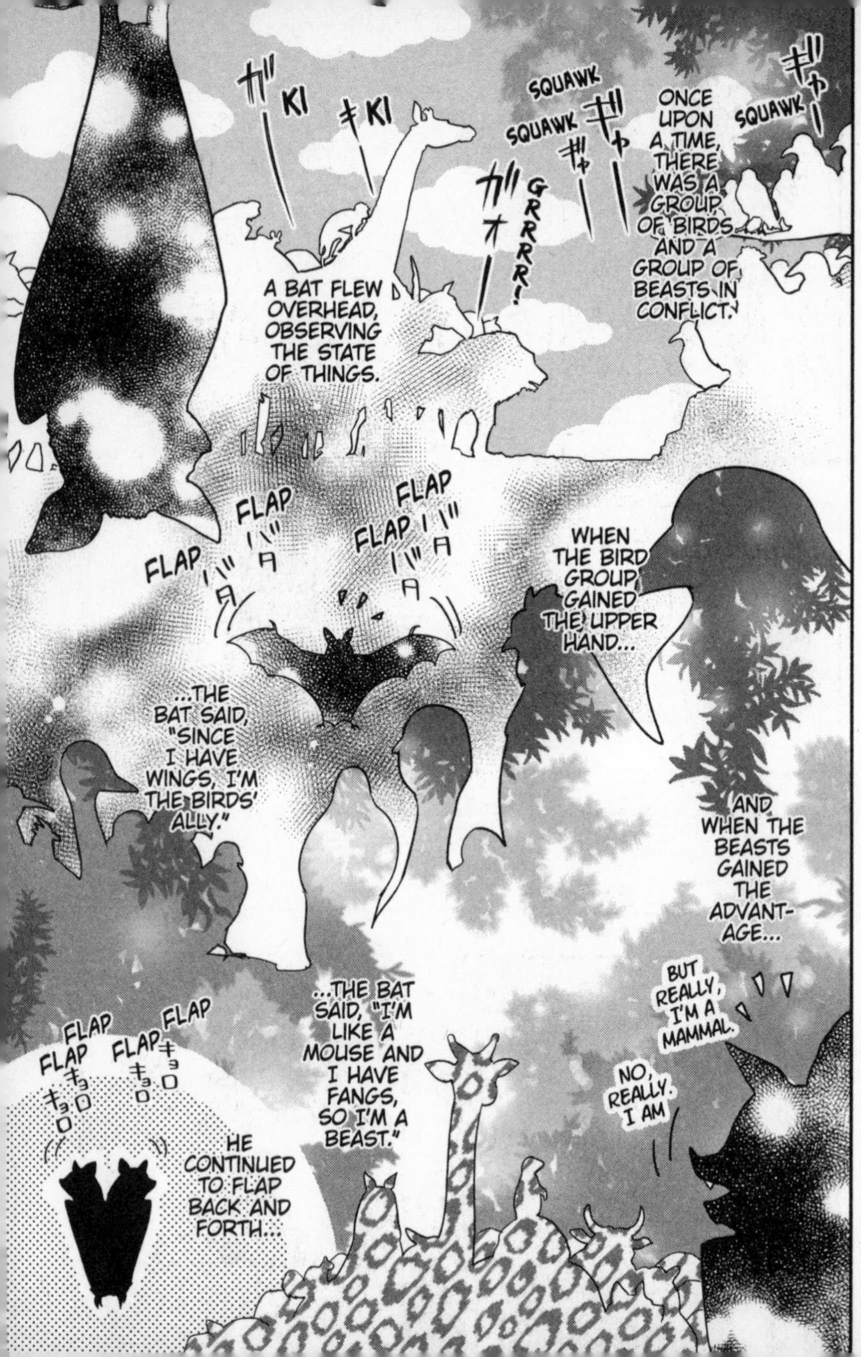
SQUAWK
ギャー
SQUAWK
ギャー
SQUAWK
ギャー
ONCE UPON A TIME, THERE WAS A GROUP OF BIRDS AND A GROUP OF BEASTS IN CONFLICT.
ガオー
GRRRR!
キ KI
ガ KI
A BAT FLEW OVERHEAD, OBSERVING THE STATE OF THINGS.
WHEN THE BIRD GROUP GAINED THE UPPER HAND...
FLAP
FLAP
FLAP
FLAP
FLAP
...THE BAT SAID, "SINCE I HAVE WINGS, I'M THE BIRDS' ALLY."
AND WHEN THE BEASTS GAINED THE ADVANTAGE...
BUT REALLY, I'M A MAMMAL.
NO, REALLY. I AM
...THE BAT SAID, "I'M LIKE A MOUSE AND I HAVE FANGS, SO I'M A BEAST."
FLAP
FLAP
FLAP
FLAP
キョロ
キョロ
キョロ
HE CONTINUED TO FLAP BACK AND FORTH...

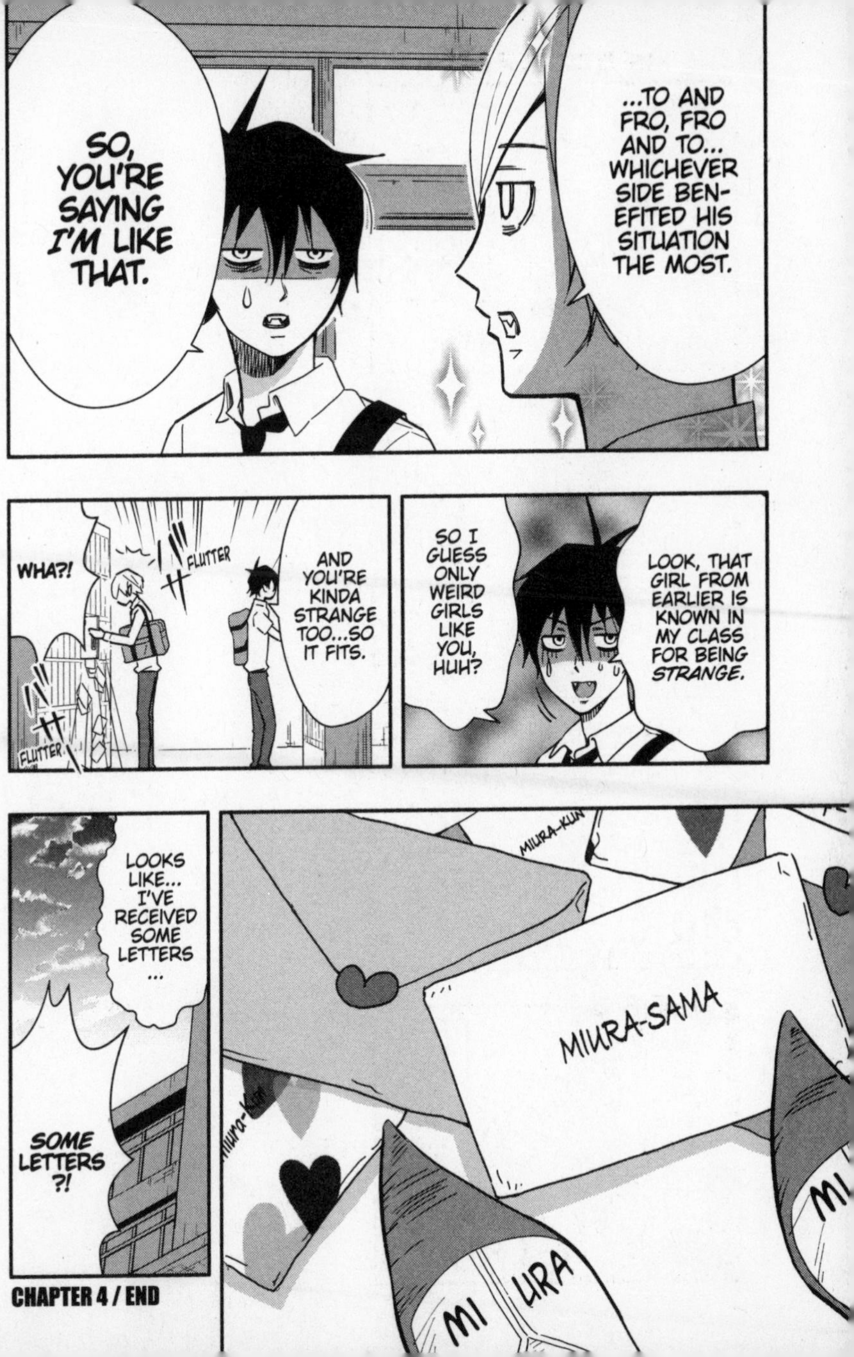
...TO AND FRO, FRO AND TO... WHICHEVER SIDE BEN-EFITED HIS SITUATION THE MOST.
SO, YOU'RE SAYING *I'M* LIKE THAT.
LOOK, THAT GIRL FROM EARLIER IS KNOWN IN MY CLASS FOR BEING *STRANGE.*
SO I GUESS ONLY WEIRD GIRLS LIKE YOU, HUH?
AND YOU'RE KINDA STRANGE TOO...SO IT FITS.
FLUTTER
WHA?!
FLUTTER
MIURA-KUN
MIURA-SAMA
Miura-kun
MI URA
MI
LOOKS LIKE... I'VE RECEIVED SOME LETTERS ...
SOME LETTERS ?!

CHAPTER 4 / END

A DAY IN THE LIFE OF MIURA

MIURA KURARA (442). HE'S USUALLY QUIET AND KEEPS TO HIMSELF.
HE'S ALWAYS READING DIFFI-CULT BOOKS
BOOKS HE'S
HE'S QUITE POPULAR WITH HIS CLASS-MATES (BOTH GUYS AND GIRLS).
MIURA'S SO COOL~!
I WANNA TALK TO HIM SOME-TIME!
BOOKS HE'S ALREADY READ
BUT HE'S HARD TO TALK TO.
AH, I'VE ALREADY READ THIS ONE.
SO MIURA RE-MAINS ALONE.

MY PATHETIC VAMPIRE LIFE

BATS

THE LATIN TERM FOR BAT IS **CHIROPTERA.**

THUMB
INDEX
MIDDLE
RING
PINKY

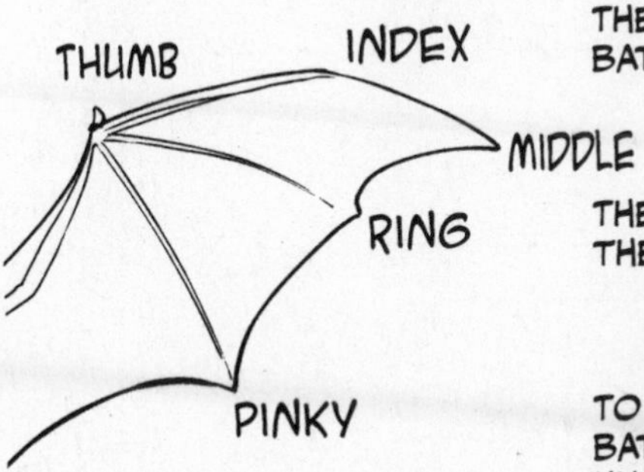

THE TWO PARTS OF THE WORD:
CHIRO IS HAND.
PTERA IS WING.

TO PUT IT MORE SIMPLY, BATS HAVE HANDS WITH HUGE PALMS ATTACHED TO THEIR WINGS...

THERE'S A MEMBRANE ATTACHED TO THE SIDE OF THEIR BODIES.

PERHAPS THAT'S WHY, LONG AGO, THE SIDES OF VESTS WORN BY VAMPIRES WERE LACED UP...

...SO THAT WHEN THE VAMPIRES TRANSFORMED INTO BATS, THEY WOULDN'T RIP THE SIDES OF THEIR VESTS.

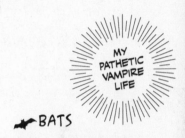

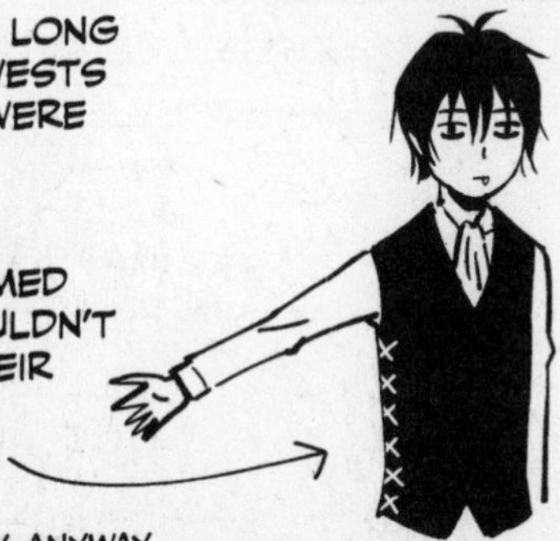

THAT'S THE STORY, ANYWAY.

CHAPTER 5 / 2ND WEEK OF JULY (134TH TIME)

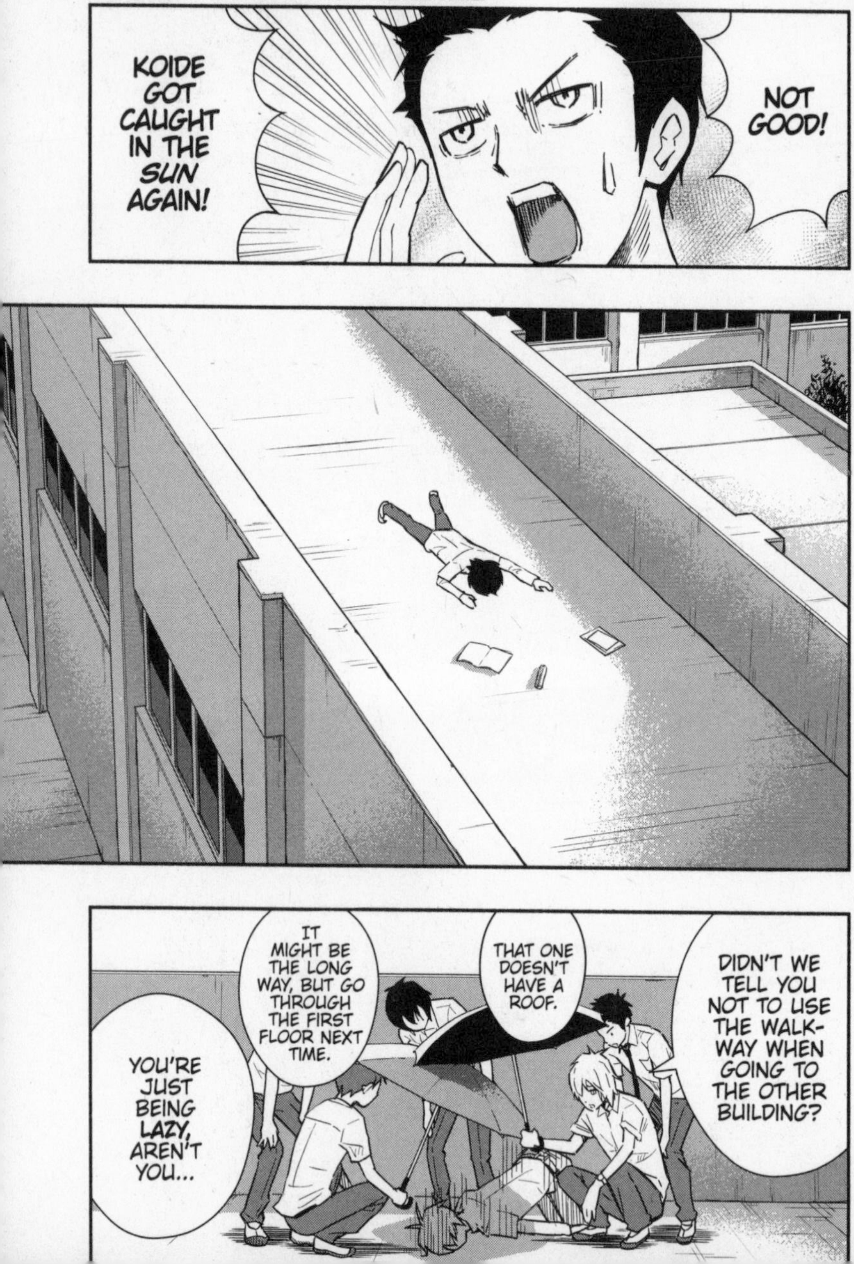
NOT GOOD!
KOIDE GOT CAUGHT IN THE SUN AGAIN!
DIDN'T WE TELL YOU NOT TO USE THE WALK-WAY WHEN GOING TO THE OTHER BUILDING?
THAT ONE DOESN'T HAVE A ROOF.
IT MIGHT BE THE LONG WAY, BUT GO THROUGH THE FIRST FLOOR NEXT TIME.
YOU'RE JUST BEING LAZY, AREN'T YOU...

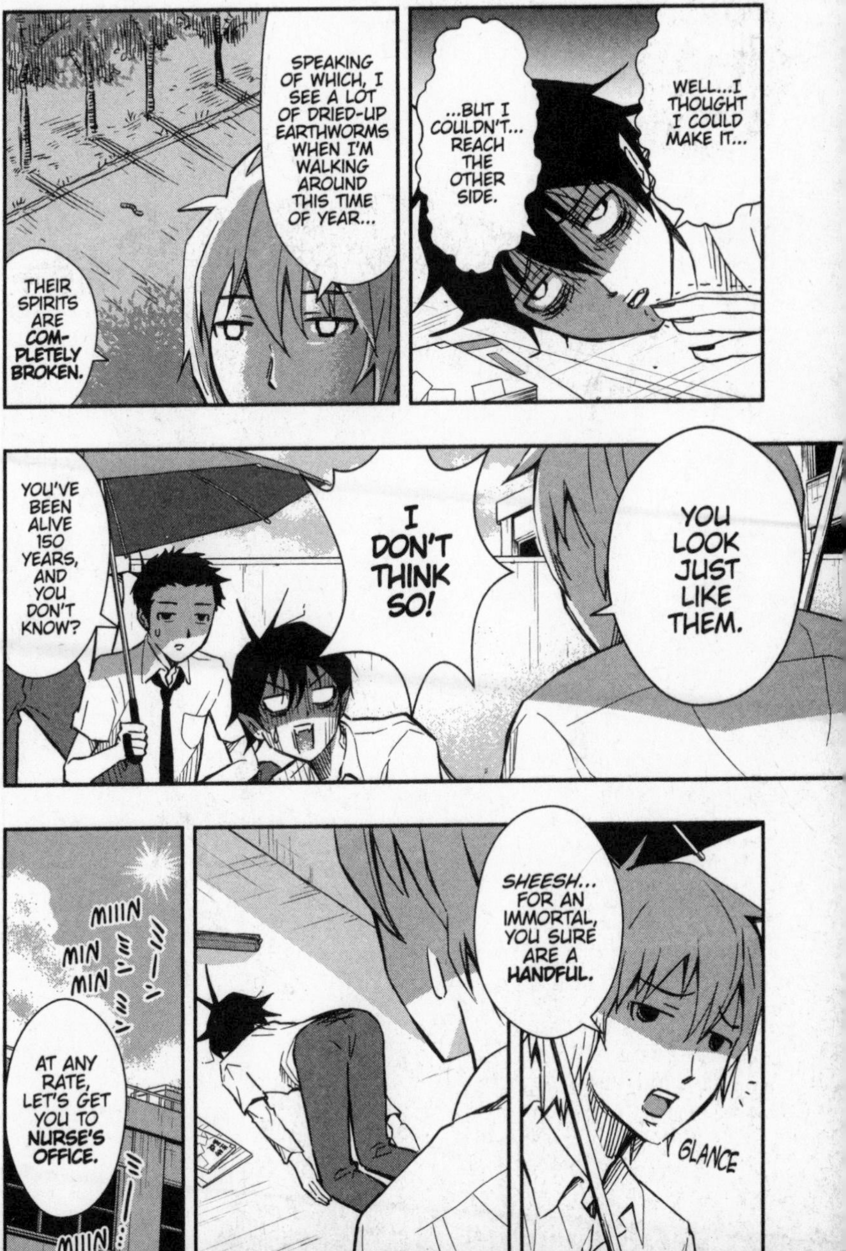
WELL...I THOUGHT I COULD MAKE IT...
...BUT I COULDN'T... REACH THE OTHER SIDE.
SPEAKING OF WHICH, I SEE A LOT OF DRIED-UP EARTHWORMS WHEN I'M WALKING AROUND THIS TIME OF YEAR...
THEIR SPIRITS ARE COMPLETELY BROKEN.
YOU LOOK JUST LIKE THEM.
I DON'T THINK SO!
YOU'VE BEEN ALIVE 150 YEARS, AND YOU DON'T KNOW?
SHEESH... FOR AN IMMORTAL, YOU SURE ARE A HANDFUL.
GLANCE
MIIIN
MIN MIN
AT ANY RATE, LET'S GET YOU TO NURSE'S OFFICE.
MIIIN...

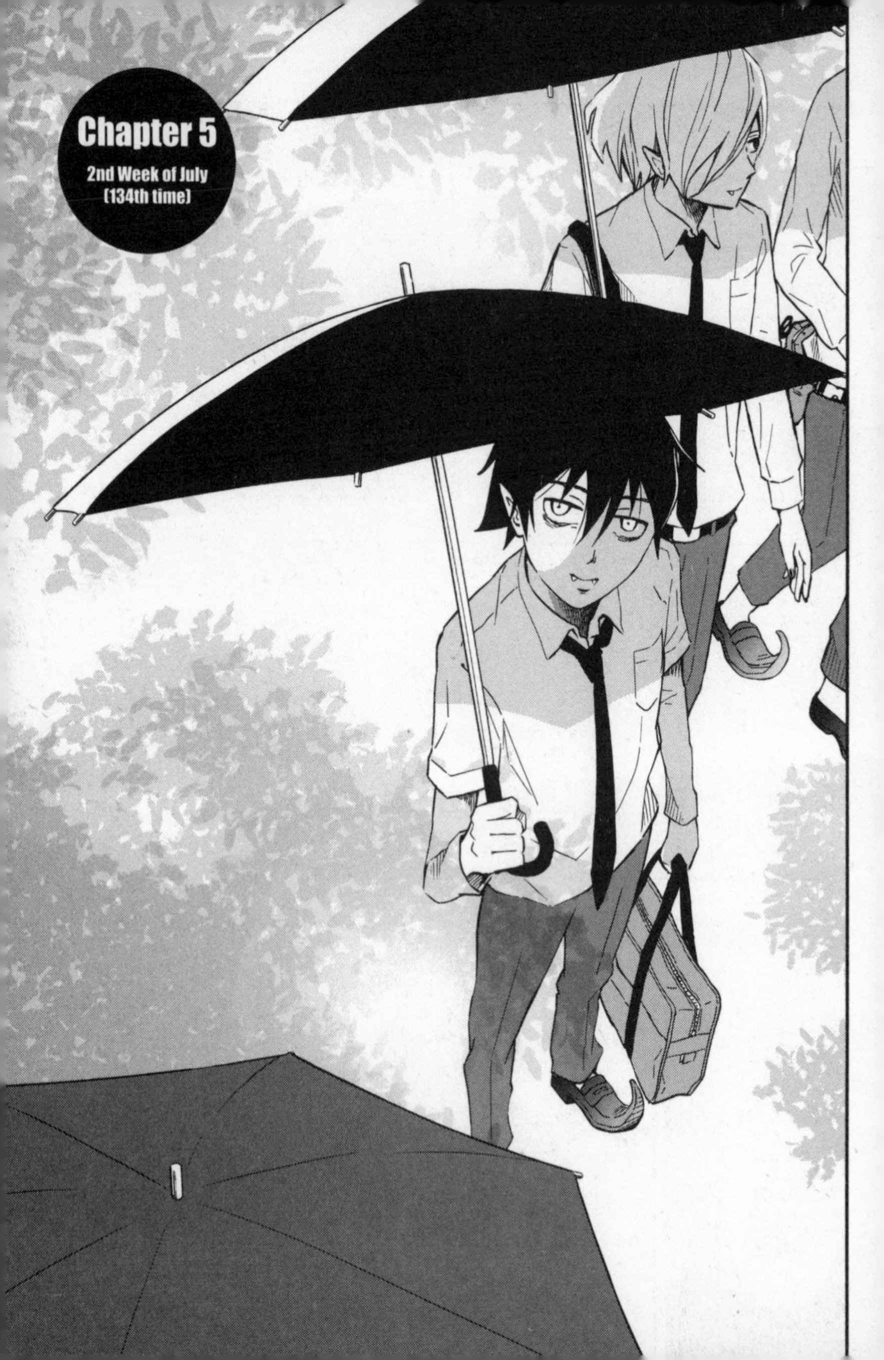
Chapter 5
2nd Week of July
(134th time)

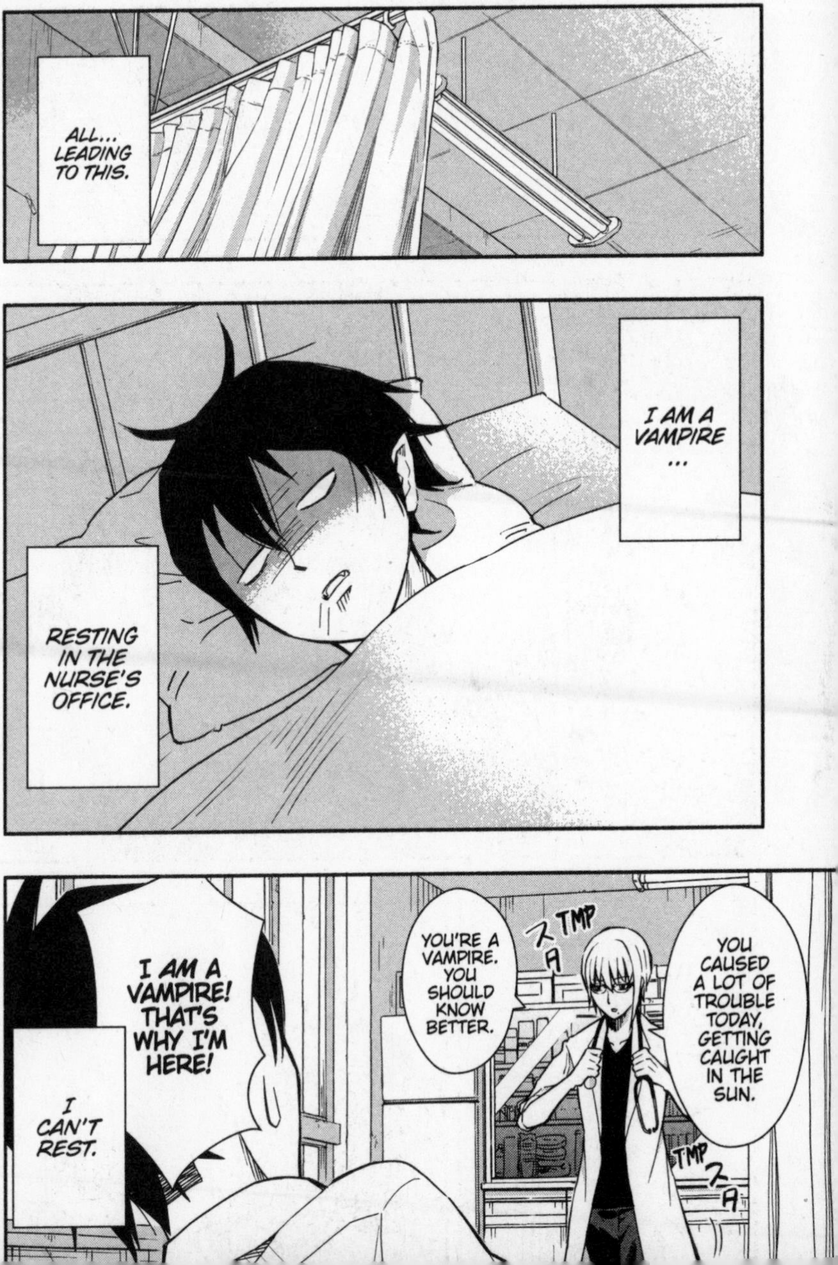
ALL... LEADING TO THIS.
I AM A VAMPIRE ...
RESTING IN THE NURSE'S OFFICE.
YOU CAUSED A LOT OF TROUBLE TODAY, GETTING CAUGHT IN THE SUN.
TMP
YOU'RE A VAMPIRE. YOU SHOULD KNOW BETTER.
TMP
I AM A VAMPIRE! THAT'S WHY I'M HERE!
I CAN'T REST.

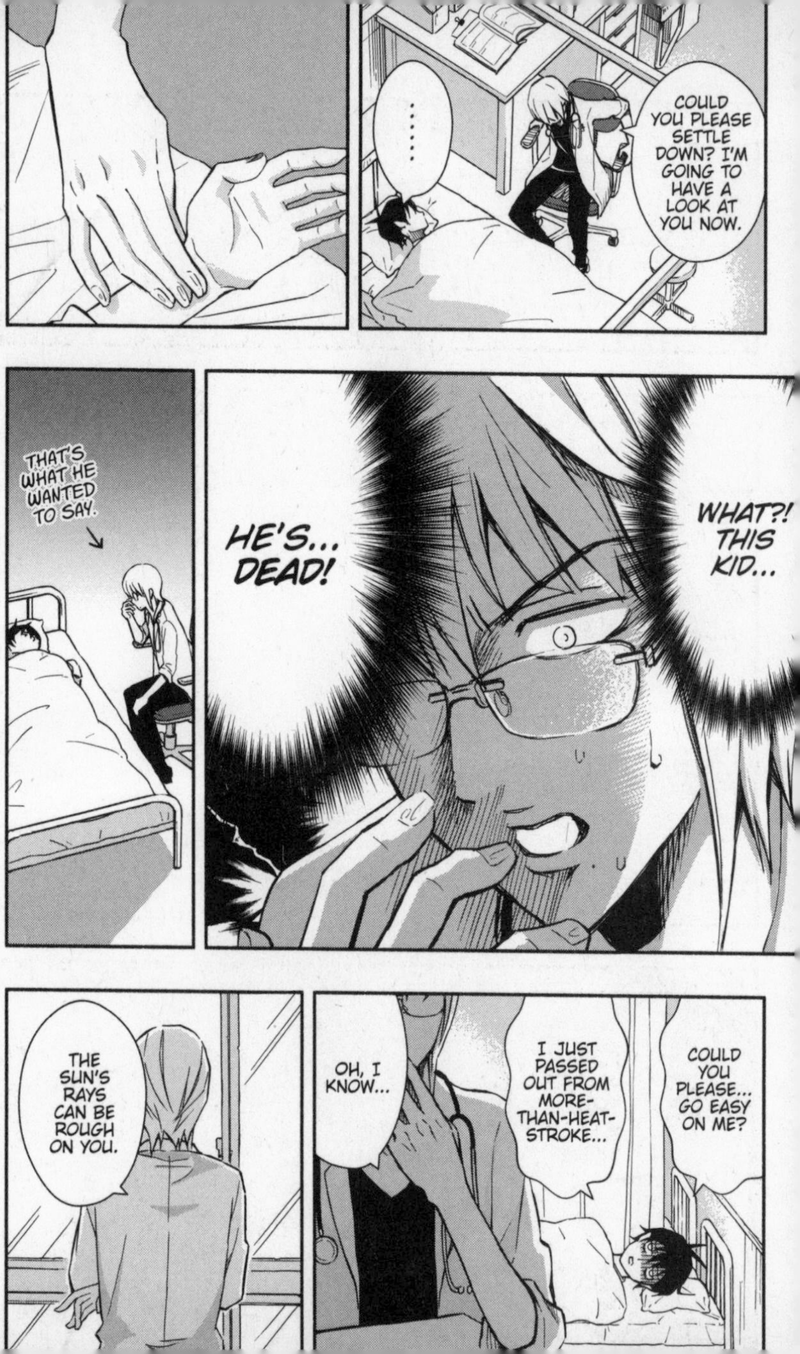
COULD YOU PLEASE SETTLE DOWN? I'M GOING TO HAVE A LOOK AT YOU NOW.
......
WHAT?! THIS KID...
HE'S... DEAD!
THAT'S WHAT HE WANTED TO SAY.
COULD YOU PLEASE... GO EASY ON ME?
I JUST PASSED OUT FROM MORE-THAN-HEAT-STROKE...
OH, I KNOW...
THE SUN'S RAYS CAN BE ROUGH ON YOU.

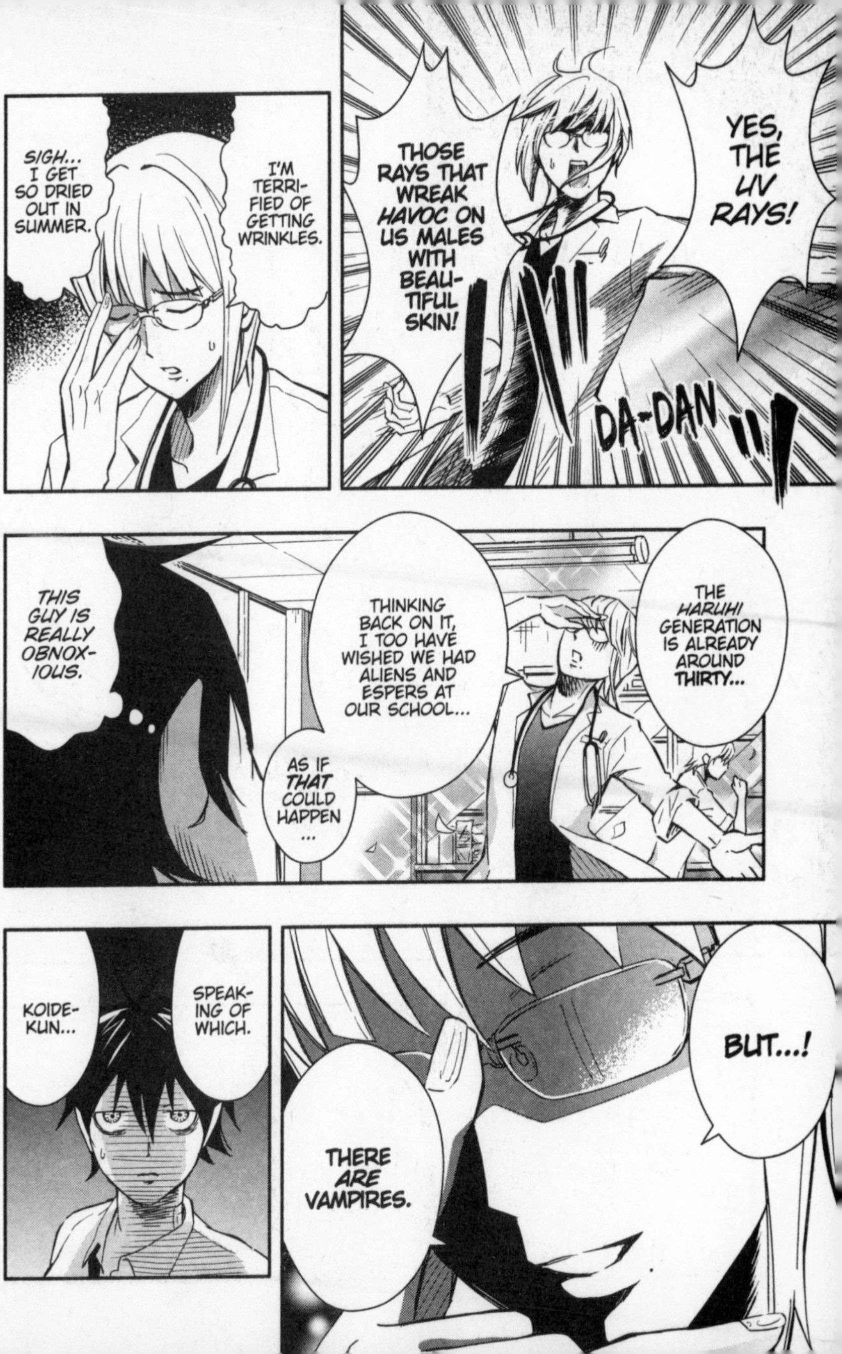
YES, THE UV RAYS!
THOSE RAYS THAT WREAK HAVOC ON US MALES WITH BEAUTIFUL SKIN!
DA-DAN!!
I'M TERRIFIED OF GETTING WRINKLES.
SIGH... I GET SO DRIED OUT IN SUMMER.
THE HARUHI GENERATION IS ALREADY AROUND THIRTY...
THINKING BACK ON IT, I TOO HAVE WISHED WE HAD ALIENS AND ESPERS AT OUR SCHOOL...
AS IF THAT COULD HAPPEN...
THIS GUY IS REALLY OBNOXIOUS.
BUT...!
THERE ARE VAMPIRES.
SPEAKING OF WHICH.
KOIDE-KUN...

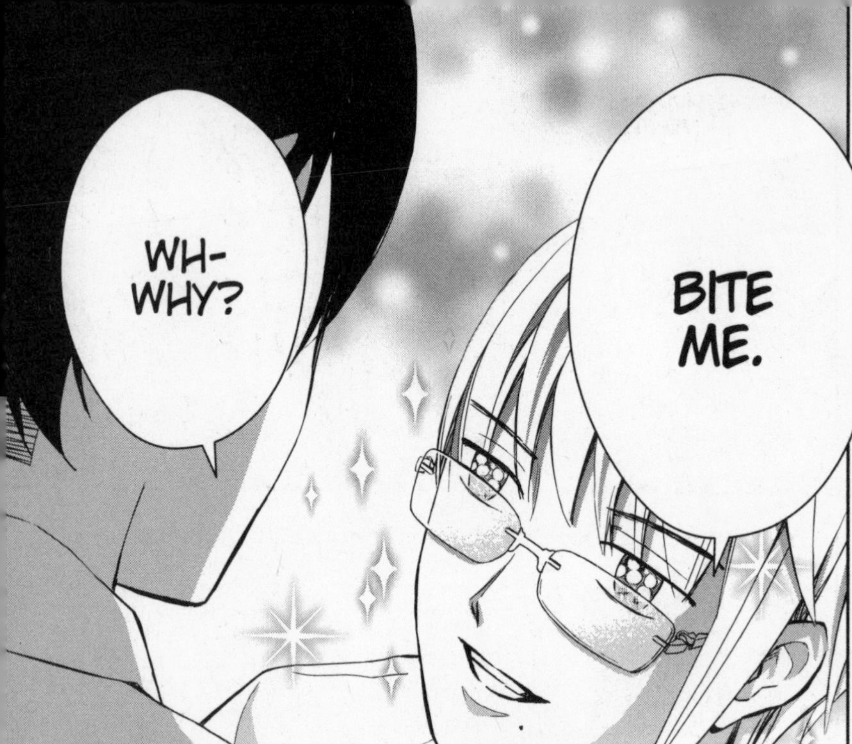
BITE ME.
WH- WHY?
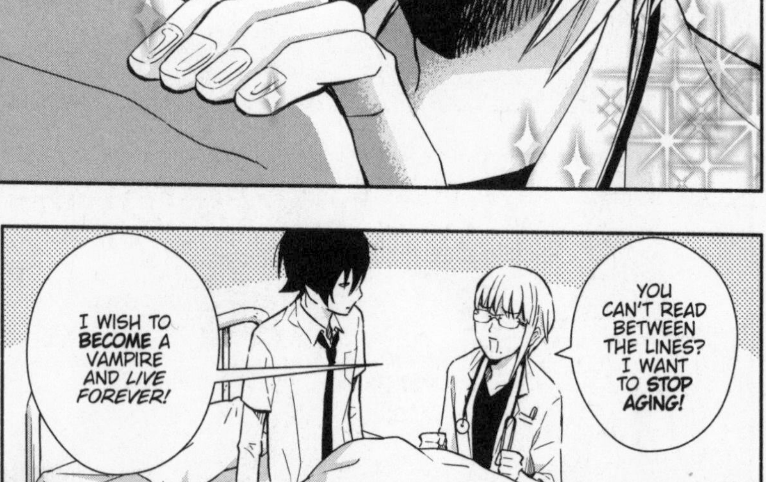
YOU CAN'T READ BETWEEN THE LINES? I WANT TO STOP AGING!
I WISH TO BECOME A VAMPIRE AND LIVE FOREVER!

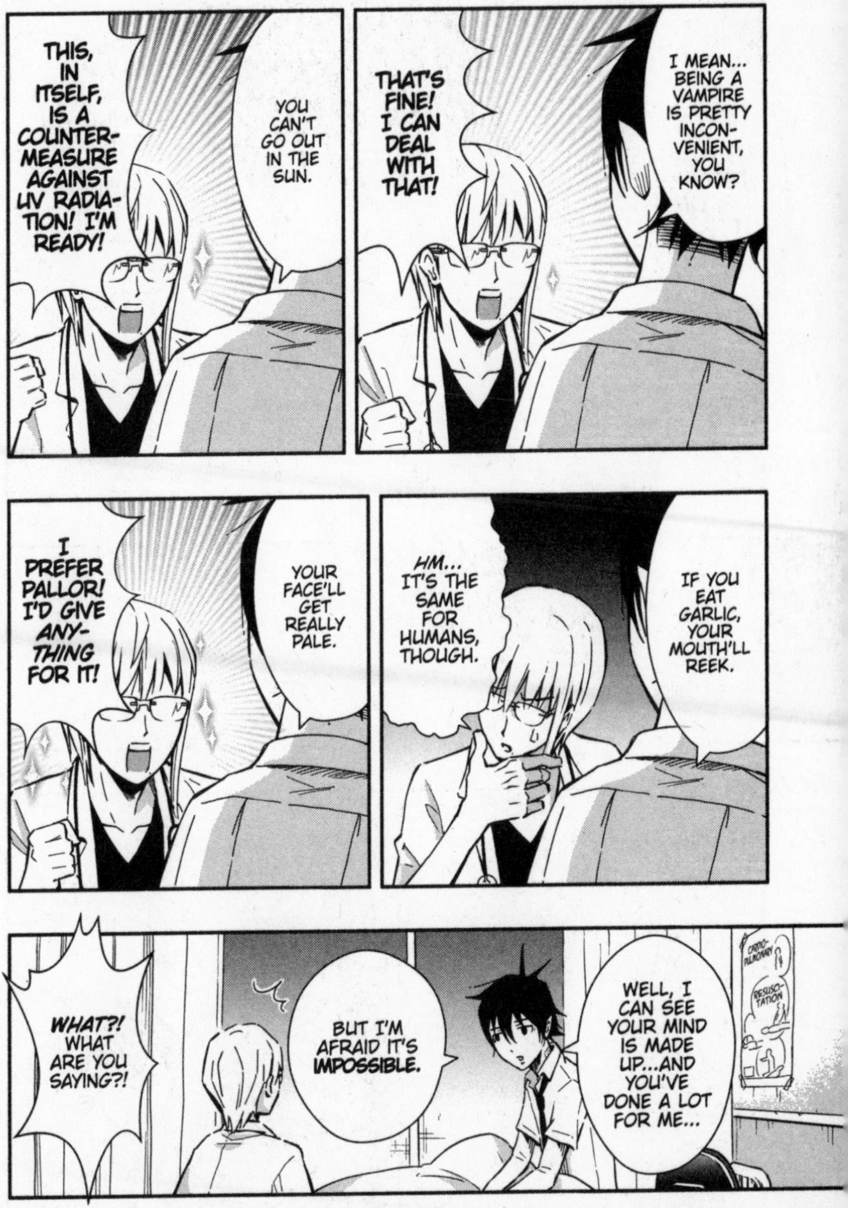
I MEAN... BEING A VAMPIRE IS PRETTY INCONVENIENT, YOU KNOW?
THAT'S FINE! I CAN DEAL WITH THAT!
YOU CAN'T GO OUT IN THE SUN.
THIS, IN ITSELF, IS A COUNTER-MEASURE AGAINST UV RADIATION! I'M READY!
IF YOU EAT GARLIC, YOUR MOUTH'LL REEK.
HM... IT'S THE SAME FOR HUMANS, THOUGH.
YOUR FACE'LL GET REALLY PALE.
I PREFER PALLOR! I'D GIVE ANYTHING FOR IT!
CARDIO-PULMONARY RESUSCITATION
WELL, I CAN SEE YOUR MIND IS MADE UP...AND YOU'VE DONE A LOT FOR ME...
BUT I'M AFRAID IT'S IMPOSSIBLE.
WHAT?! WHAT ARE YOU SAYING?!

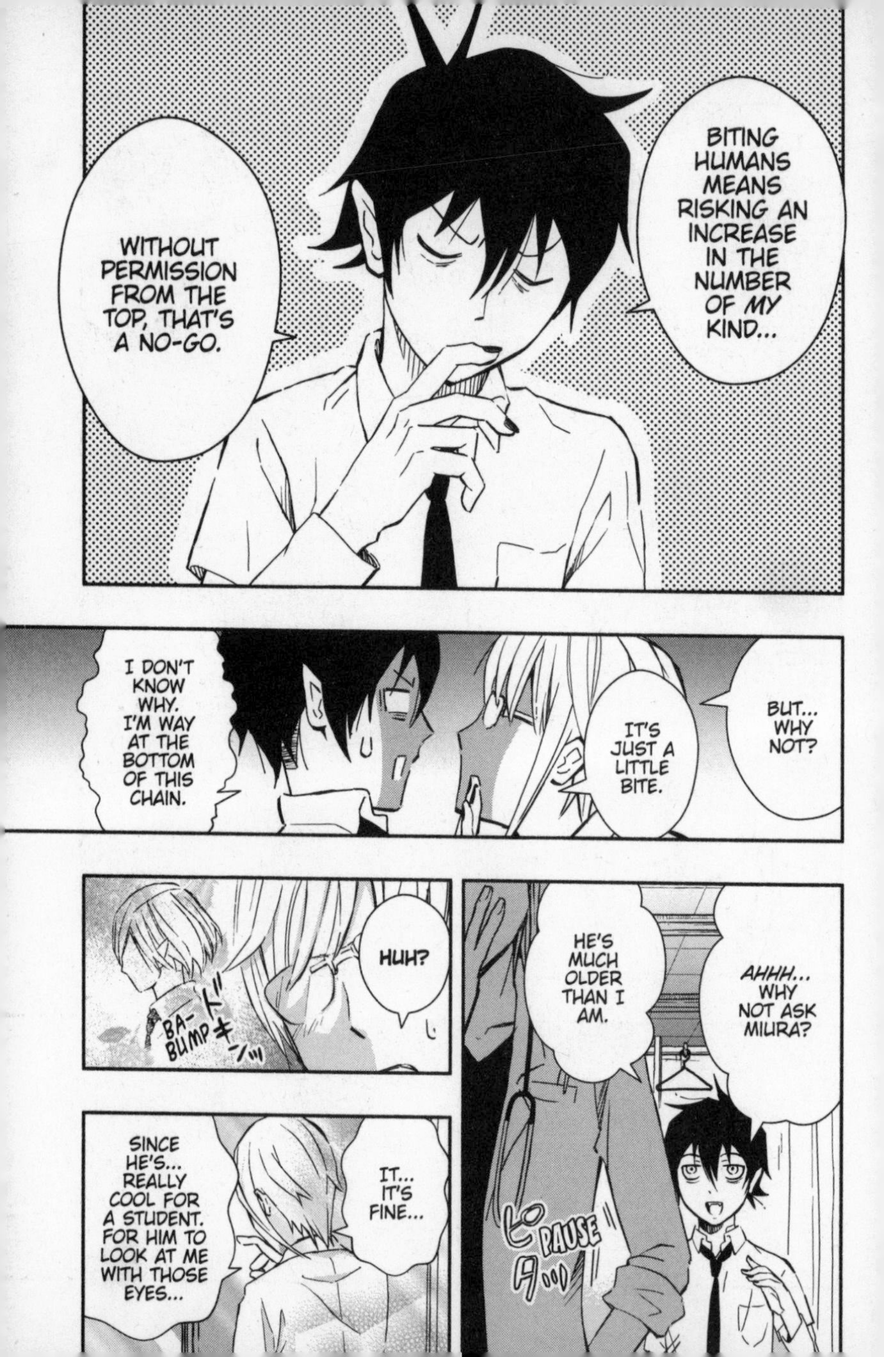
BITING HUMANS MEANS RISKING AN INCREASE IN THE NUMBER OF MY KIND...
WITHOUT PERMISSION FROM THE TOP, THAT'S A NO-GO.
BUT... WHY NOT?
IT'S JUST A LITTLE BITE.
I DON'T KNOW WHY. I'M WAY AT THE BOTTOM OF THIS CHAIN.
AHHH... WHY NOT ASK MIURA?
HE'S MUCH OLDER THAN I AM.
PAUSE
HUH?
BA-BUMP
IT... IT'S FINE...
SINCE HE'S... REALLY COOL FOR A STUDENT. FOR HIM TO LOOK AT ME WITH THOSE EYES...

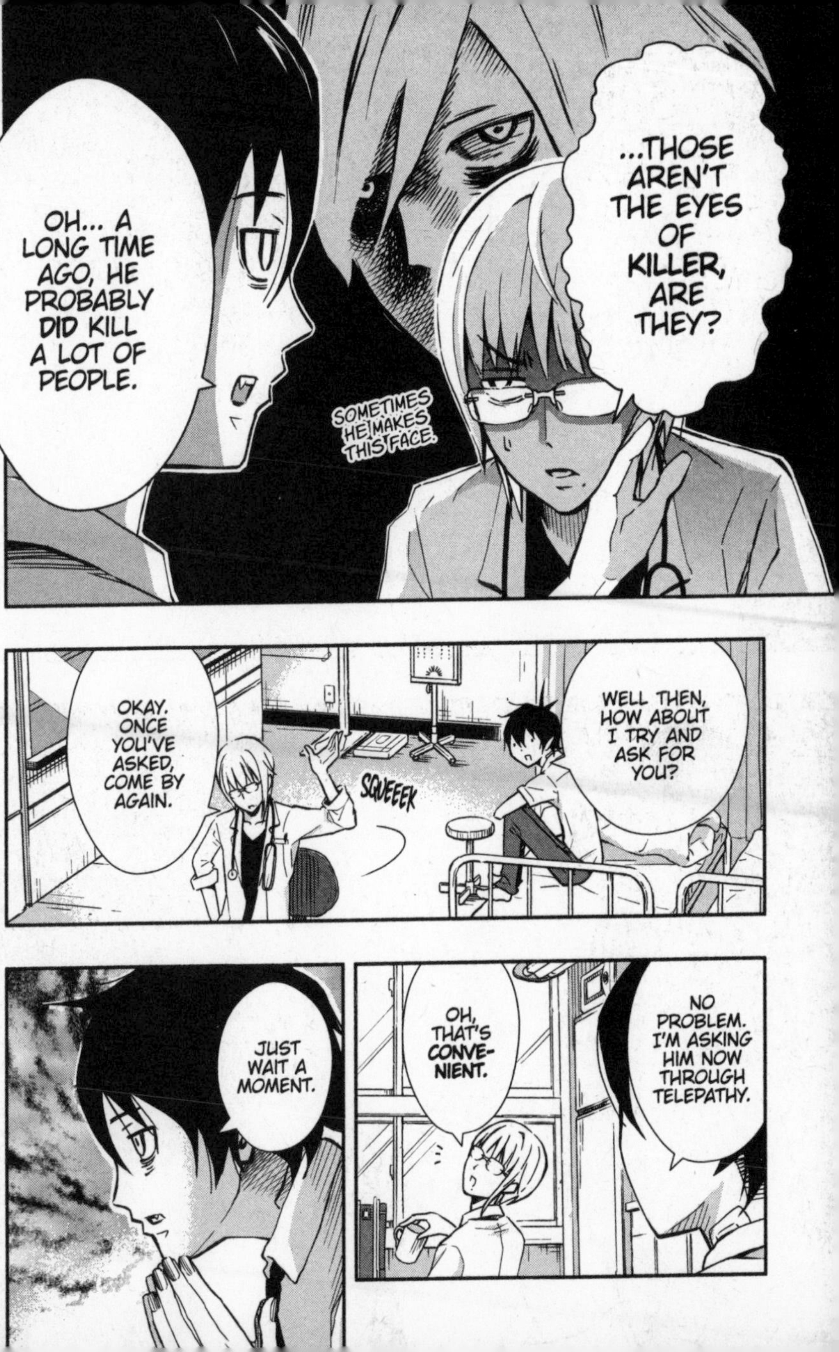
...THOSE AREN'T THE EYES OF KILLER, ARE THEY?
SOMETIMES HE MAKES THIS FACE.
OH... A LONG TIME AGO, HE PROBABLY DID KILL A LOT OF PEOPLE.
WELL THEN, HOW ABOUT I TRY AND ASK FOR YOU?
SQUEEEK
OKAY. ONCE YOU'VE ASKED, COME BY AGAIN.
NO PROBLEM. I'M ASKING HIM NOW THROUGH TELEPATHY.
OH, THAT'S CONVE-NIENT.
JUST WAIT A MOMENT.

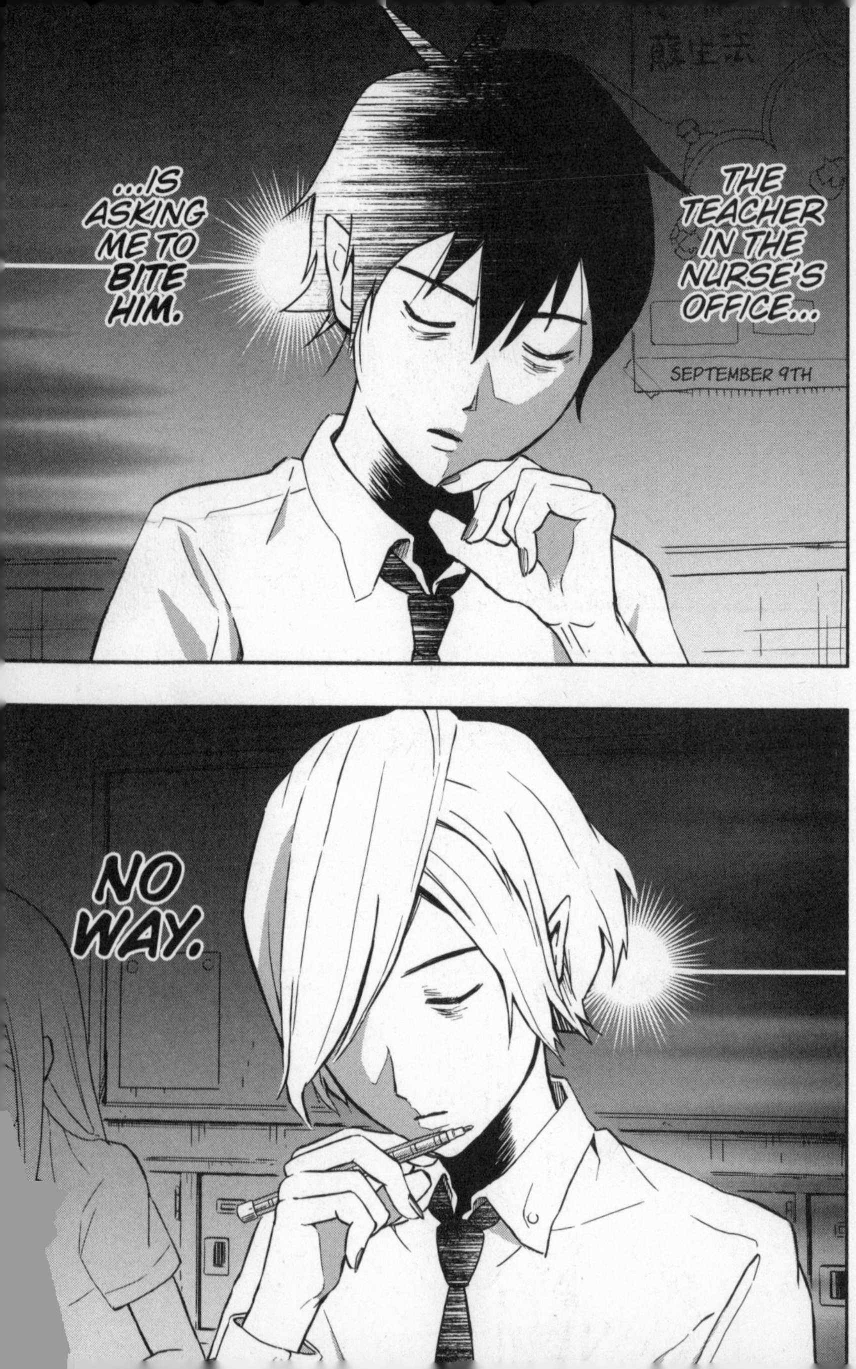
THE TEACHER IN THE NURSE'S OFFICE...
...IS ASKING ME TO BITE HIM.
SEPTEMBER 9TH
NO WAY.

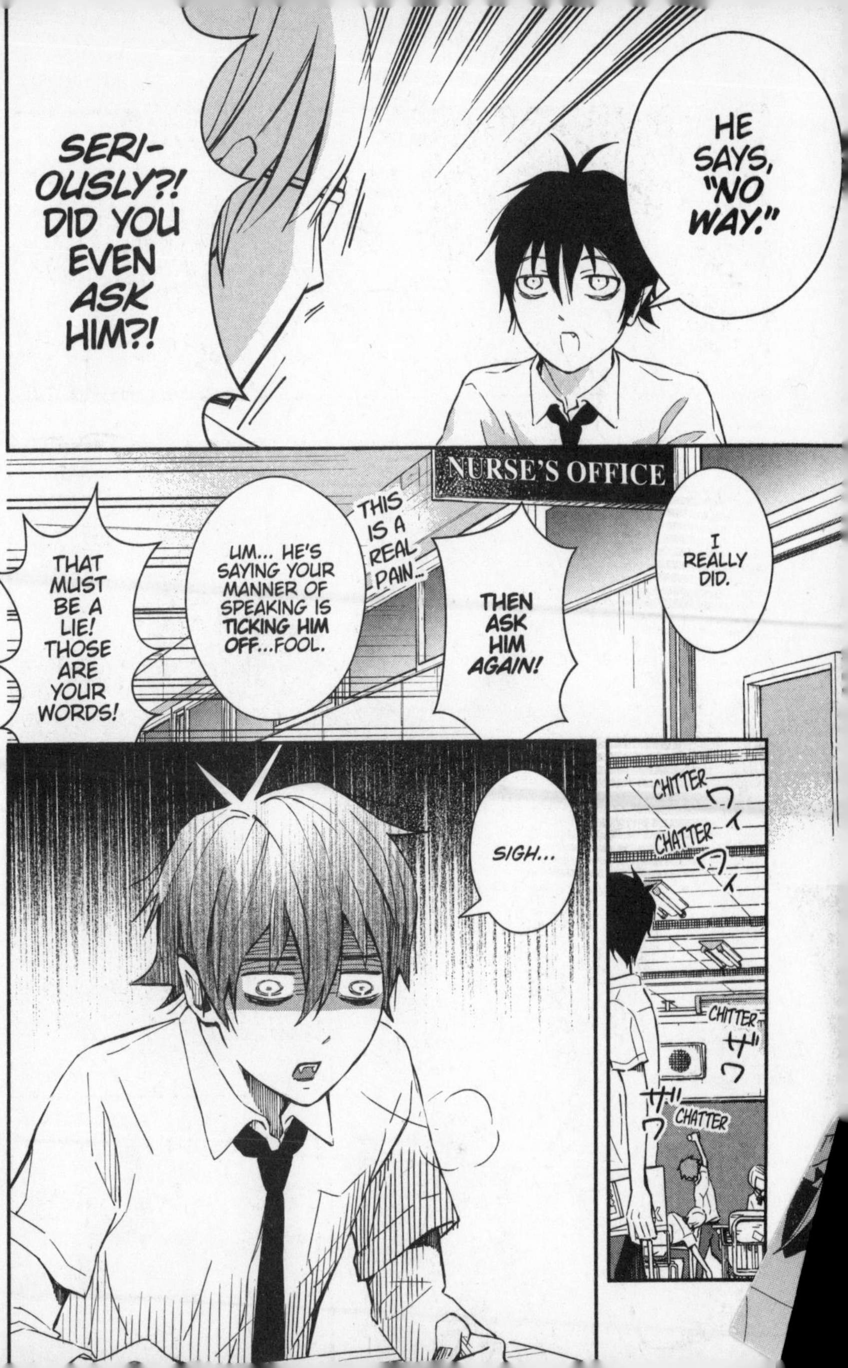
HE SAYS, "NO WAY."
SERI-OUSLY?! DID YOU EVEN ASK HIM?!
NURSE'S OFFICE
I REALLY DID.
THEN ASK HIM AGAIN!
THIS IS A REAL PAIN...
UM... HE'S SAYING YOUR MANNER OF SPEAKING IS TICKING HIM OFF...FOOL.
THAT MUST BE A LIE! THOSE ARE YOUR WORDS!
CHITTER ワイ
CHATTER ワイ
CHITTER ザワ
ザワ CHATTER
SIGH...

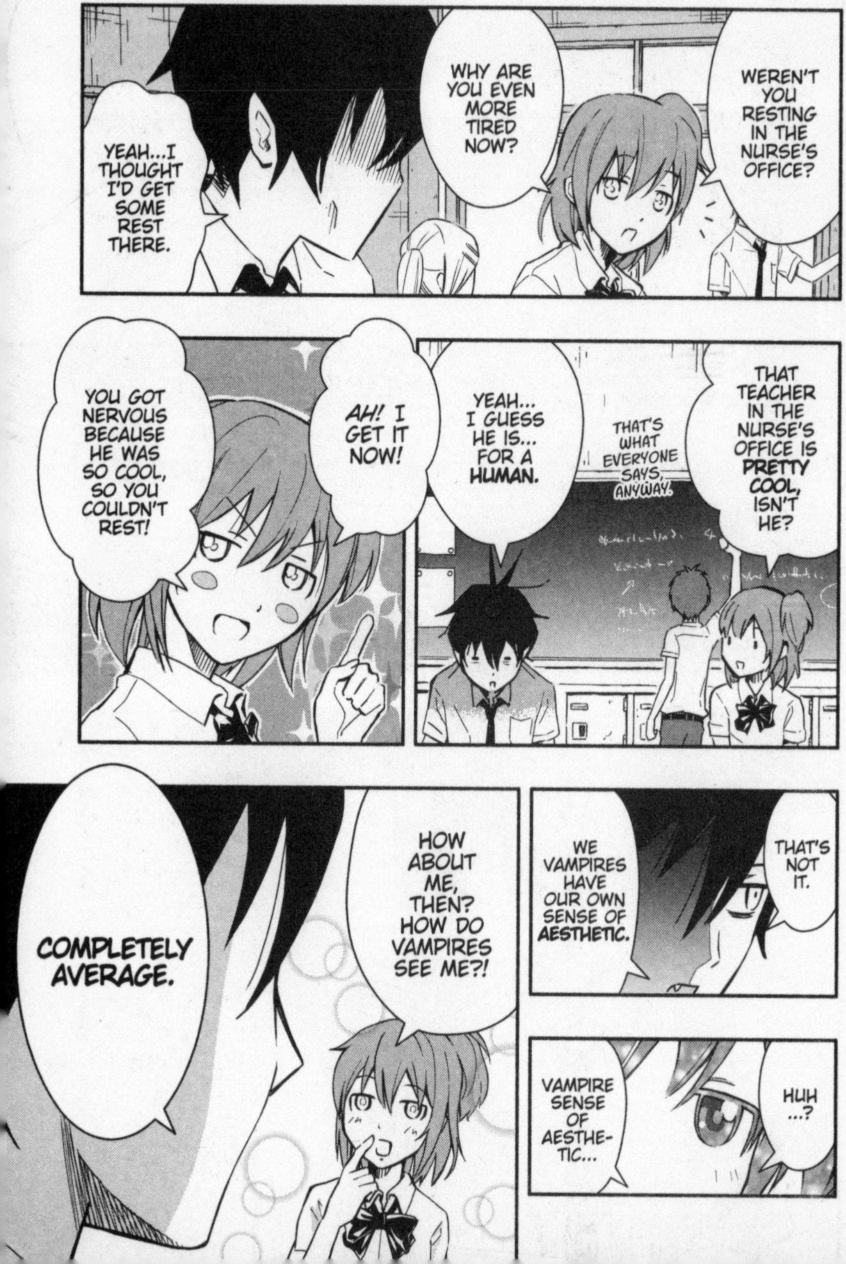
WEREN'T YOU RESTING IN THE NURSE'S OFFICE?
WHY ARE YOU EVEN MORE TIRED NOW?
YEAH...I THOUGHT I'D GET SOME REST THERE.
THAT TEACHER IN THE NURSE'S OFFICE IS **PRETTY COOL,** ISN'T HE?
THAT'S WHAT EVERYONE SAYS, ANYWAY.
YEAH... I GUESS HE IS... FOR A **HUMAN.**
AH! I GET IT NOW!
YOU GOT NERVOUS BECAUSE HE WAS SO COOL, SO YOU COULDN'T REST!
THAT'S NOT IT.
WE VAMPIRES HAVE OUR OWN SENSE OF **AESTHETIC.**
HUH ...?
VAMPIRE SENSE OF AESTHE-TIC...
HOW ABOUT ME, THEN? HOW DO VAMPIRES SEE ME?!
COMPLETELY AVERAGE.

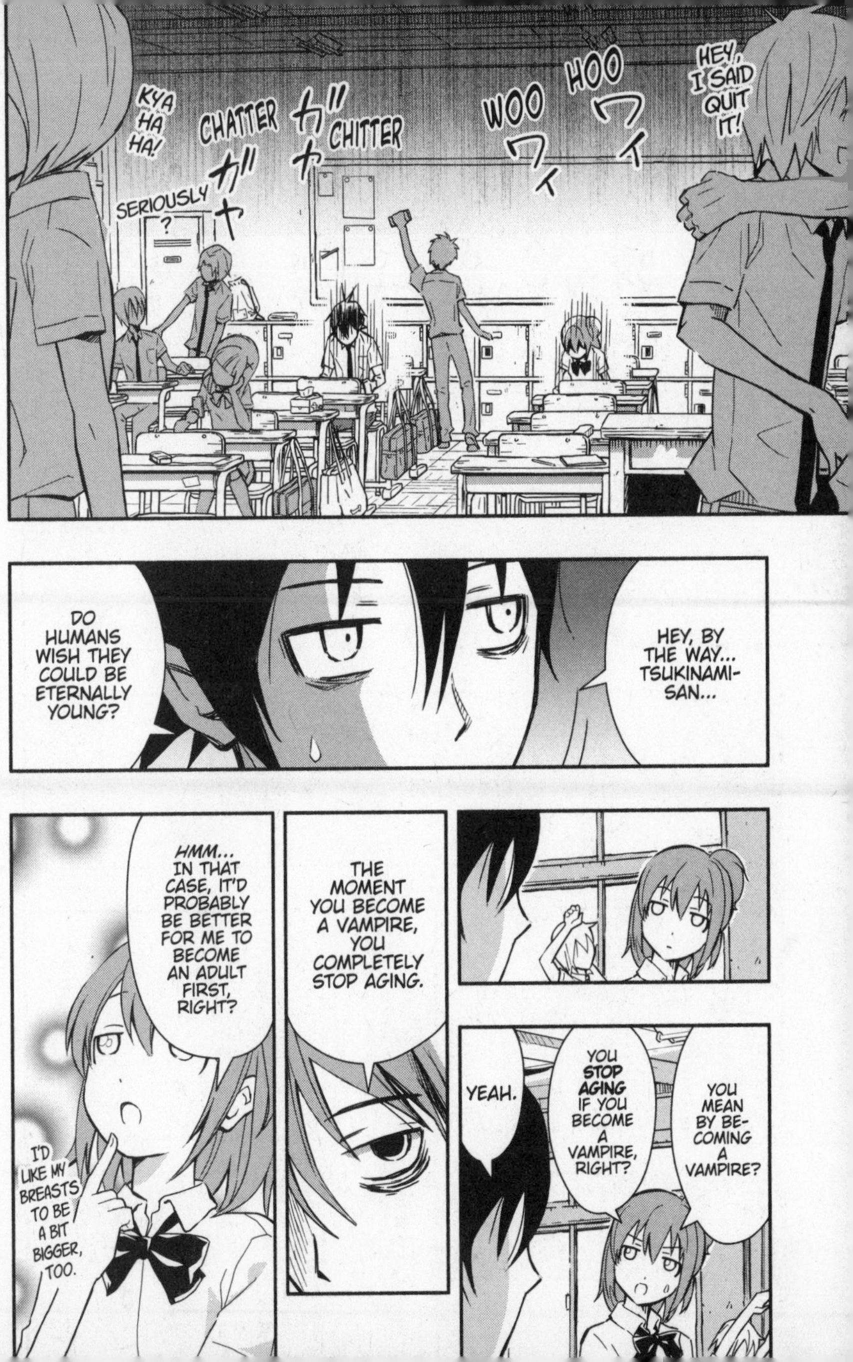
HEY, I SAID QUIT IT!
HOO ワイ
WOO ワイ
CHITTER ガヤ
CHATTER
KYA HA HA!
SERIOUSLY?
ガヤ
HEY, BY THE WAY... TSUKINAMI-SAN...
DO HUMANS WISH THEY COULD BE ETERNALLY YOUNG?
YOU MEAN BY BE-COMING A VAMPIRE?
YOU STOP AGING IF YOU BECOME A VAMPIRE, RIGHT?
YEAH.
THE MOMENT YOU BECOME A VAMPIRE, YOU COMPLETELY STOP AGING.
HMM... IN THAT CASE, IT'D PROBABLY BE BETTER FOR ME TO BECOME AN ADULT FIRST, RIGHT?
I'D LIKE MY BREASTS TO BE A BIT BIGGER, TOO.

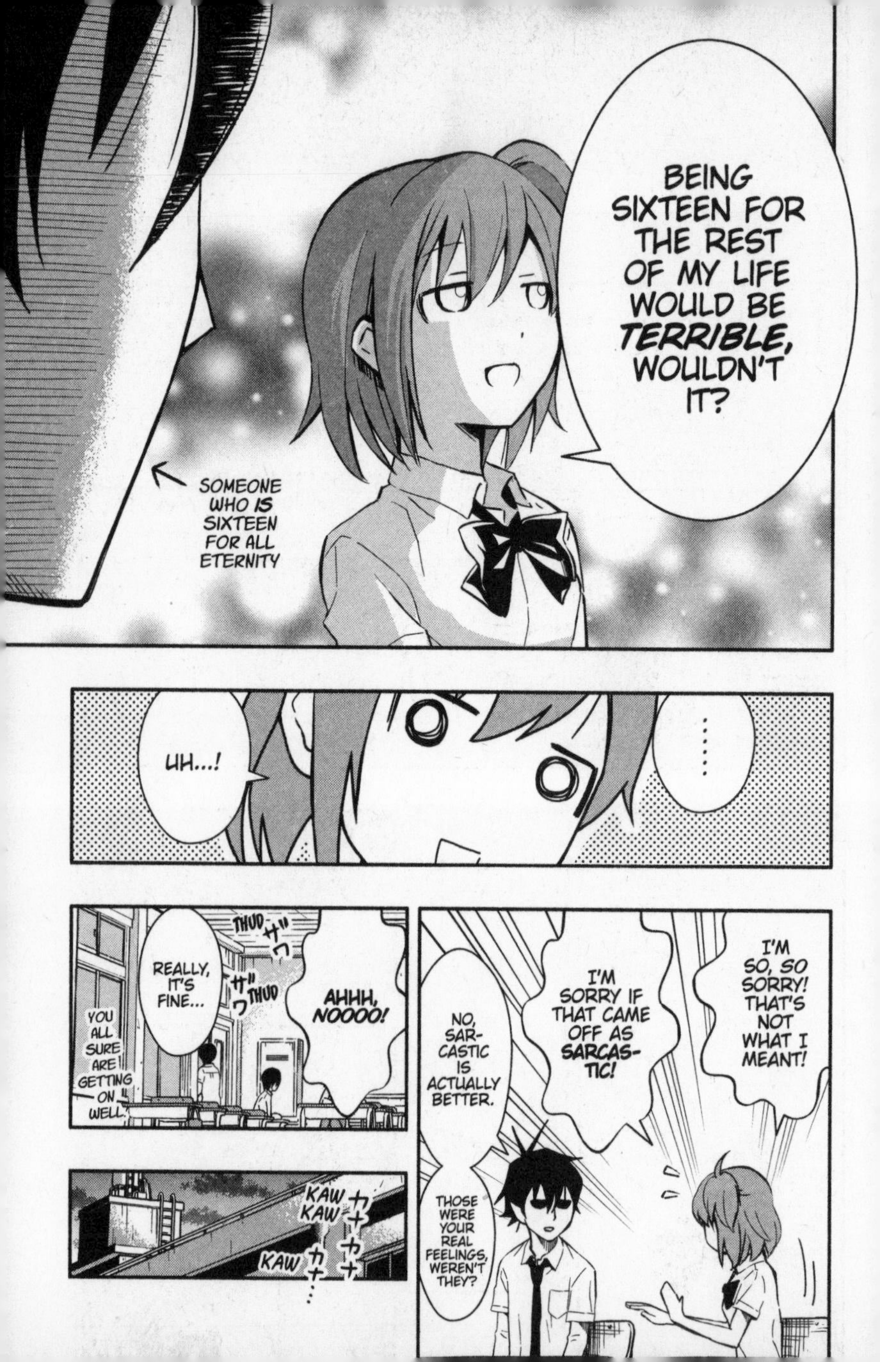
BEING SIXTEEN FOR THE REST OF MY LIFE WOULD BE TERRIBLE, WOULDN'T IT?
SOMEONE WHO IS SIXTEEN FOR ALL ETERNITY
......
UH...!
I'M SO, SO SORRY! THAT'S NOT WHAT I MEANT!
I'M SORRY IF THAT CAME OFF AS SARCASTIC!
NO, SARCASTIC IS ACTUALLY BETTER.
THOSE WERE YOUR REAL FEELINGS, WEREN'T THEY?
AHHH, NOOOO!
THUD ザワ
ザワ THUD
REALLY, IT'S FINE...
YOU ALL SURE ARE GETTING ON WELL.
KAW KAW カァカァ
KAW カァ...

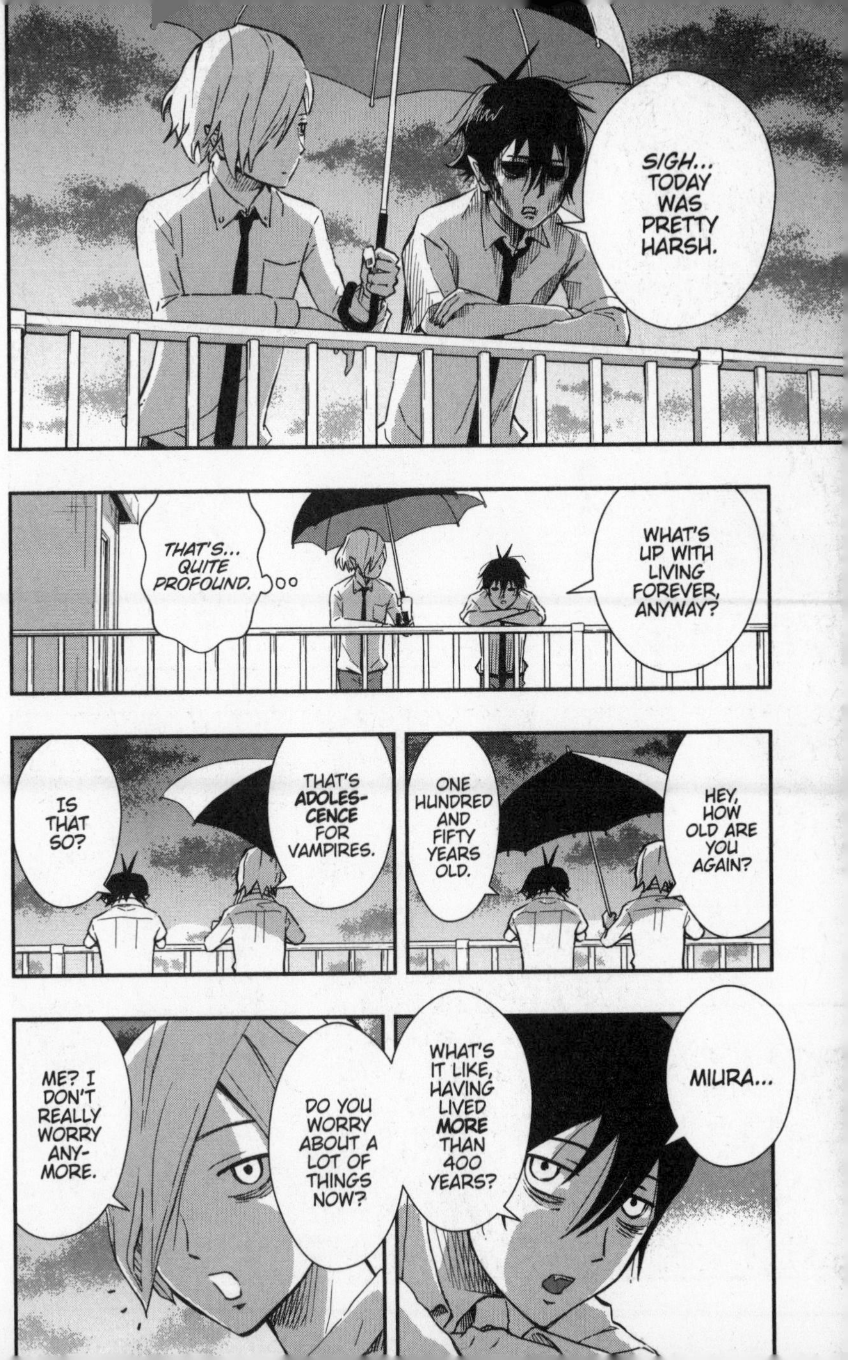
SIGH... TODAY WAS PRETTY HARSH.
WHAT'S UP WITH LIVING FOREVER, ANYWAY?
THAT'S... QUITE PROFOUND.
HEY, HOW OLD ARE YOU AGAIN?
ONE HUNDRED AND FIFTY YEARS OLD.
THAT'S **ADOLES-CENCE** FOR VAMPIRES.
IS THAT SO?
MIURA...
WHAT'S IT LIKE, HAVING LIVED **MORE** THAN 400 YEARS?
DO YOU WORRY ABOUT A LOT OF THINGS NOW?
ME? I DON'T REALLY WORRY ANY-MORE.

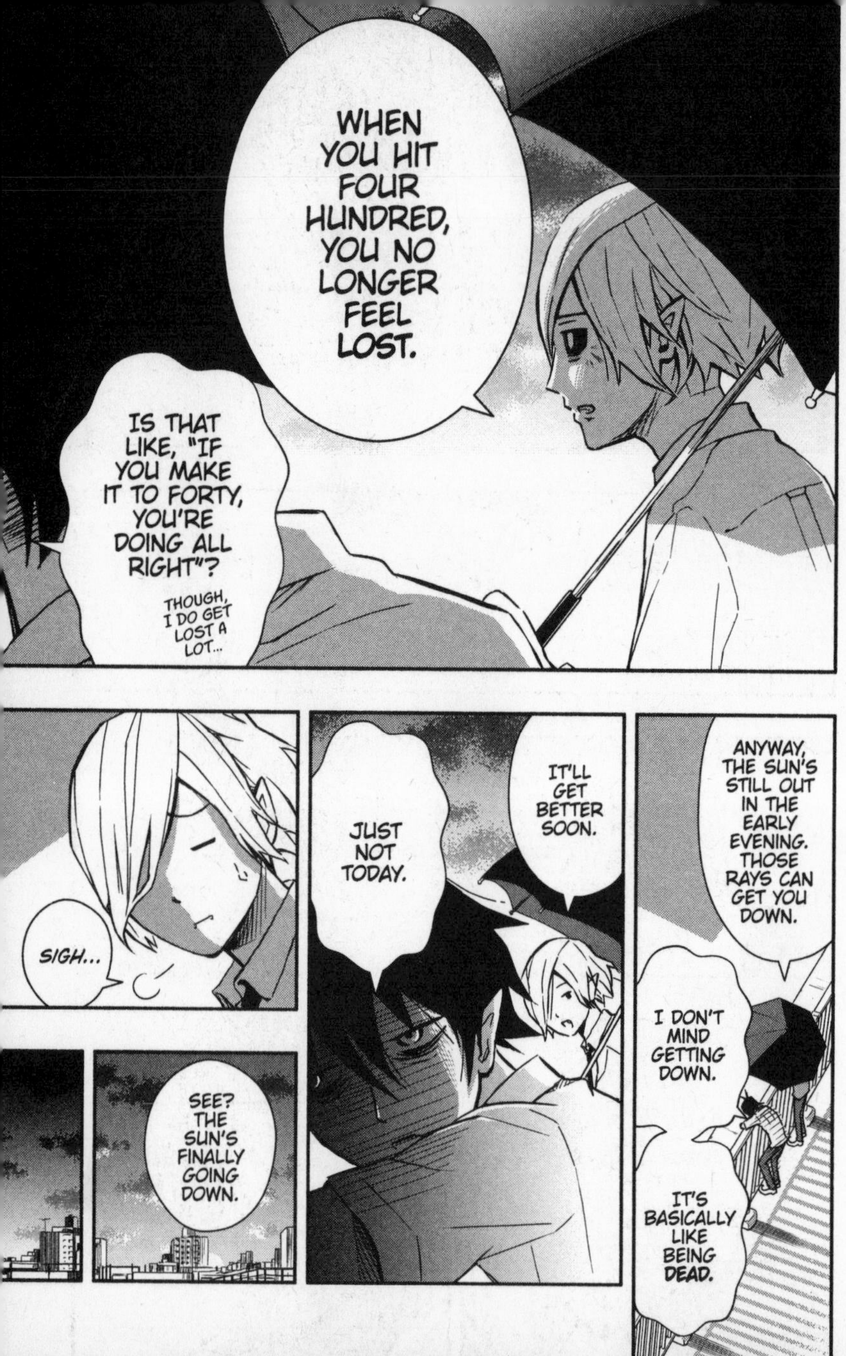
WHEN YOU HIT FOUR HUNDRED, YOU NO LONGER FEEL LOST.
IS THAT LIKE, "IF YOU MAKE IT TO FORTY, YOU'RE DOING ALL RIGHT"?
THOUGH, I DO GET LOST A LOT...
ANYWAY, THE SUN'S STILL OUT IN THE EARLY EVENING. THOSE RAYS CAN GET YOU DOWN.
I DON'T MIND GETTING DOWN.
IT'S BASICALLY LIKE BEING DEAD.
IT'LL GET BETTER SOON.
JUST NOT TODAY.
SIGH...
SEE? THE SUN'S FINALLY GOING DOWN.

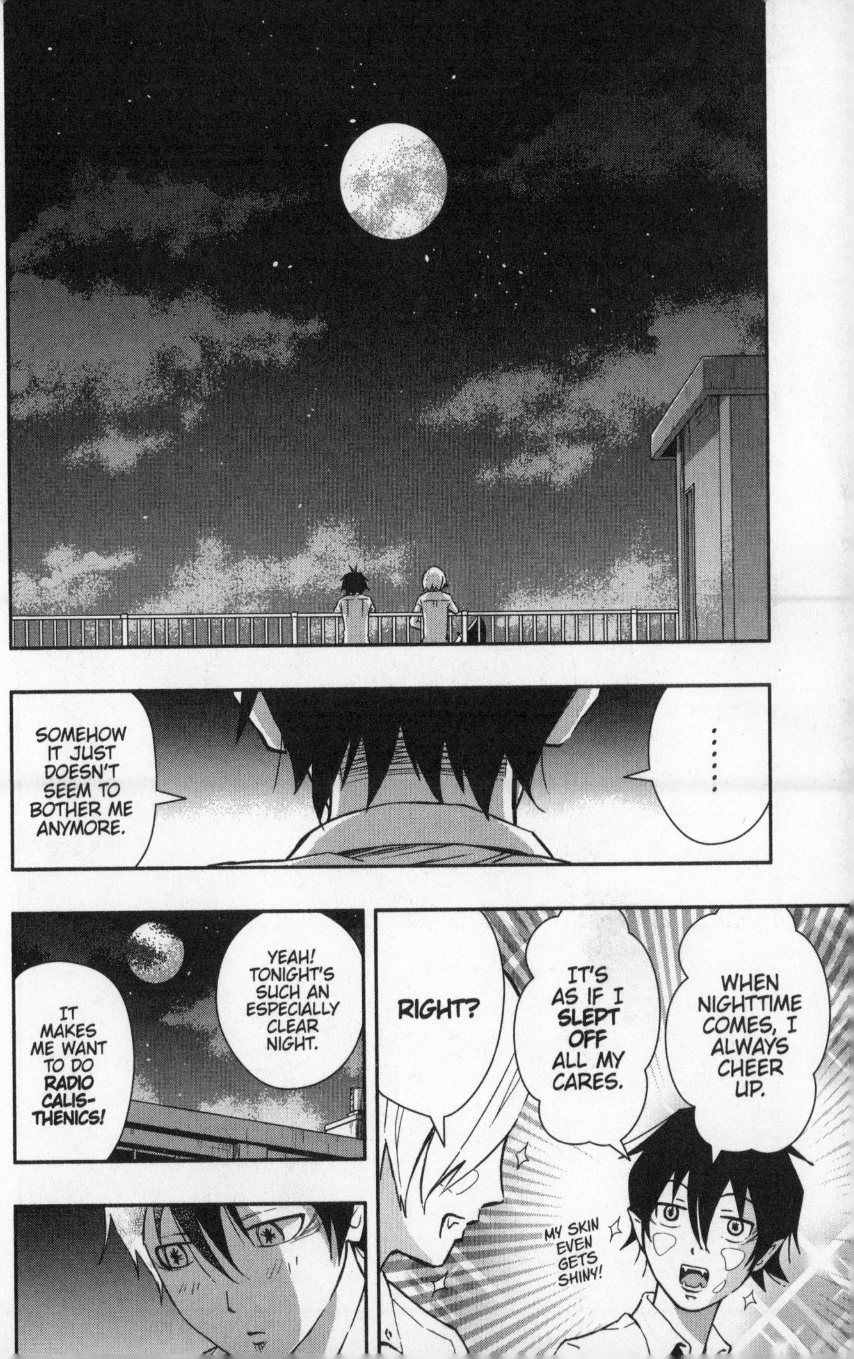
......
SOMEHOW IT JUST DOESN'T SEEM TO BOTHER ME ANYMORE.
WHEN NIGHTTIME COMES, I ALWAYS CHEER UP.
IT'S AS IF I SLEPT OFF ALL MY CARES.
RIGHT?
MY SKIN EVEN GETS SHINY!
YEAH! TONIGHT'S SUCH AN ESPECIALLY CLEAR NIGHT.
IT MAKES ME WANT TO DO RADIO CALIS-THENICS!

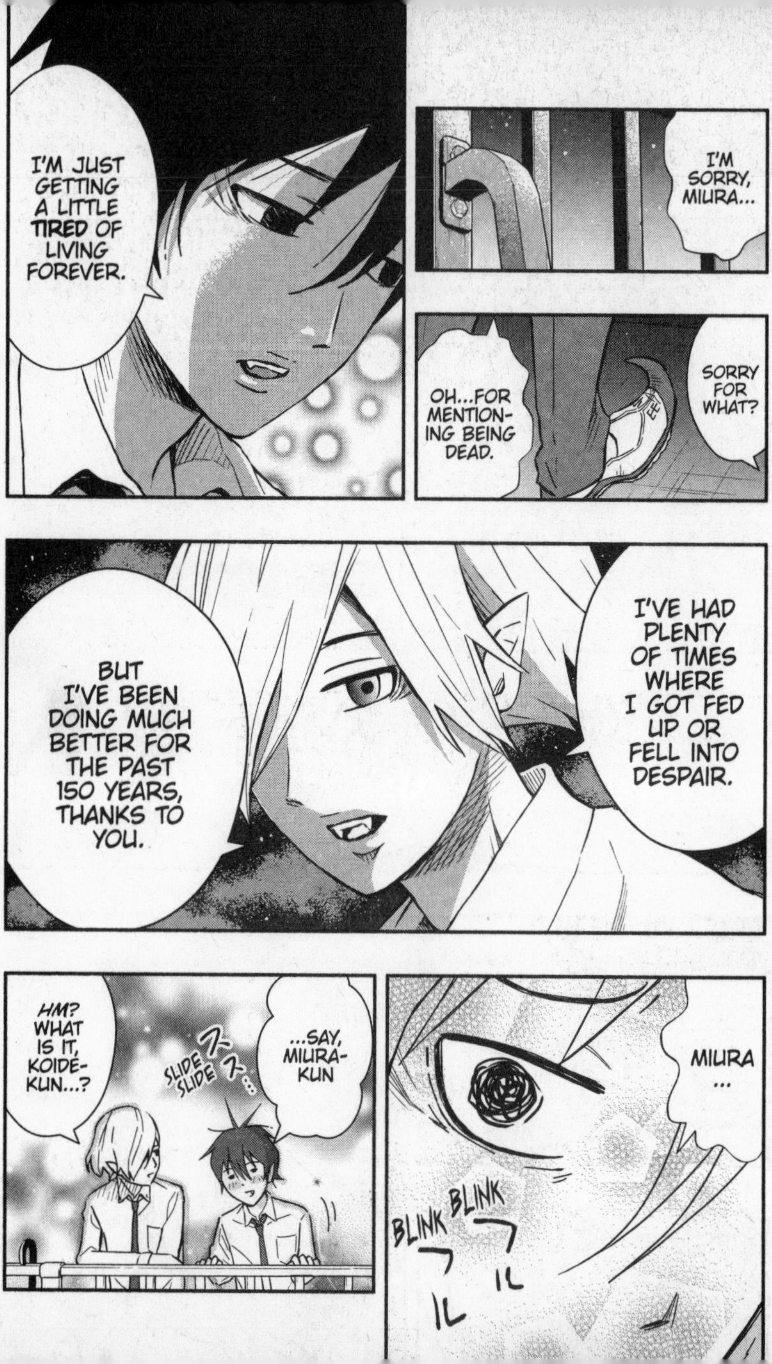
I'M SORRY, MIURA...
SORRY FOR WHAT?
OH...FOR MENTIONING BEING DEAD.
I'M JUST GETTING A LITTLE TIRED OF LIVING FOREVER.
I'VE HAD PLENTY OF TIMES WHERE I GOT FED UP OR FELL INTO DESPAIR.
BUT I'VE BEEN DOING MUCH BETTER FOR THE PAST 150 YEARS, THANKS TO YOU.
MIURA ...
BLINK BLINK
...SAY, MIURA-KUN
SLIDE SLIDE
HM? WHAT IS IT, KOIDE-KUN...?

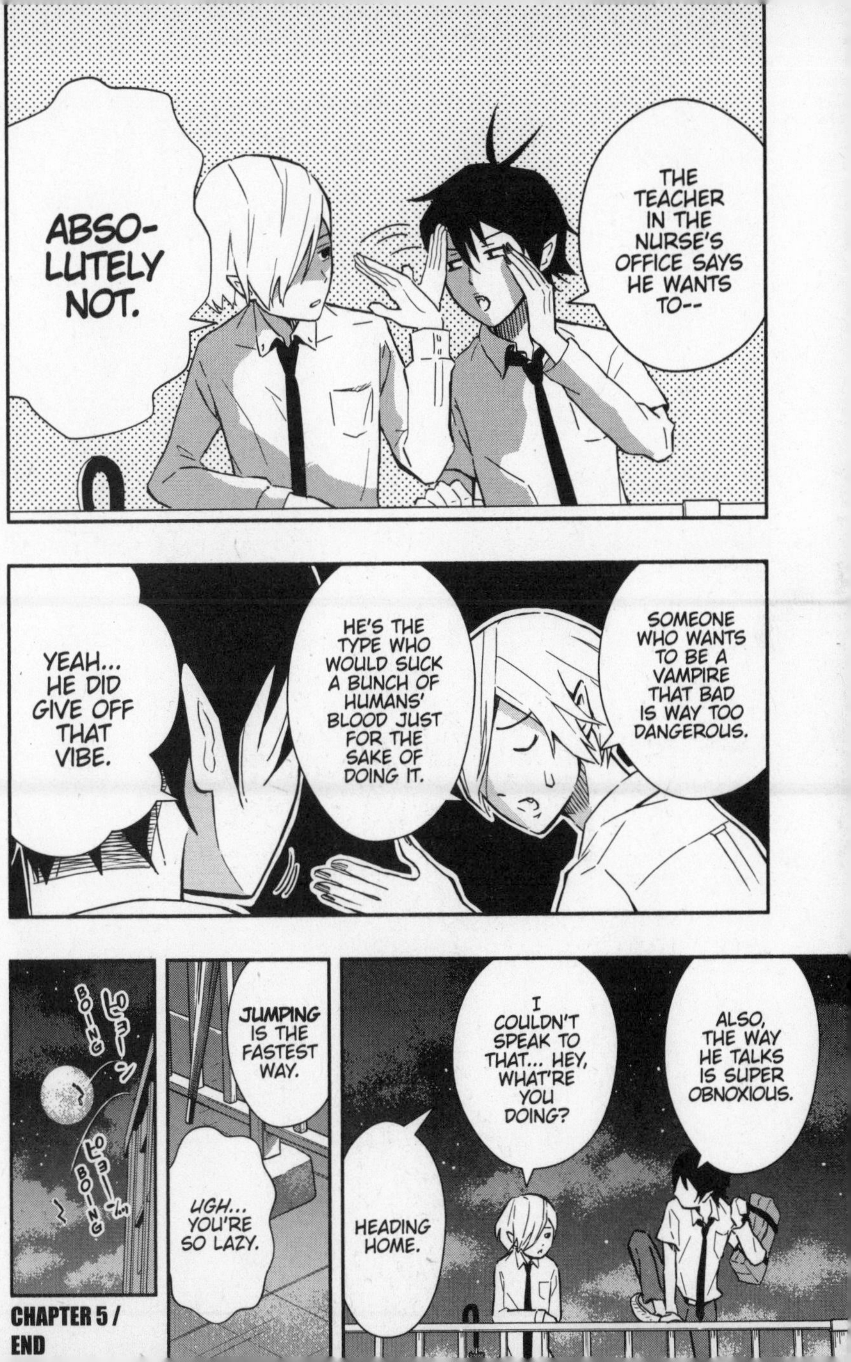
THE TEACHER IN THE NURSE'S OFFICE SAYS HE WANTS TO--
ABSOLUTELY NOT.
SOMEONE WHO WANTS TO BE A VAMPIRE THAT BAD IS WAY TOO DANGEROUS.
HE'S THE TYPE WHO WOULD SUCK A BUNCH OF HUMANS' BLOOD JUST FOR THE SAKE OF DOING IT.
YEAH... HE DID GIVE OFF THAT VIBE.
ALSO, THE WAY HE TALKS IS SUPER OBNOXIOUS.
I COULDN'T SPEAK TO THAT... HEY, WHAT'RE YOU DOING?
HEADING HOME.
JUMPING IS THE FASTEST WAY.
UGH... YOU'RE SO LAZY.
BOING
BOING
CHAPTER 5 / END

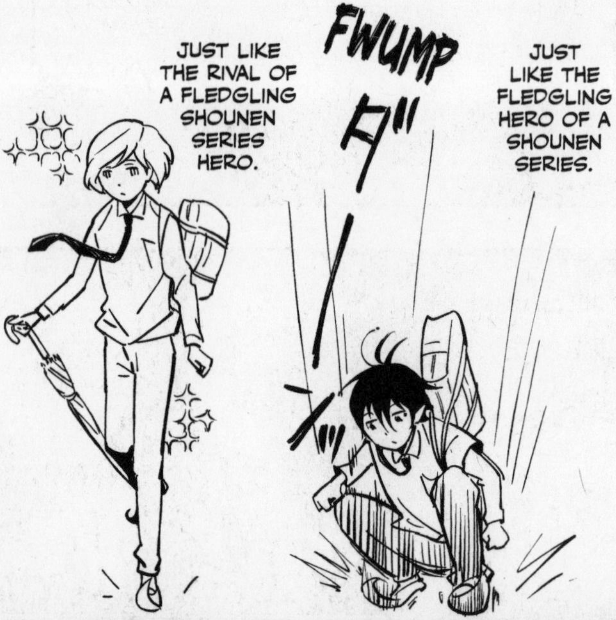
JUST LIKE THE FLEDGLING HERO OF A SHOUNEN SERIES.
FWUMP
JUST LIKE THE RIVAL OF A FLEDGLING SHOUNEN SERIES HERO.

CONFUCIUS SAID...
WHEN I WAS 150, I THREW
MYSELF INTO MY STUDIES.
AT 300, I STOOD ON MY OWN.
AT 400, I WAS NO LONGER LOST.
AT 500, I LEARNED MY DIVINE
PURPOSE.
AT 600, I COULD COMPREHEND
ANYTHING I WAS TOLD.
AND AT 700, I COULD FOLLOW
MY OWN HEART WITHOUT
RUNNING AFOUL OF THE WORLD.

THAT'S NOT WHAT CONFUCIUS SAID.

MY PATHETIC VAMPIRE LIFE

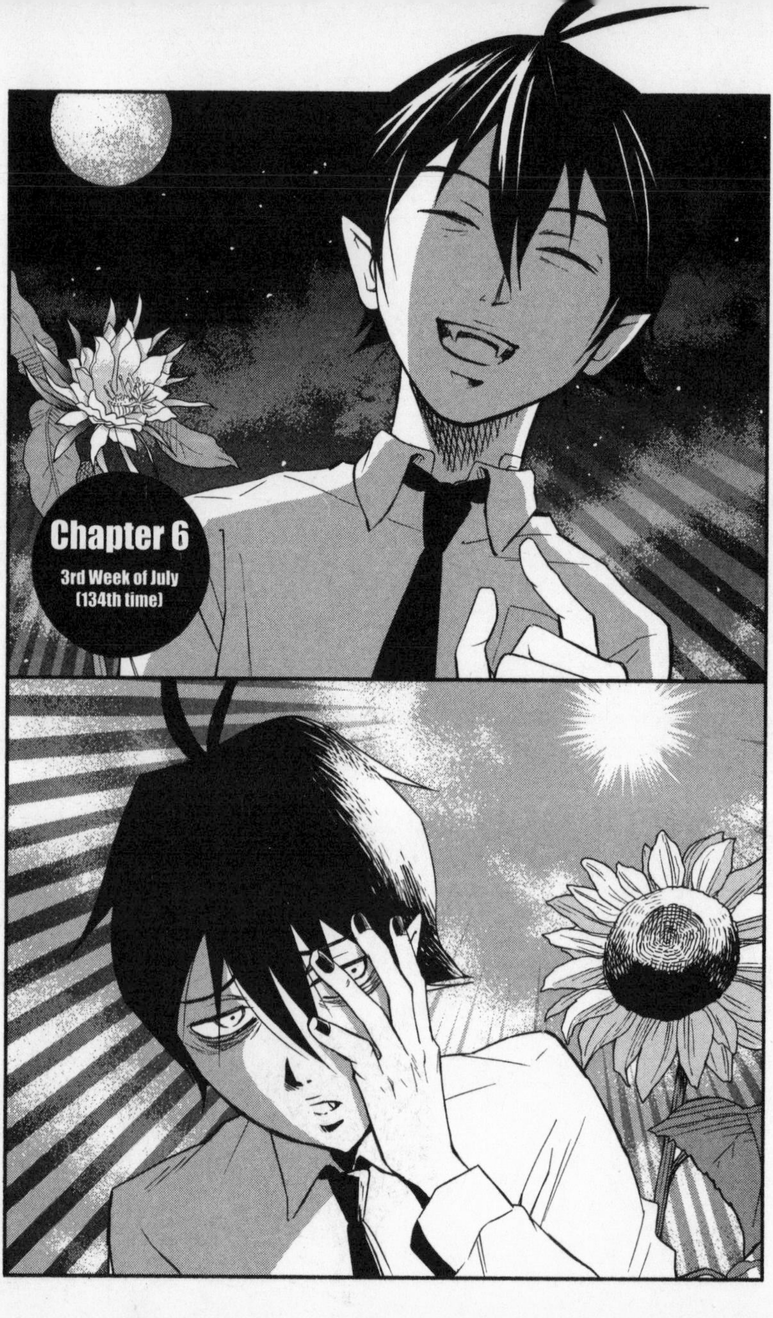
Chapter 6
3rd Week of July
(134th time)

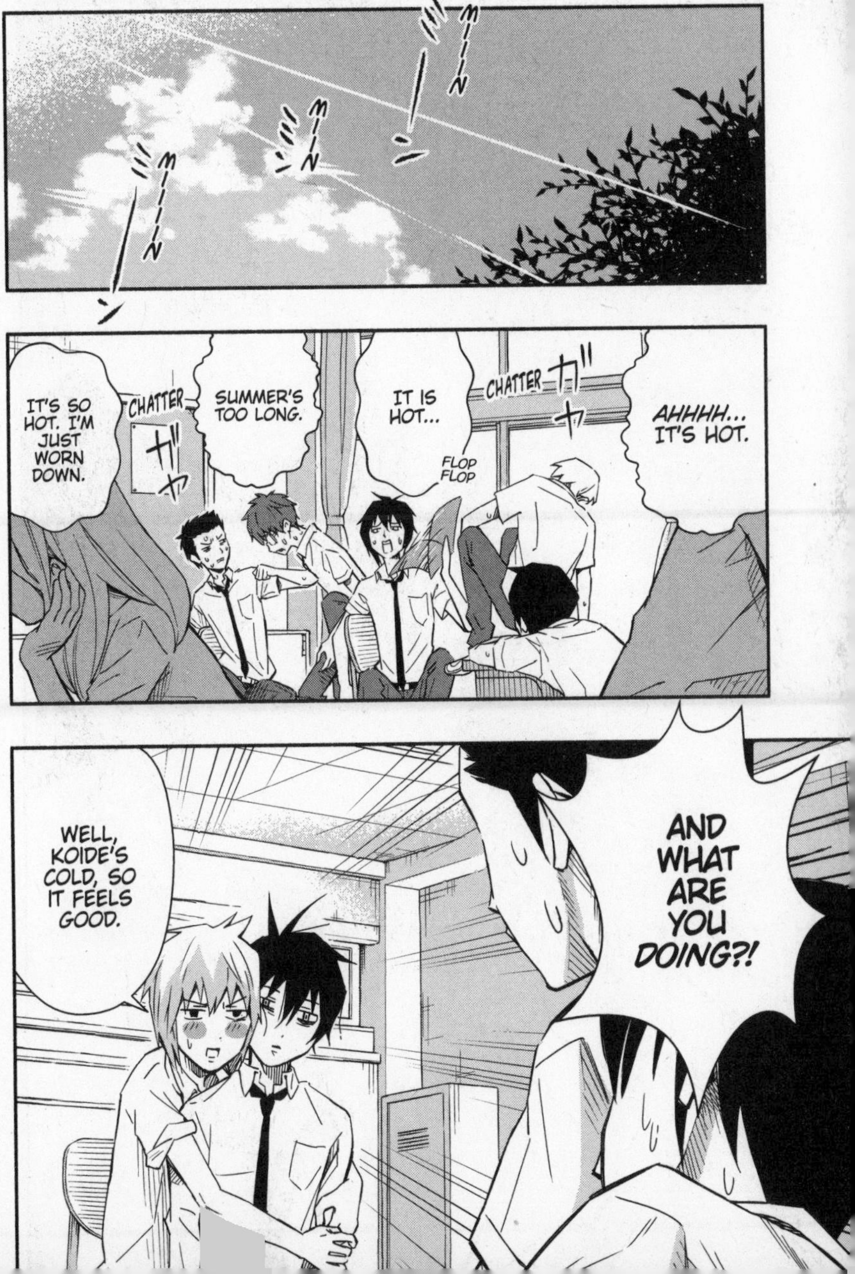
M-I-I-N
M-I-N
M-I-I-N
AHHHH... IT'S HOT.
CHATTER
IT IS HOT...
FLOP FLOP
SUMMER'S TOO LONG.
CHATTER
IT'S SO HOT. I'M JUST WORN DOWN.
AND WHAT ARE YOU DOING?!
WELL, KOIDE'S COLD, SO IT FEELS GOOD.

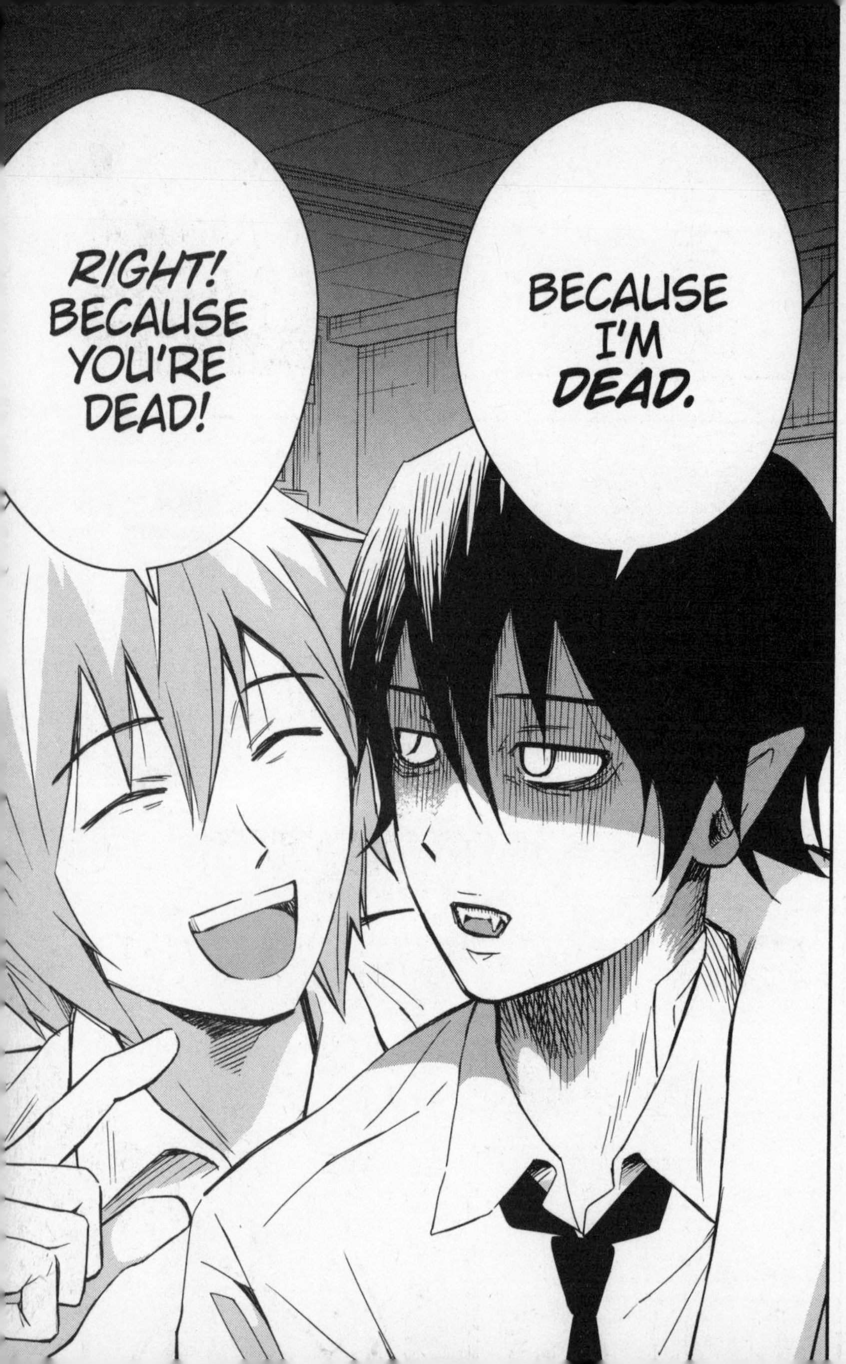
BECAUSE I'M DEAD.
RIGHT! BECAUSE YOU'RE DEAD!

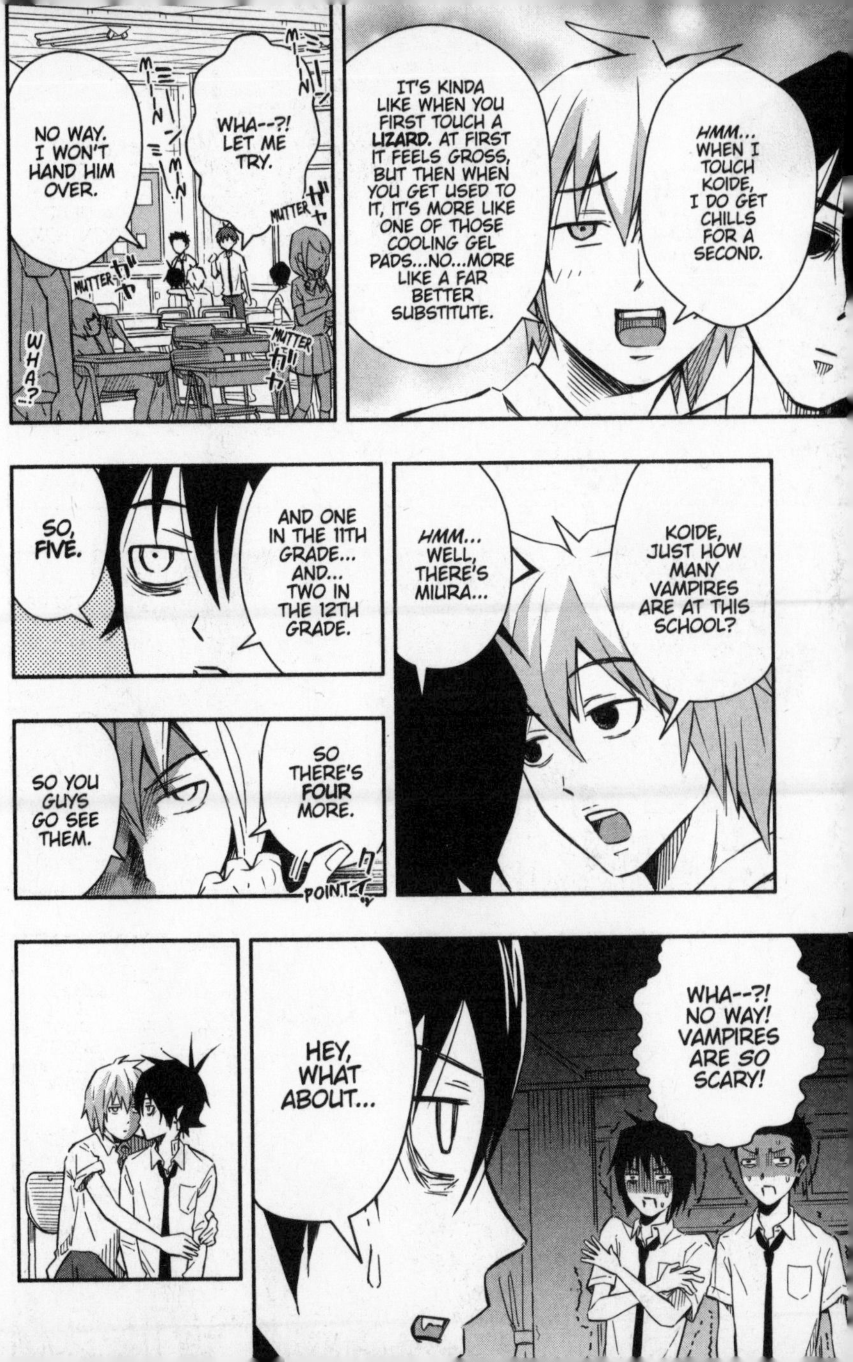
HMM... WHEN I TOUCH KOIDE, I DO GET CHILLS FOR A SECOND.
IT'S KINDA LIKE WHEN YOU FIRST TOUCH A LIZARD. AT FIRST IT FEELS GROSS, BUT THEN WHEN YOU GET USED TO IT, IT'S MORE LIKE ONE OF THOSE COOLING GEL PADS...NO...MORE LIKE A FAR BETTER SUBSTITUTE.
WHA--?! LET ME TRY.
NO WAY. I WON'T HAND HIM OVER.
MUTTER
MUTTER
MUTTER
WHA-?
KOIDE, JUST HOW MANY VAMPIRES ARE AT THIS SCHOOL?
HMM... WELL, THERE'S MIURA...
AND ONE IN THE 11TH GRADE... AND... TWO IN THE 12TH GRADE.
SO, FIVE.
SO THERE'S FOUR MORE.
SO YOU GUYS GO SEE THEM.
POINT
WHA--?! NO WAY! VAMPIRES ARE SO SCARY!
HEY, WHAT ABOUT...

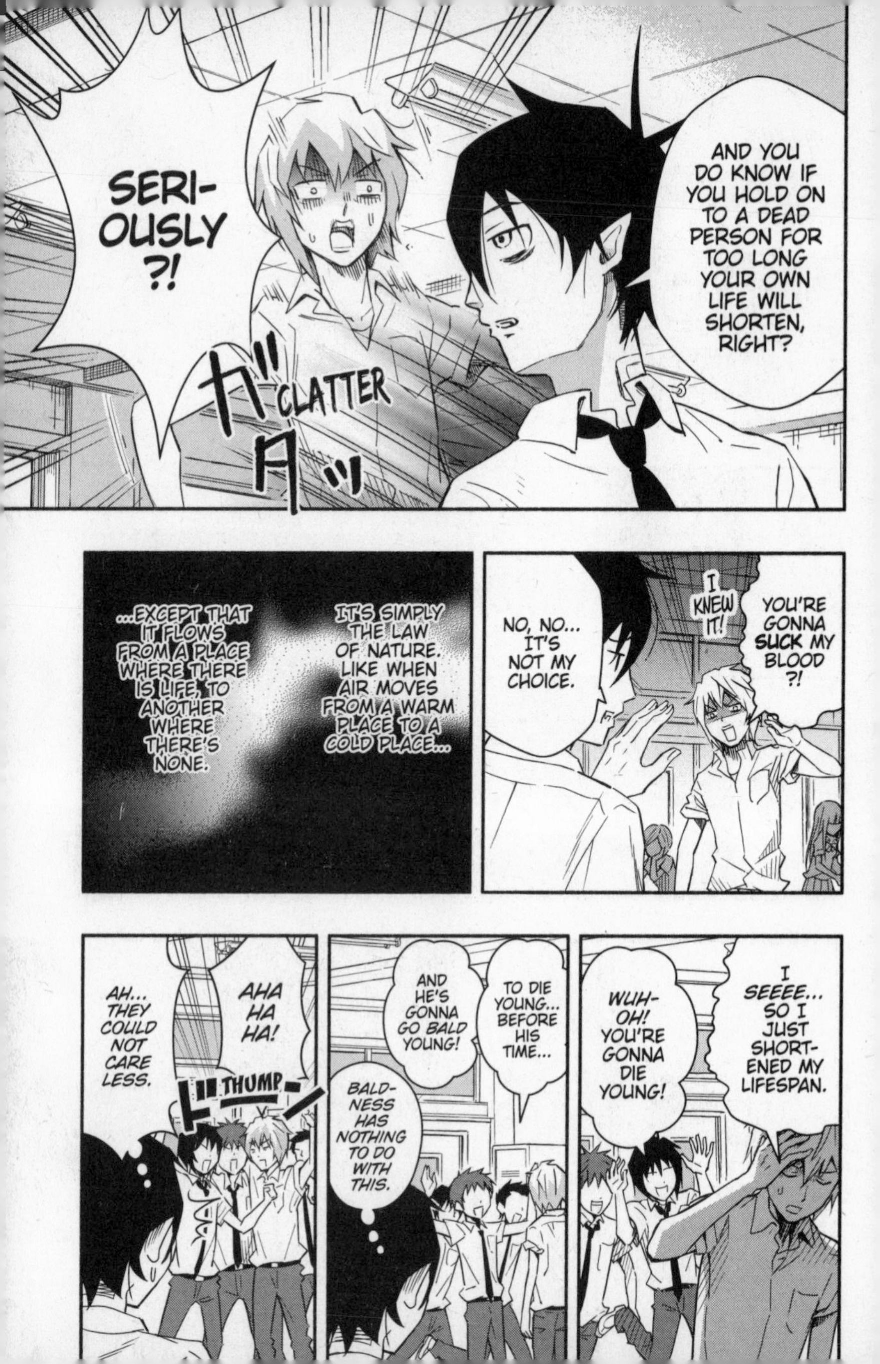
AND YOU DO KNOW IF YOU HOLD ON TO A DEAD PERSON FOR TOO LONG YOUR OWN LIFE WILL SHORTEN, RIGHT?
SERI-OUSLY?!
CLATTER
I KNEW IT!
YOU'RE GONNA SUCK MY BLOOD?!
NO, NO... IT'S NOT MY CHOICE.
IT'S SIMPLY THE LAW OF NATURE. LIKE WHEN AIR MOVES FROM A WARM PLACE TO A COLD PLACE...
...EXCEPT THAT IT FLOWS FROM A PLACE WHERE THERE IS LIFE, TO ANOTHER WHERE THERE'S NONE.
I SEEEE... SO I JUST SHORT-ENED MY LIFESPAN.
WUH-OH! YOU'RE GONNA DIE YOUNG!
TO DIE YOUNG... BEFORE HIS TIME...
AND HE'S GONNA GO BALD YOUNG!
BALD-NESS HAS NOTHING TO DO WITH THIS.
AHA HA HA!
THUMP
AH... THEY COULD NOT CARE LESS.

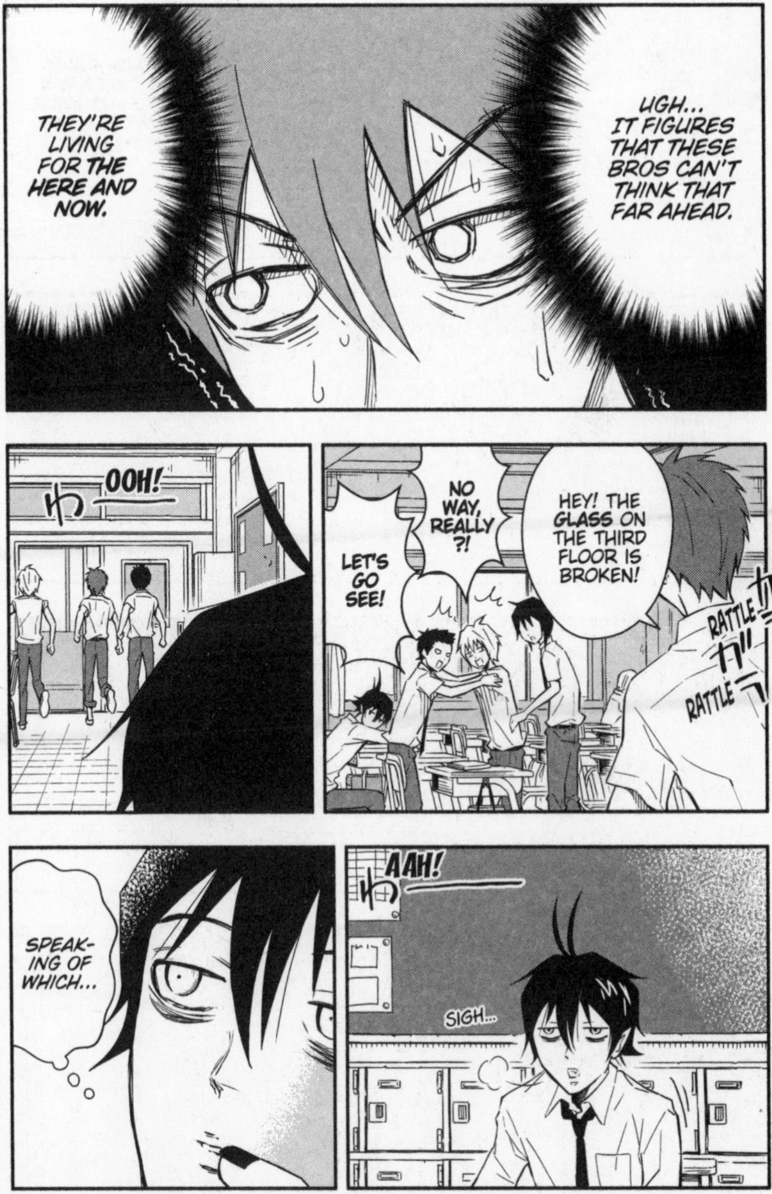
UGH... IT FIGURES THAT THESE BROS CAN'T THINK THAT FAR AHEAD.
THEY'RE LIVING FOR THE HERE AND NOW.
RATTLE
RATTLE
HEY! THE GLASS ON THE THIRD FLOOR IS BROKEN!
NO WAY, REALLY?!
LET'S GO SEE!
OOH!
AAH!
SIGH...
SPEAK-ING OF WHICH...

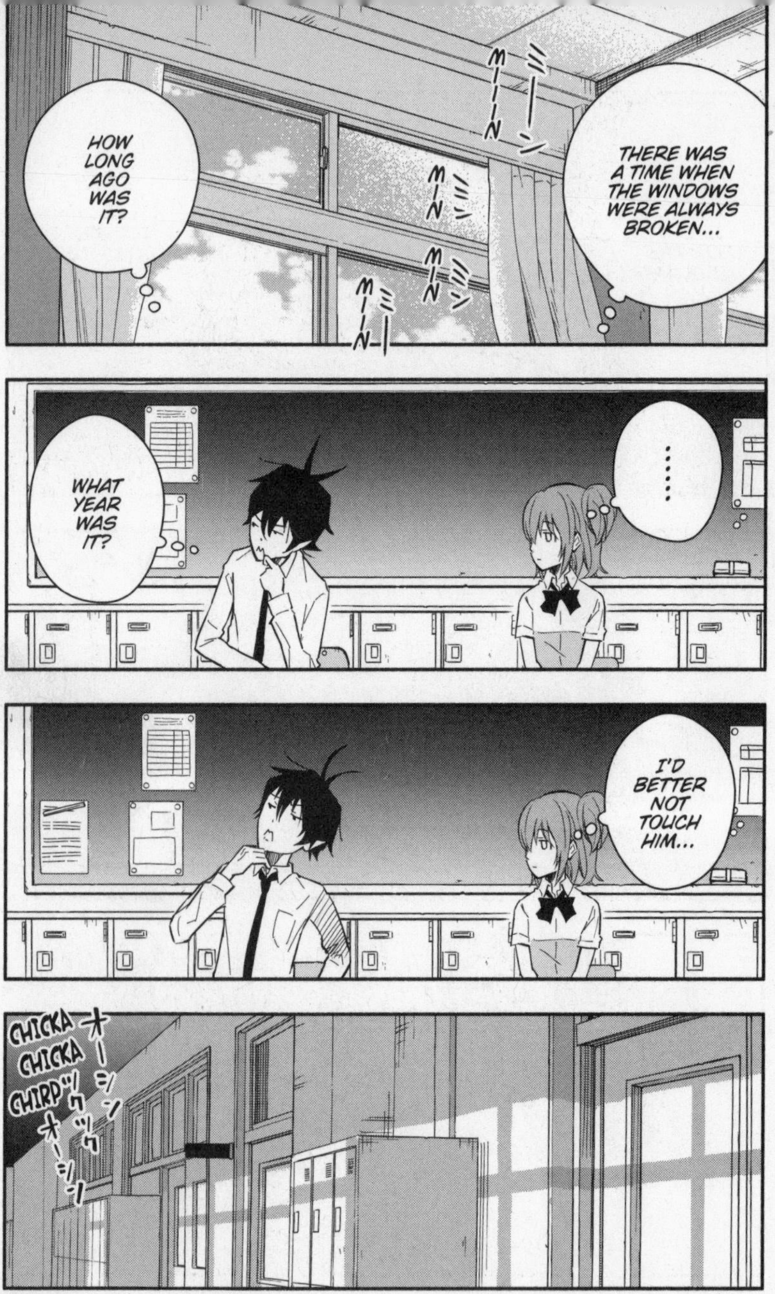
THERE WAS A TIME WHEN THE WINDOWS WERE ALWAYS BROKEN...
MI-I-N
MIN
MIN
MI-I-N
HOW LONG AGO WAS IT?
......
WHAT YEAR WAS IT?
I'D BETTER NOT TOUCH HIM...
CHICKA CHICKA CHIRP

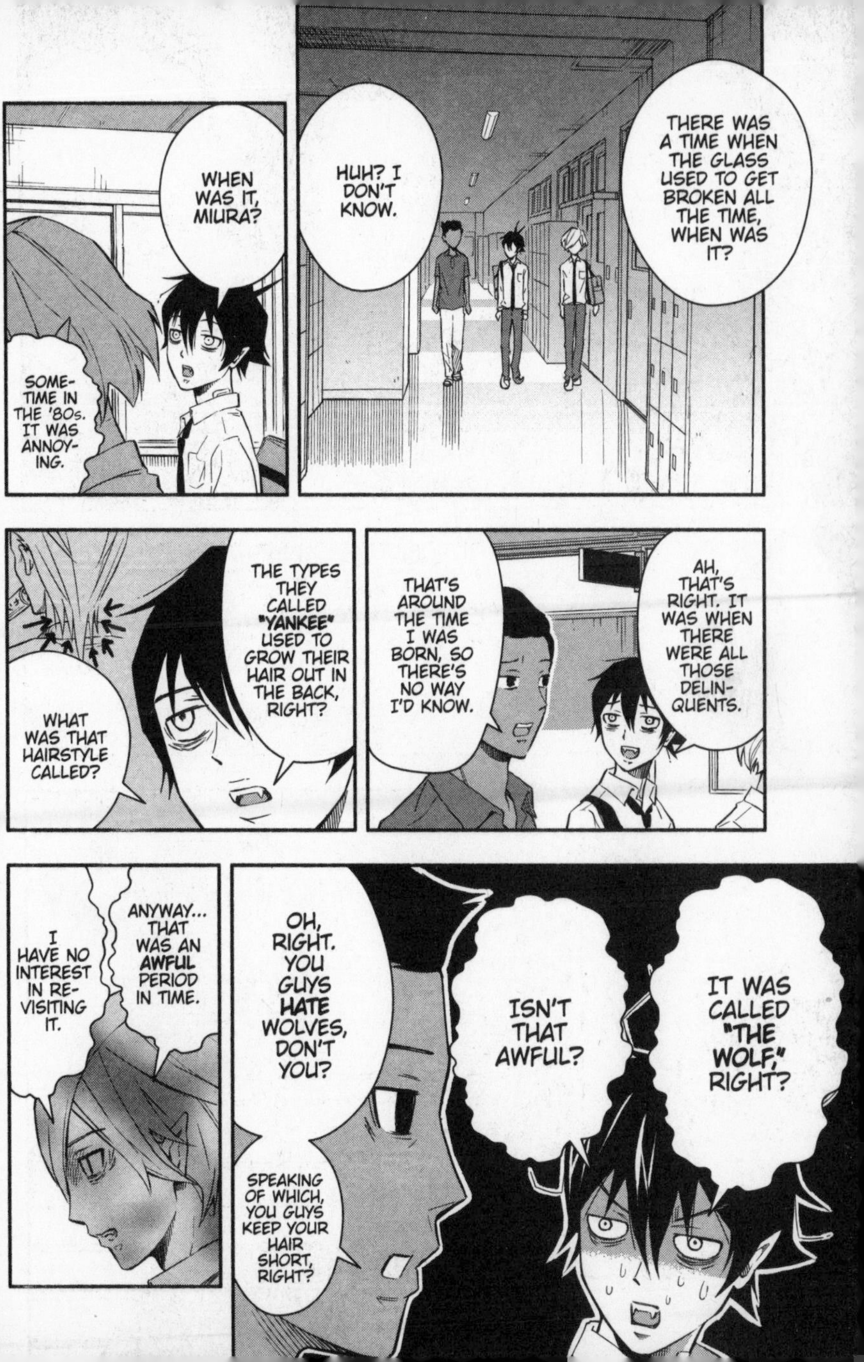
THERE WAS A TIME WHEN THE GLASS USED TO GET BROKEN ALL THE TIME, WHEN WAS IT?
HUH? I DON'T KNOW.
WHEN WAS IT, MIURA?
SOMETIME IN THE '80s. IT WAS ANNOYING.
AH, THAT'S RIGHT. IT WAS WHEN THERE WERE ALL THOSE DELINQUENTS.
THAT'S AROUND THE TIME I WAS BORN, SO THERE'S NO WAY I'D KNOW.
THE TYPES THEY CALLED "YANKEE" USED TO GROW THEIR HAIR OUT IN THE BACK, RIGHT?
WHAT WAS THAT HAIRSTYLE CALLED?
IT WAS CALLED "THE WOLF," RIGHT?
ISN'T THAT AWFUL?
OH, RIGHT. YOU GUYS HATE WOLVES, DON'T YOU?
SPEAKING OF WHICH, YOU GUYS KEEP YOUR HAIR SHORT, RIGHT?
ANYWAY... THAT WAS AN AWFUL PERIOD IN TIME.
I HAVE NO INTEREST IN REVISITING IT.

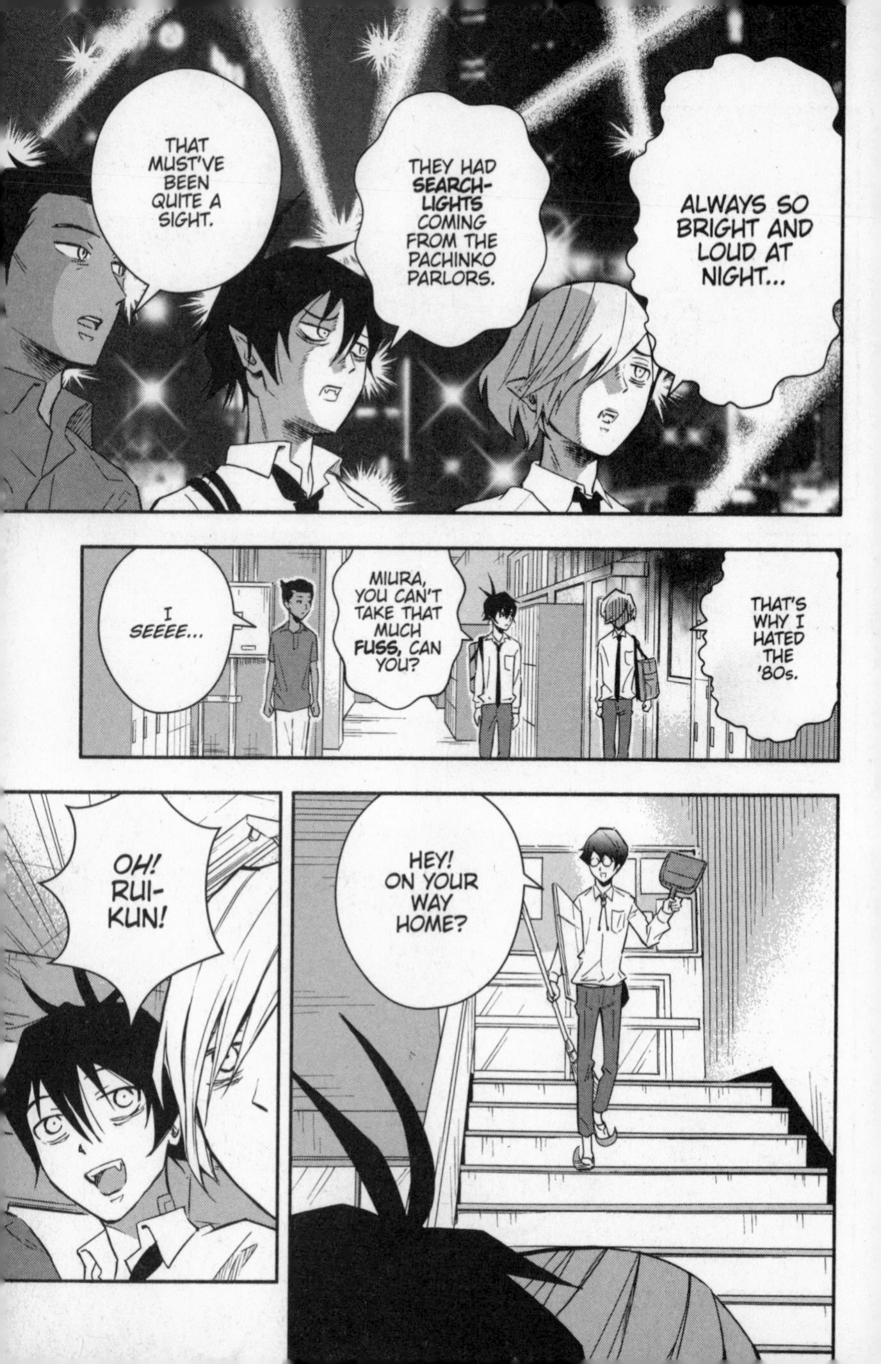
ALWAYS SO BRIGHT AND LOUD AT NIGHT...
THEY HAD SEARCH-LIGHTS COMING FROM THE PACHINKO PARLORS.
THAT MUST'VE BEEN QUITE A SIGHT.
THAT'S WHY I HATED THE '80s.
MIURA, YOU CAN'T TAKE THAT MUCH FUSS, CAN YOU?
I SEEEE...
HEY! ON YOUR WAY HOME?
OH! RUI-KUN!

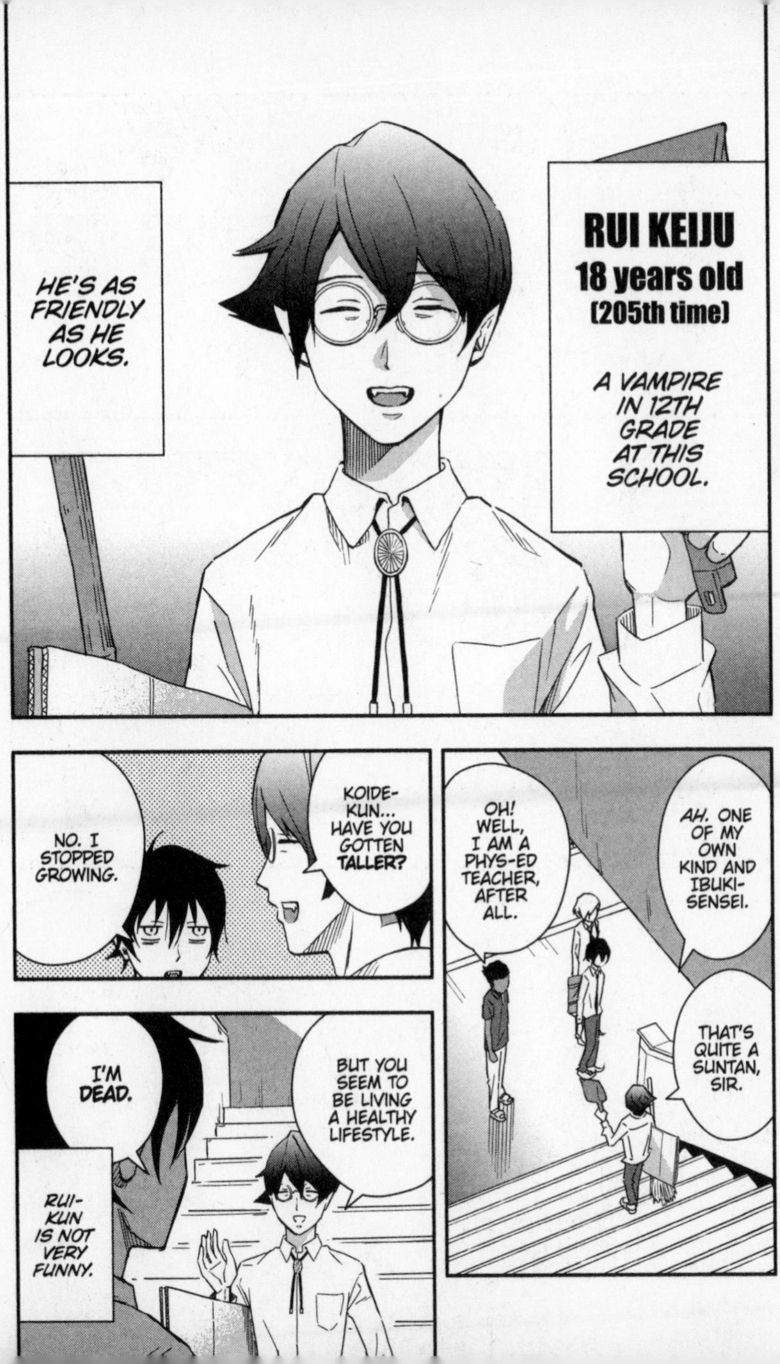
RUI KEIJU
18 years old
(205th time)
A VAMPIRE IN 12TH GRADE AT THIS SCHOOL.
HE'S AS FRIENDLY AS HE LOOKS.
AH. ONE OF MY OWN KIND AND IBUKI-SENSEI.
THAT'S QUITE A SUNTAN, SIR.
OH! WELL, I AM A PHYS-ED TEACHER, AFTER ALL.
KOIDE-KUN... HAVE YOU GOTTEN TALLER?
NO. I STOPPED GROWING.
BUT YOU SEEM TO BE LIVING A HEALTHY LIFESTYLE.
I'M DEAD.
RUI-KUN IS NOT VERY FUNNY.

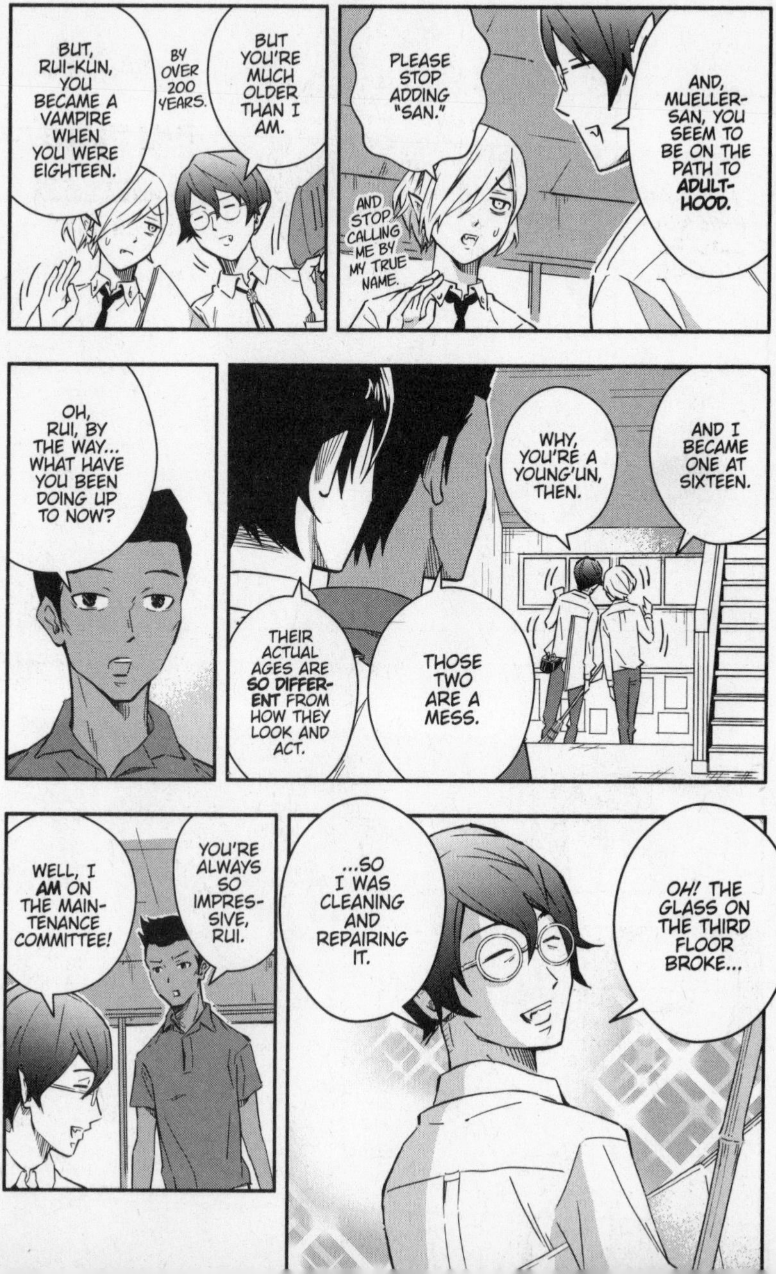
AND, MUELLER-SAN, YOU SEEM TO BE ON THE PATH TO **ADULTHOOD.**
PLEASE STOP ADDING "SAN."
AND STOP CALLING ME BY MY TRUE NAME.
BUT YOU'RE MUCH OLDER THAN I AM.
BY OVER 200 YEARS.
BUT, RUI-KUN, YOU BECAME A VAMPIRE WHEN YOU WERE EIGHTEEN.
AND I BECAME ONE AT SIXTEEN.
WHY, YOU'RE A YOUNG'UN, THEN.
THOSE TWO ARE A MESS.
THEIR ACTUAL AGES ARE **SO DIFFERENT** FROM HOW THEY LOOK AND ACT.
OH, RUI, BY THE WAY... WHAT HAVE YOU BEEN DOING UP TO NOW?
OH! THE GLASS ON THE THIRD FLOOR BROKE...
...SO I WAS CLEANING AND REPAIRING IT.
YOU'RE ALWAYS SO IMPRESSIVE, RUI.
WELL, I **AM** ON THE MAINTENANCE COMMITTEE!

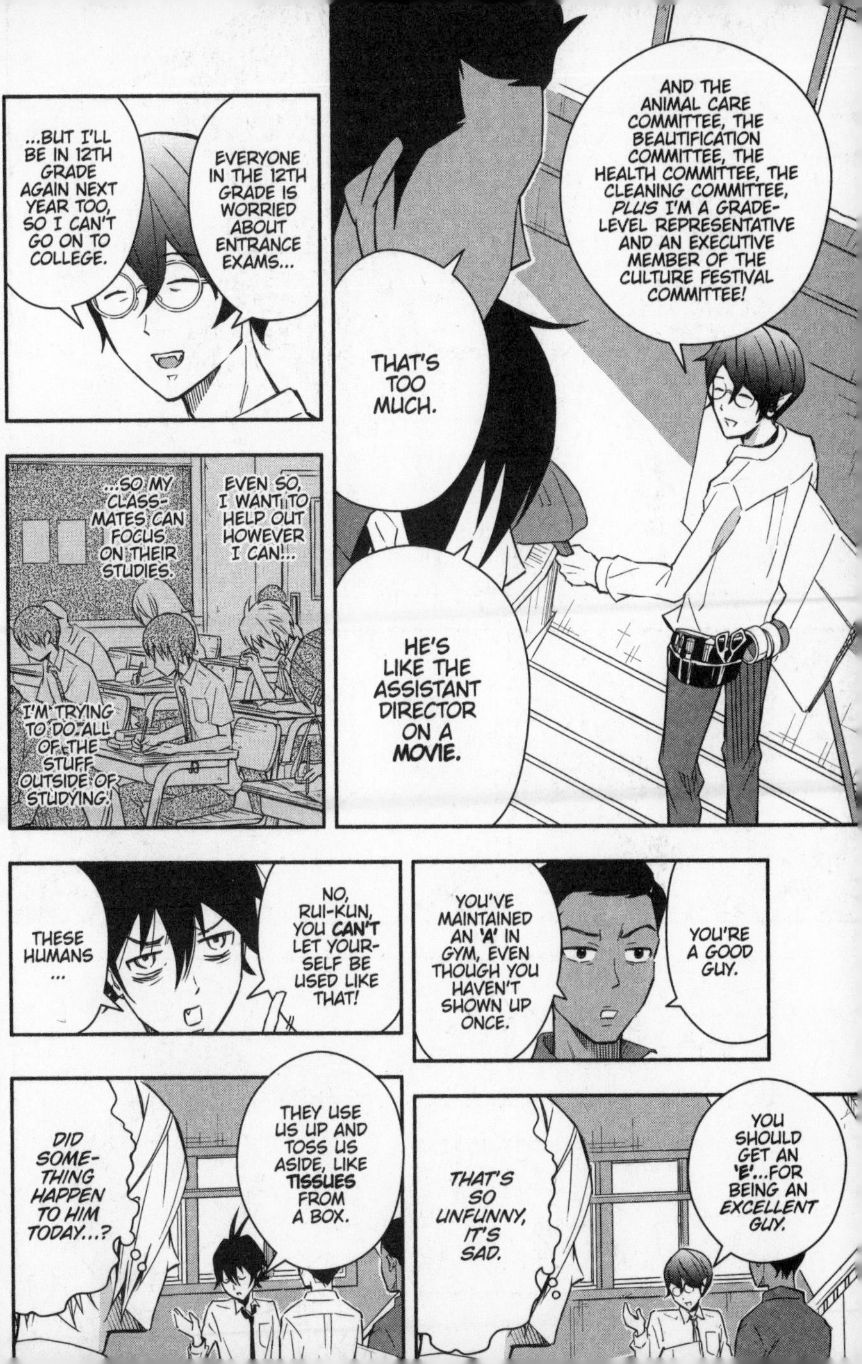
AND THE ANIMAL CARE COMMITTEE, THE BEAUTIFICATION COMMITTEE, THE HEALTH COMMITTEE, THE CLEANING COMMITTEE, *PLUS* I'M A GRADE-LEVEL REPRESENTATIVE AND AN EXECUTIVE MEMBER OF THE CULTURE FESTIVAL COMMITTEE!
THAT'S TOO MUCH.
HE'S LIKE THE ASSISTANT DIRECTOR ON A **MOVIE.**
EVERYONE IN THE 12TH GRADE IS WORRIED ABOUT ENTRANCE EXAMS...
...BUT I'LL BE IN 12TH GRADE AGAIN NEXT YEAR TOO, SO I CAN'T GO ON TO COLLEGE.
EVEN SO, I WANT TO HELP OUT HOWEVER I CAN!...
...SO MY CLASS-MATES CAN FOCUS ON THEIR STUDIES.
I'M TRYING TO DO ALL OF THE STUFF OUTSIDE OF STUDYING.
YOU'RE A GOOD GUY.
YOU'VE MAINTAINED AN **'A'** IN GYM, EVEN THOUGH YOU HAVEN'T SHOWN UP ONCE.
NO, RUI-KUN, YOU **CAN'T** LET YOUR-SELF BE USED LIKE THAT!
THESE HUMANS ...
YOU SHOULD GET AN **'E'**...FOR BEING AN *EXCELLENT* GUY.
THAT'S SO UNFUNNY, IT'S SAD.
THEY USE US UP AND TOSS US ASIDE, LIKE **TISSUES** FROM A BOX.
DID SOME-THING HAPPEN TO HIM TODAY...?

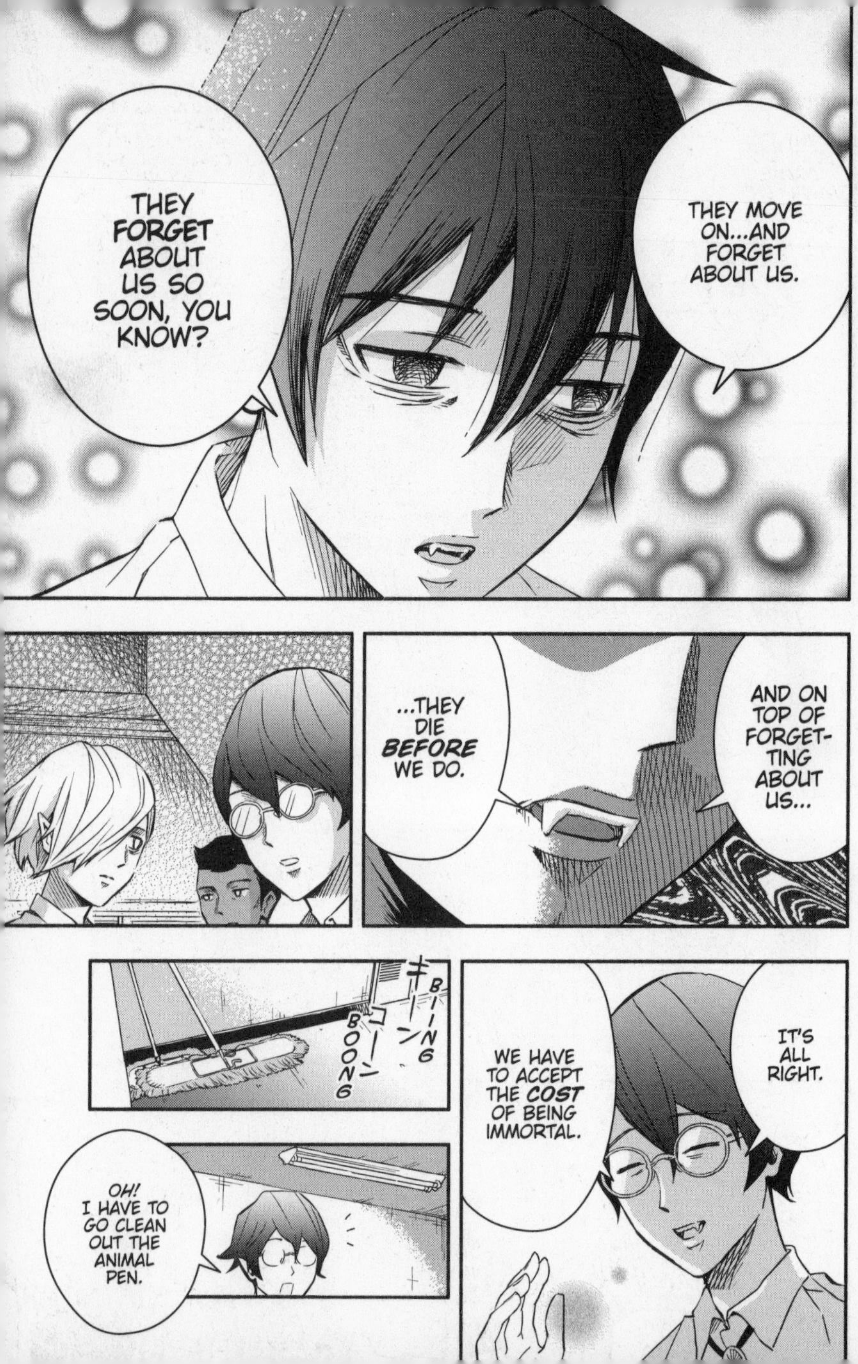
THEY MOVE ON...AND FORGET ABOUT US.
THEY **FORGET** ABOUT US SO SOON, YOU KNOW?
AND ON TOP OF FORGET-TING ABOUT US...
...THEY DIE ***BEFORE*** WE DO.
IT'S ALL RIGHT.
WE HAVE TO ACCEPT THE ***COST*** OF BEING IMMORTAL.
キーン
BIING
コーン
BOONG
OH! I HAVE TO GO CLEAN OUT THE ANIMAL PEN.

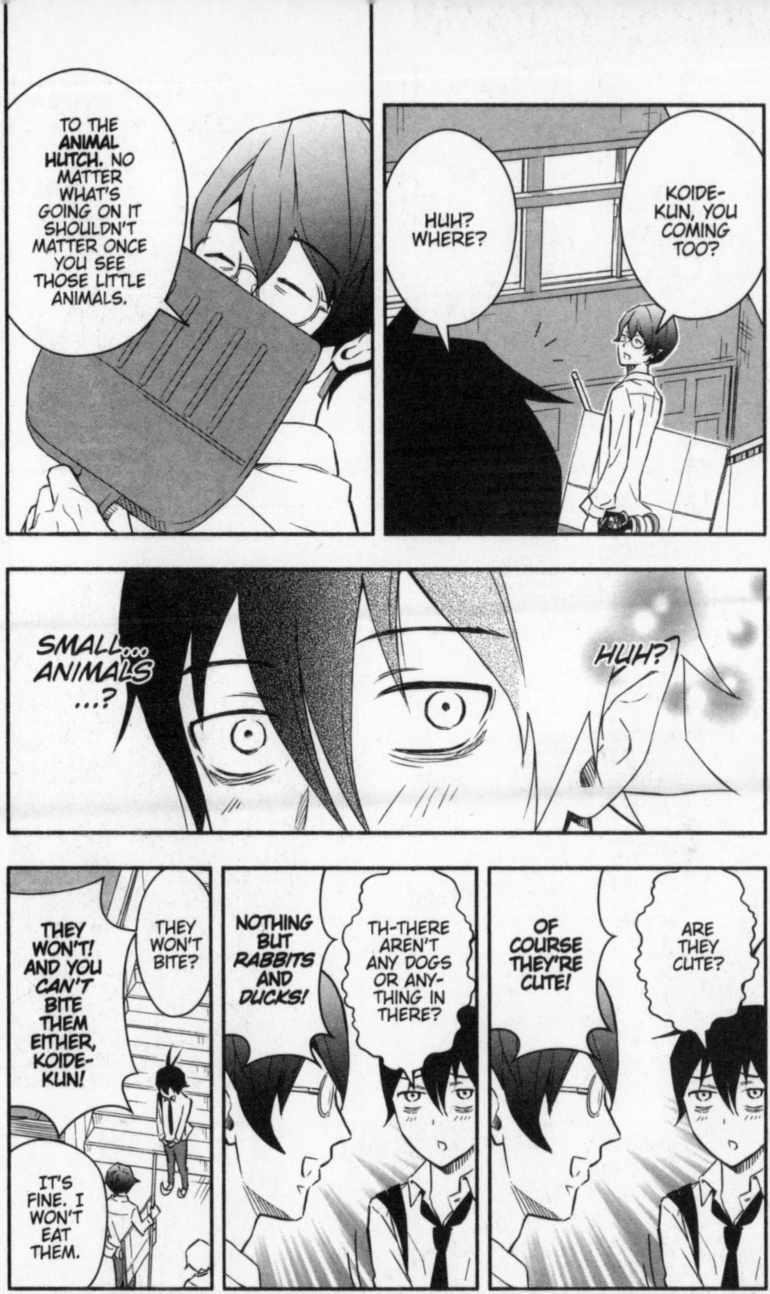
KOIDE-KUN, YOU COMING TOO?
HUH? WHERE?
TO THE ANIMAL HUTCH. NO MATTER WHAT'S GOING ON IT SHOULDN'T MATTER ONCE YOU SEE THOSE LITTLE ANIMALS.
HUH?
SMALL... ANIMALS ...?
ARE THEY CUTE?
OF COURSE THEY'RE CUTE!
TH-THERE AREN'T ANY DOGS OR ANY-THING IN THERE?
NOTHING BUT RABBITS AND DUCKS!
THEY WON'T BITE?
THEY WON'T! AND YOU CAN'T BITE THEM EITHER, KOIDE-KUN!
IT'S FINE. I WON'T EAT THEM.

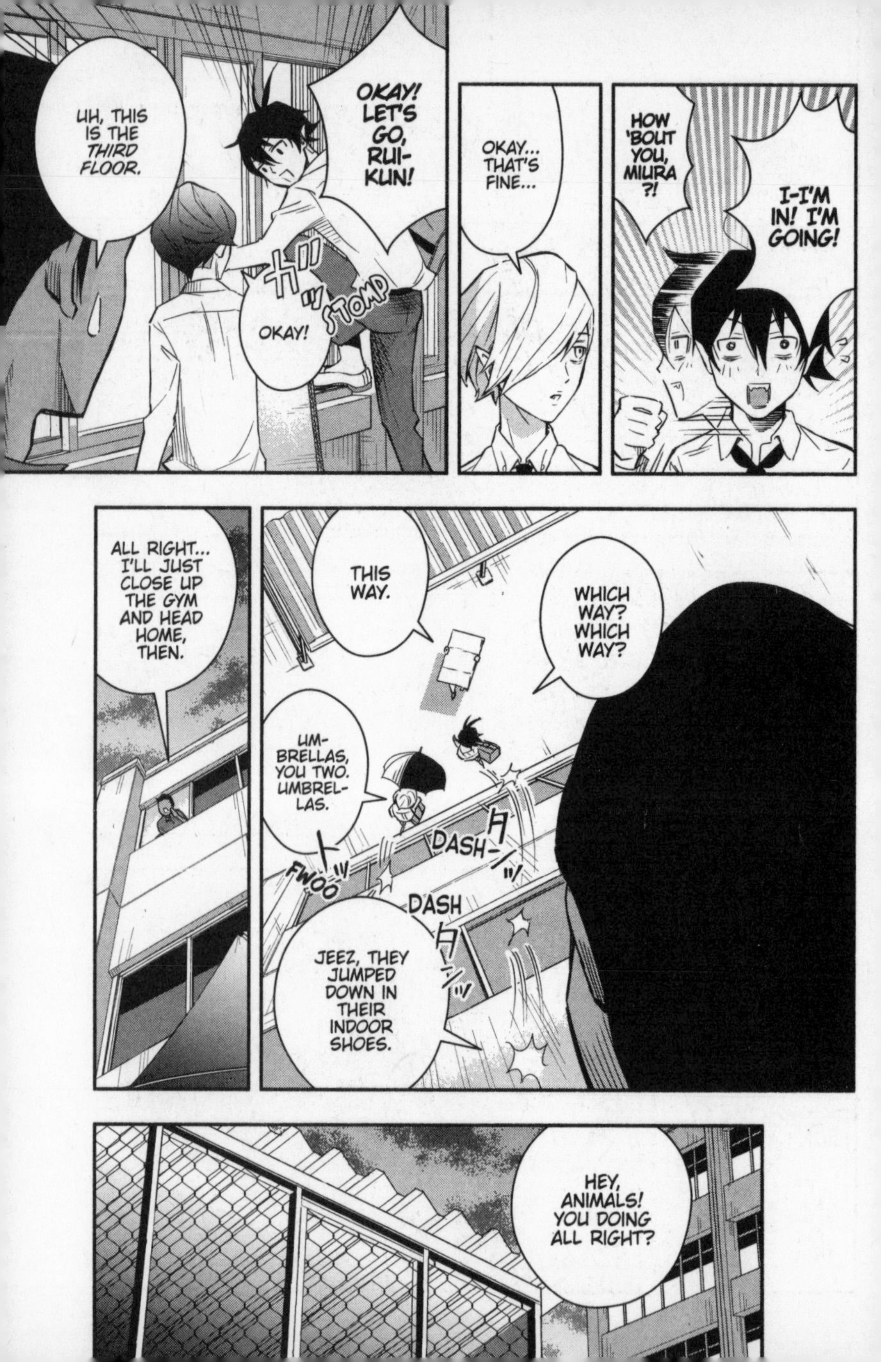
HOW 'BOUT YOU, MIURA?!
I-I'M IN! I'M GOING!
OKAY... THAT'S FINE...
OKAY! LET'S GO, RUI-KUN!
UH, THIS IS THE *THIRD FLOOR.*
STOMP
OKAY!
WHICH WAY? WHICH WAY?
THIS WAY.
UM-BRELLAS, YOU TWO. UMBREL-LAS.
DASH
FWOO
DASH
JEEZ, THEY JUMPED DOWN IN THEIR INDOOR SHOES.
ALL RIGHT... I'LL JUST CLOSE UP THE GYM AND HEAD HOME, THEN.
HEY, ANIMALS! YOU DOING ALL RIGHT?

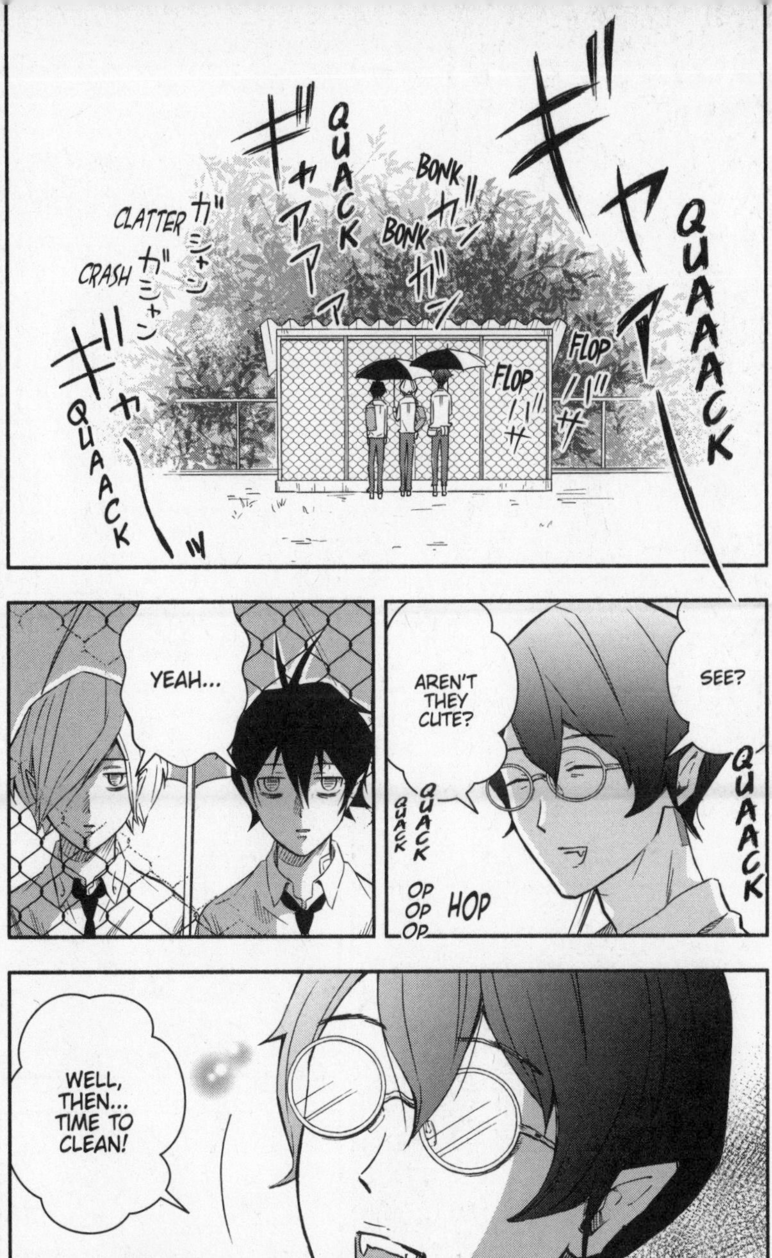
QUAAACK
FLOP
FLOP
BONK
BONK
QUACK
CLATTER
CRASH
QUAAACK
SEE?
AREN'T THEY CUTE?
QUAAACK
QUACK QUACK
HOP
OP OP OP
YEAH...
WELL, THEN... TIME TO CLEAN!

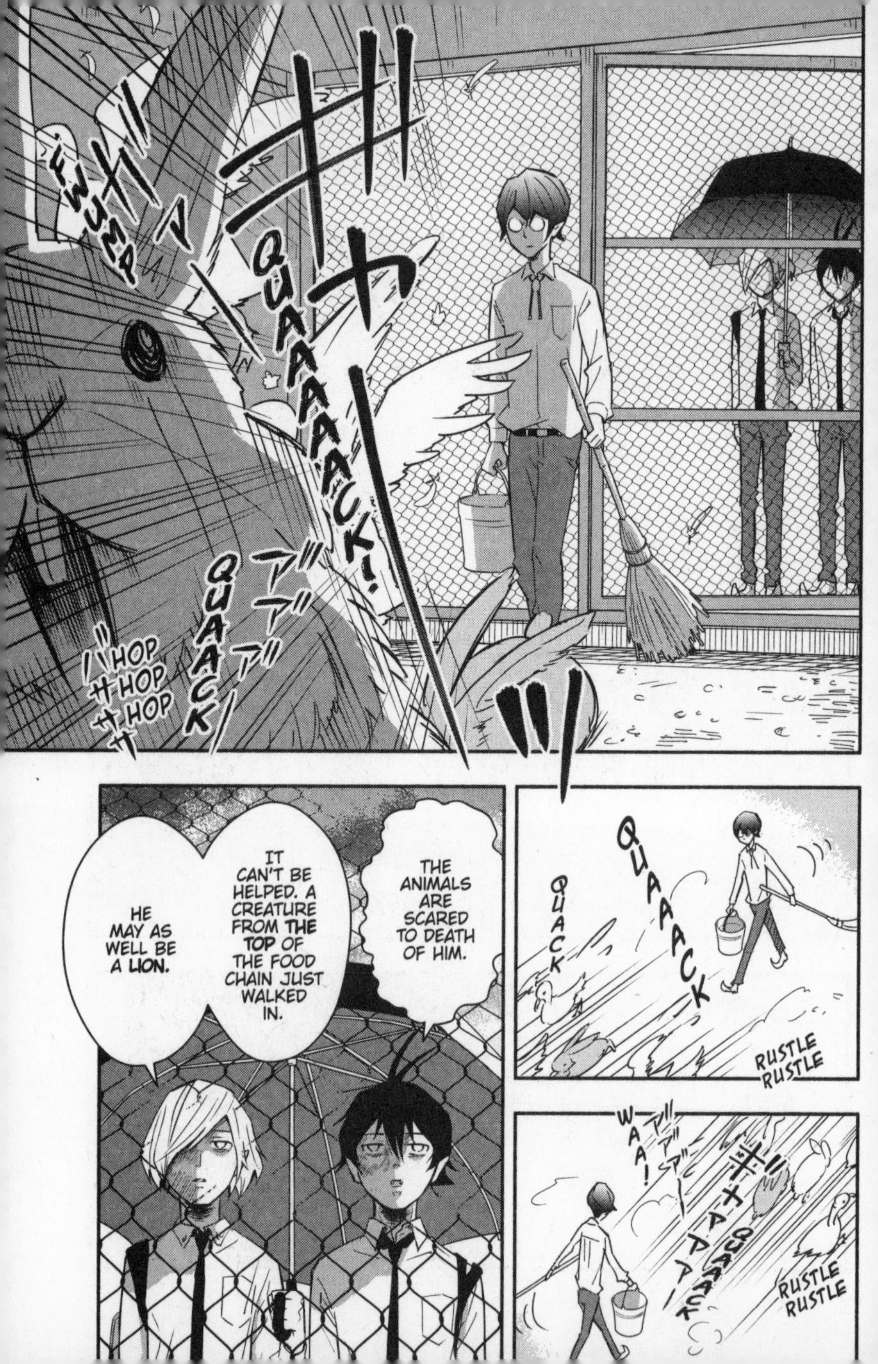
QUAAAAAACK!
FWUMP
QUAAACK
HOP HOP HOP
QUAAAACK
QUACK
RUSTLE RUSTLE
WAA!
QUAAACK
RUSTLE RUSTLE
THE ANIMALS ARE SCARED TO DEATH OF HIM.
IT CAN'T BE HELPED. A CREATURE FROM THE TOP OF THE FOOD CHAIN JUST WALKED IN.
HE MAY AS WELL BE A LION.

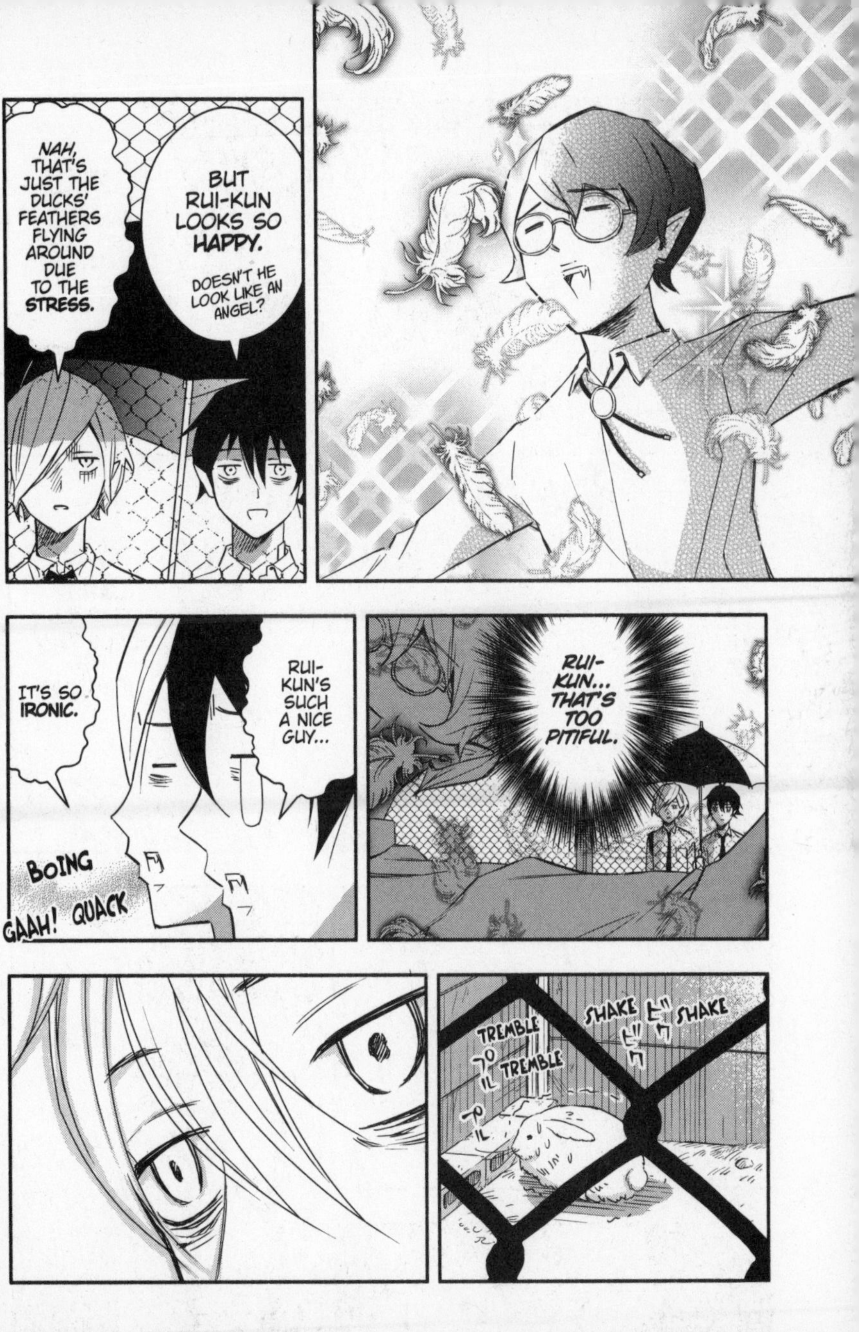
BUT RUI-KUN LOOKS SO HAPPY.
DOESN'T HE LOOK LIKE AN ANGEL?
NAH, THAT'S JUST THE DUCKS' FEATHERS FLYING AROUND DUE TO THE STRESS.
RUI-KUN... THAT'S TOO PITIFUL.
RUI-KUN'S SUCH A NICE GUY...
IT'S SO IRONIC.
BOING
QUACK
GAAH!
SHAKE SHAKE
TREMBLE TREMBLE

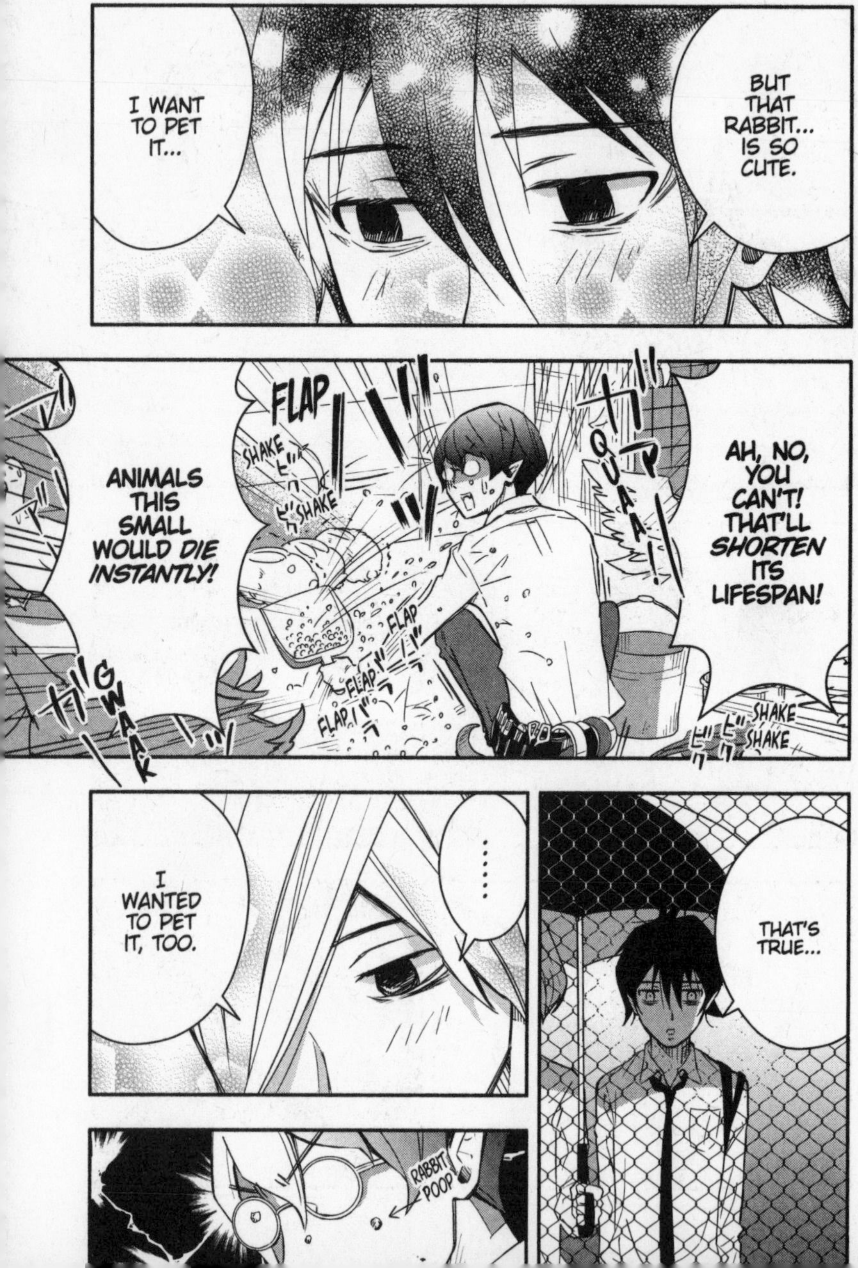
BUT THAT RABBIT... IS SO CUTE.
I WANT TO PET IT...
QUAAA!
AH, NO, YOU CAN'T! THAT'LL SHORTEN ITS LIFESPAN!
SHAKE SHAKE
FLAP
SHAKE SHAKE
FLAP FLAP FLAP FLAP
ANIMALS THIS SMALL WOULD DIE INSTANTLY!
GWAAK
THAT'S TRUE...
......
I WANTED TO PET IT, TOO.
RABBIT POOP

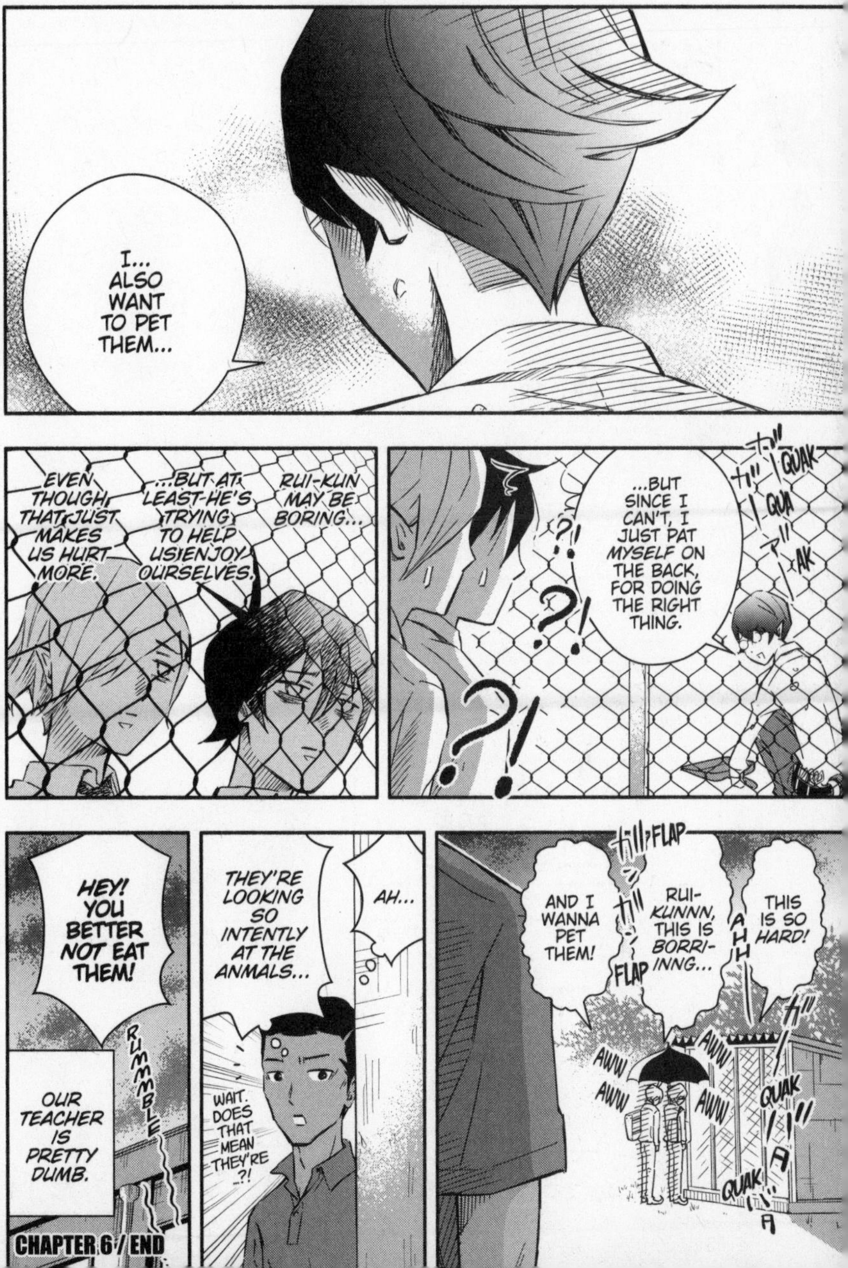
I... ALSO WANT TO PET THEM...
QUAK
QUA
AK
...BUT SINCE I CAN'T, I JUST PAT MYSELF ON THE BACK, FOR DOING THE RIGHT THING.
?!
?!
?!
RUI-KUN MAY BE BORING...
...BUT AT LEAST HE'S TRYING TO HELP US ENJOY OURSELVES.
EVEN THOUGH THAT JUST MAKES US HURT MORE.
FLAP
THIS IS SO HARD!
AHH
RUI-KUNNN, THIS IS BORRI-INNG...
AND I WANNA PET THEM!
FLAP
AWW
AWW
AWW
AWW
QUAK
QUAK
AH...
THEY'RE LOOKING SO INTENTLY AT THE ANMALS...
WAIT. DOES THAT MEAN THEY'RE ...?!
HEY! YOU BETTER NOT EAT THEM!
RUMMBLE
OUR TEACHER IS PRETTY DUMB.
CHAPTER 6 / END

A DAY IN THE LIFE OF RUI-KUN

BEAU-TIFICA-TION COM-MITTEE.
ENJOYS WATERING THE FLOWERS.
CLEAN-ING COMMIT-TEE.
ENJOYS KEEPING THE SCHOOL TIDY.
SWISH
SWISH
KEEP-ING A CLASS JOUR-NAL.
ENJOYS LOOKING BACK ON THE DAY.
SCRIBBLE
SCRIBBLE
HEALTH COMMIT-TEE.
RUI-KUN! WAIT! BITE ME!
DOESN'T REALLY ENJOY THIS PART.

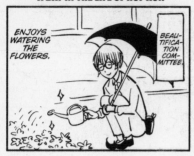

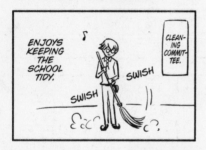

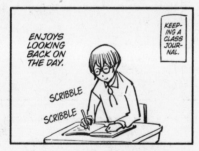

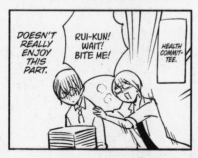

My Pathetic Vampire Life

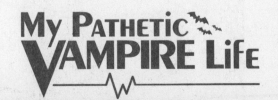

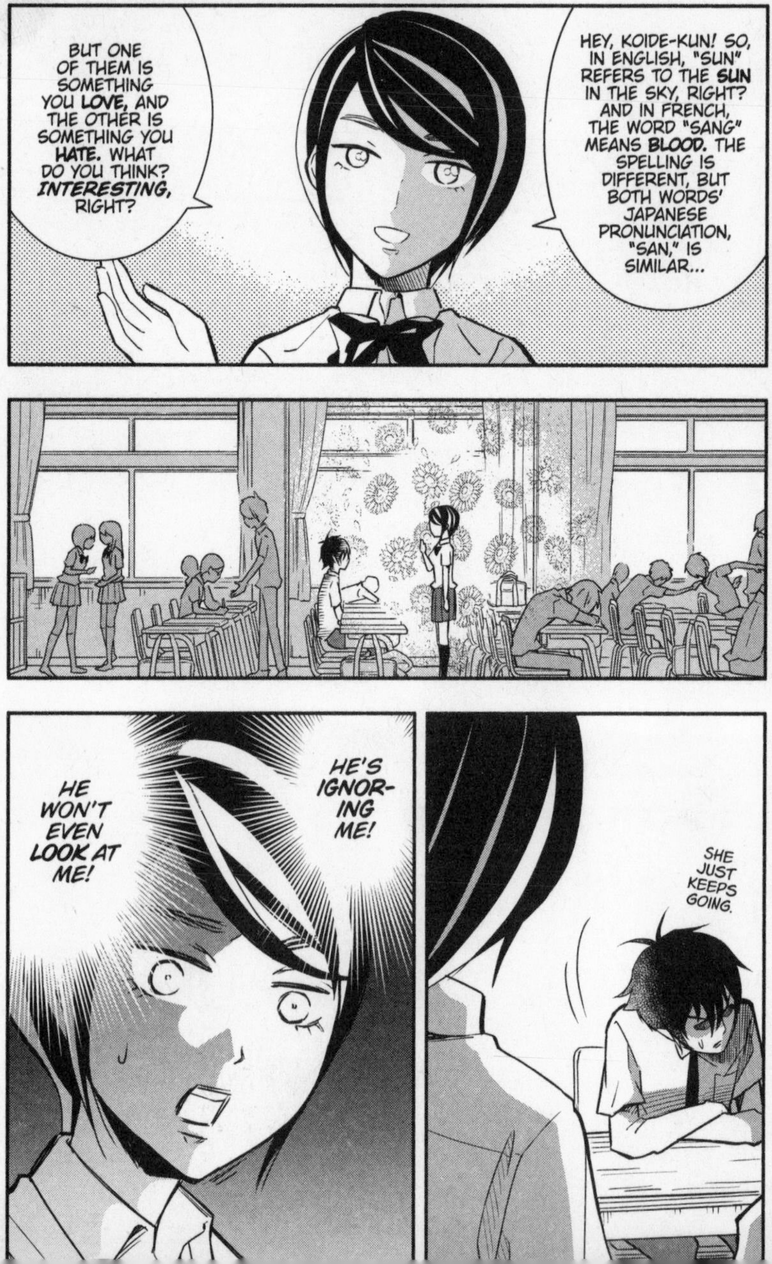
HEY, KOIDE-KUN! SO, IN ENGLISH, "SUN" REFERS TO THE SUN IN THE SKY, RIGHT? AND IN FRENCH, THE WORD "SANG" MEANS BLOOD. THE SPELLING IS DIFFERENT, BUT BOTH WORDS' JAPANESE PRONUNCIATION, "SAN," IS SIMILAR...
BUT ONE OF THEM IS SOMETHING YOU LOVE, AND THE OTHER IS SOMETHING YOU HATE. WHAT DO YOU THINK? INTERESTING, RIGHT?
SHE JUST KEEPS GOING.
HE'S IGNORING ME!
HE WON'T EVEN LOOK AT ME!

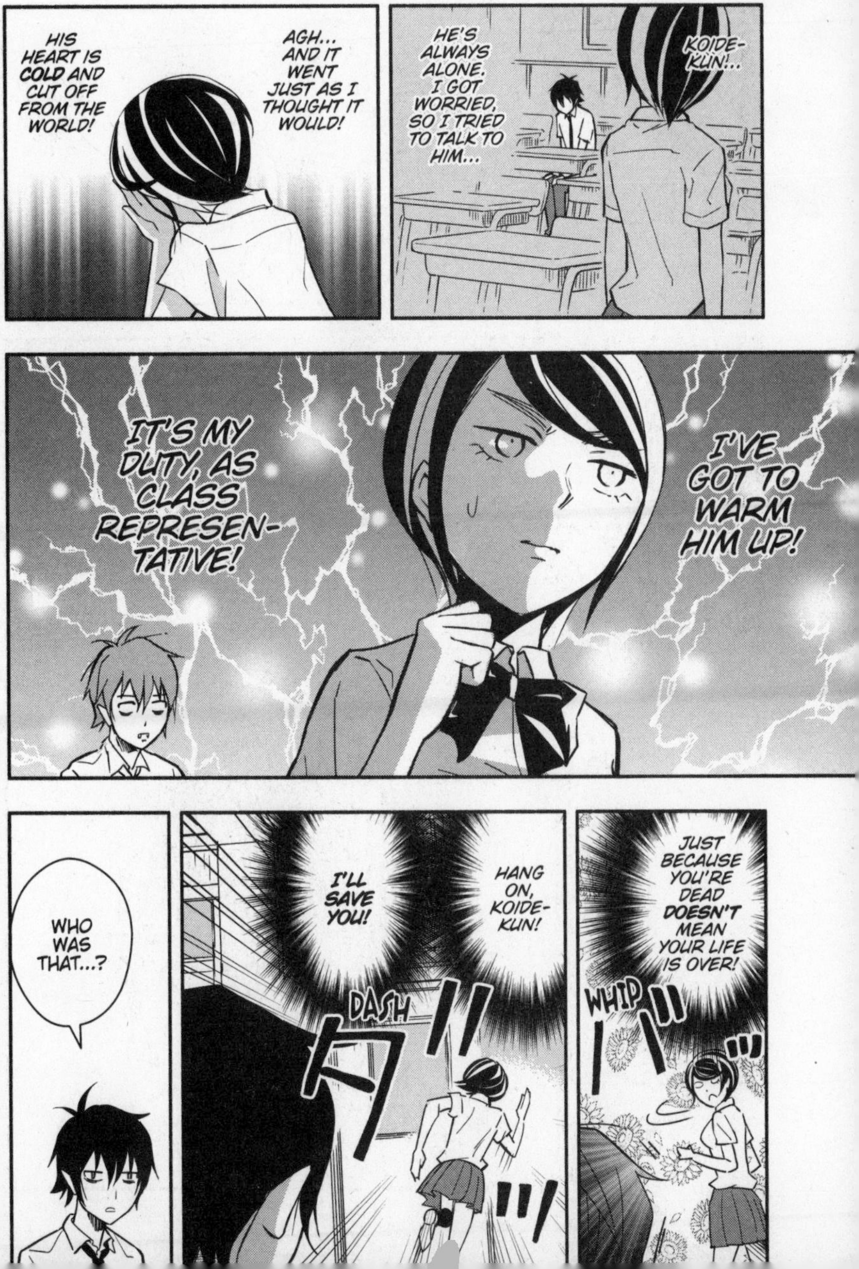
KOIDE-KUN!...
HE'S ALWAYS ALONE. I GOT WORRIED, SO I TRIED TO TALK TO HIM...
AGH... AND IT WENT JUST AS I THOUGHT IT WOULD!
HIS HEART IS COLD AND CUT OFF FROM THE WORLD!
I'VE GOT TO WARM HIM UP!
IT'S MY DUTY, AS CLASS REPRESEN-TATIVE!
JUST BECAUSE YOU'RE DEAD DOESN'T MEAN YOUR LIFE IS OVER!
WHIP
HANG ON, KOIDE-KUN!
I'LL SAVE YOU!
DASH
WHO WAS THAT...?

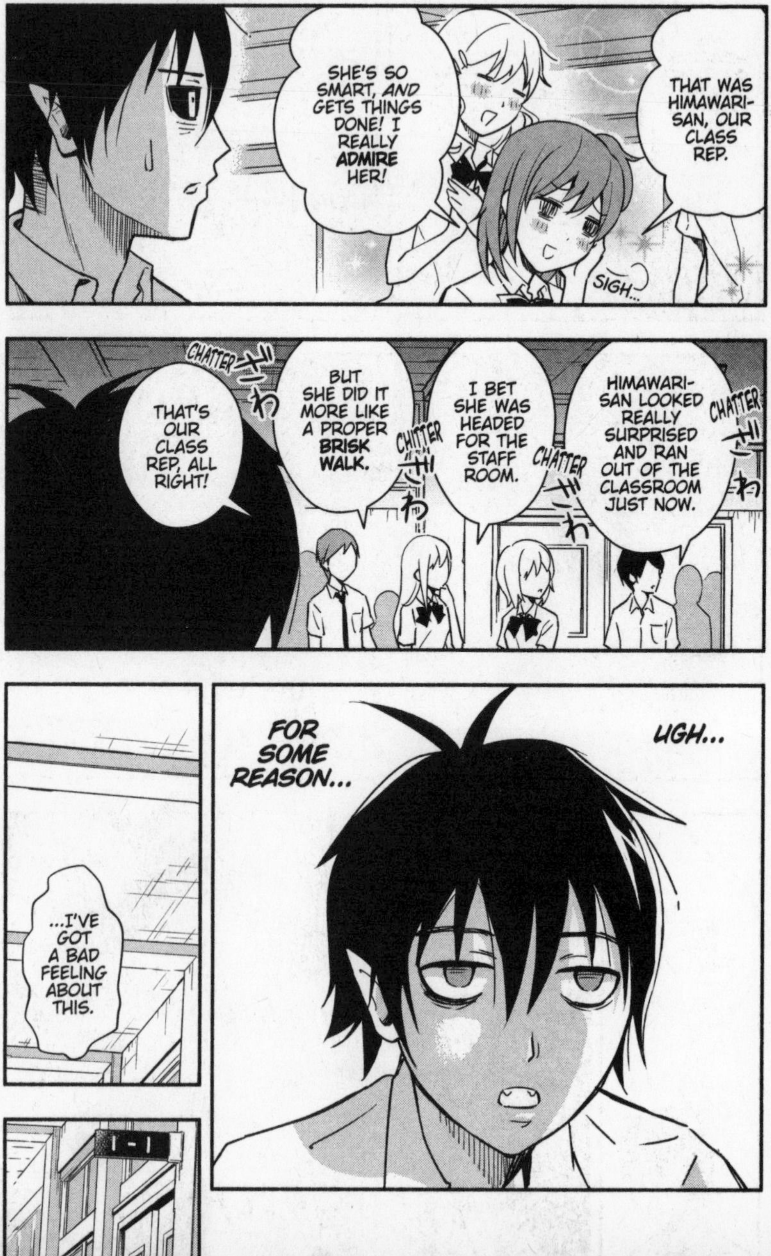
THAT WAS HIMAWARI-SAN, OUR CLASS REP.
SIGH...
SHE'S SO SMART, AND GETS THINGS DONE! I REALLY ADMIRE HER!
CHATTER
HIMAWARI-SAN LOOKED REALLY SURPRISED AND RAN OUT OF THE CLASSROOM JUST NOW.
CHATTER
I BET SHE WAS HEADED FOR THE STAFF ROOM.
CHITTER
BUT SHE DID IT MORE LIKE A PROPER BRISK WALK.
CHATTER
THAT'S OUR CLASS REP, ALL RIGHT!
UGH...
FOR SOME REASON...
...I'VE GOT A BAD FEELING ABOUT THIS.
1-1

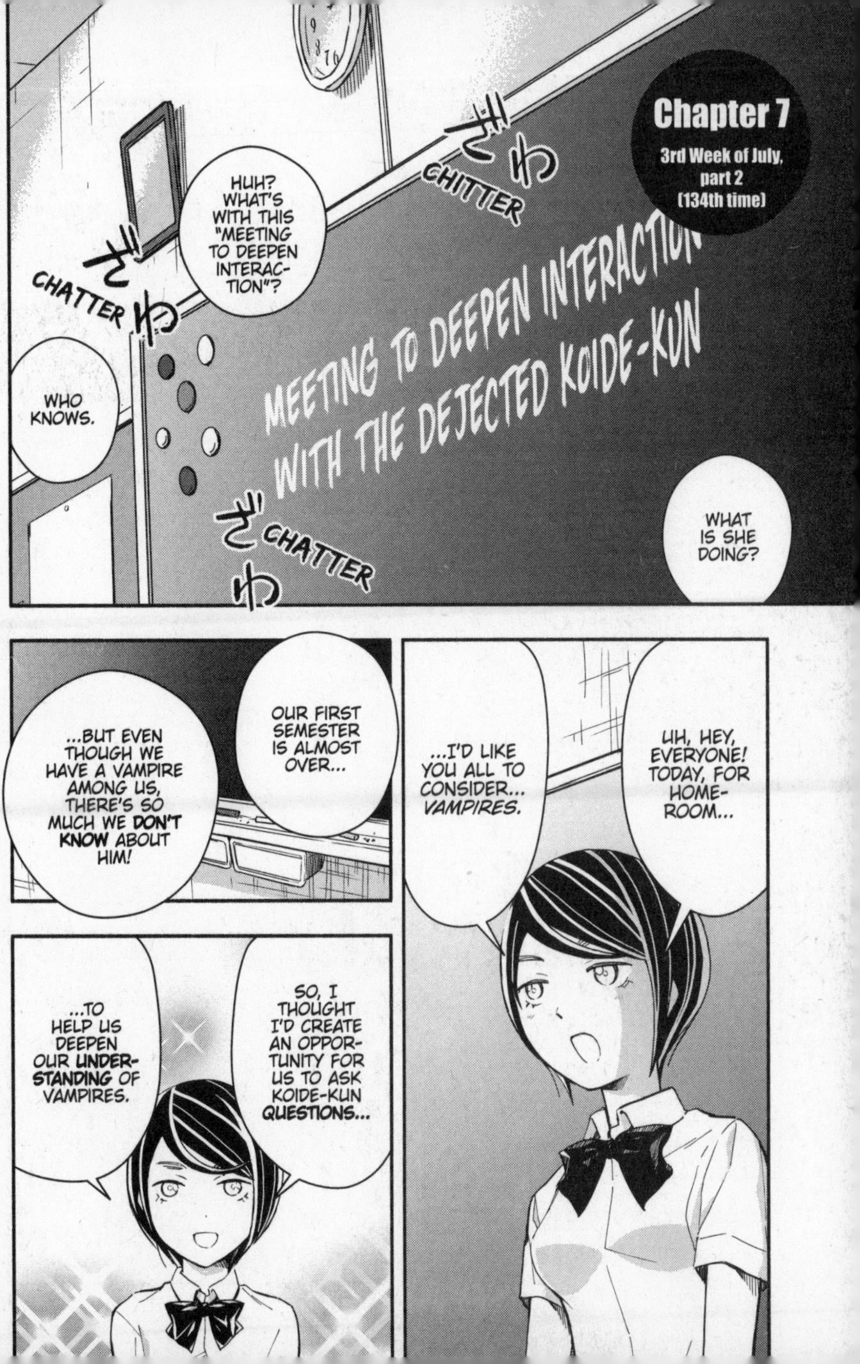
Chapter 7
3rd Week of July, part 2 (134th time)
ざわ
CHITTER
HUH? WHAT'S WITH THIS "MEETING TO DEEPEN INTERACTION"?
MEETING TO DEEPEN INTERACTION WITH THE DEJECTED KOIDE-KUN
ざわ
CHATTER
WHAT IS SHE DOING?
WHO KNOWS.
ざわ
CHATTER
UH, HEY, EVERYONE! TODAY, FOR HOMEROOM...
...I'D LIKE YOU ALL TO CONSIDER... VAMPIRES.
OUR FIRST SEMESTER IS ALMOST OVER...
...BUT EVEN THOUGH WE HAVE A VAMPIRE AMONG US, THERE'S SO MUCH WE DON'T KNOW ABOUT HIM!
SO, I THOUGHT I'D CREATE AN OPPORTUNITY FOR US TO ASK KOIDE-KUN QUESTIONS...
...TO HELP US DEEPEN OUR UNDERSTANDING OF VAMPIRES.

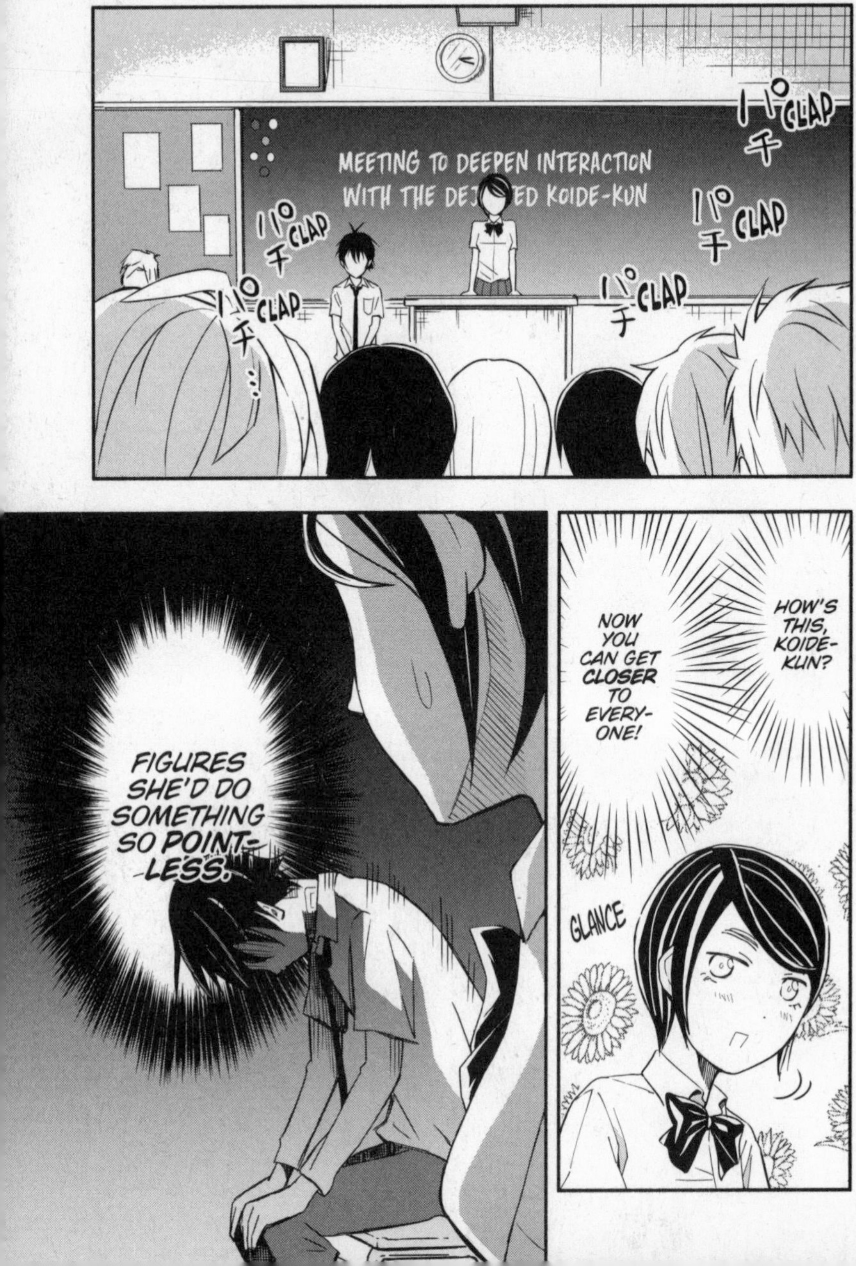
パチ CLAP
MEETING TO DEEPEN INTERACTION
WITH THE DEJ ED KOIDE-KUN
パチ CLAP
パチ CLAP
パチ CLAP
パチ CLAP
HOW'S THIS, KOIDE-KUN?
NOW YOU CAN GET CLOSER TO EVERYONE!
GLANCE
FIGURES SHE'D DO SOMETHING SO POINTLESS.

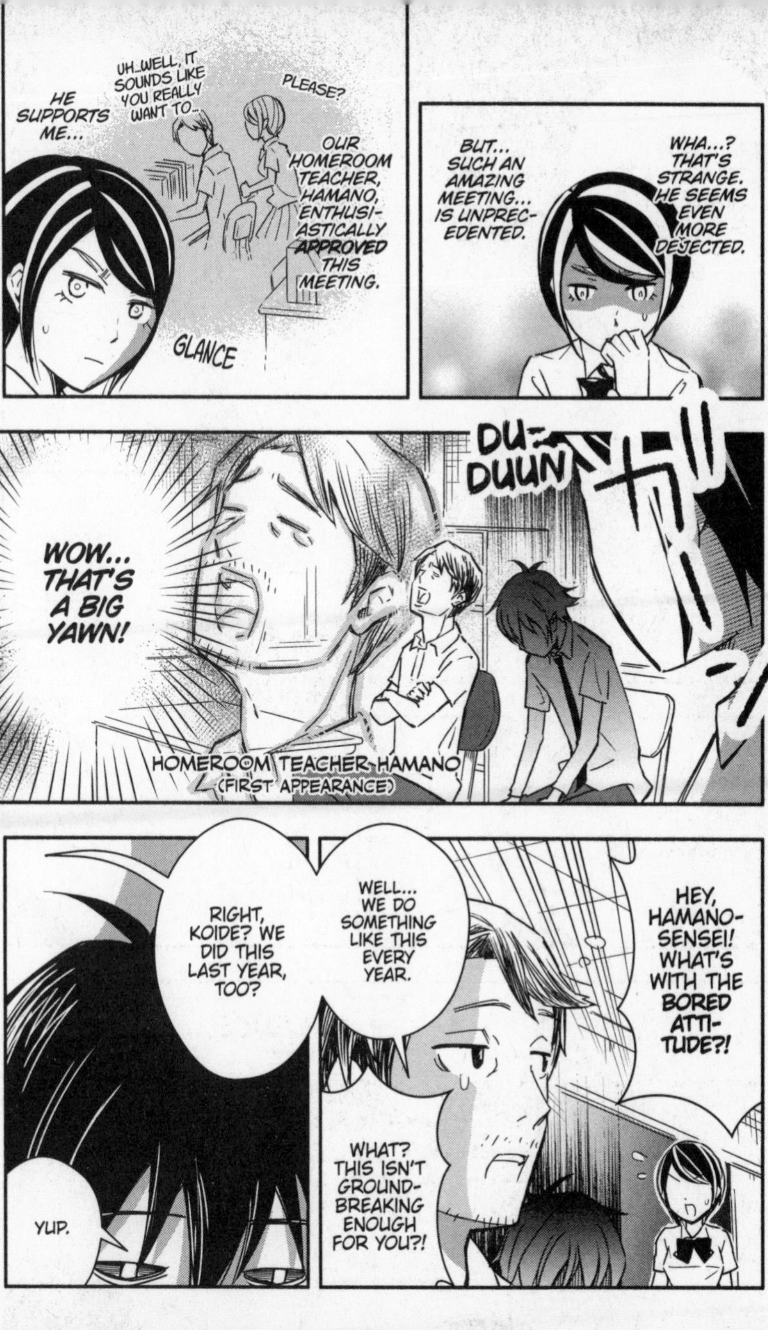
WHA...? THAT'S STRANGE. HE SEEMS EVEN MORE DEJECTED.
BUT... SUCH AN AMAZING MEETING... IS UNPRECEDENTED.
OUR HOMEROOM TEACHER, HAMANO, ENTHUSIASTICALLY APPROVED THIS MEETING.
PLEASE?
UH..WELL, IT SOUNDS LIKE YOU REALLY WANT TO..
HE SUPPORTS ME...
GLANCE
DU-DUUN
WOW... THAT'S A BIG YAWN!
HOMEROOM TEACHER HAMANO
(FIRST APPEARANCE)
HEY, HAMANO-SENSEI! WHAT'S WITH THE BORED ATTITUDE?!
WELL... WE DO SOMETHING LIKE THIS EVERY YEAR.
WHAT? THIS ISN'T GROUNDBREAKING ENOUGH FOR YOU?!
RIGHT, KOIDE? WE DID THIS LAST YEAR, TOO?
YUP.

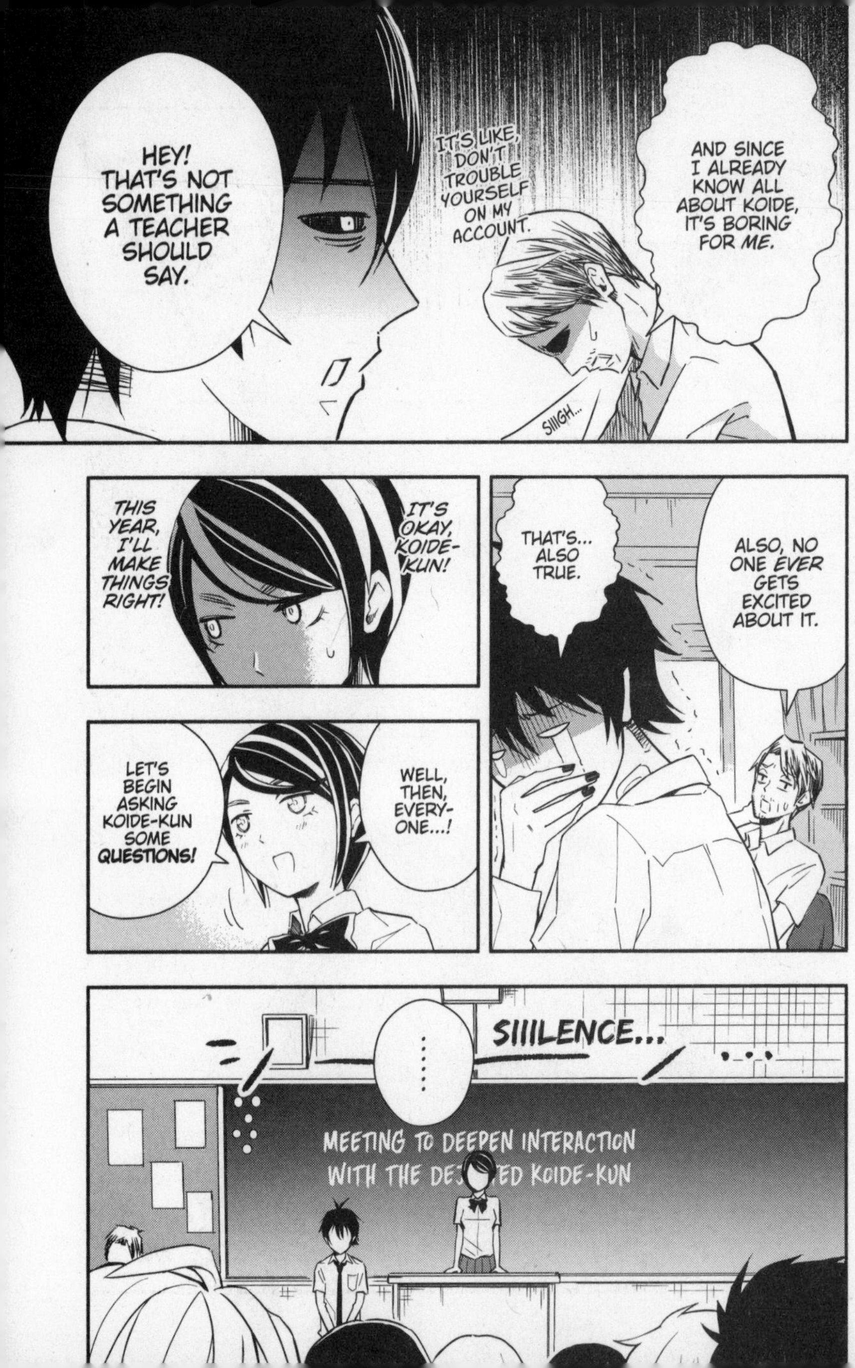
AND SINCE I ALREADY KNOW ALL ABOUT KOIDE, IT'S BORING FOR ME.
IT'S LIKE, DON'T TROUBLE YOURSELF ON MY ACCOUNT.
HEY! THAT'S NOT SOMETHING A TEACHER SHOULD SAY.
SIIIGH...
ALSO, NO ONE EVER GETS EXCITED ABOUT IT.
THAT'S... ALSO TRUE.
IT'S OKAY, KOIDE-KUN!
THIS YEAR, I'LL MAKE THINGS RIGHT!
WELL, THEN, EVERYONE...!
LET'S BEGIN ASKING KOIDE-KUN SOME QUESTIONS!
......
SIIILENCE...
MEETING TO DEEPEN INTERACTION
WITH THE DES ED KOIDE-KUN

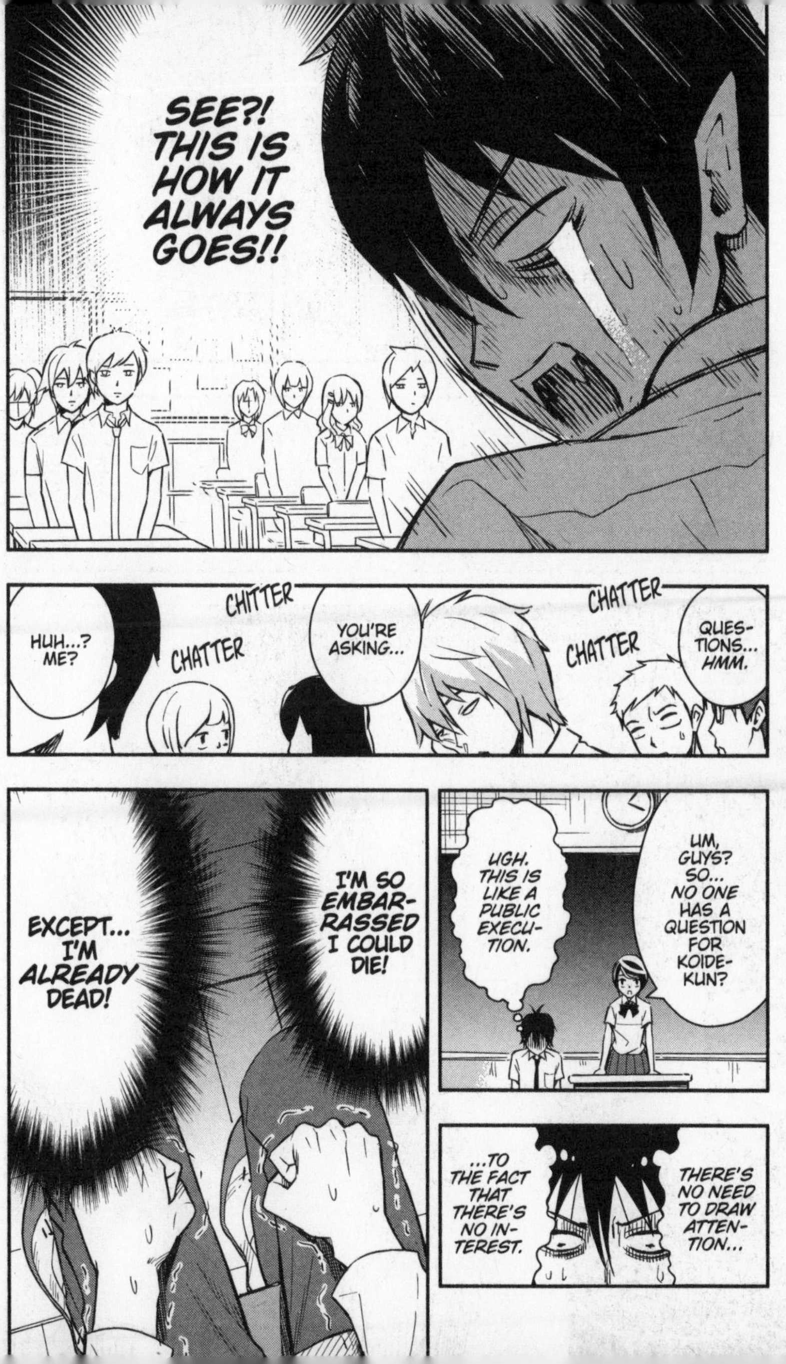
SEE?! THIS IS HOW IT ALWAYS GOES!!
QUES-TIONS... HMM.
CHATTER
CHATTER
YOU'RE ASKING...
CHITTER
CHATTER
HUH...? ME?
UM, GUYS? SO... NO ONE HAS A QUESTION FOR KOIDE-KUN?
UGH. THIS IS LIKE A PUBLIC EXECU-TION.
THERE'S NO NEED TO DRAW ATTEN-TION...
...TO THE FACT THAT THERE'S NO IN-TEREST.
I'M SO EMBAR-RASSED I COULD DIE!
EXCEPT... I'M ALREADY DEAD!

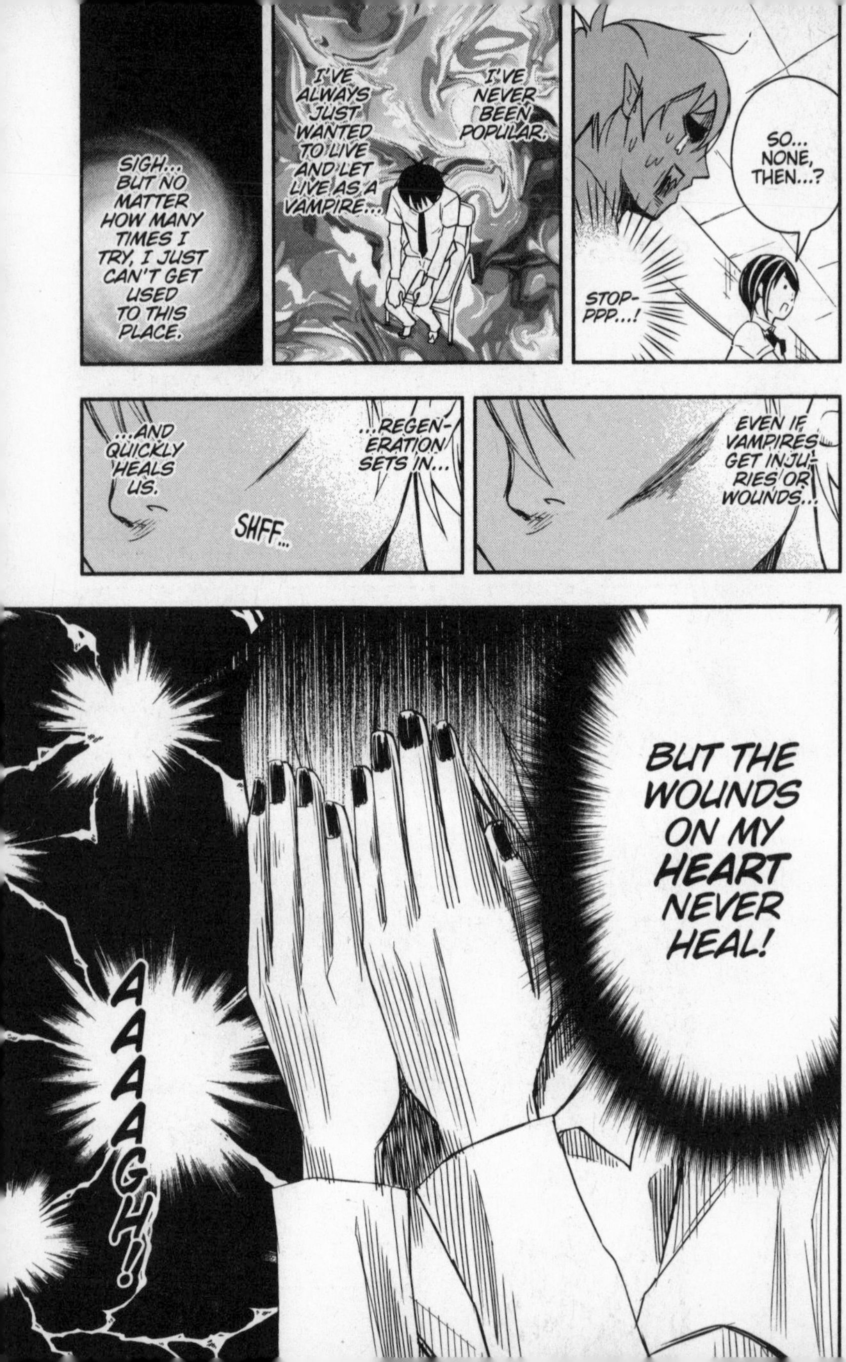
SO... NONE, THEN...?
STOP-PPP...!
I'VE NEVER BEEN POPULAR.
I'VE ALWAYS JUST WANTED TO LIVE AND LET LIVE AS A VAMPIRE...
SIGH... BUT NO MATTER HOW MANY TIMES I TRY, I JUST CAN'T GET USED TO THIS PLACE.
EVEN IF VAMPIRES GET INJURIES OR WOUNDS...
...REGENERATION SETS IN...
...AND QUICKLY HEALS US.
SHFF...
BUT THE WOUNDS ON MY HEART NEVER HEAL!
AAAAAGH!

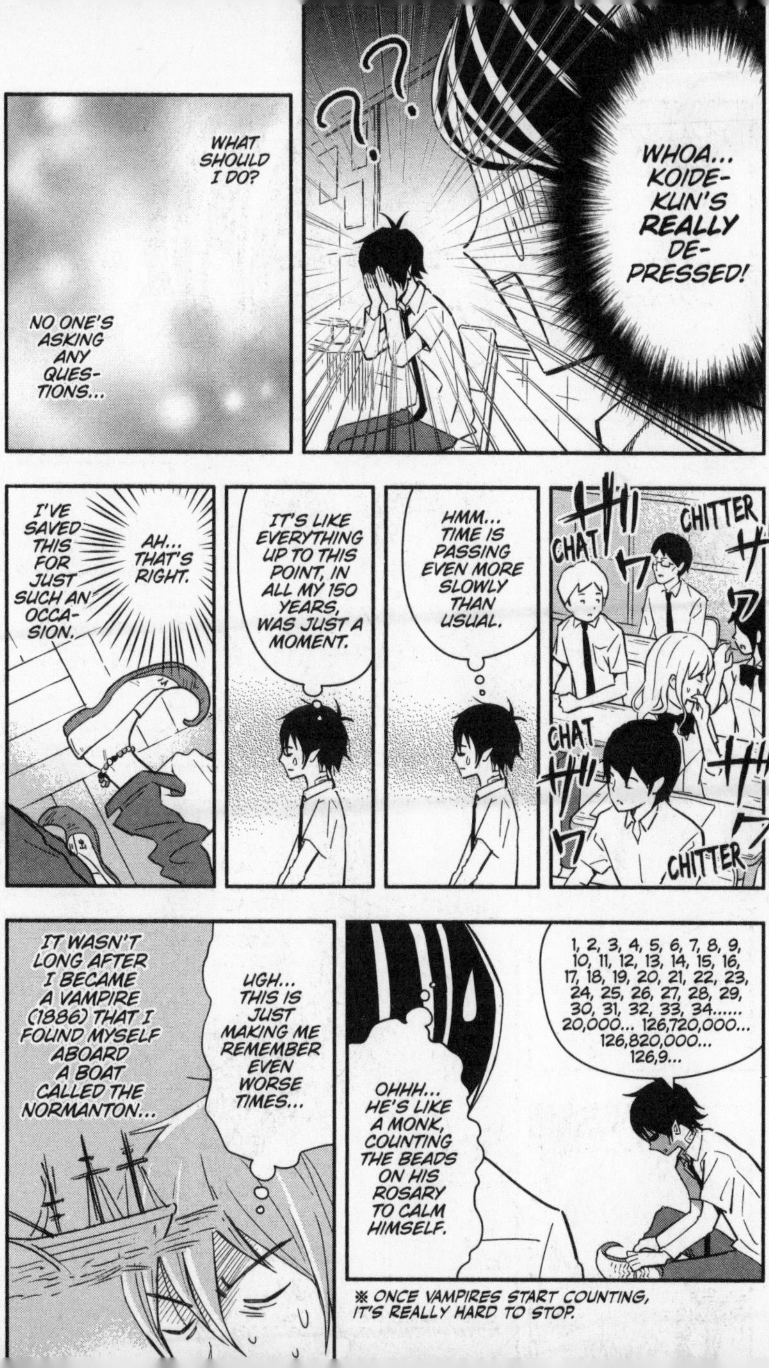
??
WHOA... KOIDE-KUN'S REALLY DE-PRESSED!
WHAT SHOULD I DO?
NO ONE'S ASKING ANY QUES-TIONS...
CHITTER
CHAT
CHAT
CHITTER
HMM... TIME IS PASSING EVEN MORE SLOWLY THAN USUAL.
IT'S LIKE EVERYTHING UP TO THIS POINT, IN ALL MY 150 YEARS, WAS JUST A MOMENT.
AH... THAT'S RIGHT.
I'VE SAVED THIS FOR JUST SUCH AN OCCA-SION.
1, 2, 3, 4, 5, 6, 7, 8, 9, 10, 11, 12, 13, 14, 15, 16, 17, 18, 19, 20, 21, 22, 23, 24, 25, 26, 27, 28, 29, 30, 31, 32, 33, 34...... 20,000... 126,720,000... 126,820,000... 126,9...
OHHH... HE'S LIKE A MONK, COUNTING THE BEADS ON HIS ROSARY TO CALM HIMSELF.
※ ONCE VAMPIRES START COUNTING, IT'S REALLY HARD TO STOP.
UGH... THIS IS JUST MAKING ME REMEMBER EVEN WORSE TIMES...
IT WASN'T LONG AFTER I BECAME A VAMPIRE (1886) THAT I FOUND MYSELF ABOARD A BOAT CALLED THE NORMANTON...

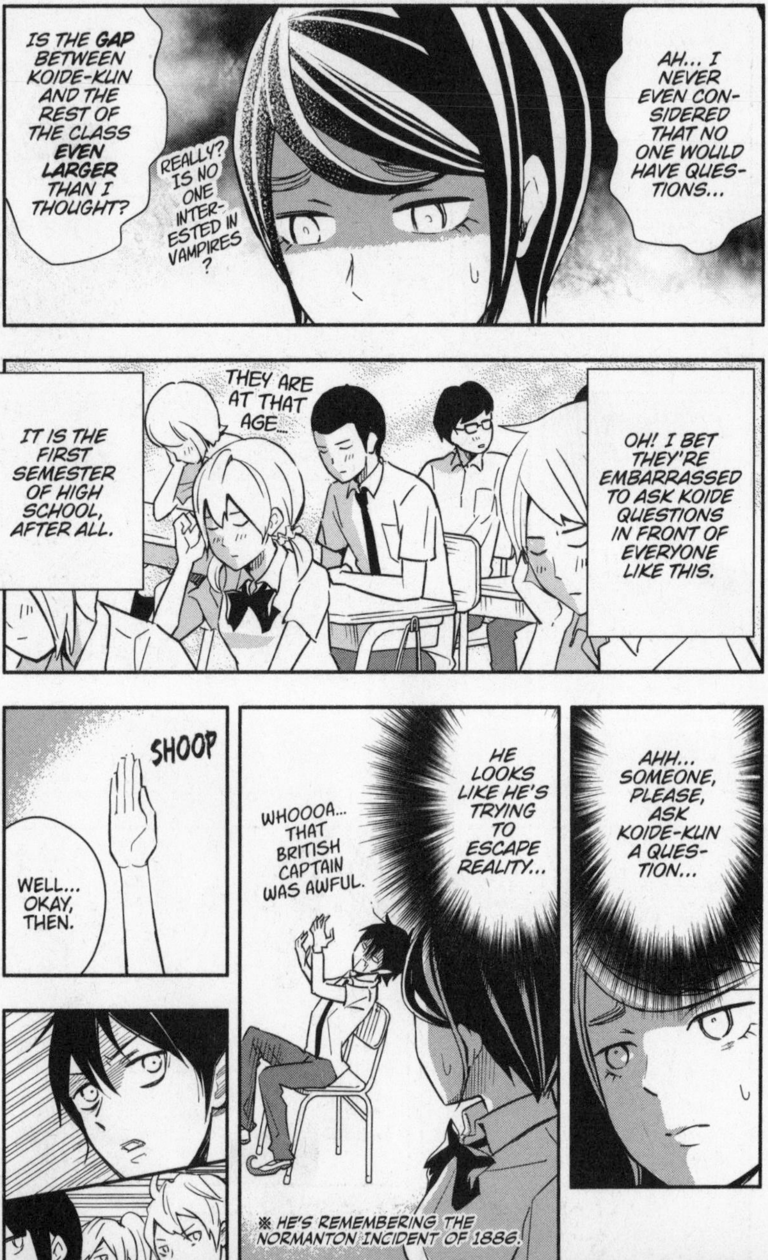
AH... I NEVER EVEN CONSIDERED THAT NO ONE WOULD HAVE QUESTIONS...
REALLY? IS NO ONE INTERESTED IN VAMPIRES?
IS THE **GAP** BETWEEN KOIDE-KUN AND THE REST OF THE CLASS **EVEN LARGER** THAN I THOUGHT?
OH! I BET THEY'RE EMBARRASSED TO ASK KOIDE QUESTIONS IN FRONT OF EVERYONE LIKE THIS.
THEY ARE AT THAT AGE...
IT IS THE FIRST SEMESTER OF HIGH SCHOOL, AFTER ALL.
AHH... SOMEONE, PLEASE, ASK KOIDE-KUN A QUESTION...
HE LOOKS LIKE HE'S TRYING TO ESCAPE REALITY...
WHOOOA... THAT BRITISH CAPTAIN WAS AWFUL.
※ HE'S REMEMBERING THE NORMANTON INCIDENT OF 1886.
SHOOP
WELL... OKAY, THEN.

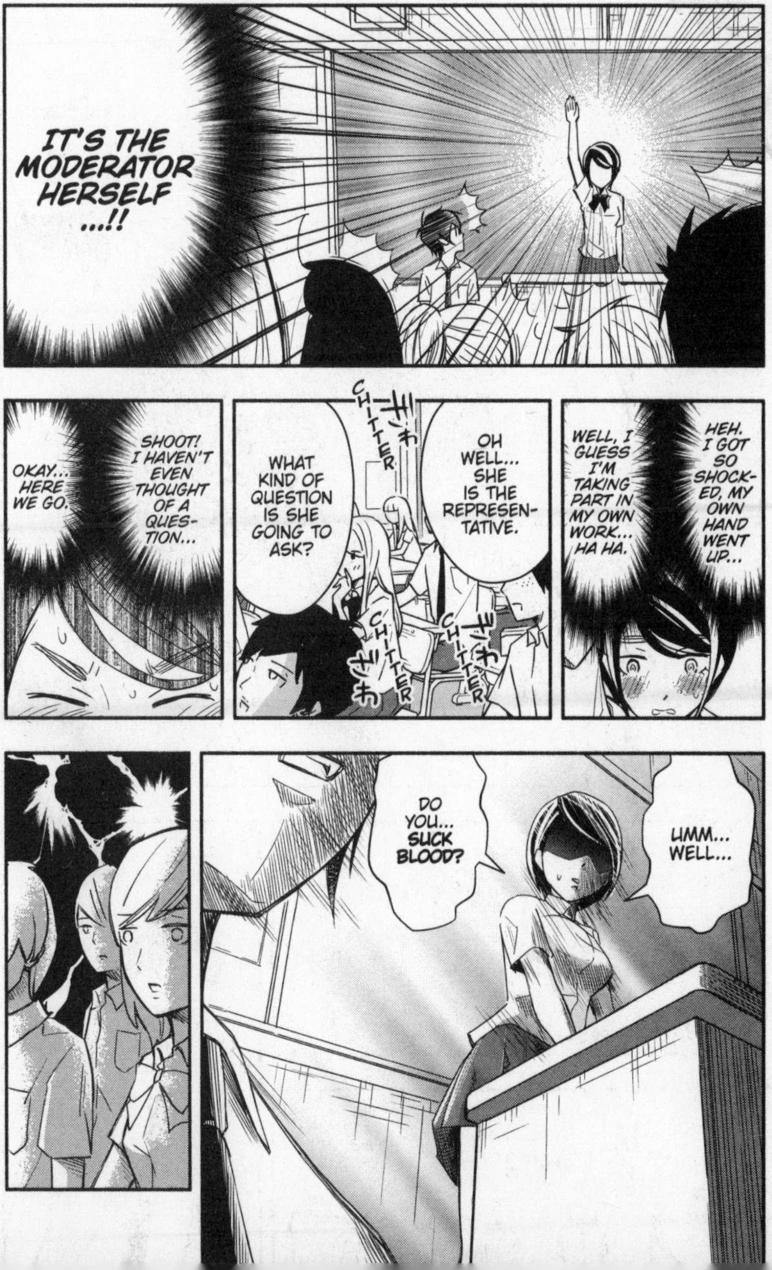
IT'S THE MODERATOR HERSELF ...!!
HEH. I GOT SO SHOCKED, MY OWN HAND WENT UP...
WELL, I GUESS I'M TAKING PART IN MY OWN WORK... HA HA.
OH WELL... SHE IS THE REPRESENTATIVE.
CHITTER
WHAT KIND OF QUESTION IS SHE GOING TO ASK?
CHITTER
CHITTER
SHOOT! I HAVEN'T EVEN THOUGHT OF A QUESTION...
OKAY... HERE WE GO.
UMM... WELL...
DO YOU... SUCK BLOOD?

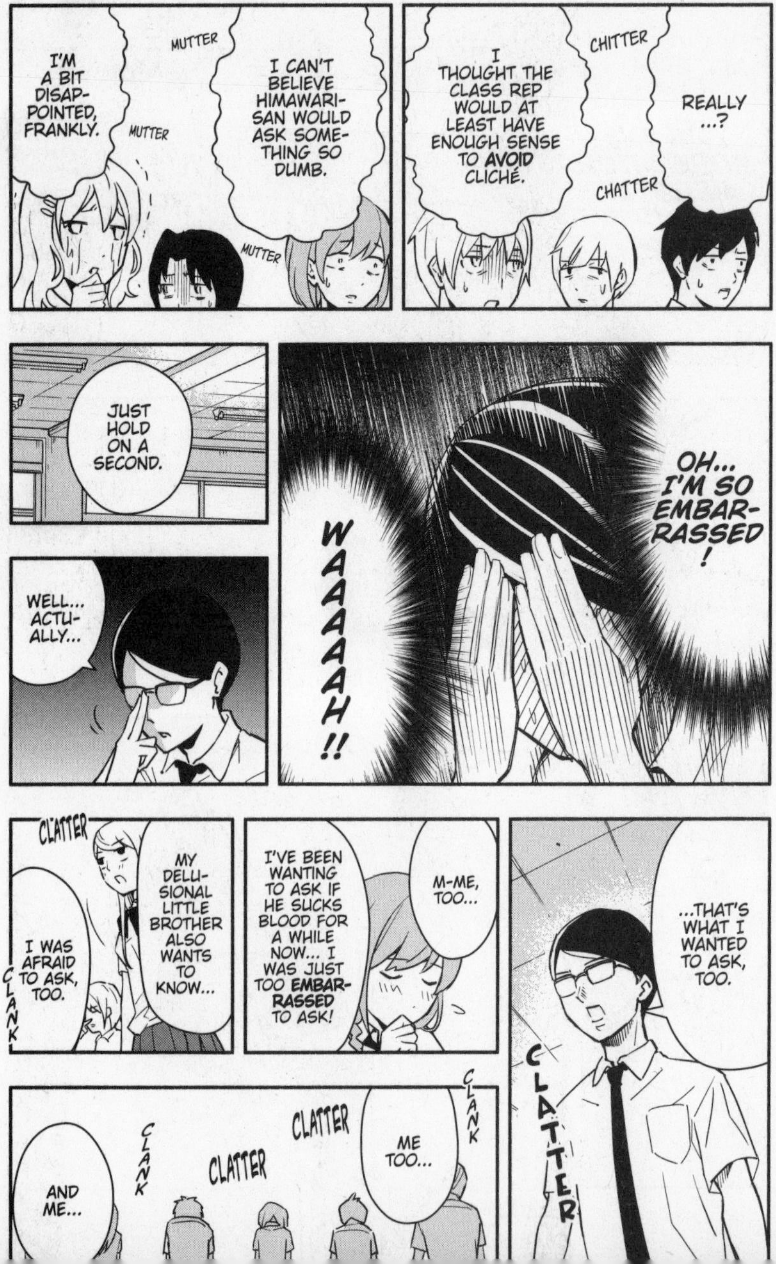
REALLY ...?
CHITTER
I THOUGHT THE CLASS REP WOULD AT LEAST HAVE ENOUGH SENSE TO **AVOID** CLICHÉ.
CHATTER
I CAN'T BELIEVE HIMAWARI-SAN WOULD ASK SOME-THING SO DUMB.
MUTTER
I'M A BIT DISAP-POINTED, FRANKLY.
MUTTER
MUTTER
OH... I'M SO EMBAR-RASSED!
WAAAAAAH!!
JUST HOLD ON A SECOND.
WELL... ACTU-ALLY...
...THAT'S WHAT I WANTED TO ASK, TOO.
CLATTER
M-ME, TOO...
I'VE BEEN WANTING TO ASK IF HE SUCKS BLOOD FOR A WHILE NOW... I WAS JUST TOO **EMBAR-RASSED** TO ASK!
MY DELU-SIONAL LITTLE BROTHER ALSO WANTS TO KNOW...
CLATTER
I WAS AFRAID TO ASK, TOO.
CLANK
CLANK
ME TOO...
CLATTER
CLATTER
CLANK
AND ME...

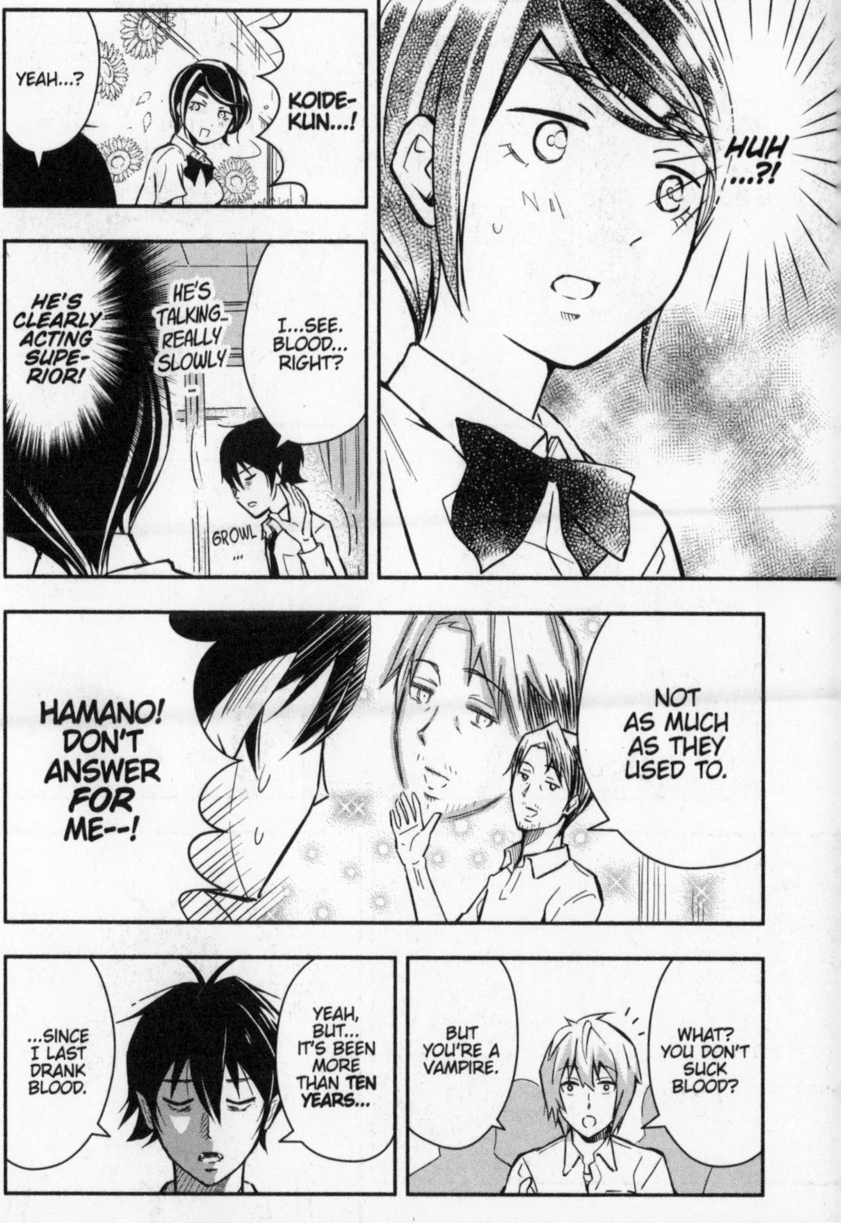
HUH ...?!
KOIDE-KUN...!
YEAH...?
I...SEE. BLOOD... RIGHT?
HE'S TALKING.. REALLY SLOWLY...
HE'S CLEARLY ACTING SUPERIOR!
GROWL ...
NOT AS MUCH AS THEY USED TO.
HAMANO! DON'T ANSWER FOR ME--!
WHAT? YOU DON'T SUCK BLOOD?
BUT YOU'RE A VAMPIRE.
YEAH, BUT... IT'S BEEN MORE THAN TEN YEARS...
...SINCE I LAST DRANK BLOOD.

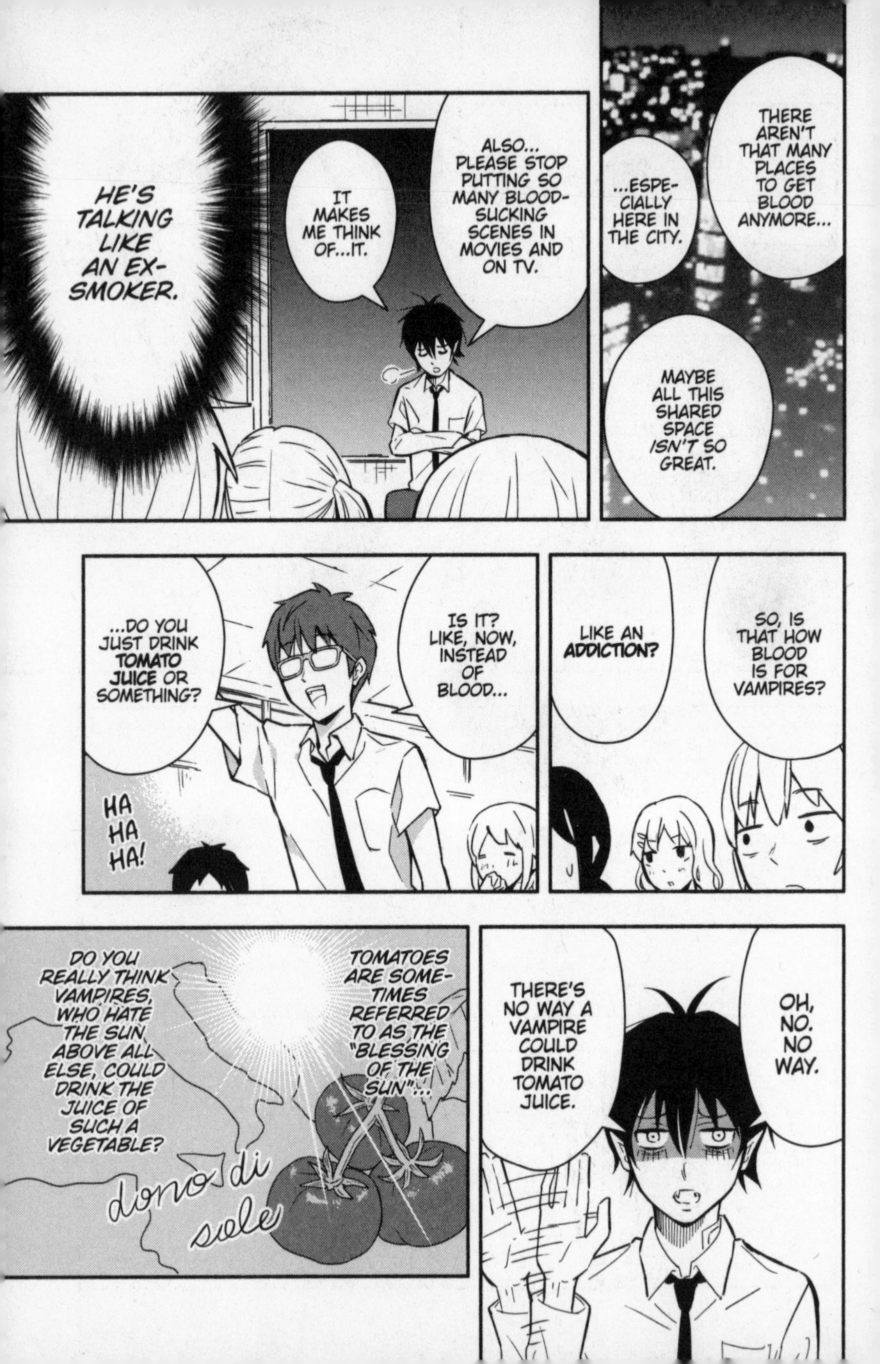
THERE AREN'T THAT MANY PLACES TO GET BLOOD ANYMORE...
...ESPE-CIALLY HERE IN THE CITY.
MAYBE ALL THIS SHARED SPACE ISN'T SO GREAT.
ALSO... PLEASE STOP PUTTING SO MANY BLOOD-SUCKING SCENES IN MOVIES AND ON TV.
IT MAKES ME THINK OF...IT.
HE'S TALKING LIKE AN EX-SMOKER.
SO, IS THAT HOW BLOOD IS FOR VAMPIRES?
LIKE AN ADDICTION?
IS IT? LIKE, NOW, INSTEAD OF BLOOD...
...DO YOU JUST DRINK TOMATO JUICE OR SOMETHING?
HA HA HA!
OH, NO. NO WAY.
THERE'S NO WAY A VAMPIRE COULD DRINK TOMATO JUICE.
TOMATOES ARE SOME-TIMES REFERRED TO AS THE "BLESSING OF THE SUN"...
DO YOU REALLY THINK VAMPIRES, WHO HATE THE SUN, ABOVE ALL ELSE, COULD DRINK THE JUICE OF SUCH A VEGETABLE?
dono di sole

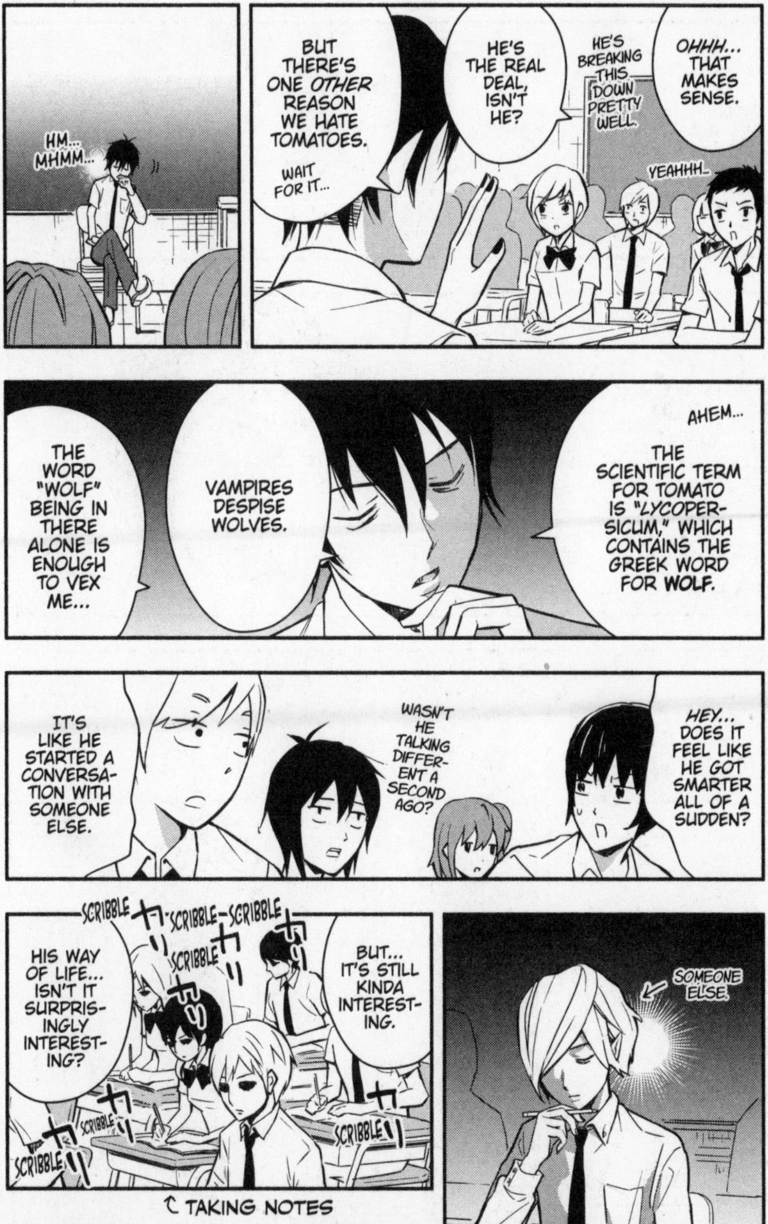
OHHH... THAT MAKES SENSE.
YEAHHH...
HE'S BREAKING THIS DOWN PRETTY WELL.
HE'S THE REAL DEAL, ISN'T HE?
BUT THERE'S ONE *OTHER* REASON WE HATE TOMATOES.
WAIT FOR IT...
HM... MHMM...
AHEM...
THE SCIENTIFIC TERM FOR TOMATO IS "*LYCOPERSICUM*," WHICH CONTAINS THE GREEK WORD FOR **WOLF**.
VAMPIRES DESPISE WOLVES.
THE WORD "WOLF" BEING IN THERE ALONE IS ENOUGH TO VEX ME...
HEY... DOES IT FEEL LIKE HE GOT SMARTER ALL OF A SUDDEN?
WASN'T HE TALKING DIFFERENT A SECOND AGO?
IT'S LIKE HE STARTED A CONVERSATION WITH SOMEONE ELSE.
SOMEONE ELSE.
SCRIBBLE
SCRIBBLE
SCRIBBLE
SCRIBBLE
BUT... IT'S STILL KINDA INTERESTING.
HIS WAY OF LIFE... ISN'T IT SURPRISINGLY INTERESTING?
SCRIBBLE
SCRIBBLE
SCRIBBLE
TAKING NOTES

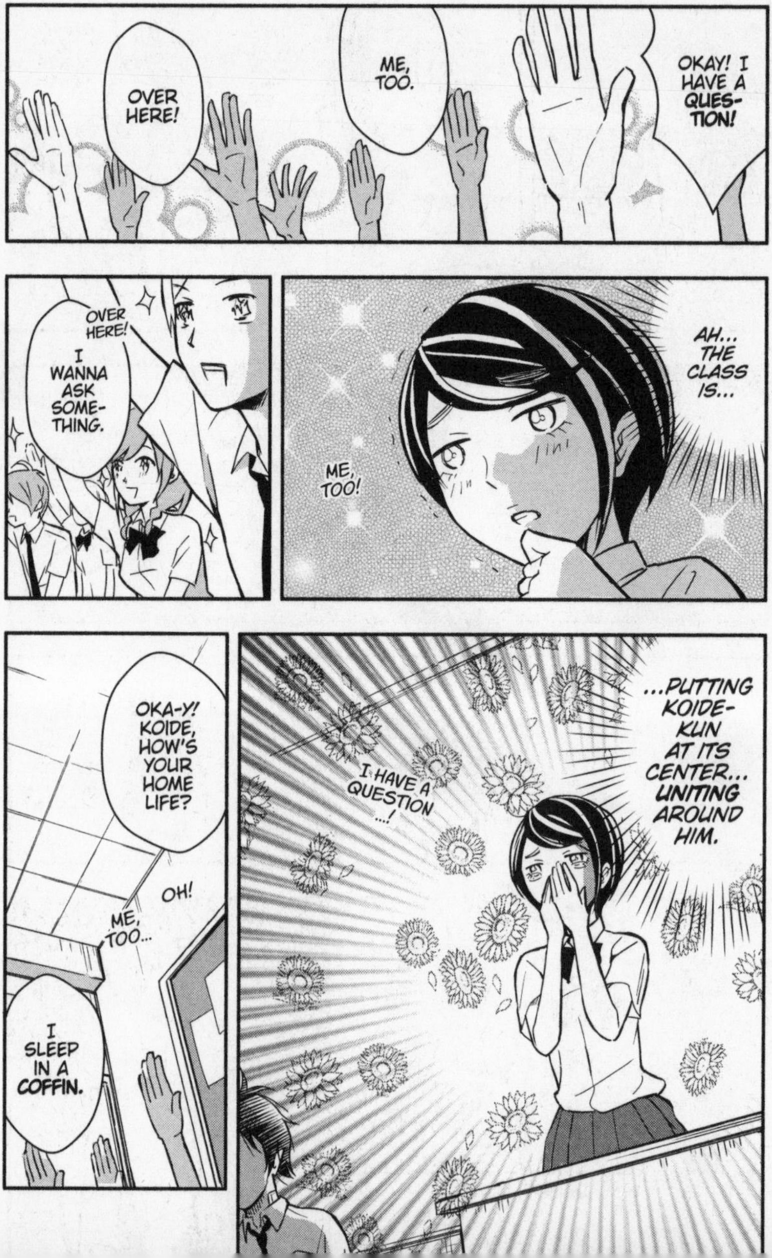
OKAY! I HAVE A QUESTION!
ME, TOO.
OVER HERE!
AH... THE CLASS IS...
ME, TOO!
OVER HERE! I WANNA ASK SOMETHING.
...PUTTING KOIDE-KUN AT ITS CENTER... UNITING AROUND HIM.
I HAVE A QUESTION ...!
OKA-Y! KOIDE, HOW'S YOUR HOME LIFE?
OH!
ME, TOO...
I SLEEP IN A COFFIN.

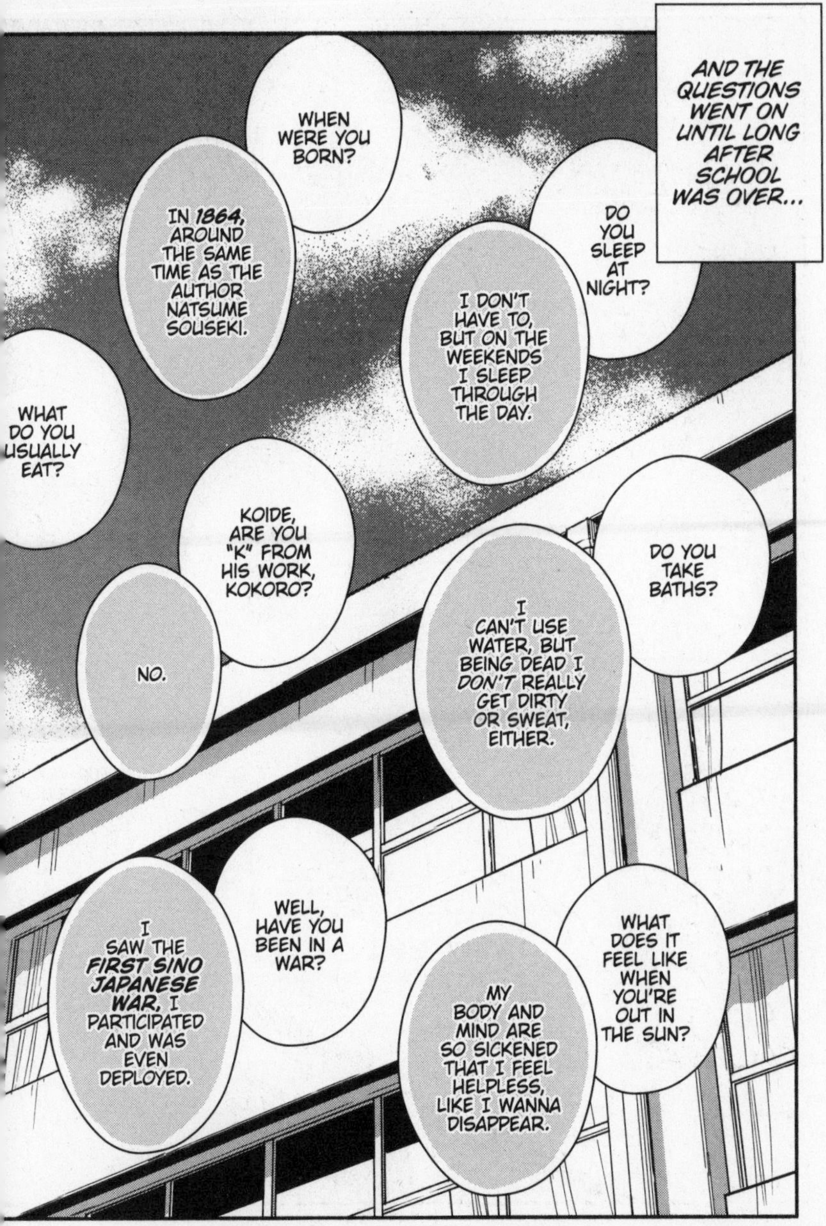
AND THE QUESTIONS WENT ON UNTIL LONG AFTER SCHOOL WAS OVER...
WHEN WERE YOU BORN?
IN *1864,* AROUND THE SAME TIME AS THE AUTHOR NATSUME SOUSEKI.
KOIDE, ARE YOU "K" FROM HIS WORK, KOKORO?
NO.
DO YOU SLEEP AT NIGHT?
I DON'T HAVE TO, BUT ON THE WEEKENDS I SLEEP THROUGH THE DAY.
WHAT DO YOU USUALLY EAT?
DO YOU TAKE BATHS?
I CAN'T USE WATER, BUT BEING DEAD I *DON'T* REALLY GET DIRTY OR SWEAT, EITHER.
WHAT DOES IT FEEL LIKE WHEN YOU'RE OUT IN THE SUN?
MY BODY AND MIND ARE SO SICKENED THAT I FEEL HELPLESS, LIKE I WANNA DISAPPEAR.
WELL, HAVE YOU BEEN IN A WAR?
I SAW THE *FIRST SINO JAPANESE WAR,* I PARTICIPATED AND WAS EVEN DEPLOYED.

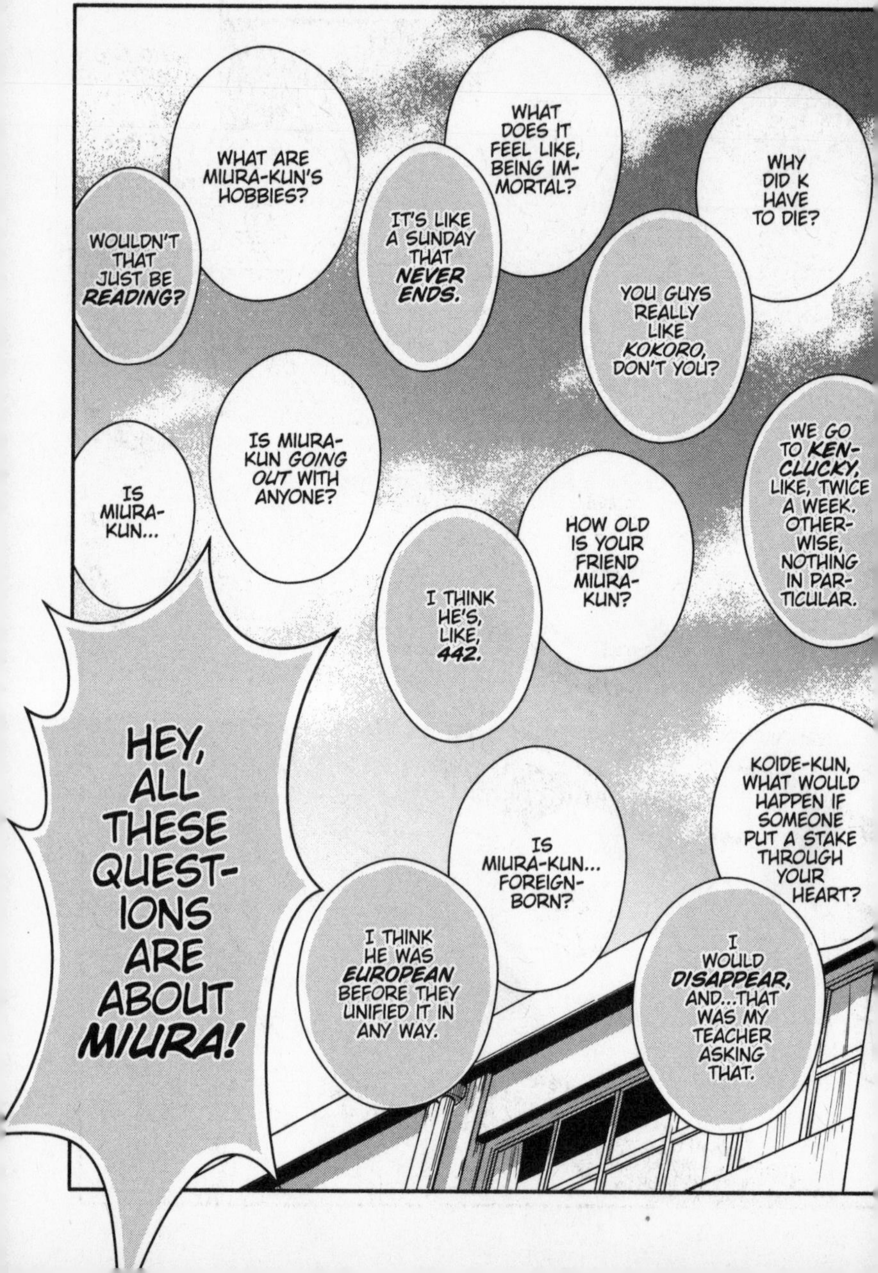

WHY DID K HAVE TO DIE?
YOU GUYS REALLY LIKE KOKORO, DON'T YOU?
WHAT DOES IT FEEL LIKE, BEING IM-MORTAL?
IT'S LIKE A SUNDAY THAT NEVER ENDS.
WHAT ARE MIURA-KUN'S HOBBIES?
WOULDN'T THAT JUST BE READING?
WE GO TO KEN-CLUCKY, LIKE, TWICE A WEEK. OTHER-WISE, NOTHING IN PAR-TICULAR.
HOW OLD IS YOUR FRIEND MIURA-KUN?
I THINK HE'S, LIKE, 442.
IS MIURA-KUN GOING OUT WITH ANYONE?
IS MIURA-KUN...
KOIDE-KUN, WHAT WOULD HAPPEN IF SOMEONE PUT A STAKE THROUGH YOUR HEART?
I WOULD DISAPPEAR, AND...THAT WAS MY TEACHER ASKING THAT.
IS MIURA-KUN... FOREIGN-BORN?
I THINK HE WAS EUROPEAN BEFORE THEY UNIFIED IT IN ANY WAY.
HEY, ALL THESE QUEST-IONS ARE ABOUT MIURA!

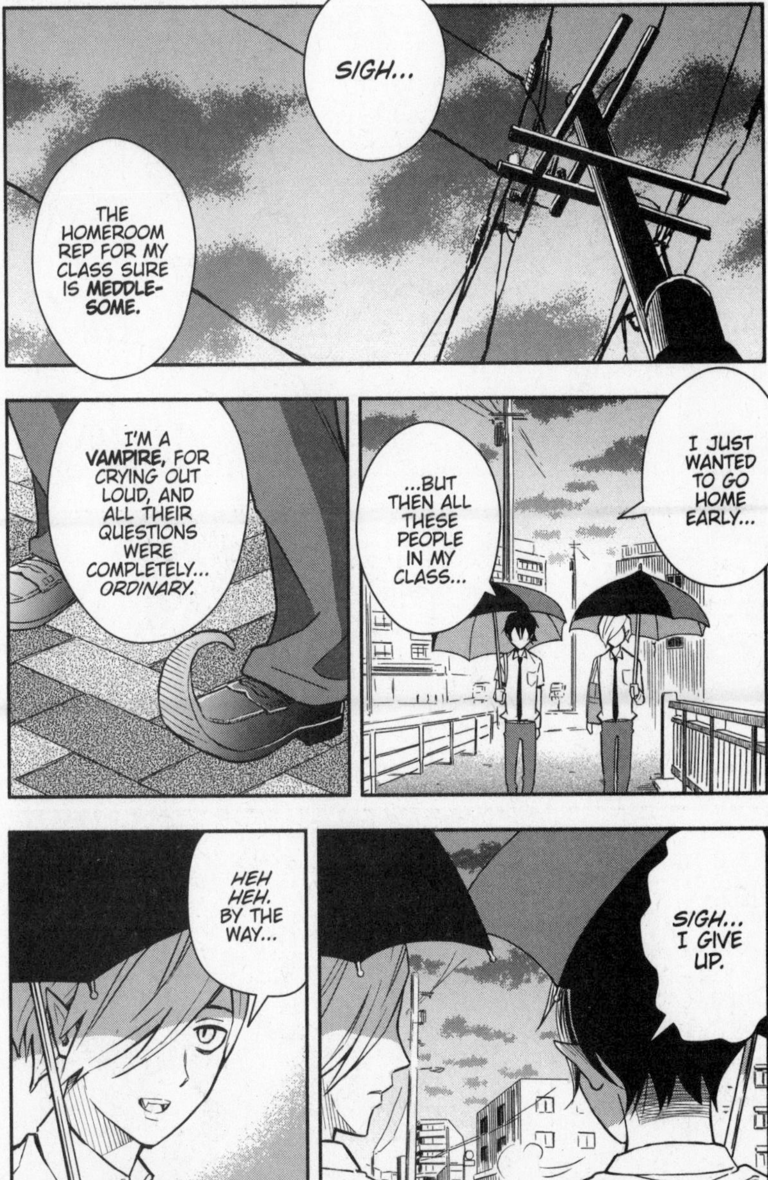
SIGH...
THE HOMEROOM REP FOR MY CLASS SURE IS MEDDLE-SOME.
I JUST WANTED TO GO HOME EARLY...
...BUT THEN ALL THESE PEOPLE IN MY CLASS...
I'M A VAMPIRE, FOR CRYING OUT LOUD, AND ALL THEIR QUESTIONS WERE COMPLETELY... ORDINARY.
SIGH... I GIVE UP.
HEH HEH. BY THE WAY...

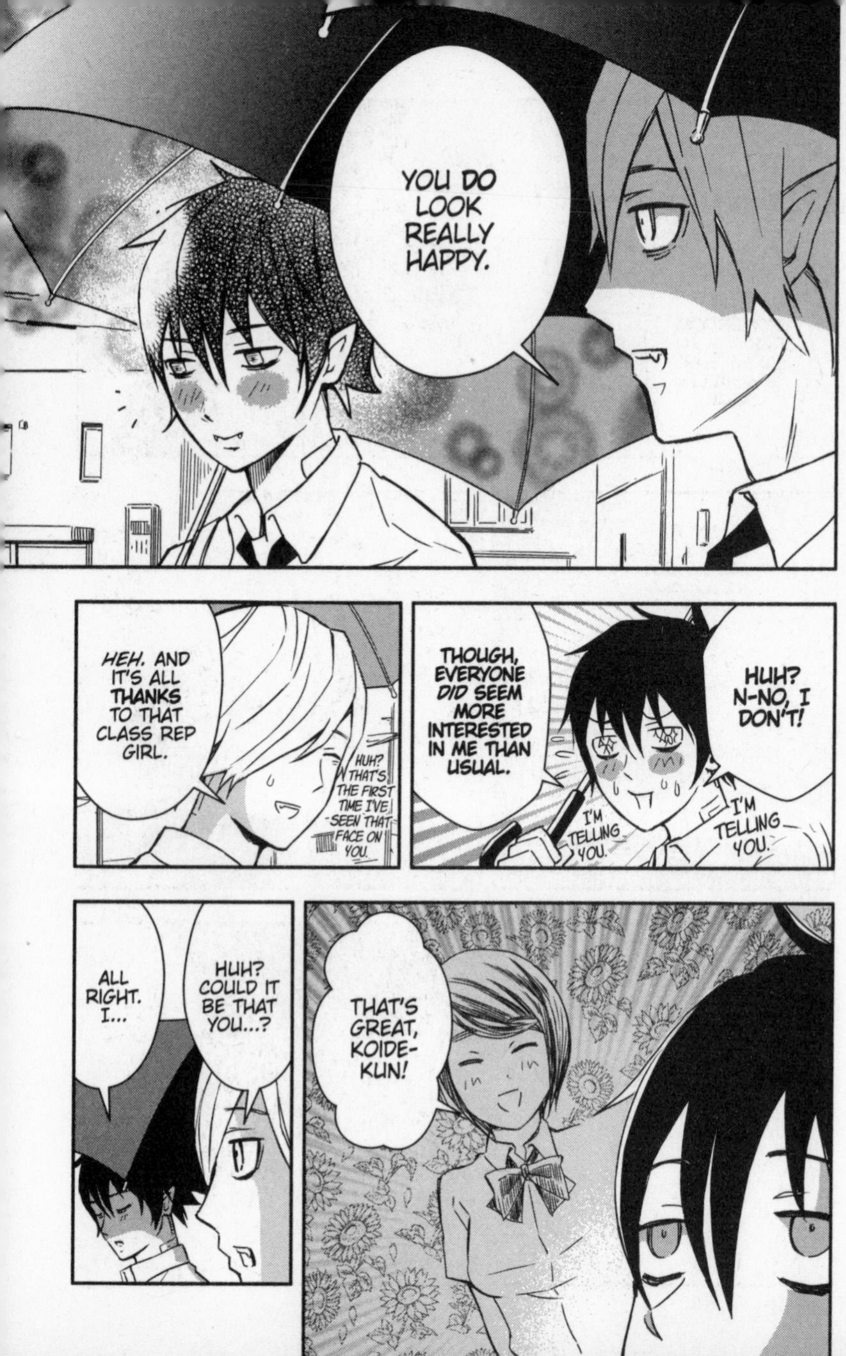
YOU DO LOOK REALLY HAPPY.
HUH? N-NO, I DON'T!
THOUGH, EVERYONE *DID* SEEM MORE INTERESTED IN ME THAN USUAL.
I'M TELLING YOU.
I'M TELLING YOU.
HEH. AND IT'S ALL THANKS TO THAT CLASS REP GIRL.
HUH? THAT'S THE FIRST TIME I'VE SEEN THAT FACE ON YOU.
THAT'S GREAT, KOIDE-KUN!
HUH? COULD IT BE THAT YOU...?
ALL RIGHT. I...

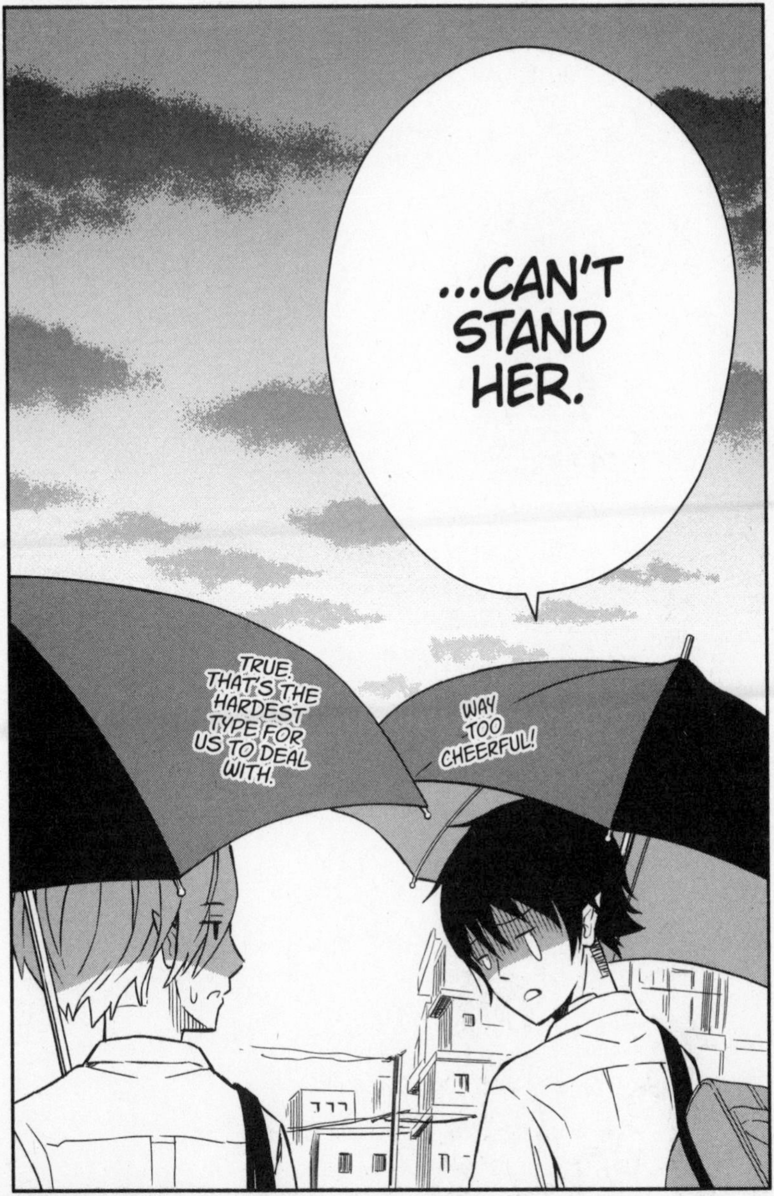
...CAN'T STAND HER.
WAY TOO CHEERFUL!
TRUE. THAT'S THE HARDEST TYPE FOR US TO DEAL WITH.

CHAPTER 7 / END

AND THEN
WE WENT TO
KENCLUCKY
(FIRST TIME IN
A WHILE).

MY PATHETIC VAMPIRE LIFE

🦇 SPEAKING OF NATSUME SOUSEKI...

IT'S WELL-KNOWN THAT, BEGINNING IN 1900, NATSUME SOUSEKI STUDIED ABROAD IN BRITAIN FOR TWO YEARS. BUT APPARENTLY HE SAID THE AIR WAS REALLY BAD IN LONDON, AND FEELING THE AIR POLLUTION WAS SO AWFUL THAT HE AVOIDED THE SUN DURING THE DAY...MAKING HIS EXISTENCE MUCH LIKE A VAMPIRE'S, NO?

COUGH COUGH

SOUSEKI, STUDYING ABROAD. 33-35 YEARS OLD.

MIURA, WHO WAS ALSO IN LONDON AT THE SAME TIME. (REAL NAME: CREMON MUELLER.)

Chapter 8

4th Week of July
(134th time)

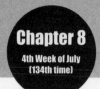

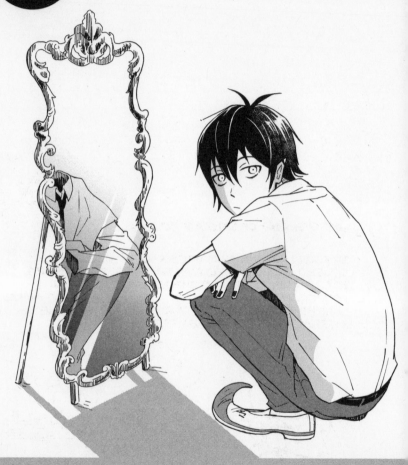

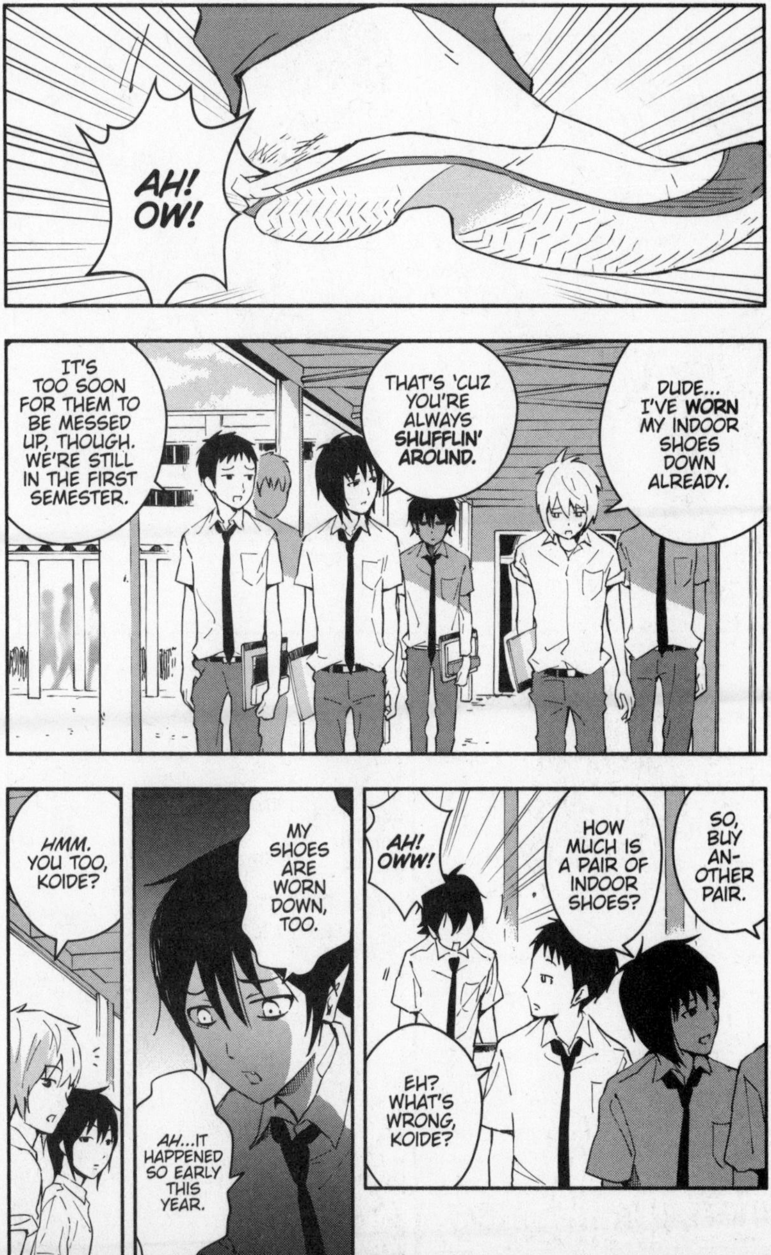
AH! OW!
DUDE... I'VE WORN MY INDOOR SHOES DOWN ALREADY.
THAT'S 'CUZ YOU'RE ALWAYS SHUFFLIN' AROUND.
IT'S TOO SOON FOR THEM TO BE MESSED UP, THOUGH. WE'RE STILL IN THE FIRST SEMESTER.
SO, BUY AN-OTHER PAIR.
HOW MUCH IS A PAIR OF INDOOR SHOES?
AH! OWW!
EH? WHAT'S WRONG, KOIDE?
MY SHOES ARE WORN DOWN, TOO.
AH...IT HAPPENED SO EARLY THIS YEAR.
HMM. YOU TOO, KOIDE?

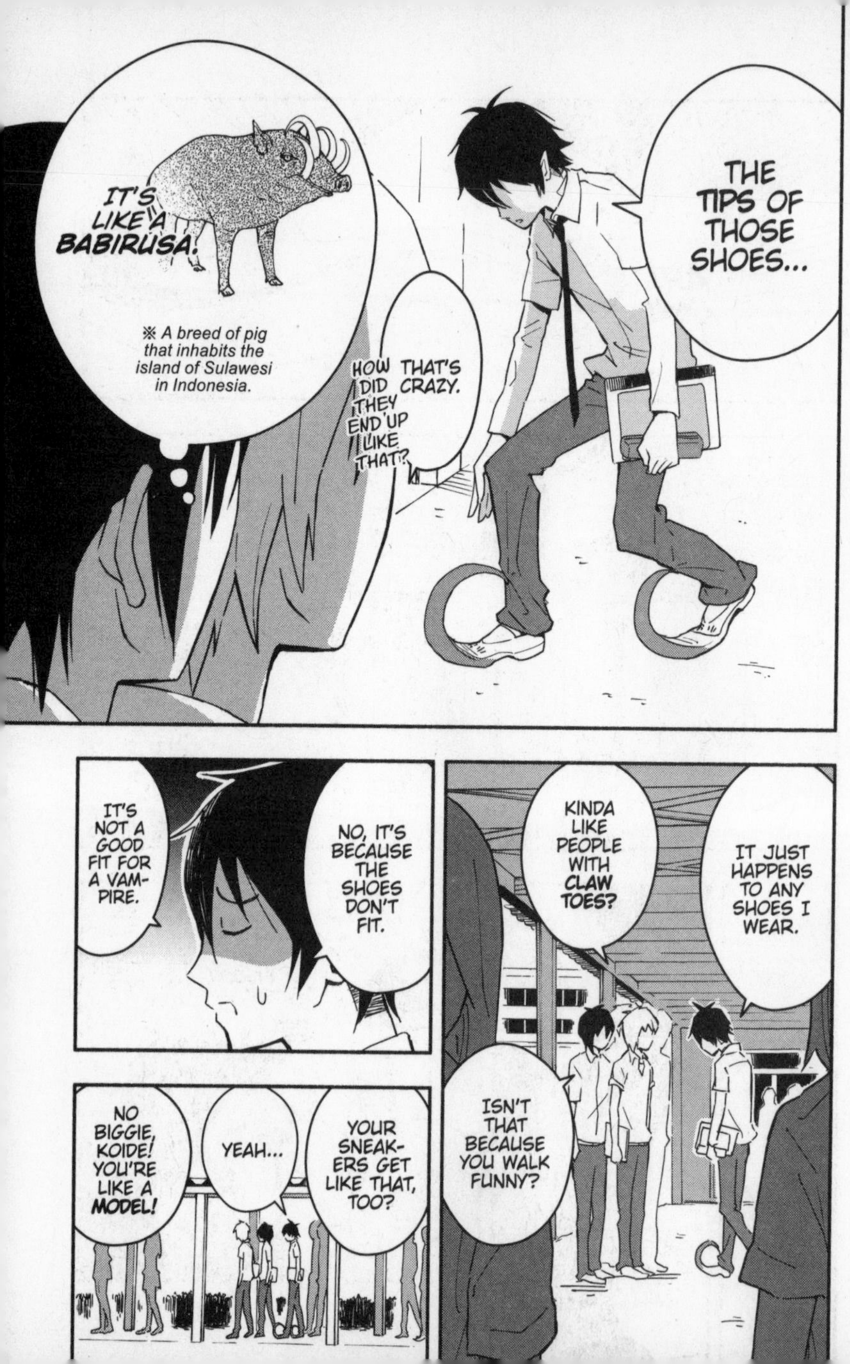
THE TIPS OF THOSE SHOES...
HOW DID THEY END UP LIKE THAT?
THAT'S CRAZY.
IT'S LIKE A BABIRUSA.
※ A breed of pig that inhabits the island of Sulawesi in Indonesia.
IT JUST HAPPENS TO ANY SHOES I WEAR.
KINDA LIKE PEOPLE WITH CLAW TOES?
ISN'T THAT BECAUSE YOU WALK FUNNY?
NO, IT'S BECAUSE THE SHOES DON'T FIT.
IT'S NOT A GOOD FIT FOR A VAM-PIRE.
YOUR SNEAK-ERS GET LIKE THAT, TOO?
YEAH...
NO BIGGIE, KOIDE! YOU'RE LIKE A MODEL!

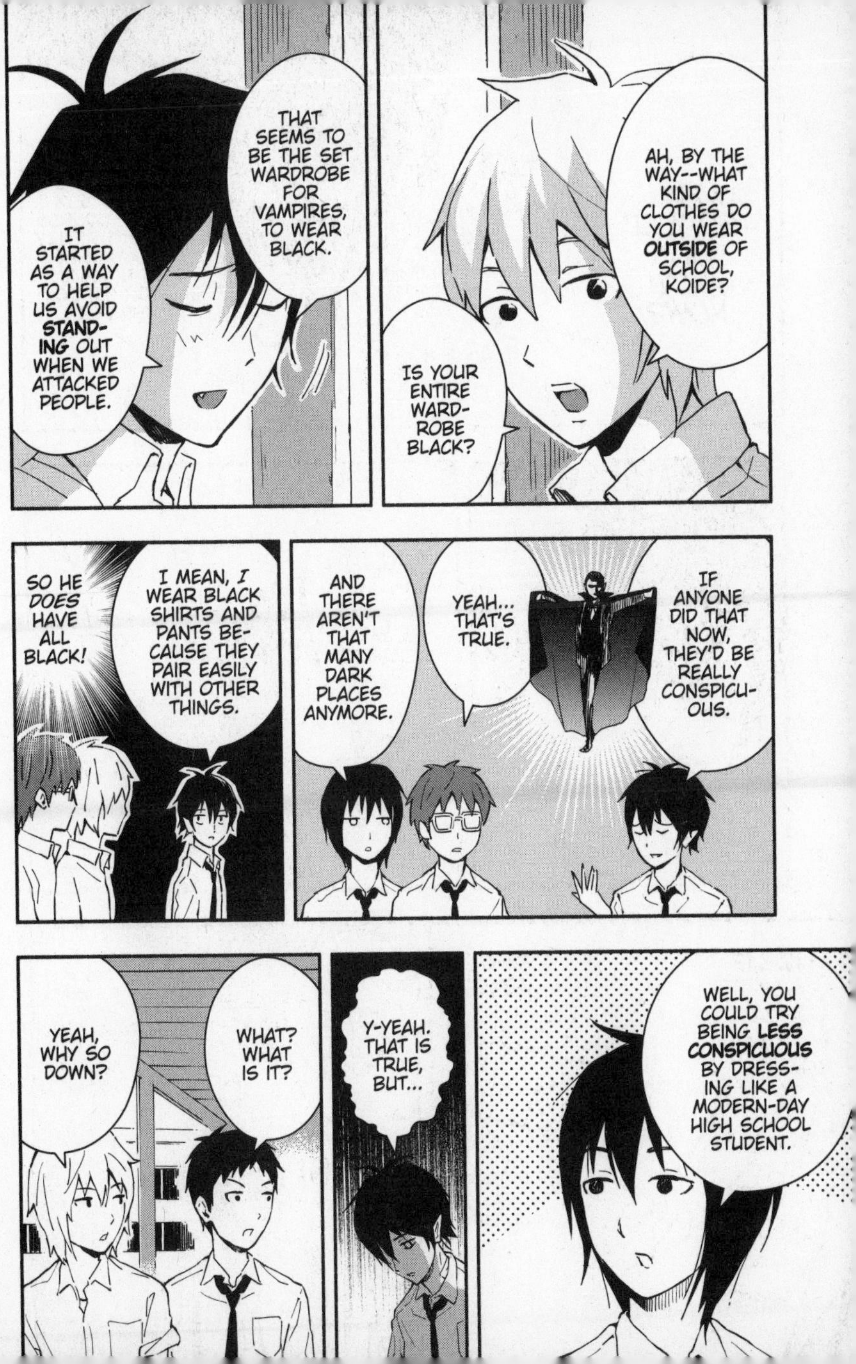
AH, BY THE WAY--WHAT KIND OF CLOTHES DO YOU WEAR **OUTSIDE** OF SCHOOL, KOIDE?
IS YOUR ENTIRE WARD-ROBE BLACK?
THAT SEEMS TO BE THE SET WARDROBE FOR VAMPIRES, TO WEAR BLACK.
IT STARTED AS A WAY TO HELP US AVOID **STAND-ING** OUT WHEN WE ATTACKED PEOPLE.
IF ANYONE DID THAT NOW, THEY'D BE REALLY CONSPICU-OUS.
YEAH... THAT'S TRUE.
AND THERE AREN'T THAT MANY DARK PLACES ANYMORE.
I MEAN, *I* WEAR BLACK SHIRTS AND PANTS BE-CAUSE THEY PAIR EASILY WITH OTHER THINGS.
SO HE *DOES* HAVE ALL BLACK!
WELL, YOU COULD TRY BEING **LESS CONSPICUOUS** BY DRESS-ING LIKE A MODERN-DAY HIGH SCHOOL STUDENT.
Y-YEAH. THAT IS TRUE, BUT...
WHAT? WHAT IS IT?
YEAH, WHY SO DOWN?

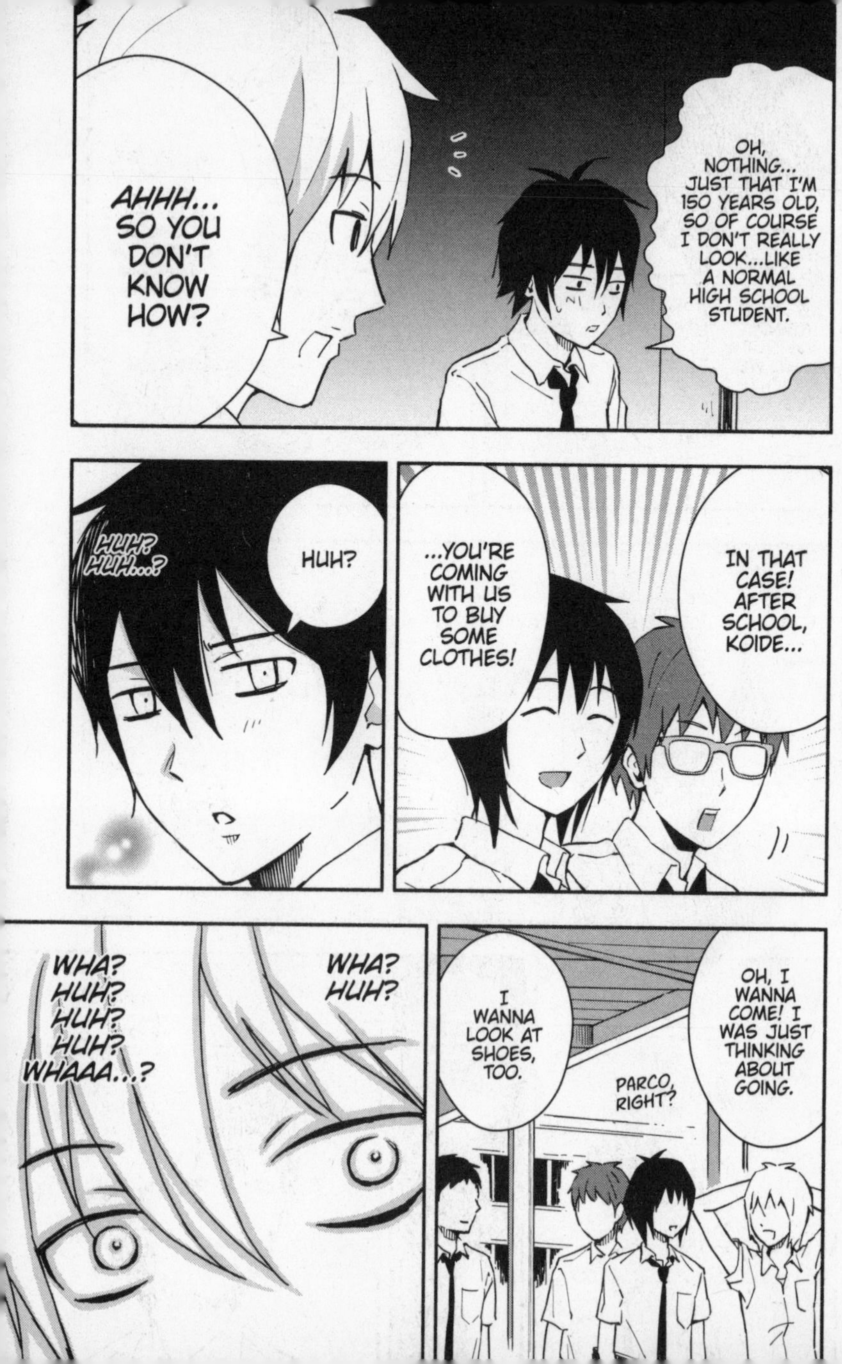
OH, NOTHING... JUST THAT I'M 150 YEARS OLD, SO OF COURSE I DON'T REALLY LOOK...LIKE A NORMAL HIGH SCHOOL STUDENT.
AHHH... SO YOU DON'T KNOW HOW?
IN THAT CASE! AFTER SCHOOL, KOIDE...
...YOU'RE COMING WITH US TO BUY SOME CLOTHES!
HUH?
HUH? HUH...?
OH, I WANNA COME! I WAS JUST THINKING ABOUT GOING.
PARCO, RIGHT?
I WANNA LOOK AT SHOES, TOO.
WHA? HUH?
WHA? HUH? HUH? HUH? WHAAA...?

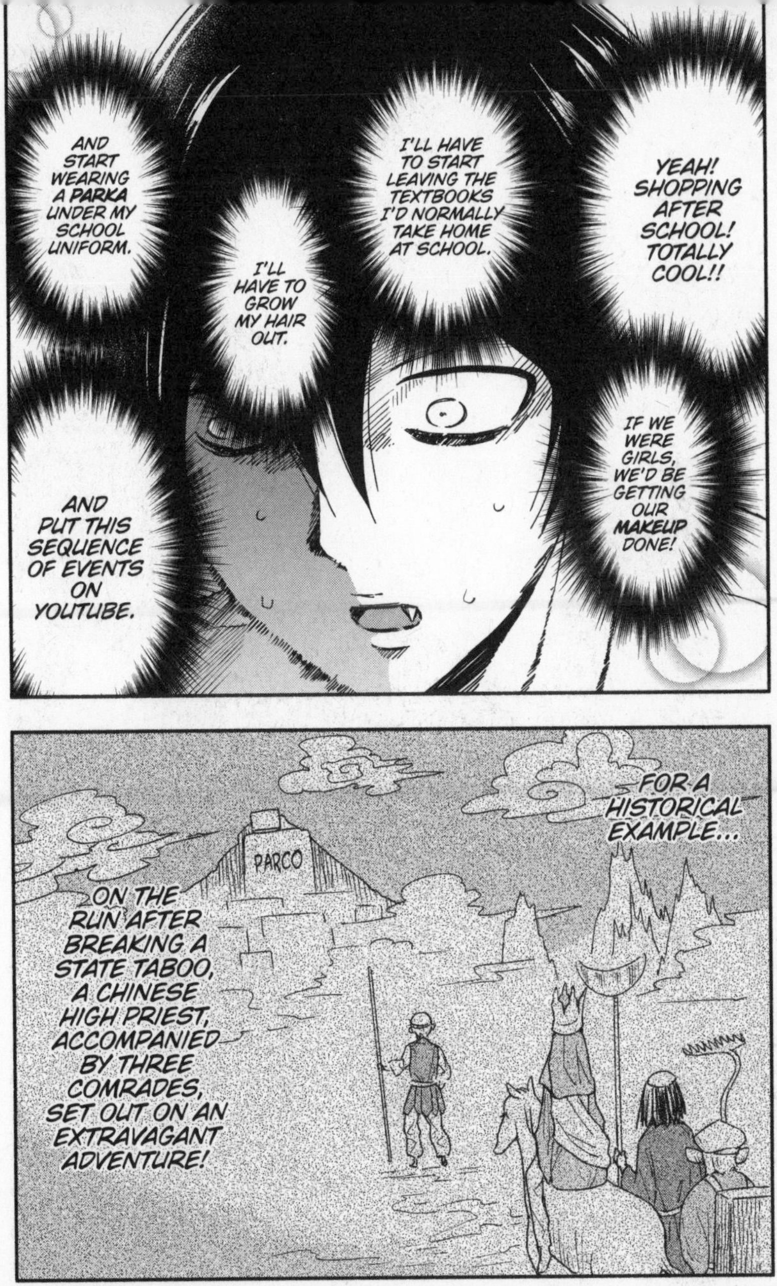
YEAH! SHOPPING AFTER SCHOOL! TOTALLY COOL!!
I'LL HAVE TO START LEAVING THE TEXTBOOKS I'D NORMALLY TAKE HOME AT SCHOOL.
AND START WEARING A **PARKA** UNDER MY SCHOOL UNIFORM.
I'LL HAVE TO GROW MY HAIR OUT.
IF WE WERE GIRLS, WE'D BE GETTING OUR **MAKEUP** DONE!
AND PUT THIS SEQUENCE OF EVENTS ON YOUTUBE.
FOR A HISTORICAL EXAMPLE...
PARCO
ON THE RUN AFTER BREAKING A STATE TABOO, A CHINESE HIGH PRIEST, ACCOMPANIED BY THREE COMRADES, SET OUT ON AN EXTRAVAGANT ADVENTURE!

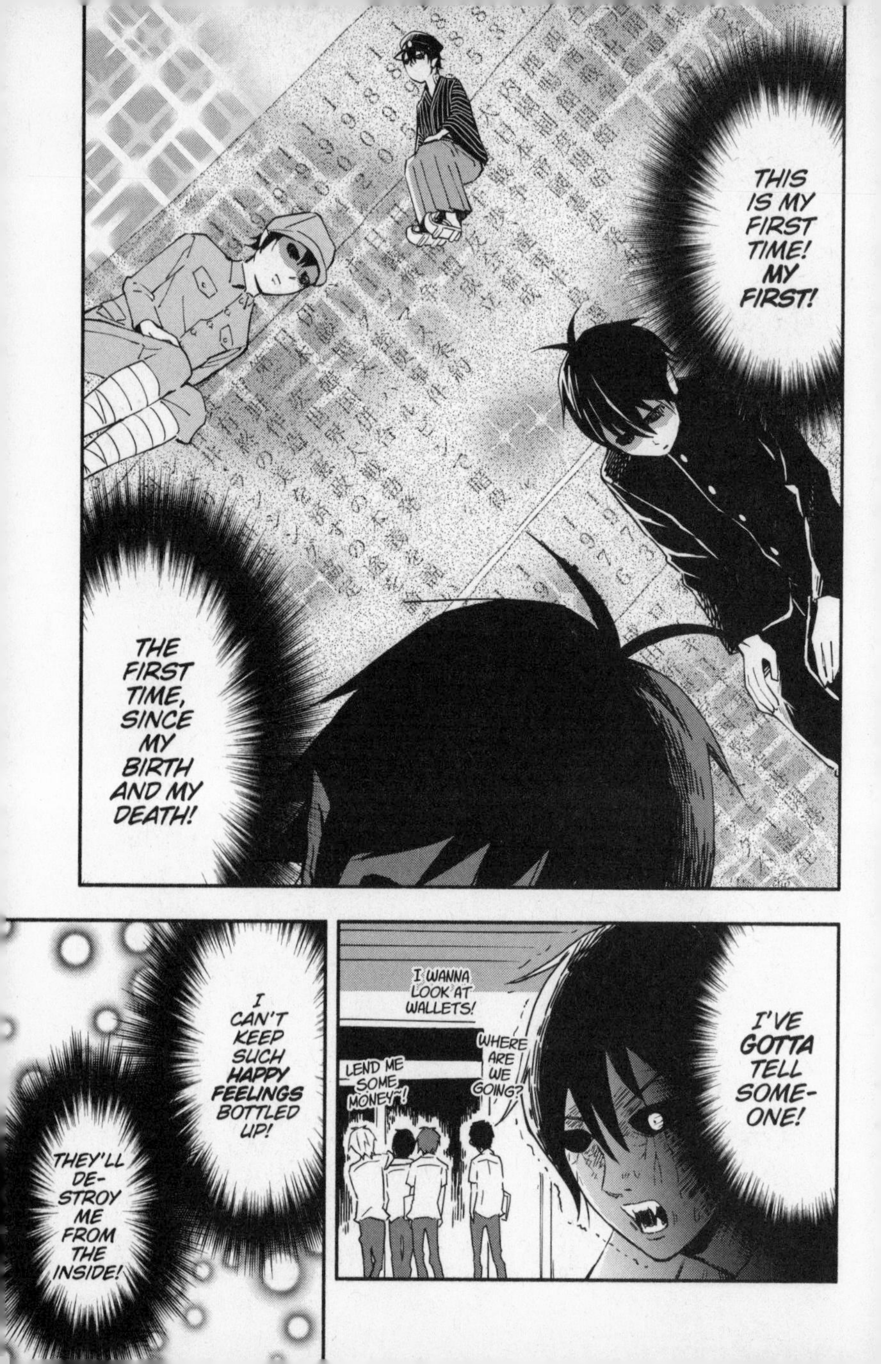
THIS IS MY FIRST TIME! MY FIRST!
THE FIRST TIME, SINCE MY BIRTH AND MY DEATH!
I'VE GOTTA TELL SOME-ONE!
I WANNA LOOK AT WALLETS!
WHERE ARE WE GOING?
LEND ME SOME MONEY~!
I CAN'T KEEP SUCH HAPPY FEELINGS BOTTLED UP!
THEY'LL DE-STROY ME FROM THE INSIDE!

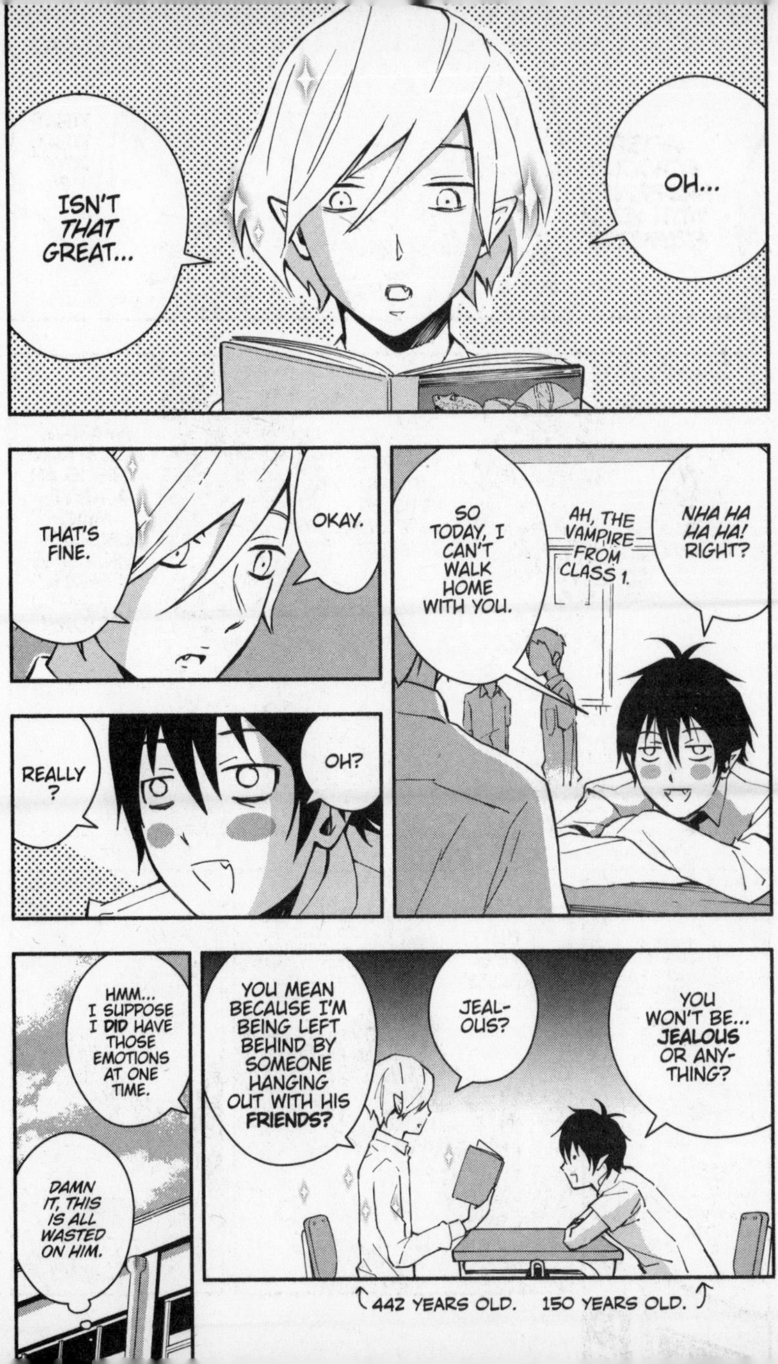
OH...
ISN'T THAT GREAT...
NHA HA HA HA! RIGHT?
AH, THE VAMPIRE FROM CLASS 1.
SO TODAY, I CAN'T WALK HOME WITH YOU.
OKAY.
THAT'S FINE.
OH?
REALLY?
YOU WON'T BE... JEALOUS OR ANY-THING?
JEAL-OUS?
YOU MEAN BECAUSE I'M BEING LEFT BEHIND BY SOMEONE HANGING OUT WITH HIS FRIENDS?
150 YEARS OLD.
442 YEARS OLD.
HMM... I SUPPOSE I DID HAVE THOSE EMOTIONS AT ONE TIME.
DAMN IT, THIS IS ALL WASTED ON HIM.

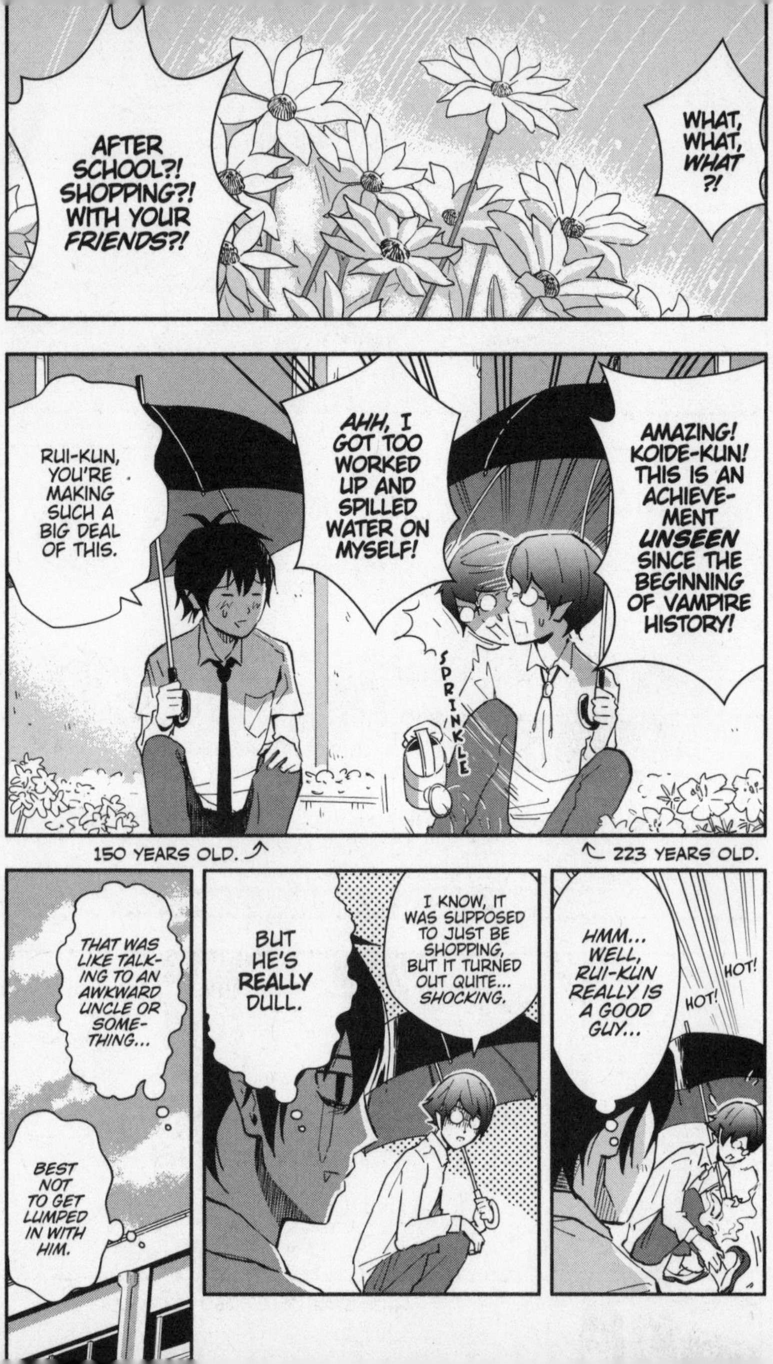
WHAT, WHAT, WHAT?!
AFTER SCHOOL?! SHOPPING?! WITH YOUR FRIENDS?!
AMAZING! KOIDE-KUN! THIS IS AN ACHIEVEMENT UNSEEN SINCE THE BEGINNING OF VAMPIRE HISTORY!
AHH, I GOT TOO WORKED UP AND SPILLED WATER ON MYSELF!
SPRINKLE
RUI-KUN, YOU'RE MAKING SUCH A BIG DEAL OF THIS.
223 YEARS OLD.
150 YEARS OLD.
HMM... WELL, RUI-KUN REALLY IS A GOOD GUY...
HOT!
HOT!
I KNOW, IT WAS SUPPOSED TO JUST BE SHOPPING, BUT IT TURNED OUT QUITE... SHOCKING.
BUT HE'S REALLY DULL.
THAT WAS LIKE TALKING TO AN AWKWARD UNCLE OR SOMETHING...
BEST NOT TO GET LUMPED IN WITH HIM.

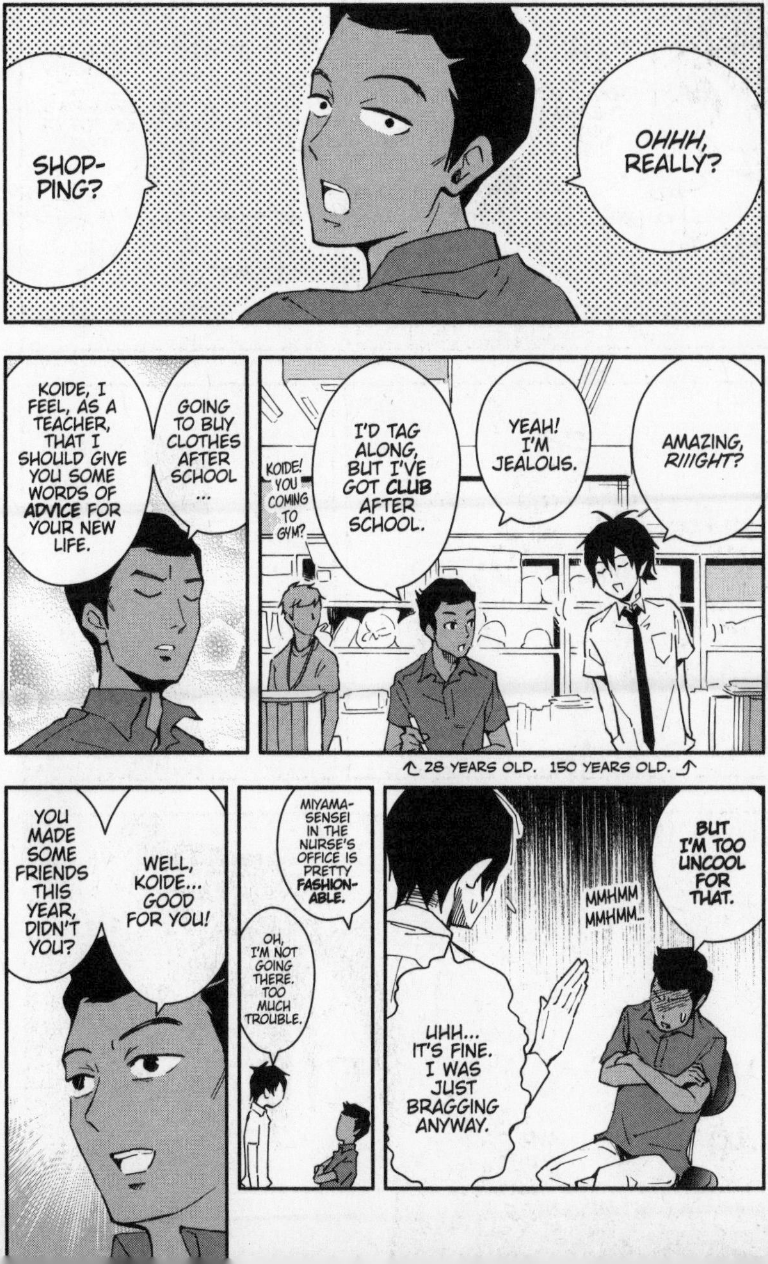
OHHH, REALLY?
SHOP-PING?
AMAZING, *RIIIGHT?*
YEAH! I'M JEALOUS.
I'D TAG ALONG, BUT I'VE GOT **CLUB** AFTER SCHOOL.
KOIDE! YOU COMING TO GYM?
GOING TO BUY CLOTHES AFTER SCHOOL ...
KOIDE, I FEEL, AS A TEACHER, THAT I SHOULD GIVE YOU SOME WORDS OF **ADVICE** FOR YOUR NEW LIFE.
↑ 28 YEARS OLD. 150 YEARS OLD. ↑
BUT I'M TOO UNCOOL FOR THAT.
MMHMM MMHMM...
UHH... IT'S FINE. I WAS JUST BRAGGING ANYWAY.
MIYAMA-SENSEI IN THE NURSE'S OFFICE IS PRETTY **FASHION-ABLE.**
OH, I'M NOT GOING THERE. TOO MUCH TROUBLE.
WELL, KOIDE... GOOD FOR YOU!
YOU MADE SOME FRIENDS THIS YEAR, DIDN'T YOU?

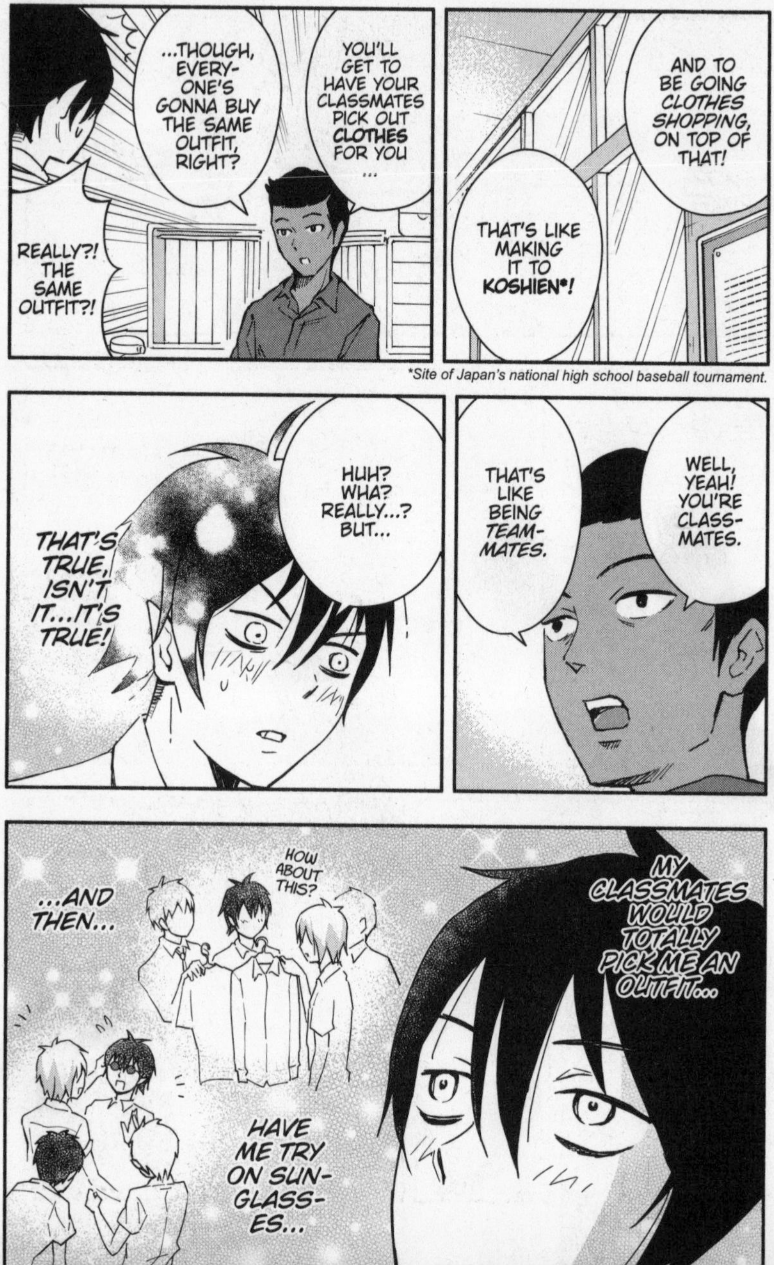
AND TO BE GOING CLOTHES SHOPPING, ON TOP OF THAT!
THAT'S LIKE MAKING IT TO KOSHIEN*!
YOU'LL GET TO HAVE YOUR CLASSMATES PICK OUT CLOTHES FOR YOU ...
...THOUGH, EVERY-ONE'S GONNA BUY THE SAME OUTFIT, RIGHT?
REALLY?! THE SAME OUTFIT?!
WELL, YEAH! YOU'RE CLASS-MATES.
THAT'S LIKE BEING TEAM-MATES.
HUH? WHA? REALLY...? BUT...
THAT'S TRUE, ISN'T IT...IT'S TRUE!
MY CLASSMATES WOULD TOTALLY PICK ME AN OUTFIT...
...AND THEN...
HOW ABOUT THIS?
HAVE ME TRY ON SUN-GLASS-ES...

*Site of Japan's national high school baseball tournament.

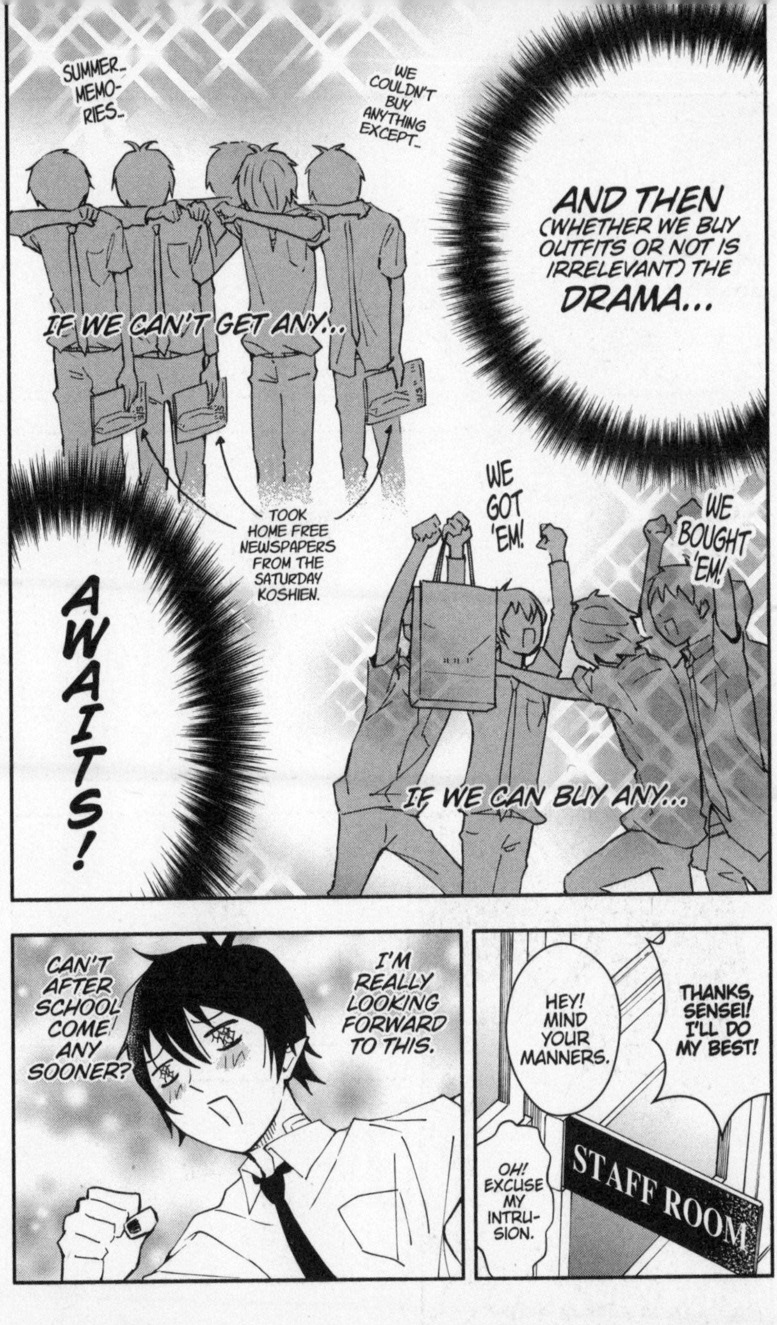
AND THEN (WHETHER WE BUY OUTFITS OR NOT IS IRRELEVANT) THE DRAMA...
WE COULDN'T BUY ANYTHING EXCEPT...
SUMMER... MEMORIES...
IF WE CAN'T GET ANY...
TOOK HOME FREE NEWSPAPERS FROM THE SATURDAY KOSHIEN.
WE BOUGHT 'EM!
WE GOT 'EM!
AWAITS!
IF WE CAN BUY ANY...
THANKS, SENSEI! I'LL DO MY BEST!
HEY! MIND YOUR MANNERS.
STAFF ROOM
OH! EXCUSE MY INTRUSION.
I'M REALLY LOOKING FORWARD TO THIS.
CAN'T AFTER SCHOOL COME ANY SOONER?

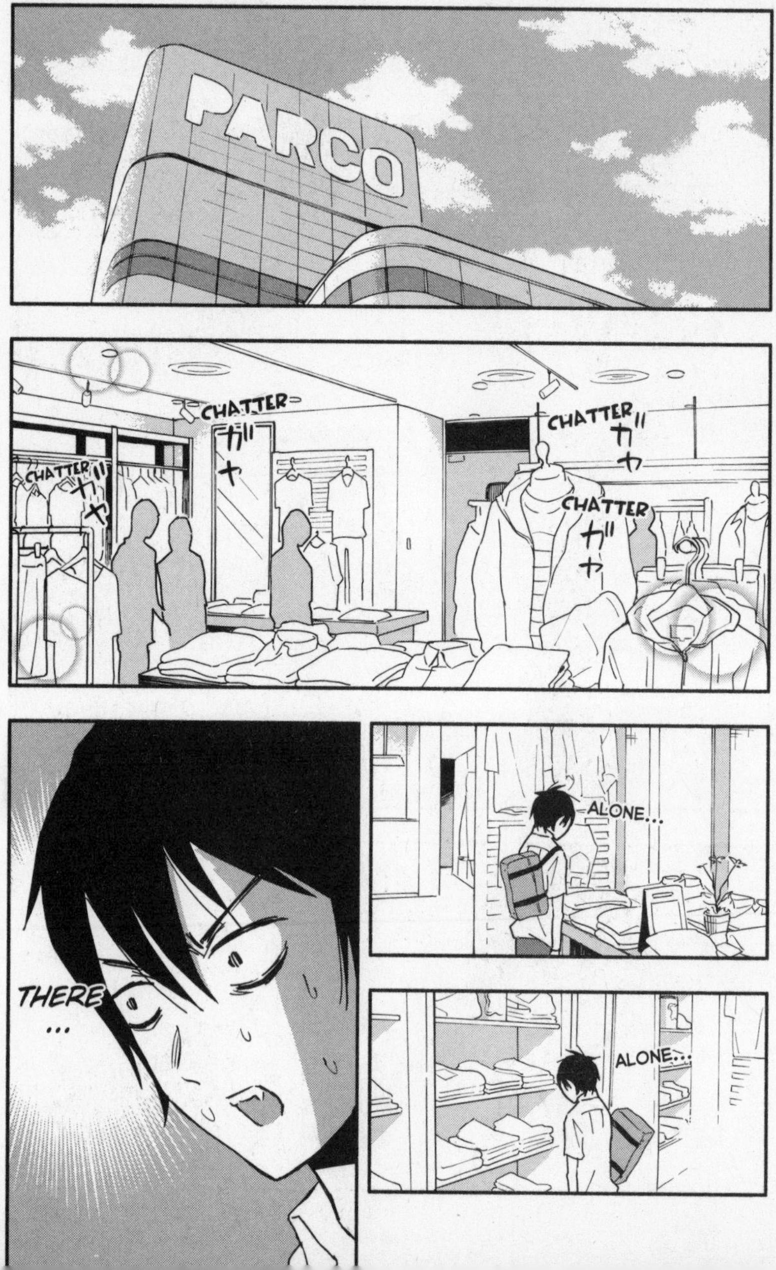
PARCO
CHATTER
ガヤ
CHATTER
ガヤ
CHATTER
ガヤ
CHATTER
ガヤ
ALONE...
ALONE...
THERE
...

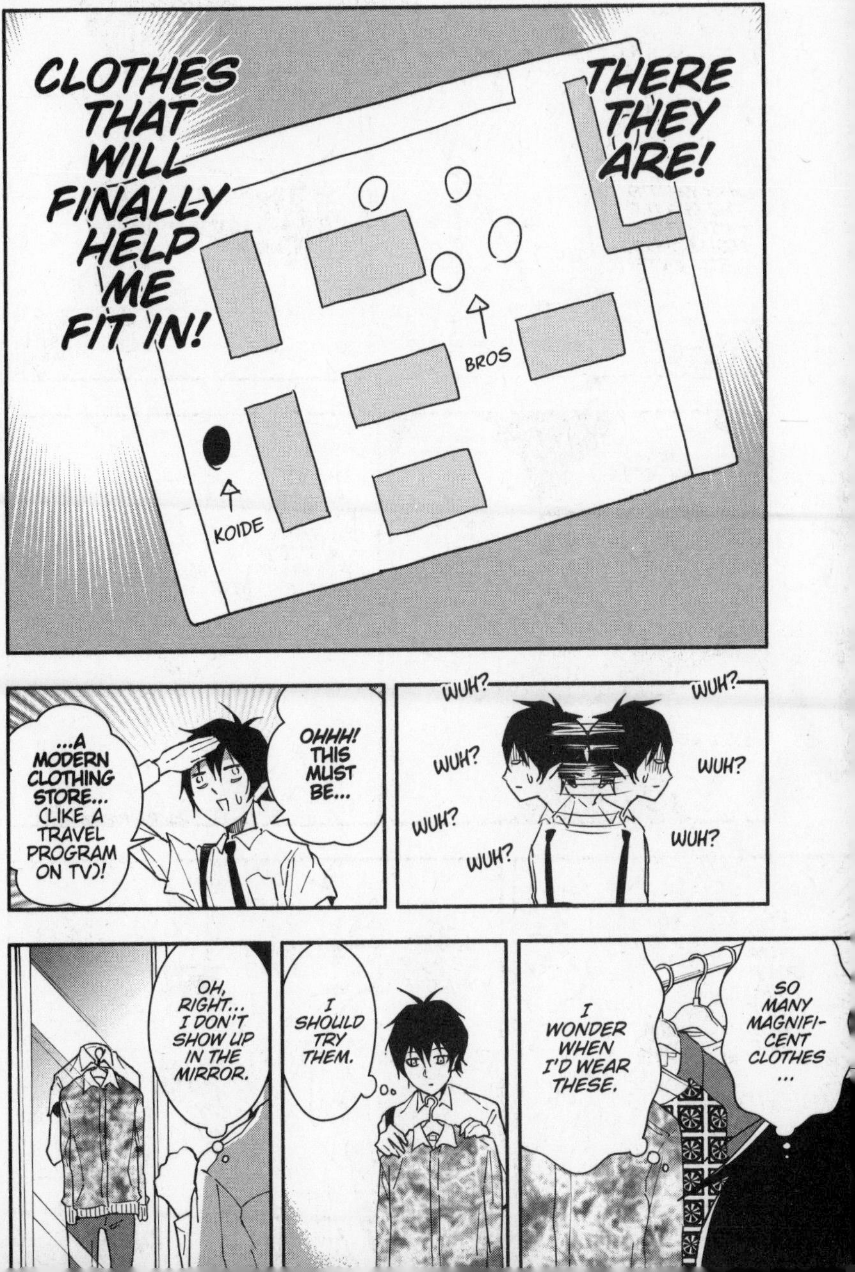
THERE THEY ARE!
CLOTHES THAT WILL FINALLY HELP ME FIT IN!
BROS
KOIDE
WUH?
WUH?
WUH?
WUH?
WUH?
WUH?
WUH?
OHHH! THIS MUST BE...
...A MODERN CLOTHING STORE... (LIKE A TRAVEL PROGRAM ON TV)!
SO MANY MAGNIFICENT CLOTHES...
I WONDER WHEN I'D WEAR THESE.
I SHOULD TRY THEM.
OH, RIGHT... I DON'T SHOW UP IN THE MIRROR.

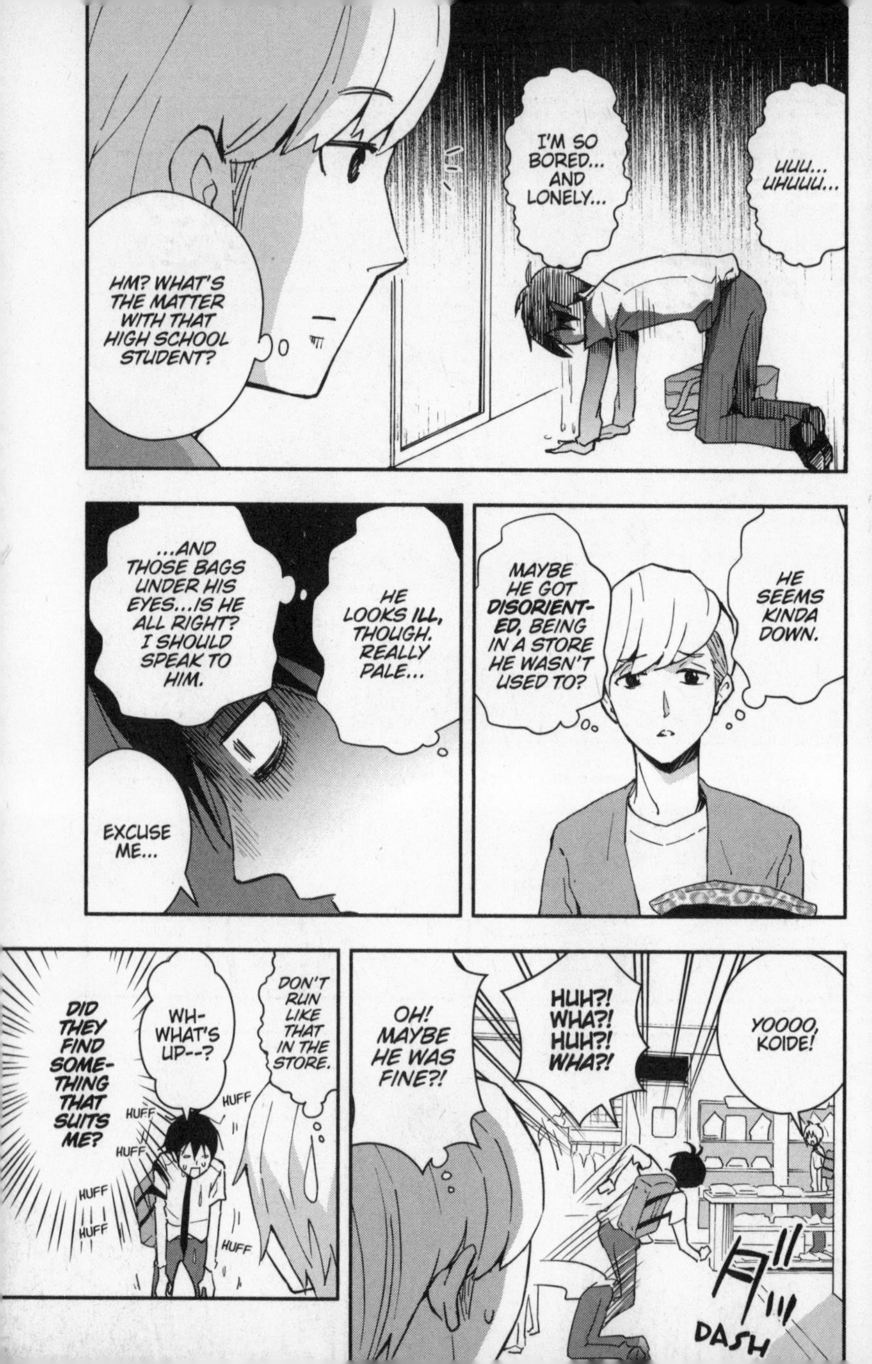
UUU... UHUUU...
I'M SO BORED... AND LONELY...
HM? WHAT'S THE MATTER WITH THAT HIGH SCHOOL STUDENT?
HE SEEMS KINDA DOWN.
MAYBE HE GOT DISORIENT-ED, BEING IN A STORE HE WASN'T USED TO?
HE LOOKS ILL, THOUGH. REALLY PALE...
...AND THOSE BAGS UNDER HIS EYES...IS HE ALL RIGHT? I SHOULD SPEAK TO HIM.
EXCUSE ME...
YOOOO, KOIDE!
HUH?! WHA?! HUH?! WHA?!
OH! MAYBE HE WAS FINE?!
DASH
DON'T RUN LIKE THAT IN THE STORE.
WH-WHAT'S UP--?
HUFF HUFF HUFF HUFF HUFF HUFF
DID THEY FIND SOME-THING THAT SUITS ME?

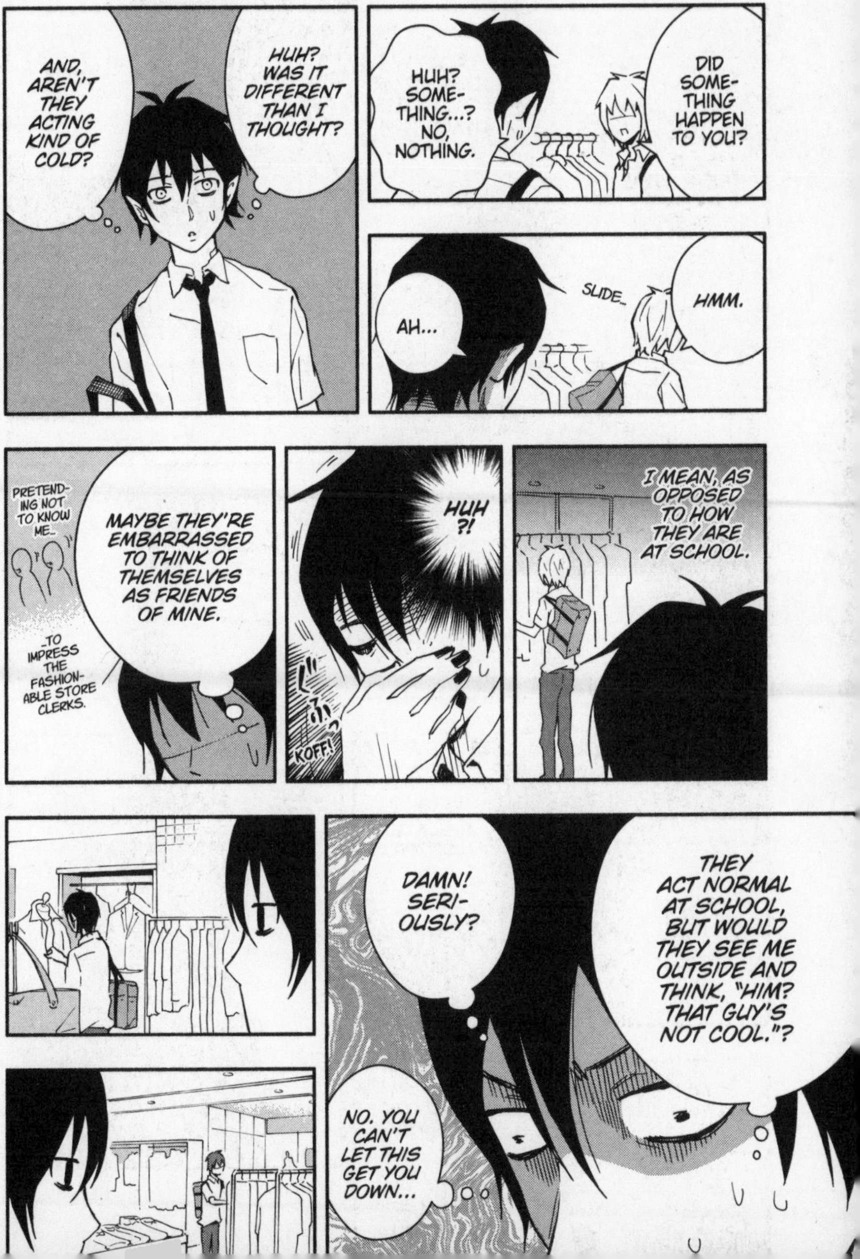
DID SOMETHING HAPPEN TO YOU?
HUH? SOMETHING...? NO, NOTHING.
HMM.
SLIDE...
AH...
HUH? WAS IT DIFFERENT THAN I THOUGHT?
AND, AREN'T THEY ACTING KIND OF COLD?
I MEAN, AS OPPOSED TO HOW THEY ARE AT SCHOOL.
HUH ?!
KOFF!
MAYBE THEY'RE EMBARRASSED TO THINK OF THEMSELVES AS FRIENDS OF MINE.
PRETENDING NOT TO KNOW ME...
...TO IMPRESS THE FASHIONABLE STORE CLERKS.
THEY ACT NORMAL AT SCHOOL, BUT WOULD THEY SEE ME OUTSIDE AND THINK, "HIM? THAT GUY'S NOT COOL."?
DAMN! SERIOUSLY?
NO. YOU CAN'T LET THIS GET YOU DOWN...

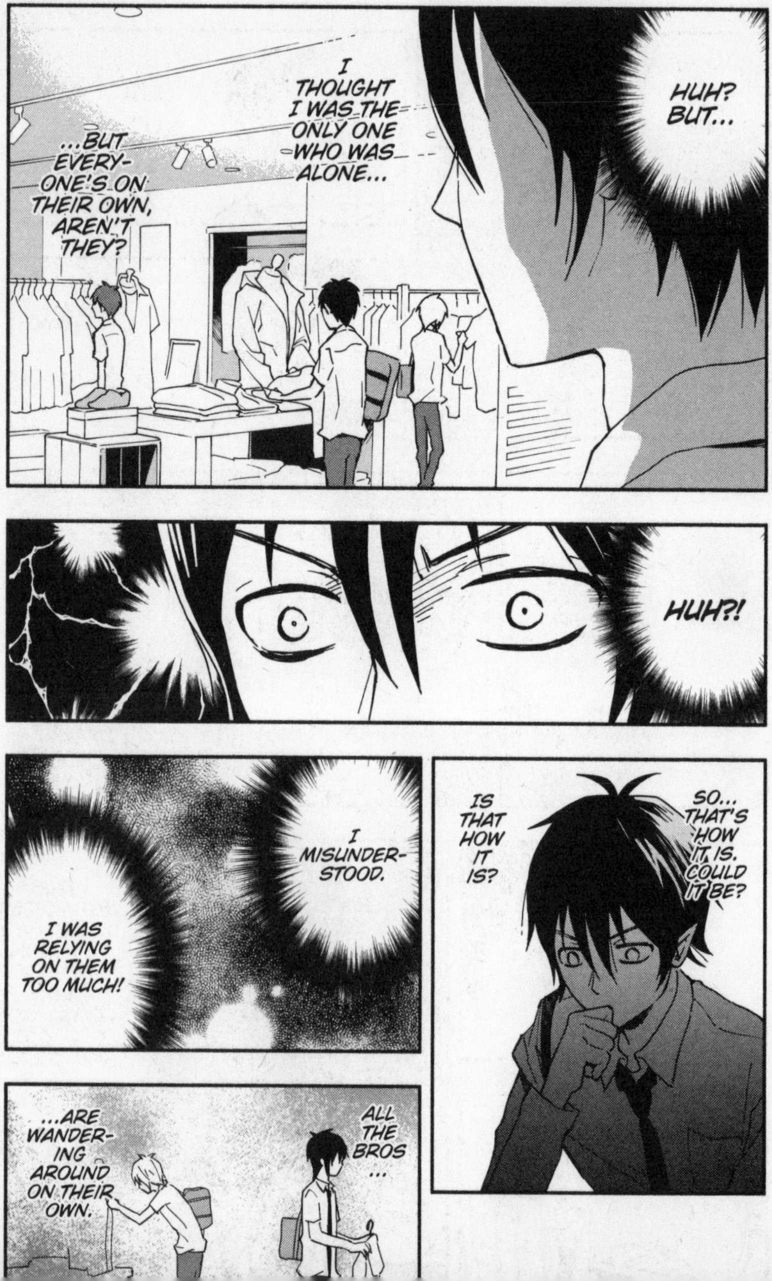
HUH? BUT...
I THOUGHT I WAS THE ONLY ONE WHO WAS ALONE...
...BUT EVERY-ONE'S ON THEIR OWN, AREN'T THEY?
HUH?!
SO... THAT'S HOW IT IS. COULD IT BE?
IS THAT HOW IT IS?
I MISUNDER-STOOD.
I WAS RELYING ON THEM TOO MUCH!
ALL THE BROS...
...ARE WANDER-ING AROUND ON THEIR OWN.

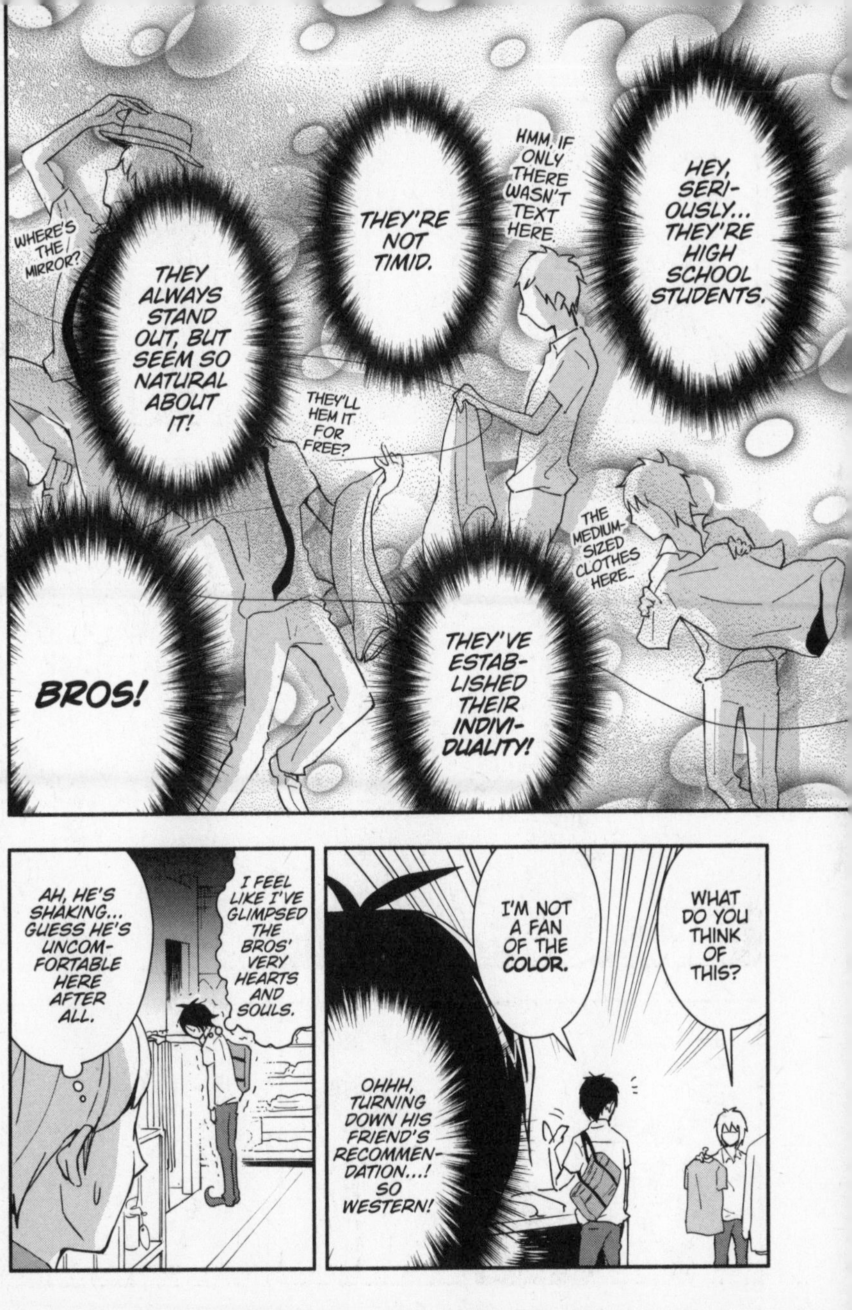
HEY, SERIOUSLY... THEY'RE HIGH SCHOOL STUDENTS.
HMM, IF ONLY THERE WASN'T TEXT HERE.
THEY'RE NOT TIMID.
THEY ALWAYS STAND OUT, BUT SEEM SO NATURAL ABOUT IT!
WHERE'S THE MIRROR?
THEY'LL HEM IT FOR FREE?
THE MEDIUM-SIZED CLOTHES HERE..
THEY'VE ESTABLISHED THEIR INDIVIDUALITY!
BROS!
WHAT DO YOU THINK OF THIS?
I'M NOT A FAN OF THE COLOR.
OHHH, TURNING DOWN HIS FRIEND'S RECOMMENDATION...! SO WESTERN!
I FEEL LIKE I'VE GLIMPSED THE BROS' VERY HEARTS AND SOULS.
AH, HE'S SHAKING... GUESS HE'S UNCOMFORTABLE HERE AFTER ALL.

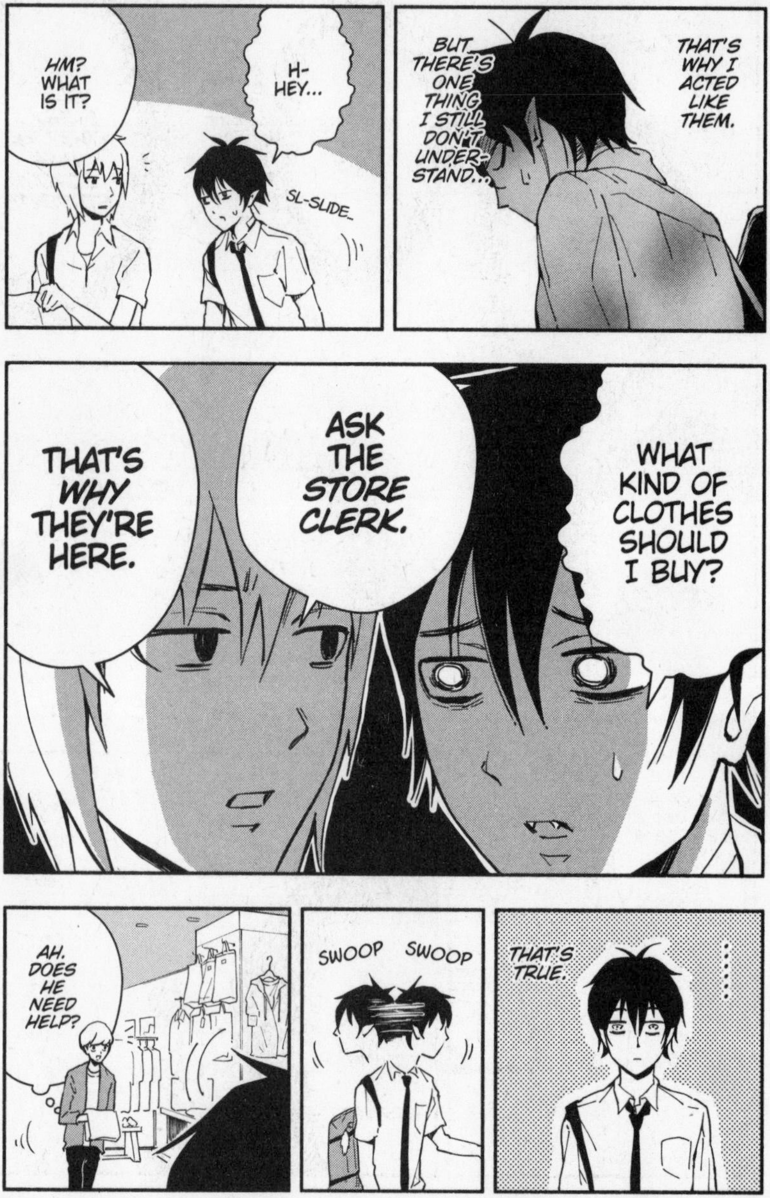
THAT'S WHY I ACTED LIKE THEM.
BUT THERE'S ONE THING I STILL DON'T UNDERSTAND...
H-HEY...
HM? WHAT IS IT?
SL-SLIDE..
WHAT KIND OF CLOTHES SHOULD I BUY?
ASK THE STORE CLERK.
THAT'S WHY THEY'RE HERE.
......
THAT'S TRUE.
SWOOP SWOOP
AH. DOES HE NEED HELP?

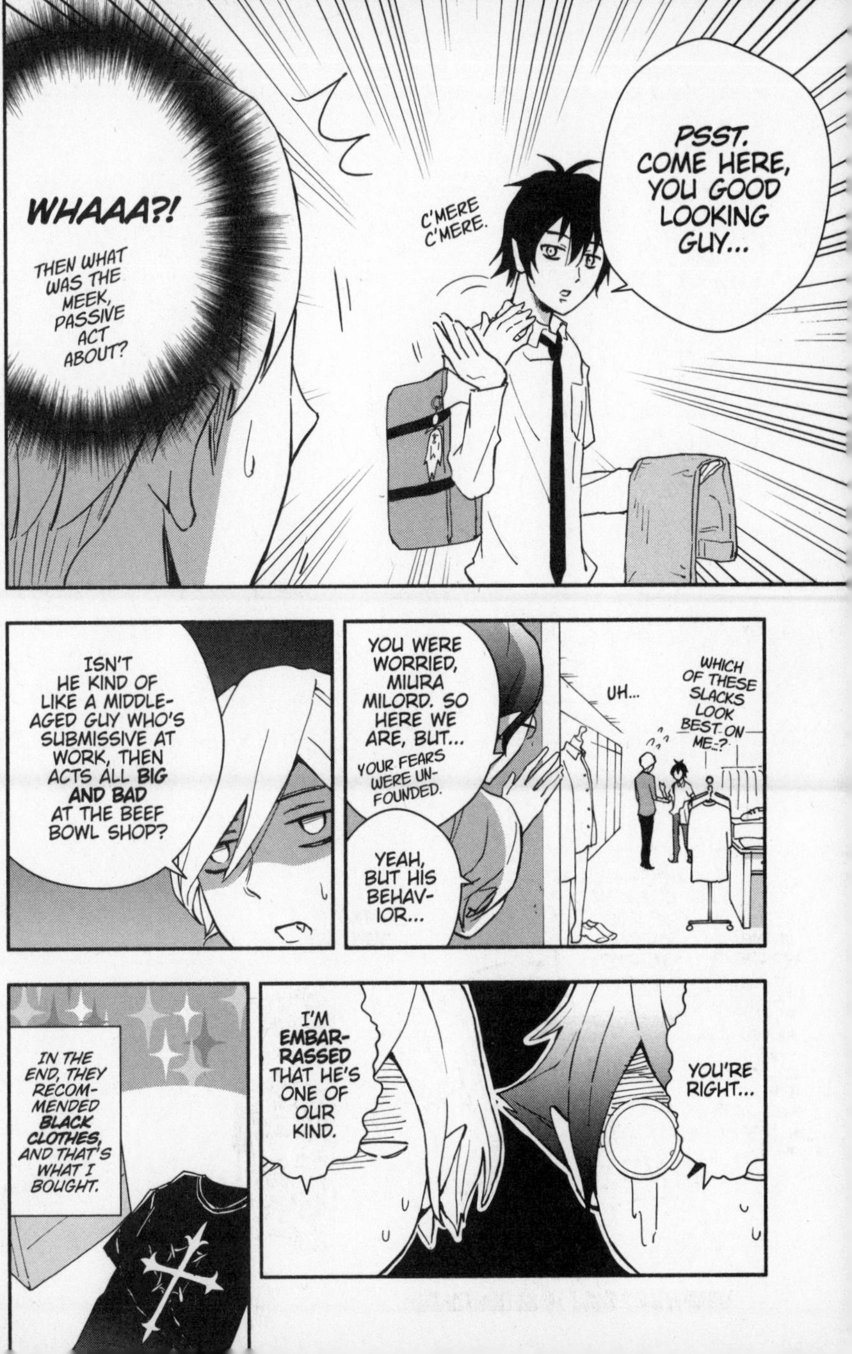
PSST. COME HERE, YOU GOOD LOOKING GUY...
C'MERE C'MERE.
WHAAA?!
THEN WHAT WAS THE MEEK, PASSIVE ACT ABOUT?
WHICH OF THESE SLACKS LOOK BEST ON ME..?
UH...
YOU WERE WORRIED, MIURA MILORD. SO HERE WE ARE, BUT...
YOUR FEARS WERE UN-FOUNDED.
YEAH, BUT HIS BEHAV-IOR...
ISN'T HE KIND OF LIKE A MIDDLE-AGED GUY WHO'S SUBMISSIVE AT WORK, THEN ACTS ALL **BIG AND BAD** AT THE BEEF BOWL SHOP?
YOU'RE RIGHT...
I'M **EMBAR-RASSED** THAT HE'S ONE OF OUR KIND.
IN THE END, THEY RECOM-MENDED **BLACK CLOTHES,** AND THAT'S WHAT I BOUGHT.

THAT DEPENDS.
HE'S WEARING IT, EVEN IF THE CROSS HURTS HIM.

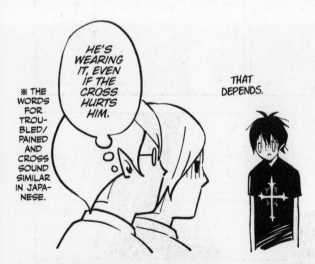

※ THE WORDS FOR TROUBLED/PAINED AND CROSS SOUND SIMILAR IN JAPANESE.

CHAPTER 8 / END / TO BE CONTINUED...

🦇 GLOSSARY

✝ SEPTUAGINT HIGH SCHOOL

REFERS TO THE "SEPTUAGINT" (A GREEK
TRANSLATION OF THE OLD TESTAMENT).
NO SPECIAL MEANING. IT JUST SOUNDED GOOD.

✝ KENCLUCKY

I'VE HEARD MICHAEL JACKSON LOVED IT. THAT
ISN'T EXACTLY WHY, BUT I FIGURED VAMPIRES
MUST LOVE IT TOO. NO SPECIAL REASON.

sogooood

✝ FALSE PSYCHIC

I REMEMBER READING A BOOK ABOUT
NAPOREONZU (A MAGICIAN) AND HOW HE
USED MAGIC TO PERFORM TELEPATHY...

✝ DALI

SALVADOR DALI. HE PAINTED
SEVERAL FAMOUS PAINTINGS
INCLUDING THE ONE WITH THE
MELTING CLOCKS. DALI'S NAME
WAS WRITTEN ON MIURA'S CHEEK.
NOW, WHICH OF KOIDE'S "BRO"
CLASSMATES DID IT IS UNDER
DEBATE, BUT ALL AGREE: IT WAS
REALLY SURREAL.

✝ MIURA'S 4TH WIFE

A POPULAR BUT STRANGE GIRL IN
KOIDE'S CLASS. SHE FELT THAT
(WHAT SHE THOUGHT WAS) MIU-
RA'S SENSE OF HUMOR BROUGHT
HIM CLOSER TO HER, SO SHE
ACCIDENTALLY CONFESSED HER
FEELINGS. SHE'S PRETTY
DIFFICULT TO USE
IN THE STORY,
SO THIS WAS
HER LAST
APPEARANCE.

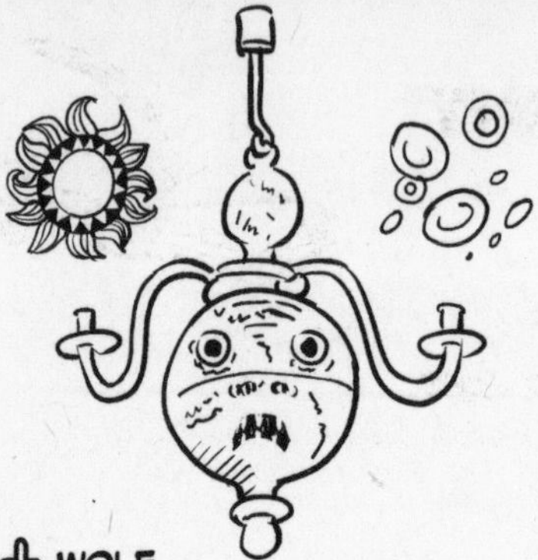

✝ SUN & SANG

THE ENGLISH WORD, "SUN" IS FOR THE SUN ITSELF. THE FRENCH WORD "SANG" MEANS BLOOD AND IS PRONOUNCED THE SAME WAY.

✝ HOMEROOM TEACHER, HAMANO

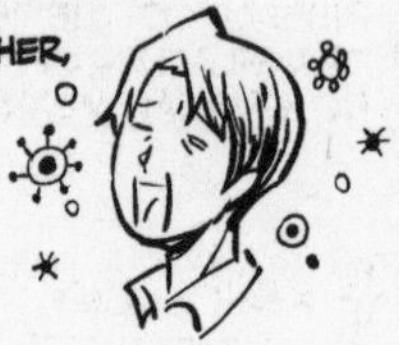

42 YEARS OLD.
AN UNLUCKY AGE.

✝ WOLF

THE OLD HAIRSTYLE OF THE "YANKEE" TYPES. THEY WOULD GROW THEIR HAIR OUT IN THE BACK. IT'S ALSO CALLED THE JUMBO CUT, NAMED FOR A FAMOUS GOLFER.

IN AMERICA, IT'S REFERRED TO AS A MULLET, NAMED FOR A TYPE OF FISH.

IN AMERICA, IT'S ALSO REFERRED TO AS THE WORLD'S WORST HAIRSTYLE.

✝ SEARCHLIGHTS COMING FROM PACHINKO SHOPS

I'VE RECEIVED INFORMATION THAT NOW EVEN SOME PACHINKO PARLORS (UNCOMMON IN SIZE) HAVE SEARCHLIGHTS ON THE ROOF.

✝ MIYAMA-SENSEI

THE TEACHER IN THE NURSE'S OFFICE. 28 YEARS OLD. LIKES LIGHT NOVELS. FASHIONABLE. INCIDENTALLY, THE P.E. TEACHER'S NAME IS IBUKI.

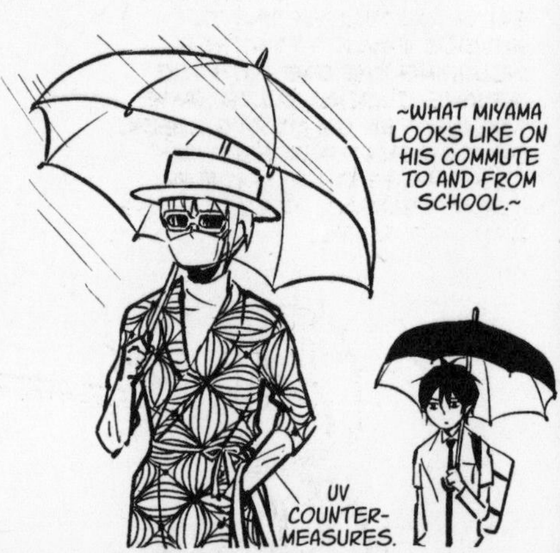
~WHAT MIYAMA LOOKS LIKE ON HIS COMMUTE TO AND FROM SCHOOL.~
UV COUNTER-MEASURES.

✝ IBUKI-SENSEI

PHYS. ED TEACHER.
28 YEARS OLD. DARK COMPLEXION. IS A PAIN.

AFTERWORD

IT'S A COMMON, FRUSTRATED REFRAIN: FAILING TO CREATE AN EFFECTIVE PERSONA FOR YOURSELF UPON ENTERING SCHOOL, WHERE IDENTITY IS LESS OF A SURE THING AND MORE OF A NECESSITY.

SOMEONE WHO'S GENUINELY CHEERFUL, BUT PLAYS IT COOL. (SOMEONE WHO CHARMS THEIR CLASSMATES. WHO DOESN'T WAIT FOR GOLDEN WEEK TO DO WHAT THEY LIKE.)

SOMEONE WHO'S GLOOMY, BUT TRIES TO BEHAVE LIKE A CHEERFUL TYPE. (THIS IS HELL, BY THE WAY.) IF YOU DO THIS, THE RESULT WILL BE PROFOUND FAILURE, EVERY TIME.

URGH... I NEED A REDO...

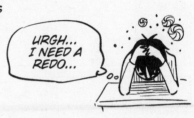

THINK OF IT LIKE THIS: YOU WANT TO GO BACK INTO THE PAST VIA TIME TRAVEL, BUT SINCE TIME TRAVEL IS SCIENTIFICALLY IMPOSSIBLE, YOU HOLD ON TO HOPE FOR THE FUTURE POSSIBILITY OF TIME TRAVEL. BUT THEN IT STILL SEEMS IMPOSSIBLE, SCIENTIFICALLY SPEAKING...

ANYHOW, I TRIED HAVING A VAMPIRE REPEAT HIGH SCHOOL OVER AND OVER.

I KNEW FROM THE START THAT I WANTED TO HAVE A MALE VAMPIRE HIGH SCHOOL STUDENT AS THE MAIN CHARACTER, SO I DREW NUMEROUS DRAFTS FROM THERE.

HERE'S AN EARLY ONE. →

LOOK.
ISN'T MY SKIN TOO PALE?
WHICH I GUESS MEANS ...
I'M A VAMPIRE, AFTER ALL.

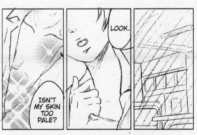

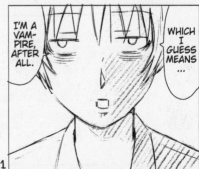

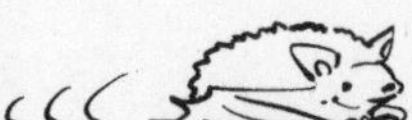

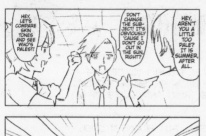

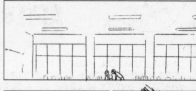

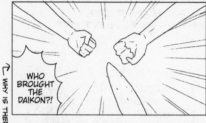

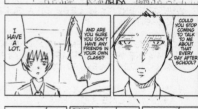

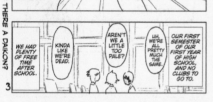

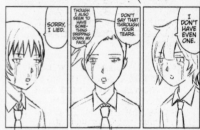

COULD YOU STOP COMING TO TALK TO ME ABOUT THAT EVERY DAY AFTER SCHOOL?
AND ARE YOU SURE YOU DON'T HAVE ANY FRIENDS IN YOUR OWN CLASS?
I HAVE A LOT.
I DON'T HAVE EVEN ONE.
DON'T SAY THAT THROUGH YOUR TEARS.
THOUGH I ALSO SEEM TO HAVE SOMETHING DRIPPING DOWN MY FACE.
SORRY, I LIED.
HEY, AREN'T YOU A LITTLE TOO PALE? IT IS SUMMER, AFTER ALL.
DON'T CHANGE THE SUBJECT! IT'S OBVIOUSLY 'CAUSE I DON'T GO OUT IN THE SUN, RIGHT?
HEY, LET'S COMPARE SKIN TONES AND SEE WHO'S PALEST!
WHO BROUGHT THE DAIKON?!
OUR FIRST SEMESTER OF OUR FIRST YEAR OF HIGH SCHOOL, AND NO CLUBS TO GO TO.
UH, WE'RE ALL PRETTY MUCH THE SAME.
AREN'T WE A LITTLE TOO PALE?
KINDA LIKE WE'RE DEAD.
WE HAD PLENTY OF FREE TIME AFTER SCHOOL.
3
← WHY IS THERE A DAIKON?

SO, I DREW 5-6 CHAPTERS OF THIS, BUT I COULDN'T SOLIDIFY THE CHARACTERS, THE SETTING, OR THE PLOT.

AND AS YOU CAN SEE, IT WAS BASICALLY UNINTERESTING, SO I DID NUMEROUS DRAFTS, OVER AND OVER.

THIS ISN'T GOING WELL AT ALL, EH--?

FINALLY, WORRIED THAT IT WOULDN'T GO WELL AT ALL, I DEBATED WITH MY FATHER AND RECEIVED THIS MESSAGE FROM MY MOTHER, WHICH I'D LIKE TO QUOTE HERE:

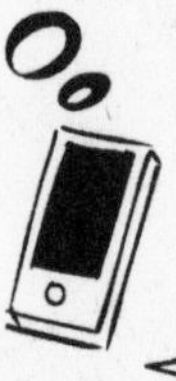

SKILLED PEOPLE ARE GREAT, BUT THAT CAN BE A LONELY LIFE. LIVING AS LONG AS KOIDE-KUN HAS, WHAT MIGHT IT BE LIKE FOR HIM? EVEN IF THERE'S A WAY TO AVOID IT, AND EVEN IF BEING IMMORTAL IS IMAGINARY, YOU CAN STILL GET THROUGH THIS. HUMANS ARE BORN, LIVING THEIR LIVES ON THE PATH TO DEATH. DO YOUR BEST, WITHOUT WAVERING.

← SHE'S SAYING SOMETHING PROFOUND ABOUT KOIDE.

THANK YOU FOR READING *MY PATHETIC VAMPIRE LIFE* VOLUME 1 ALL THE WAY TO THE END!

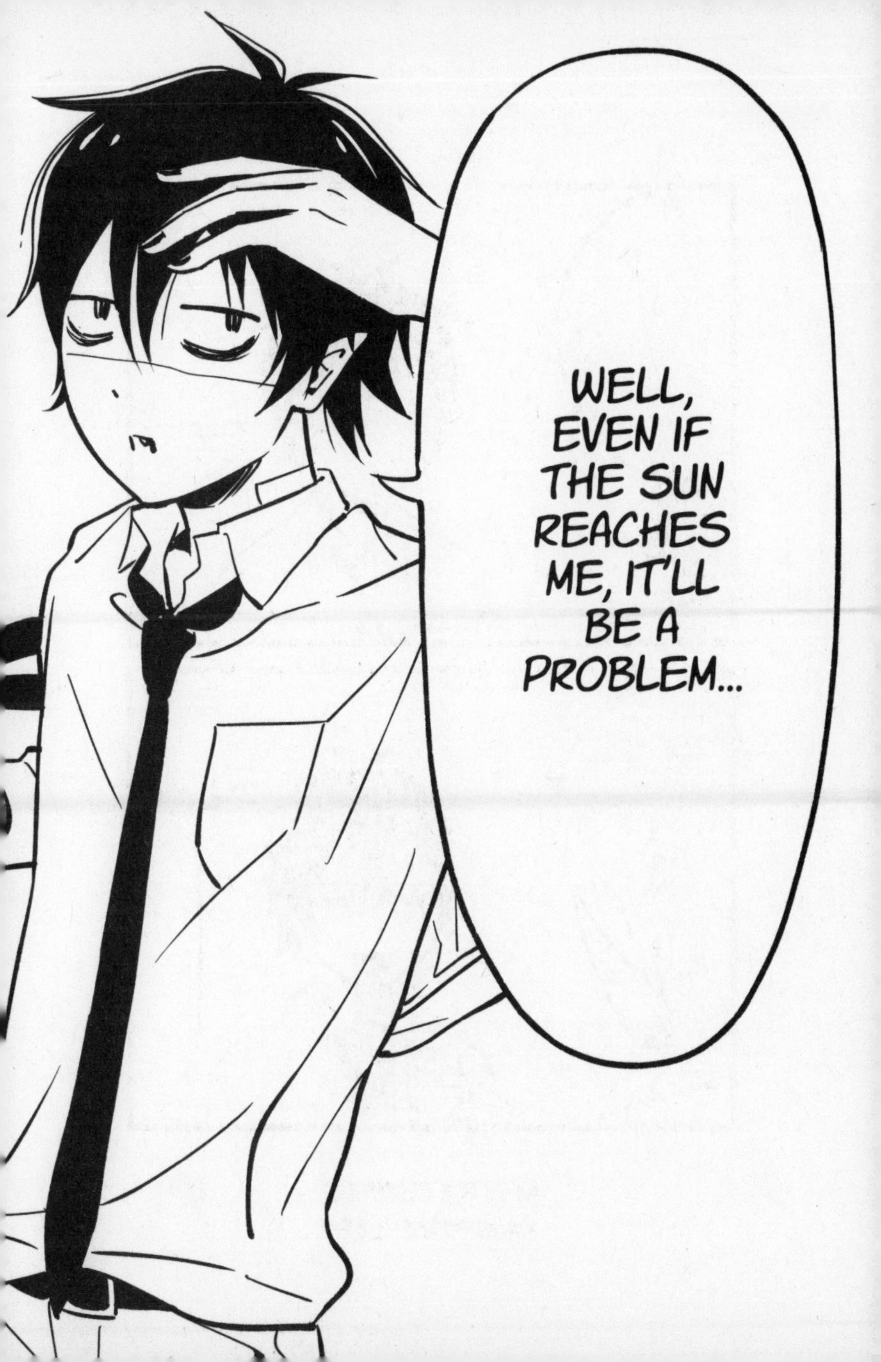
WELL, EVEN IF THE SUN REACHES ME, IT'LL BE A PROBLEM...

Tomato Juice
SLURP
Tomato Juice
BLEH

MY PATHETIC
VAMPIRE LIFE

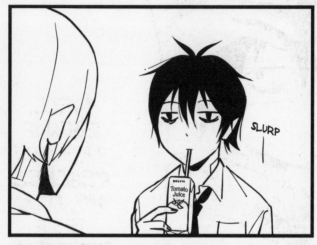

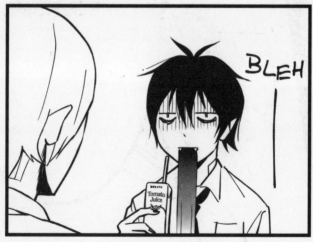

SEVEN SEAS ENTERTAINMENT PRESENTS

W9-CJF-934

My Pathetic VAMPIRE Life

story and art by ISHIKAWA ROSE　vol. 1

TRANSLATION
Amber Tamosaitis

ADAPTATION
Carol Fox

LETTERING
Rina Mapa

LOGO DESIGN
Karis Page

COVER DESIGN
Nicky Lim

PROOFREADER
Lee Otter
Janet Houck

PRODUCTION MANAGER
Lissa Pattillo

EDITOR-IN-CHIEF
Adam Arnold

PUBLISHER
Jason DeAngelis

MY PATHETIC VAMPIRE LIFE VOL. 1
© Ishikawa Rose 2014
All rights reserved.
First published in Japan in 2014 by Futabasha Publishers Ltd., Tokyo.
English version published by Seven Seas Entertainment, LLC.
Under license from Futabasha Publishers Ltd.

Seven Seas books may be purchased in bulk for promotional, educational, or
business use. Please contact your local bookseller or the Macmillan Corporate
and Premium Sales Department at 1-800-221-7945, extension 5442, or by
e-mail at MacmillanSpecialMarkets@macmillan.com.

Seven Seas and the Seven Seas logo are trademarks of
Seven Seas Entertainment, LLC. All rights reserved.

ISBN: 978-1-626923-49-2

Printed in Canada

First Printing: October 2016

10 9 8 7 6 5 4 3 2 1

FOLLOW US ONLINE: *www.gomanga.com*

READING DIRECTIONS

This book reads from *right to left*, Japanese style.
If this is your first time reading manga, you start
reading from the top right panel on each page and
take it from there. If you get lost, just follow the
numbered diagram here. It may seem backwards at
first, but you'll get the hang of it! Have fun!!

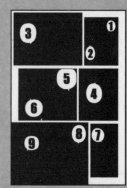